GLOBAL ISSUES

GENOCIDE AND INTERNATIONAL JUSTICE

Rebecca Joyce Frey

Foreword by Dr. Dori Laub
Yale University School of Medicine

Facts On File
An imprint of Infobase Publishing

Dedicated to the memory of my father,
Clayton S. Frey, Jr.,
82nd Airborne, World War II,
who saw what genocide looks like

GLOBAL ISSUES: GENOCIDE AND INTERNATIONAL JUSTICE

Copyright © 2009 by Infobase Publishing

Facts On File, Inc.
An imprint of Infobase Publishing
132 West 31st Street
New York NY 10001

Library of Congress Cataloging-in-Publication Data

Frey, Rebecca Joyce.
  Genocide and international justice/Rebecca Joyce Frey; foreword author Dori Laub.
      p. cm.—(Global issues)
  Includes bibliographical references and index.
  ISBN 978-0-8160-7310-8
1. Genocide—History. 2. Crimes against humanity—History. I. Title.

HV6322.7.F74 2009
  345'.0251—dc22   2008055852

Facts On File books are available at special discounts when purchased in bulk quantities for businesses, associations, institutions, or sales promotions. Please call our Special Sales Department in New York at (212) 967-8800 or (800) 322-8755.

You can find Facts On File on the World Wide Web at http://www.factsonfile.com

Text design by Erika K. Arroyo
Cover design by Salvatore Luongo and Alicia Post
Illustrations by Dale Williams

Printed in the United States of America

MP MSRF 10 9 8 7 6 5 4 3 2 1

This book is printed on acid-free paper and contains 30 percent postconsumer recycled content.

CONTENTS

PART II: Primary Sources

PART III: Research Tools

List of Maps and Tables

Foreword:
A Letter to Young Readers

This book starts with the most appropriate question—Why study geno-cide—when the sheer mass of material is overwhelming but also "[when] the contents of that mass are the new materials of nightmares." I would like in my foreword to elaborate on this question and address it to the young readers for whom this book is intended. Why should you be burdened by the horrors endured, witnessed, or perpetrated by your parents or forefathers? Are there lessons you need to learn from them? Are there events you are obligated to memorialize?

First and foremost, a young man or woman entering adulthood in the 21st century needs to know the world he or she is going to negotiate as it really is. The television soap opera, the sensational action movie, the science fiction plot, and, above all, commercials all portray a life experience that is illusory at best and are intended to draw viewers' attention away from life's core experiences. Such core experiences include love, intimacy, bonding, loyalty, bereavement, loss, merciless violence, betrayal, abandonment, aloneness, desolation, separa-tion, utter helplessness, illness, death, and many more. Such core experiences are fraught with conflict, terror, sadness, and pain and are hard to bear, often resulting in a turning away, a sense of numbness and dissociation from the terrifying and painful. Mass media and entertainment often provide comfort and closure to such existential pain: the movie that always has a happy ending, where good prevails over evil or death that is contextualized as heroism—as a sacrifice for the greater good. The commercial goes even further. It capitalizes on this trend, attempting to substitute the pleasures of consumerism for the stark deprivations that are commonplace, even in regular day-to-day life, not to mention periods of war and social upheaval.

Music, art, and serious literature and drama have found ways of authenti-cally representing and conveying to an audience what life is all about. But such representation is not limited to fiction. The events that happened in the 20th century exceeded the imaginary, went beyond all fiction. The number of people murdered, exiled, and bereaved in the genocides, world wars, regional wars, revolutions, brutal repressions, and upheavals exceeded that of any other century in human history. One may never know the exact figure, but probably 100 million people lost their lives. And it was in these very situations of extremity, when all frames of reference broke down, all boundaries dissolved, when people were no longer protected by what is customary, expected, by values they all believed they shared, that their lives came to be stark, merciless, unmitigated, and raw experiences. The banalities of daily living fell by the wayside under the impact of such extreme experience, and the naked merciless truth became unavoidable.

Those who lived through such extremes gained an additional knowledge, which cannot be found or learned anywhere else. They became the witnesses to that experience, and the teachers who can impart that special knowledge. And for you, the new generation, it is crucial to obtain that knowledge. You need such knowledge not for the purpose of partaking in the suffering of the past century, nor for the sake of memorializing it—but for the skills it imparts that will enable you to effectively navigate life as it really is and not as we like to imagine it.

Dr. Rebecca Frey in this book rightfully points to Gregory Stanton's seven stages of genocide, with denial being "a stage in a society's transition to genocide that typically begins before mass extermination" and persists and keeps resurfacing long into its aftermath. In the section of chapter 1 entitled "Understanding Genocide by Studying the Holocaust," she puts special emphasis on this phenomenon of societal denial that follows genocide. This is precisely why students often face an uphill battle in their attempts to acquire historical information. The most direct way they can do this, beyond researching facts about incidents, is listening to or reading the testimonies given by survivors. There is an experiential truth in such testimonies that goes beyond the facts. Yet it is the dogged, unwavering pursuit of truth that made it possible for those who were affected and severely traumatized to emotionally survive. It is not possible to restore any normalcy in life, without knowing the traumata one has experienced and acknowledging them. This is also why the pervasive societal denial of genocide constitutes not only an assault on truth, but also an assault on the survivors. As students of this field, your adherence to truth not only prevents its annihilation, but also prepares you to confront and master much of what is difficult in life.

How does the present book assist you in obtaining the knowledge you need?

The first part of the book introduces you to basic concepts and a wide spectrum of relevant historical events. It acquaints you with the map, so to speak. You read of genocidal events happening over many centuries (even millennia) and on many continents, including our own. Its prose is rather gentle in the hope of raising your interest and your curiosity to go deeper into the topic.

When you proceed to Part II, Primary Sources, you come to read the documents and witness accounts of those involved. If you wish, you can become really absorbed in events and imagine yourself in those places at those times.

If your interest is aroused and your imagination is stimulated and you wish to pursue the topic further, you can proceed to Part III, Research Tools, the most valuable part of this book, which puts at your disposal an array of options that will help you access in-depth information on the topics of your choice. There is plenty of guidance to continue the itinerary you have chosen.

I wish you a safe and fruitful journey in reading this book.

—Dr. Dori Laub
Yale University School of Medicine
Cofounder of the Holocaust Survivors' Film Project

PART I

At Issue

1

Introduction

WHY STUDY GENOCIDE?

Genocide is a term of fairly recent origin, having been coined in 1944 by a Polish legal scholar named Raphael Lemkin (1900–59) in relation to the Holocaust, or Shoah. The term was so strange to its first readers, in fact, that Lemkin wrote an article the following year for the general public in which he explained his introduction of a new word for an ancient crime:

> ... *[Hitler] had said, "Natural instincts bid all living human beings not merely conquer their enemies but also destroy them. In former days it was the victor's prerogative to destroy tribes, entire peoples."*
>
> *Hitler was right. The crime of the Reich in wantonly and deliberately wiping out whole peoples is not utterly new in the world. It is only new in the civilized world as we have come to think of it. It is so new in the traditions of civilized man that he has no name for it. It is for this reason that I took the liberty of inventing the word, "genocide." The term is from the Greek word* genes *meaning tribe or race and the Latin* cide *meaning killing. Genocide tragically enough must take its place in the dictionary of the future beside other tragic words like homicide and infanticide. . . . The term does not necessarily signify mass killings although it may mean that.*
>
> *More often it refers to a coordinated plan aimed at destruction of the essential foundations of the life of national groups so that these groups wither and die like plants that have suffered a blight. The end may be accomplished by the forced disintegration of political and social institutions, of the culture of the people, of their language, their national feelings and their religion. It may be accomplished by wiping out all basis of personal security, liberty, health and dignity. When these means fail the machine gun can always be utilized as a last resort. Genocide is directed against a national group as an entity and the attack on individuals is only secondary to the annihilation of the national group to which they belong.[1]*

More than half a century after Lemkin's first publications, however, the term *genocide* seems almost commonplace. It has been applied in a variety of contexts apparently far removed from the mass murders of the 1940s to such matters as the use of birth control by African-American women[2] and the killing of animals for food.[3]

Until the 1970s comparatively few historians or researchers in other fields were interested in the topic. That relative lack of interest changed rapidly in response to a number of events. First was the recurrence of genocide as defined by Lemkin—in Cambodia in 1975–79, in the former Yugoslavia in 1991, in Rwanda in 1994—all of them evidence that Hitler's attempt to exterminate Jews and members of other groups deemed to be "life unworthy of life" (*lebensunwertes Leben*) was not a historical anomaly. Second was the release of secret government archives following the collapse of the Soviet Union in 1991. These documents revealed details of the brutality perpetrated by Soviet leaders from the time of the Russian Revolution in 1917 through the 1980s. The opening of the archives led to scholarly questioning not only of the Soviet regime, but of such other repressive regimes as Maoist China and Japan in the 1930s. Still another factor in the revived interest in genocide was the apparent inability of such international organizations as the United Nations, once regarded as humankind's best hope for avoiding future wars, to prevent genocide from occurring or to act decisively when it does occur. The number of published books and articles on genocide began to rise exponentially in the 1990s; genocide studies became a separate field of academic inquiry, leading to the establishment of periodicals and university departments devoted exclusively to the subject; research centers were funded; and museums were built to remind people of the horrors of the recent as well as the remote past.

The question remains, however, as to why anyone would want to involve themselves in a subject like genocide. It is not only that the sheer mass of material is overwhelming but also that the contents of that mass are the raw material of nightmares. Verbal descriptions of the methods of execution; photographs of the dead; survivors' testimonies and courtroom proceedings; artistic, musical, and literary commemorations or reenactments—none is easy to read, listen to, or look at. There are numerous survivors of genocide who eventually attempt or commit suicide, such as the poet Paul Celan (1920–70) and the writers Primo Levi (1919–87) and Jean Améry (1912–78). Nor is this reaction to genocide limited to survivors. Iris Chang (1968–2004), a journalist who wrote a historical account of the Japanese destruction of Nanking, committed suicide, while Roméo Dallaire (1946–   ), the former commander of the United Nations peacekeeping force in Rwanda, suffered an episode of severe depression in 2000. The term *secondary* or *vicarious traumatization,* also called *compassion fatigue,* has been coined to describe the various posttraumatic syndromes that affect psychotherapists and other medical professionals who treat survivors of genocide.[4] The symptoms of vicarious traumatization include numbness and withdrawal; emotional overreaction; anger at the survivor; a feeling of complete paralysis; loss of trust in one's own relationships; a pervasive feeling of personal danger; and nightmares.[5]

Further, the horrors of genocide affect many of the children and even grandchildren of survivors. Studies of the descendants of Holocaust survivors (children born after the end of World War II) indicate that many have difficulty with intimate relationships and creating separate families for themselves.[6]

Perhaps the most disturbing aspect of recent instances of genocide is the failure of international legal bodies and nongovernmental organizations (NGOs) to prevent or mitigate these atrocities. To mention only one example, the genocide in Darfur—which started in 2003 and is ongoing as this book goes to press—has become a notable instance of the United Nation's nearly complete loss of credibility as a peacekeeping force. UN deputy secretary general Mark Malloch Brown, speaking at a Brookings Institution event, admitted that in Darfur,

> *. . . there is a little bit of bluff playing, in that we're saying to President Bashir of Sudan, give us consent for deployment or else. And there's a lot of questions about what plausibly the "or else" is. And President Bashir looks at us and he thinks he's seen us blink, and that makes it hugely difficult to credibly address this issue of winning his consent to our deployment.[7]*

One reason why this failure to act on the part of once-trusted institutions is so disquieting is that it leads to some unpleasant questions about human nature itself. Human beings are social animals who have lived in groups since the Neolithic period, about 10,000 years ago. Genocide is typically planned and carried out by groups of people who have decided that other people constitute a group threat or nuisance of some kind. It is a recurrent tragedy that has taken place in many different cultures throughout history, under every known form of government, using a wide variety of weapons and other methods. Genocide has been committed by bands of hunter-gatherers, by nomadic tribes on horseback, and by organized armies with modern weaponry. It has occurred in tribal cultures, under absolute monarchs, under dictatorships of the political Left as well as the political Right, and in parliamentary democracies. It has occurred in peacetime, as a prelude to war, during war, and in the aftermath of war. It is this collective dimension of genocide that makes it impossible for students of the subject to dismiss it as an aberration on a par with mass murders carried out by deranged individuals.

The Bureau of Justice Statistics of the U.S. Department of Justice defines mass murder as "the murder of four or more victims at one location, within one event." Some instances within recent memory make for unpleasant reading, such as the deaths in 1987 of 43 passengers on a Pacific Southwest Airlines plane that crashed when a passenger, angry at having been fired earlier that day by USAir, shot the pilot and copilot,[8] or the shooting of 72 people, 35 of whom died, in Tasmania in April 1996 by a disturbed 28-year-old man with below-normal intelligence, or the rampage that killed 33 on the campus of Virginia Tech in April 2007.[9] But these events, horrifying as they are, do not usually cause the reader to ask whether there is something about the human condition in itself that leads to mass killings of this type. They are usually attributed to the abnormal brain structure, personal history, or psychopathology of the individual perpetrator. It is a simple matter for casual readers to assure themselves that they would never carry out such crimes, no matter what the provocation.

Genocide, however, will not yield to this form of analysis. Inevitably the thoughtful reader must ask under what social pressures or in which settings could I participate in genocide. This is particularly important because older explanations of genocide, such as economic self-interest or the organizational development of nation-states, are beginning to yield to a renewed emphasis on belief structures, whether religious or ideological, as a major factor in violence between human groups. Neuroscientist Bruce Wexler predicts that such violence is likely to increase rather than diminish in the near future because of what he terms the "global mixing of cultures." In the past, people could simply keep their distance—literally and imaginatively—from those whose cultural and behavioral differences were disturbing to them. But now, "retreat from the intercultural contact zones [is] impossible and battles for control of the cultural environment [are] commonplace."[10] His conclusion implies that genocide is not likely to disappear from the planet any time soon.

Much of the material in this and the following chapters is depressing and upsetting. It is not at all unusual for students of genocide—in any age group—to experience symptoms of vicarious traumatization. In fact, the writer of a college-level textbook on genocide issues a warning: ". . . I encourage you—especially if you are just beginning your studies—to be attentive to signs of personal stress. Talk about it with your fellow students, your colleagues, or family and friends. . . . If that doesn't help, seek counseling through the resources available on your campus or in your community."[11]

Why, then, study genocide? One suggestion that has been made is to remember the "positive examples of bravery and love for others that the study of genocide regularly provides,"[12] as well as the actions of the perpetrators. Another writer, a researcher in psychology who organized a four-day meeting between children of concentration camp survivors and children of German Nazis, has suggested that people can develop the strength to deal with the pain of historical injustice on the individual level and "use that strength to transcend our personal hurts in order to apprehend other people and their hurts. It offers the possibility of a future free from the damaging legacy of the past."[13] But perhaps the best reason for studying the darkest side of human history is also personal, namely, a strengthened resolve to make one's life count for something, not to waste one's opportunities to do good and to contribute to the world. The words of Charlotte Delbo (1913–85), a French playwright who was sent to Auschwitz in 1943 for her participation in the Resistance and who later wrote about her experiences in the camp, may serve as encouragement. Her plea stands at the end of a lengthy poem titled "Prayer to the Living, to Forgive Them for Being Alive":

I beg you
do something
learn a dance step
something to justify your existence
something that gives you the right
to be dressed in your skin in your body hair
learn to walk and to laugh
because it would be too senseless
after all
for so many to have died
while you live
doing nothing with your life.[14]

SOME DEFINITIONS AND BOUNDARIES
The Many Names of Mass Death

In addition to the emotional and psychological difficulty of studying a topic like genocide, the student is confronted with a bewildering labyrinth of academic arguments about the concept of genocide itself. Some writers define the term very narrowly to avoid its being applied too frequently and thus losing effectiveness; these are sometimes called "hard" positions. Others are more inclusive, maintaining that a rigid insistence on the meeting of certain criteria (such as the number of victims or the survival of some members of the group) rules out too many instances of mass killing that certainly qualify as genocide from a moral perspective. These wider definitions of genocide are called "soft" positions and are often encountered in contemporary accounts and later analyses of genocide in the ancient and medieval periods.

Prior to Raphael Lemkin's introduction of *genocide* as a legal term, historians—whether contemporaries of the event or later writers—had only such general terms as "mass slaughter," "massacre," "barbarism," or "execution." Some ancient historians described large-scale killings in almost antiseptic terms. For example, the Greek historian Thucydides, describing the Athenians' killing of the men of Melos during the Peloponnesian War, says simply that ". . . the Melians surrendered at discretion to the Athenians, who put to death all the grown men whom they took, and sold the women and children for slaves, and subsequently sent out five hundred colonists and inhabited the place themselves."[15] Later writers were more likely to express indignation. Comparably, Benjamin Franklin's 1764 account of the vigilante killing of a group of Conestoga Indians who had been offered protection by the governor is quite passionate: "What could [the Indians' leader] or the other poor old Men and Women do? What had little Boys and Girls done; what could Children of a Year old, Babes at the Breast, what could they do, that they too must be shot and hatcheted?—Horrid to relate!—and in their Parents Arms! This is done by no civilized Nation in *Europe*. Do we come to *America* to learn and practise the Manners of *Barbarians*?"[16] The Sand Creek Massacre of 1864 was described as "indiscriminate slaughter" in the course of a witness's testimony before Congress the following year.[17] The term *massacre* was used by an American consul in Armenia in a letter to Ambassador Henry Morgenthau in Constantinople in regard to the deportations and mass killings of Armenians in 1915. After describing specific episodes of group executions and large-scale death from malnutrition and thirst, the consul stated, "The entire movement seems to be the most thoroughly organized and effective massacre this country has ever seen."[18]

The use of the term *genocide* by itself, however, does not necessarily add clarity to discussions of these events. Some researchers in the field of what has been called comparative genocide studies have proposed a set of categories to structure the historical data.

- *Perpetrators or agents.* Who are the groups or persons responsible for the killing? Are they representatives of the government? The titular ruler or rulers of the country? Private individuals? One well-known writer on genocide, R. J. Rummel, has introduced the terms *politicide* and *demo-*

cide to denote mass killings carried out by a government. Thus democide is "The murder of any person or people by a government, including genocide, politicide, and mass murder," while politicide is "The murder of any person or people by a government because of their politics or for political purposes."[19] One question that Rummel's definitions raise, however, is the role of non-state agents in genocide. The possibility of freelance terrorists who are not formally associated with any government but are nonetheless motivated by the desire to destroy members of a specific ethnic, political, racial, or religious group expands the definition of agency.

- *Victims.* The victims of genocide are usually understood to be social minorities vulnerable to attacks by perpetrators. The victim groups may be either self-identified (as in the case of Native American tribes, religious communities, and similar groupings) or they may be labeled by the perpetrators (as in the case of Cambodia's so-called New People, or city dwellers, who were given that name by the Khmer Rouge in 1975). Identifying the victims in an instance of genocide has led to coining such words as *urbicide,* which denotes the destruction of an urban lifestyle as well as the buildings and infrastructure of a city; *gendercide,* which denotes the selective killing of either males (as in the Armenian genocide of 1915) or females (as in the practice of sex-specific abortions);[20] and *omnicide,* to describe the fanatical desire to kill the entire human race.[21]

- *Objectives.* Scholars do not always agree as to whether the complete physical extermination of a group is the essential objective of genocide, whether territorial displacement accompanied by mass killing is sufficient to qualify an event as genocide, or whether the perpetrators must intend to destroy the group's culture or language. If the first definition is accepted, most of the mass killings of antiquity could not be considered genocide because the immediate goals of such conquerors as Alexander the Great and Julius Caesar were the acquisition of territory and the defeat of opposing armies, not the liquidation of all the civilian populations in the countries they invaded. On the other hand, if the third definition of the goal of genocide is accepted, then such acts as the late 19th- and early 20th-century federal boarding school program for Native Americans in the United States could be considered genocidal, insofar as that program led to the extinction of literally hundreds of Native American languages as well as intense distress on the part of individuals.[22]

- *Scale.* There seems to be a growing agreement that the number of persons killed in an instance of genocide should not be a defining factor in and of itself. For example, most of the massacres of Native Americans in what is now the United States during the 18th and 19th centuries involved fewer victims than recent aviation accidents involving jumbo jets, yet few historians would deny that the deaths of the 20 Conestoga Indians in Pennsylvania in 1764 or those of the 180 Cheyenne killed at Sand Creek in Colorado a century later were genocidal killings. For one thing, the perpetrators of genocide for most of human history lacked the technology for killing people on an industrial scale; thus, setting fire to captured cities, poisoning wells, and throwing plague-infected bodies over the walls of besieged cities were the major means of inflicting mass casualties, and they were not instantaneous. World War I (1914–18) is usually considered the watershed event in this regard. Prior to the Great War, as it was known before 1939, the notion of 60,000 battle casualties per day over a period of days (including 20,000 deaths) was unthinkable;[23] yet, after the battle of the Somme in July 1916, such figures became commonplace. In all, the war cost the lives of 10 million soldiers and 2 million civilians—a high price tag on 20th-century military technology.[24] Some historians consider the death toll of World War I to have been a factor in encouraging the sheer mercilessness of the mass killings in Armenia in 1915 and Russia in the 1930s. In addition to the numbers, the weapons used in World War I allowed for mass slaughter at a distance, which may have encouraged genocidal attitudes and behaviors in the decades following. It is psychologically easier for perpetrators to shoot, gas, or incinerate people targeted for genocide when they do not have to get close enough to recognize them as individuals and as fellow human beings.

- *Policies and strategies.* Some scholars follow Lemkin's precedent in including various forms of cultural destruction, including the breakup of family units or attacks on such institutions as libraries and universities, as forms of genocide even if they do not result in widespread death. Others, however, still maintain that mass killing is an essential element in defining a particular event as genocide.

- *Motive and intention.* Some scholars use motivation as a way to classify or categorize genocides. They usually distinguish four motives: 1) Genocides carried out to settle ethnic, religious, or racial differences. This category would include the Armenian genocide of 1915, the genocide in the former Yugoslavia in the early 1990s, and the genocide in Rwanda in 1994. 2) Genocides perpetrated to terrorize the populations of recently conquered lands. This category would include many ancient and medieval instances of genocide, including the sacking of

Tyre by Alexander the Great (332 B.C.E.), the destruction of Carthage by the Romans at the end of the Third Punic War (146 B.C.E.), and the massacres in Central Asia carried out by Genghis Khan and later Mongol rulers in the 13th and 14th centuries. 3) Genocides carried out to acquire or increase wealth. The mass killings in Mexico and Peru by the Spanish conquistadores in the 16th century and the German massacre of the Herero in southwestern Africa in 1904 would be examples of this type of genocide. 4) Genocides carried out to enforce a political ideology. This category would include the mass killings of civilians in the Vendée in 1794 through 1796 in the aftermath of the French Revolution, as well as the Great Terror in Russia in the 1930s under Stalin and the genocide that took place in Cambodia in the 1970s under the Khmer Rouge regime. The distinction between *motive* and *intention* is often discussed in this context, particularly with reference to the rapid decline of the Native American population in the New World in the 16th and 17th centuries as a result of repeated disease epidemics. That the European colonial powers—England, France, the Netherlands, Portugal, and Spain—were willing to expand their territorial possessions, extend their trade routes, and exploit the wealth of the new lands by violent as well as peaceful means is not open to doubt. But it is difficult to see how the introduction of communicable diseases into populations that had little or no biological immunity to them can be considered an intentional act, particularly in an era in which the modern germ theory of disease had not yet been defined. Some scholars use such terms as "second-degree genocide" to categorize mass death resulting from conquest or warfare even though it is not directly intended.[25]

Raphael Lemkin and the 1948 United Nations Convention

Much of the contemporary debate about the boundaries and subtypes of genocidal acts can be traced to disagreements over the legacy of Raphael Lemkin, the Polish-born lawyer who gave a name to a crime previously nameless. According to Samantha Power, who has studied Lemkin's private papers, the future legal scholar became interested in atrocities in 1913, when he was only 12 years old. He had read *Quo Vadis,* a novel by the Polish writer Henryk Sienkiewicz, whose subject matter was the emperor Nero's persecution of Christians in the first century. He asked his mother, a painter and linguist who homeschooled her children, about such other instances of mass murder as the Mongol invasions of Central Asia, the sack of Carthage, and the 16th-century massacre of the French Huguenots. He later wrote, "I was an impressionable youngster . . . appalled by the frequency of the evil . . . and, above all, by the impunity coldly relied on by the guilty."[26] After going to university and then to law school in the 1920s, Lemkin set to work on drafting an international law that would commit governments to end the targeted destruction of national or ethnic groups. It was a task that occupied him throughout the 1930s and early 1940s.

Lemkin was living and working in Poland when the Germans invaded the country in September 1939. After narrowly escaping death when the Luftwaffe bombed the train on which he was riding, Lemkin eventually made his way to Lithuania, then to neutral Sweden, and ultimately to the United States, where he arrived in April 1941. By June 1942 he was serving as a consultant to the Board of Economic Warfare in Washington and by 1944 he joined the War Department as an expert on international law. However, his efforts to lobby various people at the top levels of the Roosevelt administration regarding conditions in Nazi-occupied Europe—including Henry Wallace, then the vice president—were without success. Frustrated, Lemkin thought back to a conference in Madrid that he had attended in 1933, when he presented a paper at a law conference on the mass killings in Armenia. He had suggested drafting a law that would outlaw "barbarity"—which he defined as "the premeditated destruction of national, racial, religious and social collectivities"—and "vandalism"—by which he meant "the destruction of works of art and culture, being the expression of the particular genius of those collectivities."[27] He remembered a speech given in August 1941 by Winston Churchill, in which the British prime minister spoke of the horrors inflicted by the Nazis as "a crime without a name." Lemkin decided he would devise a name to fit the crime. In 1944 he published a lengthy book titled *Axis Rule in Occupied Europe,* in which he collected all the rules and decrees that Hitler's regime imposed on 19 different European countries and territories. Although the book initially received criticism and was dry and legalistic, it introduced the word *genocide.* Lemkin had formed the new word with care: In one of his surviving notebooks, he scribbled the phrase "the word," drew a circle around it, and drew a line between the circle and the phrase "moral judgement."[28]

After the war, Lemkin spent the next three years persuading the newly formed United Nations to pass a law against genocide. After a year of drafting the Convention on the Prevention and Punishment of the Crime of Genocide, it was scheduled for a vote. On December 9, 1948, the 55 delegates in the General Assembly unanimously voted to approve the convention. The convention defined genocide as

Introduction

. . . any of the following acts committed with intent to destroy, in whole or in part, a national, ethnical, racial or religious group, as such:

(a) Killing members of the group;

(b) Causing serious bodily or mental harm to members of the group;

(c) Deliberately inflicting on the group conditions of life calculated to bring about its physical destruction in whole or in part;

(d) Imposing measures intended to prevent births within the group;

(e) Forcibly transferring children of the group to another group.

Although the convention has been faulted for its vagueness—among other matters, it did not give precise definition to "national, ethnical, racial or religious" groups, nor did it define what acts might constitute "serious bodily or mental harm"—its passage in 1948 was nonetheless a landmark event. It closed one of the major loopholes left by the Nuremberg tribunal that had brought high-ranking leaders of Nazi Germany to justice in 1946, namely that only crimes committed during wartime could be prosecuted. The 1948 convention made rebel groups as well as nation-states liable to prosecution without regard to whether they are at war with another country or acting only against internal "enemies of the people."

The two major weaknesses of the convention are its omission of political groups from the list of protected entities—an absence generally attributed to the influence of the Soviet Union—and the long delay of the United States in ratifying the convention. It could not become official international law until 20 of the original 55 members of the General Assembly ratified it. Lemkin was aware that the League of Nations had been powerless to stop the European dictators of the 1930s because the United States had never joined the League. By October 1950 the convention had acquired the needed number of ratifications (it entered into force on January 12, 1951), but without the United States to enforce the convention, it would remain a dead letter. Ratification by the Senate was stalled during the 1950s, in part by Southern lawmakers who were afraid that they could be accused of genocide because of their support for racial segregation in their home states. Although the passage of the convention through the U.S. Senate was shepherded by Senator William Proxmire (1915–2005) from 1967 onward, it was not until February 11, 1986, that the Senate adopted a ratification resolution; and not until October 19, 1988, that the Senate passed the Genocide Convention Implementation Act, sometimes called the Proxmire Act. The act was signed into law on November 4 by President Ronald Reagan (1911–2004), who gave credit to Raphael Lemkin for his role in changing the course of international law.

UNDERSTANDING GENOCIDE BY STUDYING THE HOLOCAUST

Although Adolf Hitler's attempt to exterminate the Jews in the 1930s and early 1940s was not the earliest instance of genocide, or even the earliest 20th-century example, it has become the template for evaluating and defining other genocides. In fact, one of the liveliest debates within contemporary genocide studies is whether the Holocaust is in some sense a uniquely terrible event "unlike any other and thus [endowed] with special significance for all humanity,"[29] or whether the attribution of uniqueness to the Holocaust somehow diminishes the sufferings of the victims of other genocides. The reader will want to keep this ongoing debate in mind throughout the remainder of this book.

Discussion of the Holocaust will be divided into three major sections: background, course of events, and aftermath. The sections will be coordinated with the stages of genocide as defined by Gregory Stanton, the founder of Genocide Watch, and by Raul Hilberg, a major historian of the Holocaust.[30]

Background

CLASSIFICATION

Stanton regards the first stage in any society's progression toward genocide as classification in the sense that people divide into two large groups, us and them. With regard to the Holocaust in particular, Hilberg describes this stage as Hitler's "undertaking of defining Jews as such."[31] The issue here is not comparing different human groups with one another; most human cultures define themselves at least in part by contrasting themselves with others. *Barbarian,* for example, was not always an uncomplimentary word; it was first used by the Greek historian Herodotus (484–425 B.C.E.) to describe the beginnings of enmity between the Greek city-states and the Persian Empire in 490 B.C.E. When Herodotus described non-Greeks as *barbaroi* or barbarians, he meant only that their customs, dress, language, and religion were different from those of the Athenians or Spartans. Later Greek writers began to use the word to mean "rude" or "brutal," and Latin writers borrowed the term to mean something closer to "uncivilized" or "uncultured" rather than "people of a different culture."[32] There is evidence that a tendency to divide people into us and them is hardwired in the human brain; humans have been shown in a variety of experiments to have a definite preference for the known and familiar over the unfamiliar.[33] This kind of division—of splitting one's social world into people like me and people who are different—is not by itself a necessary precursor to genocide. In complex societies with many different ethnic groups, religions, or languages represented, genocide is less likely to occur than in societies divided sharply into two major groups.

From a long-term historical perspective, the Holocaust was the climactic episode in a long history of persecution of the Jews. From the time of King Nebuchadnezzar of Babylon's destruction of Jerusalem in 587 B.C.E. to the Roman general Titus's sack of Jerusalem in 70 C.E., through the Middle Ages and into the 19th century, the Jews were often targeted as the quintessential outsiders in Western societies. In 19th-century Eastern Europe, Jews were frequently the victims of pogroms, or organized massacres, in which the population of a town or city might kill or injure several hundred Jews. Some pogroms were motivated by the so-called blood libel, namely the belief that Jews murdered Christian children in order to obtain their blood for making ceremonial bread for Passover.[34] A particularly brutal pogrom broke out in 1903 in a Russian town called Kishinev when the murder of a Christian boy was blamed on the Jews. It is noteworthy that this long history of suffering was one reason why many Jews did *not* leave Europe during the 1930s, when the danger they were in was increasingly obvious, at least to some observers. The Jews of Eastern Europe were so accustomed to episodic violence interspersed with relatively peaceful periods that they did not expect a policy of complete extermination. When Raphael Lemkin tried to persuade his parents to leave Poland with him, they refused, on the grounds that they would have to suffer but would "survive somehow." Lemkin also noted the words of a village baker who told him, "There is nothing new in the suffering of Jews, especially in time of war. . . . The main thing for a Jew is not to get excited and to outlast the enemies."[35]

Hitler's scheme of classification, however, went beyond the usual distinction between Jew and non-Jew on the basis of religious practice; he interpreted Jewish identity as a matter of race. The boundaries between German Jews and the nominally Christian majority had begun to blur in the 19th century. Prussia was the first state in Europe to grant Jews full civic privileges, which it did in 1812. German Jews were generally safe from pogroms, unlike their coreligionists in Russia. Many attended universities. Some married into Christian families or became Christians themselves; the composer Felix Mendelssohn (1809–47), for example, was baptized as a Christian in 1812 when his father renounced Judaism. What Hitler did in effect was to reclassify Jews as a distinctive race rather than a minority religious group.[36] In 1935 Hitler secured the passage of the Nürnberger Gesetze, or Nuremberg Laws, which divided Germans into three groups according to the number of Jewish grandparents they had: people with no Jewish grandparents were of "German blood," those with one or two were of "mixed blood," and those with three or four were of "Jewish blood." The second of the two laws denaturalized Jews (stripped them of their citizenship), thus dividing the German population into two political groups, "citizens of the Reich" and "nationals."

Hitler's emphasis on the purity of "German blood" derived from a general Nazi preoccupation with eugenics, or the belief that human mating and reproduction should be scientifically controlled in order to improve the hereditary qualities or characteristics of an ethnic group or nation. Two years before the Nuremberg Laws, the Nazis had already promulgated the Law for the Prevention of Hereditarily Diseased Offspring to enforce the sterilization of persons suffering from epilepsy, schizophrenia, "innate mental deficiency," Huntington's disease, hereditary blindness or deafness, chronic alcoholism, and several other diseases or mental disorders known or thought to be genetically transmitted. By 1935, when the Nuremberg Laws were passed, about 300,000 people had already been forcibly sterilized.[37] The Nuremberg Laws themselves were intended to prevent intermarriage or sexual intercourse between Jews and persons of "German blood" as well as to define the two groups according to "race." The same attitude toward classification on the basis of race was evident in Nazi attitudes toward Roma[38] (Gypsies); the 1935 marriage laws that forbade "Germans" to marry Jews were extended in 1936 to Roma. Even before the Nuremberg Laws, the Nazis had also begun to target homosexual males (they generally ignored lesbians) on the grounds that gay men were "useless" people who were not contributing to the expansion of the "pure German" population.[39] In terms of classification, gay men were segregated from other prisoners even within the concentration camps.

SYMBOLIZATION

The second stage that Stanton identifies in a culture's progression to genocide is symbolization, defined as the wearing of distinctive clothing, badges, or other symbols. Like classification, symbolization is universally human; there is nothing necessarily sinister in wearing items of jewelry or clothing that identify people as adherents of a particular religion, members of the clergy or a religious order, married rather than single, or children rather than adults. Many cultures throughout history have symbolized a young person's official coming of age by clothing him or her in the garb of an adult member of the society. The Roman boy, for example, assumed the toga virilis around age 15; this pure white garment not only marked him as an adult, but also as a Roman citizen; noncitizens were forbidden to wear togas.[40] Similarly, married men among the Old Order Amish in the United States grow beards even in the early 2000s as an indication that they are full adult members of the community, while unmarried men must be clean-shaven.

Symbolization does not become a problem or a precursor of genocide as long as the adoption of the symbolic garments or other items is voluntary and is not intended to identify members of the group for later segregation and extermination. Hitler's regime, however, compelled Jews in Germany to wear an identifying Star of David, usually in yellow with the German word *Jude* (Jew) in the center, either as an armband or sewn on the outer clothing. Similarly, male homosexuals were identified by a badge with a pink triangle. Thus set apart, they were often singled out for particularly brutal treatment in the concentration camps.[41]

DEHUMANIZATION

Dehumanization is the stage at which ordinarily benign forms of classification and symbolization are used to fan hatred for the groups set apart. The targeted groups are typically labeled as less than human; they may be compared to rats, lice, maggots, and other vermin; to hermaphrodites (the Nazis referred to homosexual men as *Mannweiber,* literally "men-women"); or to plague and other infectious diseases. Heinrich Himmler (1900–45), the head of Hitler's Schutzstaffel (SS) and the officer in charge of the concentration camps, published a decree on Roma titled "On Combating the Gypsy Plague" in 1938, and spoke of the mass murder of the Jews as "exactly the same as delousing."[42] The comparison of the targeted group to a cancer or disease that must be eliminated if the rest of the body politic is to live also encourages such atrocities as medical experiments on members of the dehumanized group, who are now seen as useful laboratory animals for the acquisition of scientific information. Thus, physicians in Hitler's Germany could be recruited to perform experiments that involved starving people to death, injecting them with chemicals or disease agents, or performing surgery without anesthesia. Similar experiments were conducted by the Japanese on Allied and Chinese prisoners of war in such camps as the infamous Unit 731.[43]

Course of Events

ORGANIZATION, POLARIZATION, AND PREPARATION

A society's transition from prejudice and discrimination to outright killing is often made through its organizations, either the takeover of existing institutions or the formation of new ones. Dehumanization of the Jews and other minority groups in Hitler's Germany was facilitated and intensified by the economic dislocation of the 1930s. The collapse of the American stock market in October 1929 was followed by a series of similar financial crises around the world, leading to the Great Depression of the early 1930s. Germany had already been struggling with a currency devalued by extreme inflation since

1923; the depression compounded the country's economic problems by creating massive unemployment. After Hitler was given nearly complete control over the government's legislative powers by the Enabling Act of March 1933 (Ermächtigungsgesetz), the Nazis swiftly made use of German economic institutions to ruin Jews financially. Hilberg regards Hitler's seizure of Jewish business firms, or "Aryanization," as the second phase in the destruction of the Jews.[44] Jews were dismissed from positions in the civil service, hospitals, banks, and universities; their businesses were boycotted; and they were heavily fined for even minor infractions of the new laws. In November 1938, Jewish-owned shops and factories as well as synagogues were physically attacked throughout Germany in a wave of violence known as Kristallnacht, or the Night of Broken Glass.

Hitler made use of another feature of the modern state on his path to mass murder—namely the growth of efficient bureaucracies in the government and other institutions. Large organizations can be effective tools of genocide because they separate most of their members from the actual killing at the same time that they can gain access to the most advanced technology for carrying out the killing. Studies of violent groups as different as street gangs and terrorist cells have shown that people participate more willingly in violent acts when they can disclaim the harm they do by displacing responsibility for it on the demands of the organization, whether that organization is identified as the state, the company, the brotherhood, or the cause. Similarly, a variety of experiments in social psychology have shown that a very effective strategy for gaining the compliance of a group member is to "create opportunities for the diffusion of responsibility, such that the one who acts [to commit genocide] won't be held liable."[45] As Aaron Beck, a contemporary psychiatrist, has noted of the various categories of state employees who participated in the Holocaust, these people generally saw themselves as honest and reliable workers. "The personnel who moved the victims along the deadly assembly line from home to gas chamber did not consider themselves evil. . . . This self-righteousness was true of the police who rounded up the Jews, the engineers who transported them on trains, and the guards who herded them into concentration camps."[46] Robert Jay Lifton, a psychiatrist who has written several books about the involvement of doctors and scientists in genocide, has identified two additional aspects of large-scale bureaucracies that allow them to become agents of genocide: The first is that "bureaucracy helps render genocide unreal."[47] This it does not only by manipulating language—such words as "deportation" or "resettlement" may become euphemisms for killing—but also by creating a kind of group mind-set in which decisions can be made that are not only disastrous but, in hindsight, irrational as well. Keeping the organization going becomes its own rationale and purpose, "as clarity of cause and effect gives way to a sense not only of inevitability but of necessity."[48]

After war broke out in September 1939, Germany was initially successful in conquering Poland and other nations to the east. The Nazis made use of two organizational tactics for controlling and then killing Jews. The first was ghettoization, which Hilberg calls "concentration." Ghettoization refers to the physical separation of the targeted group from the majority population—in the case of the Holocaust, the confinement of the Jews within very small areas of conquered cities, limiting the availability of food and sanitation measures, and thereby causing death indirectly through starvation and outbreaks of disease due to overcrowding. It is estimated that several hundred thousand Jews died of malnutrition, cholera, and typhus in the ghettoes of Eastern Europe.

The second tactic was the formation of special paramilitary organizations and other groups of professional killers that constituted a kind of bureaucratization of murder. After 1938, four battalions of death squads called Einsatzgruppen followed the German armies into the conquered territories of Eastern Europe, where they carried out mass executions of Jews, Roma, and other targeted groups, usually by machine-gunning the victims or shooting them in the head with pistols. After Hitler invaded the Soviet Union in June 1941, the Einsatzgruppen rounded up and killed at least 1.2 million Jews.[49]

MASS EXTERMINATION

Stanton considers mass extermination a relatively late stage in a nation's path to genocide. Hitler's regime turned to assembly-line extermination relatively late in the course of the Holocaust. There were several reasons for this development. One was that killing by gunfire did not proceed quickly or efficiently enough to satisfy the leaders of the regime. The second was the psychological stress on the members of the death squads; the close-range shooting of women and children in particular became known as *Seelenbelastung*, or burdening of the soul, because it led to what would now be called post-traumatic stress disorder (PTSD) in the perpetrators. The technicians of the Einsatzgruppen then devised mobile vans with exhaust pipes turned inward to suffocate the victims with carbon monoxide while they were being driven to their mass graves.[50]

Even this refinement was not enough. In the summer of 1941, the task of devising an *Endlösung der Judenfrage,* or Final Solution to the Jewish Problem, was given to Reinhard Heydrich (1904–42), the Reich governor of Bohemia and Moravia.[51] By November 1941, the first death camps were under construction in eastern Poland. Concentration camps for slave labor had been in use in Germany itself since 1933, but the six death camps

(Belzec, Sobibor, Treblinka, Chelmno, Majdanek, and Auschwitz-Birkenau) were built specifically for mass extermination. In January 1942, Heydrich chaired the Wannsee Conference, named for the suburb of Berlin in which it was held. Although Heydrich was assassinated in June 1942, the large-scale killing of Jews in the death camps had already begun. Between 3 and 3.25 million Jews died in the gas chambers[52] of these camps between 1942 and the spring of 1945, when the camps were liberated by the advancing Allied armies.

DENIAL

Stanton regards denial as a stage in a society's transition to genocide that typically begins before mass extermination and overlaps chronologically with the dehumanization of the target group and the setting up of organizational machinery for mass killing. Denial is a psychological defense that many people have encountered in families and other small groups. A problem arises—perhaps substance abuse, perhaps early symptoms of cancer or another serious illness—and people avoid confronting it by denying its magnitude or even its very existence. Denial takes place on a national and international scale in instances of genocide when people in the society itself or outside observers refuse to recognize what is happening or call it by its proper name.

In the case of the Holocaust, there is ample evidence from government archives as well as personal correspondence that detailed accounts of the activities of the Einsatzgruppen and the construction of the death camps were known to diplomats and other officials in the West. In early 1942, Jan Karski (1914–2000), a young Polish diplomat and a Roman Catholic, disguised himself as a Jew by wearing the armband with the yellow Star of David. Karski managed to sneak into the Warsaw ghetto through a tunnel and later to pose as a Ukrainian soldier in order to infiltrate Belzec, the first of the death camps. Karski then escaped to the United States at the end of 1942 and reported what he had seen.[53] He obtained an interview with Felix Frankfurter (1882–1965), an associate justice of the U.S. Supreme Court who had been born in Vienna and had come to the United States at the age of 12. After listening to Karski, Frankfurter told him that he did not believe him. He explained to Karski, "I do not mean that you are lying. I simply said I cannot believe you."[54] Frankfurter, himself a Jew whose first language was German, simply could not take in the enormities that Karski was describing, nor could most people. An organized plan for the annihilation of an entire people on the basis of what they were rather than for anything they had done was unimaginable to people in the early 1940s. American diplomats in Europe hesitated to relay what they regarded as incredible rumors in official

reports. Szmul Zygielbojm (1895–1943), a member of the Polish government-in-exile based in London, who had been traveling around Europe and
the United States since 1940 trying to convince people of the horrors that
the Nazis were inflicting on Eastern Europe, committed suicide in May 1943
when he learned that his modest proposals to expand the number of Jewish
refugees admitted to the unoccupied countries of Europe and his request for
the Allies to bomb Auschwitz and the Warsaw ghetto had been rejected.[55]
The Nazis, of course, were only too happy to reinforce public denial in the
West by ritual disclaimers.

As Jan Karski's bravery indicates, however, there were people who saw
clearly and did not hesitate to do what they could to convey information
to the outside world or to rescue people from the Nazi genocide. Some,
like Raoul Wallenberg (1912–47?), were diplomats who made use of their
access to visas and other forms of influence to prevent deportations and
help Jews escape to freedom. Wallenberg, who has been called the Swedish Angel of Rescue, is credited with having rescued tens of thousands of
Hungarian Jews.[56] Other rescuers were ordinary men and women who hid
Jewish families, sometimes in their own homes, sometimes in orphanages,
convents, schools, or hospitals. In many cases Jews were helped by a chain of
sympathetic persons over a period of months or years until they could finally
leave Europe. Many of these courageous individuals paid with their lives.
Yad Vashem, the Holocaust Martyrs' and Heroes' Remembrance Authority
in Israel, has an archive of material concerning these "righteous Gentiles,"
who included Roman Catholic, Eastern Orthodox, Lutheran, Calvinist, and
Baptist Christians as well as Muslims in Bosnia and Albania.[57]

Aftermath

THE INTERNATIONAL MILITARY TRIBUNAL OF 1946

The Holocaust has the distinction of being the first major genocide whose
high-ranking perpetrators were put on trial before the world at large. While
the Armenian genocide of 1915 was followed by Turkish domestic courts-
martial after the end of World War I, the lack of a public international
prosecution of the leaders of the Armenian genocide is thought to have
encouraged Adolf Hitler to think that he could annihilate the Jews and escape
punishment.[58]

The public indignation that did arise when news of the deportations
and slaughter of the Armenians reached the Allied powers and the United
States in 1915 represented a historical turning point, however, because
it reflected widespread acceptance of a new category of criminal offense,
namely war crimes. The reader should note here that the notion of respect

for the life and well-being of all people simply because they are human is a very recent development. For most of the course of recorded history, people restricted regard for the life and property of others to those who belonged to the same tribe, clan, or social class as themselves. People outside the restricted category were fair game for exploitation or worse.[59] The ancient Roman saying, *Vae victis*, or "woe to the defeated," was usually interpreted to mean that victors could do as they pleased with defeated or subjugated peoples. The idea that there are limits to what a victorious army can do to captured combatants or civilians in their path, and that those who violate these limits should be prosecuted for crimes afterward, grew slowly out of several different sources. These sources ranged from such practices as the Truce of God or the Peace of God in medieval Europe (which restricted armed combat to certain seasons of the year and placed clergy and other noncombatants under special protection) to theories about international law and the desirability of a body or institution that would mediate international disputes. A French writer, perhaps a monk, named Émeric Crucé (1590–1648) is thought to have been the first person to propose a meeting place (he suggested Venice) for representatives from all European countries to discuss conflicts before they escalated into full-fledged war. Crucé's plan was noteworthy for its suggested inclusion of the emperor of the Turks, leaders of the European Jewish communities, and the kings of Persia and China as well as European monarchs.[60]

Another strand of thought that contributed to the notion of establishing a legal system of some kind to prosecute and punish war crimes grew out of what is called just war theory. Just war theory in the West began with Augustine of Hippo (354–430), a Christian bishop in North Africa who was familiar with Roman law and derived some of his thinking from it. Augustine maintained that human law (in his case, Roman law) is a reflection of the rational aspect of divine law. Thus, a government under law is a creation of human reason for the common good rather than a function of arbitrary will. A government that remains within the limits set by divine and natural law can legitimately wage war under certain conditions. By the 15th century, Augustine's thoughts about the legitimacy of war under certain conditions had been codified into two parts: The first concerned *jus ad bellum*, or the legality of going to war. For a war to be considered just, it had to have a just cause (to punish evil or defend against an attack); to be conducted by a rightful authority; to use proportional force (not doing more harm than good); that it be undertaken as a last resort; that it have a reasonable hope of success; and that it have peace as its goal. The second part of just war theory concerned *jus in bello*, or lawful actions in waging

22

war. *Jus in bello* had two primary principles, the principle of immunity of noncombatants and the principle of using proportionate means (that is, not using weapons that cause unnecessary destruction). From the 16th through the 18th centuries, such writers as Hugo Grotius (1583–1645) and John Locke (1632–1704) expanded and extended the notion of moral limitations on reasons for as well as the conduct of warfare. Grotius in particular is sometimes called the father of international law on the basis of a book he published in 1625, *De jure belli ac pacis libri tres,* or *On the Laws of War and Peace.* Grotius advocated a system of principles of natural law, held to be binding on all people and nations regardless of religion or local custom.

Philosophical treatises about the desirability of restrictions on warfare through the creation of a body of international law gave way during the 19th century to the formation of actual organizations to work toward these goals. The first of the four sets of treaties known as the Geneva Conventions—the international legal framework that obliges signatories to uphold human rights in conflict and in peacetime—came about in 1863 as a result of the efforts of Henri Dunant (1828–1910), the founder of the International Committee of the Red Cross. Dunant, a Swiss businessman and humanitarian, had been horrified by the suffering of soldiers on the battlefield in 1859 during the second Italian war for independence from Austria. The Geneva Conventions were first applied to the treatment of wounded soldiers and prisoners of war and gradually extended to include protection of noncombatants.

Following the adoption of the First Geneva Convention, there were two important peace conferences at The Hague in 1899 and 1907 respectively. The first conference, summoned by Russia, dealt with the laws regulating land warfare. The document drafted at the conference entered into force on September 4, 1900. It outlawed certain forms of modern technology in warfare, including the use of aerial bombing and chemical weapons. The Hague Convention of 1907 was signed in October 1907 by representatives of the participating nations and entered into force on January 26, 1910. It dealt primarily with naval warfare, including rules regarding ships at sea when war breaks out and for conversion of merchant ships into warships.

It was the Second Hague Convention of 1907, which the United States had signed, that served as the underlying legal basis for the creation of an international court to try the surviving leaders of Hitler's regime as war criminals. Although British prime minister Winston Churchill had initially favored immediate execution of any captured high-ranking Nazis, he was persuaded by the United States to agree to a formal trial by the end of the war. In addition, no one wanted the repetition of such episodes of summary justice (immediate trial and punishment without a jury trial) as the immediate machine-gunning of more than 100 disarmed German soldiers during the U.S. Army's liberation of the concentration camp at Dachau on April 29, 1945.[61] On August 8, 1945, the Allied powers issued a decree known as the London Charter (or Nuremberg Charter), which set forth three categories of crimes for which "the major war criminals of the European Axis countries"[62] could be punished: war crimes, crimes against peace, and crimes against humanity. Because the court to be established was given jurisdiction only over violations of the laws of war, it could not punish instances of genocide committed by the Nazi leaders prior to September 1, 1939.

The trials of the German war criminals were held in the city of Nuremberg from 1945 through 1949. The first of these trials, and the best known, was the trial of 24 of the major leaders of Hitler's government under the jurisdiction of the International Military Tribunal, or IMT. The tribunal consisted of eight judges, four primary judges and four alternates, representing France, the Soviet Union, the United Kingdom, and the United States. Twelve of the defendants were sentenced to death, one (Martin Bormann) in absentia.[63] Hermann Göring, the former commander of the Luftwaffe, committed suicide the night before his scheduled execution. The others were hanged on October 16, 1946.

REAPPEARANCE OF DENIAL

One of the more discouraging developments following the Holocaust was the persistence and eventual resurfacing of denial in spite of the (West) German government's acknowledgment of responsibility for the Holocaust and the laws against Holocaust denial passed as early as 1947 by Austria, Belgium, France, and other European countries. Holocaust denial presently takes two forms: the first, outright refusal to acknowledge that the mass murder of Jews and Roma happened at all, and the second, denial that it happened to the extent that mainstream scholars maintain. Some strategies for minimizing the genocide of the Holocaust include:

- *Maintaining that the Holocaust was an unintentional rather than a deliberate by-product of World War II.* This form of minimization commonly takes the form of arguing that most of the victims of the Holocaust died from disease or starvation related to food rationing rather than from deliberate killing.

- *Arguing that the Holocaust was a form of self-defense against the threat posed by world Jewry to the German state.* This type of self-defense argument, which is based on conspiracy thinking, has also been used by those who deny the Armenian genocide of 1915 and the Rwandan genocide of 1994.

- *Accusing the present state of Israel of conducting its own version of the Holocaust.* Shimon Samuels has documented examples from European media in the 1980s of the use of Holocaust language to describe Israel during the 1982 war between Lebanon and Israel. Such phrases as "the Israeli Luftwaffe" and the "Palestinian Holocaust" appeared repeatedly in European newspapers.[64]

- *Questioning the accuracy of the casualty figures given by mainstream historians.* Some Holocaust deniers maintain that the figure of 6 to 10 million dead is an exaggeration and that many Jews and members of other targeted groups emigrated or escaped to other countries.

- *Maintaining that the perpetrators of the Holocaust were the real victims.* In regard to the Holocaust, some observers focus on the documented suffering of Germans during World War II (mass rapes committed by Soviet soldiers; the fire-bombings of Hamburg and Dresden in 1943 and 1945; mass Soviet executions of German prisoners of war, etc.) in order to downplay or deny the significance of the Holocaust, not just to write a complete history of the period.[65]

In the West, most Holocaust deniers are fringe academics like David Irving in the United Kingdom,[66] Arthur Butz in the United States,[67] or Robert Faurisson in France.[68] There have, however, also been worrisome incidents involving nonacademic individuals physically attacking well-known Holocaust survivors, such as the lone assailant who waylaid the renowned theorist of the Holocaust, Elie Wiesel, in the elevator of a San Francisco hotel in February 2007.[69] In the Arab world, Holocaust denial is commonly found in political speeches and mainstream journalism, to such an extent that some schoolteachers in Great Britain were reported in 2007 as avoiding teaching about the Holocaust "to avoid offending Muslim pupils."[70]

What are some of the reasons underlying Holocaust denial? Several have been proposed by various observers:

- *Ideology.* Anti-Semitism in the Arab world continues to fester as an excuse for the economic and political problems of the region. Political groups on the far Left in the West sometimes engage in Holocaust denial in order to portray Israel as the villain in its dealings with the Palestinians. Nationalism appears to be the most common ideology leading to Holocaust denial on the part of skinheads and neo-Nazi groups.

- *Individual discomfort with imputations of collective guilt.* People whose ancestors were perpetrators of genocide or who belong to an ethnic group identified with the commission of genocide often express resentment or pain when judged according to such generalizations as "all Germans are anti-Semitic Nazis." The daughter of a Nazi described to her psychologist how she felt when the daughter of a Holocaust survivor said that she looked like an SS woman: "It hurts when somebody says that. . . . I mean I'm not seen, you know, as a person, and I think that's what hurts very much. . . . [being put in] the same category of something that we all know we hate."[71] In some cases, discomfort with generalized accusations can eventually lead to denial of genocide. Adult offspring of Nazi leaders often deny the Holocaust.

- *Differences in perspective between perpetrators and victims.* Research in the social sciences indicates that victims and perpetrators regard both the wrongdoing itself and the time frame quite differently. Victims generally consider the memory of past injustices crucial to understanding the present, whereas perpetrators tend to reason that people should let bygones be bygones. In addition, victims tend to feel the sting of injustice keenly, whereas perpetrators are more likely to maintain that what took place wasn't so bad. One social psychologist explains these discrepancies in terms of what he calls the magnitude gap: "What the perpetrator gained was generally smaller than what the victim lost, and so the perpetrator has less reason to replay that memory."[72]

- *Insistence by Holocaust deniers on unlimited freedom of speech.* The issue of genocide denial in general and Holocaust denial in particular is often bound up with debates on the limits of free speech. In some countries, including Germany, Holocaust denial is punished by fines, prison terms, or deportation, but other countries, including the United States, prefer surveillance and infiltration of neo-Nazi and other anti-Semitic organizations. As of 2009, there are scholars on both sides of this issue. Some writers, including Robert Jay Lifton and Roger Smith, believe that denial of the Holocaust (and other genocides) should be punished on the grounds that denial increases the likelihood of future genocides and adds to the suffering of genocide survivors. Lifton has argued that Japan's societywide denial of its genocidal behavior during World War II created the psychological conditions that fostered such cults as Aum Shinrikyō,[73] a millennial cult that looked forward to violent destruction of the world and promised survival and power to cult members. Lifton regards Japanese denial of World War II atrocities as unresolved guilt and shame that made an apocalyptic movement extremely attractive to a younger generation of Japanese. Other scholars, however, maintain that prosecution of such authors as Irving and Faurisson does little more than give their opinions undeserved publicity and that it is better to answer their publications with well-reasoned argumentation and documentation than to punish them through the legal system.

CONCLUSION

It is not likely that international laws against genocide will be enforced at any time in the near future. One reason is that no international body, not even the United Nations with its 192 member states as of 2008, can claim to represent all states that consider themselves to be independent entities. In addition, some member states do not regard the United Nations as an independent organization with the right to intervene in troubled situations but only as an association whose 192 members must reach agreement before acting. Second, the lack of consensus regarding a definition of genocide hinders the enforcement of laws against genocide. As a result, the international community's response to such events as the Rwandan genocide of 1994 has been reaction after the fact rather than proactive measures to stop genocides as they occur.

An additional factor that complicates the enforcement of international laws against genocide as of 2008 is the emergence of non-state actors, both secessionist groups within existing nation-states and terrorist organizations that operate across national borders. Neither ethnic separatists who do not consider themselves bound by the laws of the state that claims them as citizens nor terrorists who are loyal to transnational causes are likely to accept international laws about genocide as binding. Last, the spread of nuclear weapons technology to small groups independent of nation-states raises the possibility of a genocidal attack that could be carried out before the United Nations or other international bodies could effectively intervene.

---

[1] Raphael Lemkin. "Genocide—A Modern Crime." *Free World* 4 (April 1945): 39. Available online. URL: http://www.preventgenocide.org/lemkin/freeworld1945.htm. Accessed March 21, 2007. Spelling and punctuation in the original.

[2] See, for example, W. A. Darity and C. B. Turner. "Family Planning, Race Consciousness, and the Fear of Race Genocide." *American Journal of Public Health* 62 (1972): 1,454–1,459.

[3] An animal rights organization called People for the Ethical Treatment of Animals (PETA) stirred up a major controversy in the United States in 2003 by an advertising campaign that compared meat consumption to the Holocaust. Such organizations as the Anti-Defamation League (ADL) and the Southern Poverty Law Center protested PETA's "Holocaust on Your Plate" publicity material. PETA formally apologized in 2005. See the ADL's article, "Holocaust

Imagery and Animal Rights," August 2, 2005. Available online. URL: http://www.adl.org/Anti_semitism/holocaust_imagery.asp. Accessed March 21, 2007.

[4] K. M. Palm, M. A. Polusny, and V. M. Follette. "Vicarious Traumatization: Potential Hazards and Interventions for Disaster and Trauma Workers." *Prehospital Disaster Medicine* 19 (January–March 2004): 73–78.

[5] Dori Laub, M.D. "Bearing Witness or the Vicissitudes of Listening." In *Testimony: Crises of Witnessing in Literature, Psychoanalysis, and History.* New York: Routledge, 1992, pp. 57–74; Christine Courtois, Ph.D. "Vicarious Traumatization of the Therapist." *National Center for PTSD Newsletter* (Spring 1993), 8–9.

[6] Luci Ruedenberg-Wright. "The Second and Third Generations: Where Do We Go from Here?" Paper delivered at the 29th annual conference of the Association for Jewish Studies, Boston, Mass., December 21–23, 1997. Available online. URL: http://www.lrw.net/~lucia/pubs/ajs/. Accessed March 25, 2007.

[7] Quoted in Daniel Allott. "A Non-Credible Threat: Why Khartoum Continues to Kill." *Weekly Standard* (3/23/07). Available online. URL: http://weeklystandard.com/Content/Public/Articles/000/000/013/409tpapb.asp. Accessed March 27, 2007.

[8] National Transportation Safety Board. Docket DCA88MA008, approved January 4, 1989. Available online. URL: http://www.ntsb.gov/NTSB/brief.asp?ev_id=20001213X32679&key=1. Accessed March 26, 2007.

[9] Numerous news reports called attention to the fact that a professor who died in order to give the students in his classroom a few extra seconds to escape from the killer was a Holocaust survivor. See, for example, Haviv Rettig. "Israeli Who Saved Virginia Students Buried as Hero." *Jerusalem Post* (4/20/07). Available online. URL: http://www.jpost.com/servlet/Satellite?cid=1176152841184&pagename=JPost%2FJPArticle%2FShowFull. Accessed April 22, 2007.

[10] Bruce E. Wexler, M.D. *Brain and Culture: Neurobiology, Ideology, and Social Change.* Cambridge, Mass.: MIT Press, 2006, pp. 230–231.

[11] Adam Jones. *Genocide: A Comprehensive Introduction.* New York: Routledge, 2006, p. xxi.

[12] Jones. *Genocide*, p. xxi.

[13] Mona Sue Weissmark. *Justice Matters: Legacies of the Holocaust and World War II.* New York: Oxford University Press, 2004, p. 180.

[14] Charlotte Delbo. *Auschwitz and After.* Translated by Rosette C. Lamont. New Haven, Conn.: Yale University Press, 1995, p. 230.

[15] Thucydides. *Peloponnesian War* V: 17.

[16] Benjamin Franklin. "A Narrative of the Late Massacres, in Lancaster County, of a Number of Indians, Friends of this Province, by Persons Unknown, With Some Observations on the Same." Available online. URL: http://www.historycarper.com/resources/twobf3/massacre.htm. Accessed March 27, 2007.

[17] Congressional testimony of Mr. John S. Smith, Washington, March 14, 1865. Available online. URL: http://www.pbs.org/weta/thewest/resources/archives/four/sandcrk.htm#smith. Accessed March 27, 2007.

[18] Consul Leslie A. Davis to Ambassador Henry Morgenthau. Quoted in Donald E. Miller and Lorna Touryan Miller. *Survivors: An Oral History of the Armenian Genocide.* Berkeley, Calif.: University of California Press, 1999, p. 21.

[19] R. J. Rummel. *Death by Government*. Chapter 2, "Definition of Democide." Available online. URL: http://www.hawaii.edu/powerkills/DBG.CHAP2.HTM. Accessed March 28, 2007.

[20] Douglas A. Sylva. "The Lost Girls." *Weekly Standard* (3/21/07). Available online. URL: http://www.theweeklystandard.com/Content/Public/Articles/000/000/013/415gcfae.asp. Accessed March 28, 2007.

[21] Robert Jay Lifton, M.D. *Destroying the World to Save It: Aum Shinrikyō, Apocalyptic Violence, and the New Global Terrorism*. New York: Henry Holt and Company, 2000, pp. 301–302.

[22] See, for example, Elsie Allen's account of her boarding school experience in Covelo, California, in 1911, in Herbert W. Luthin, ed. *Surviving Through the Days: A California Indian Reader*. Berkeley, Calif.: University of California Press, 2002, pp. 560–562.

[23] There were a few battles in the ancient world that cost lives on this scale, such as the 40,000 to 50,000 Persians who died fighting Alexander the Great at Gaugamela in 331 B.C.E. and the 60,000 to 70,000 Romans slaughtered or captured by Hannibal at Cannae in 216 B.C.E., but these were one-day combats that ended at sundown—unlike the incessant gunfire and bombardments that characterized World Wars I and II.

[24] John Terraine. *The Great War*. Ware, England: Wordsworth Editions, 1998, p. 369.

[25] Jones. *Genocide*, p. 83.

[26] Raphael Lemkin. Unfinished autobiography. Quoted in Samantha Power. *A Problem from Hell: America and the Age of Genocide*. New York: Basic Books, 2002, p. 20.

[27] Raphael Lemkin. "The Evolution of the Genocide Convention." Unpublished papers in the New York Public Library. Quoted in Power. *Problem from Hell*, p. 21.

[28] Power. *Problem from Hell*, p. 42. The spelling is Lemkin's.

[29] Alan S. Rosenbaum. "Introduction to the First Edition." In Alan S. Rosenbaum, ed. *Is the Holocaust Unique? Perspectives on Comparative Genocide*, 2nd ed. Boulder, Colo.: Westview Press, 2001, p. 7.

[30] Gregory H. Stanton. "The Eight Stages of Genocide." Available online. URL: http://www.genocidewatch.org/eightstages.htm. Accessed March 1, 2007. I have combined Stanton's eight stages into six.

[31] Raul Hilberg. "The Anatomy of the Holocaust." In *The Holocaust: Ideology, Bureaucracy, and Genocide. The San José Papers.* Edited by Henry Friedlander and Sybil Milton. New York: Kraus International Publications, 1980, pp. 86–87.

[32] The etymology of *barbarian* is summarized in Wexler. *Brain and Culture*, p. 199.

[33] Wexler. *Brain and Culture*, p. 155.

[34] Although Jews have been the most frequent victims of a blood libel, other groups have suffered from it as well, including the ancient Carthaginians, Christians in the Roman Empire, Roma (Gypsies), the medieval Cathars, and, most recently, the Chinese.

[35] Quoted in Power. *Problem from Hell*, pp. 24–25.

[36] Robert Gellately has suggested that World War II itself should be reinterpreted as "overwhelmingly a race war.... In [Germany's] race war against the Jews, it murdered an estimated 5 to 6 million people. The Nazis also went after the "Gypsies." ... Robert Gellately.

"The Third Reich, the Holocaust, and Visions of Serial Genocide." In *The Specter of Genocide: Mass Murder in Historical Perspective*. Edited by Robert Gellately and Ben Kiernan. New York: Cambridge University Press, 2003, p. 263.

[37] Jones. *Genocide*, p. 173.

[38] Contemporary scholars usually prefer the term *Roma* (or *Romani*) for the peoples known colloquially as Gypsies. *Gypsy* is presently considered a derogatory term because of its association with *gyp* and should be avoided except in historical descriptions or explanations of the meaning of Roma.

[39] Michael Burleigh. *Ethics and Extermination: Reflections on Nazi Genocide*. Cambridge: Cambridge University Press, 1997, p. 162.

[40] The corresponding garment for freeborn adult women was the stola; a woman who wore the toga virilis was publicly identifying herself as a prostitute.

[41] Richard Plant. *The Pink Triangle: The Nazi War against Homosexuals*. New York: Henry Holt, 1986, p. 166.

[42] Quoted in Robert Jay Lifton. *The Nazi Doctors: Medical Killing and the Psychology of Genocide*. New York: Basic Books, 2000, p. 477. Himmler's use of the comparison was preceded almost a century earlier in reference to Native Americans. When asked why he planned to kill the children in a Native American village as well as the adult males, an officer of the U.S. Army said, "Because nits make lice." Quoted in David E. Stannard. *American Holocaust: The Conquest of the New World*. New York: Oxford University Press, 1992, p. 131.

[43] Arnold C. Brackman. *The Other Nuremberg: The Untold Story of the Tokyo War Crimes Trials*. New York: William Morrow, 1987, pp. 242–269; see also George Weller and Anthony Weller. *First into Nagasaki: The Censored Eyewitness Dispatches on Post-Atomic Japan and Its Prisoners of War*. New York: Crown Publishing Group, 2006.

[44] Hilberg. "Anatomy of the Holocaust," p. 90.

[45] Philip Zimbardo, Ph.D. "When Good People Do Evil." *Yale Alumni Magazine*. January/February 2007, p. 44.

[46] Aaron T. Beck, M.D. *Prisoners of Hate: The Cognitive Basis of Anger, Hostility, and Violence*. New York: HarperCollins, 1999, p. 176.

[47] Lifton. *The Nazi Doctors*, p. 495.

[48] Lifton. *The Nazi Doctors*, p. 496.

[49] Jones. *Genocide*, p. 152.

[50] Hilberg. "Anatomy of the Holocaust," pp. 95–96.

[51] A detailed account of the decision and chain of command can be found in Christopher R. Browning. *The Origins of the Final Solution*. London: William Heinemann, 2004.

[52] The gas used was hydrogen cyanide, released when small absorbent disks or pellets impregnated with hydrocyanic acid (known as Zyklon B) were exposed to air. Zyklon B had originally been developed as a pesticide during World War I and was used to delouse German soldiers to control the spread of typhus. Zyklon B was first tested as an agent of mass murder on Roma children in 1940 and Soviet prisoners of war in 1941.

[53] Karski came to the United States after the end of World War II, earning a Ph.D. from Georgetown University in 1952 and becoming a citizen of the United States in 1954. His

wartime service was largely forgotten until the publication of a biography in 1994. See E. Thomas Wood and Stanislaw M. Jankowski. *Karski: How One Man Tried to Stop the Holocaust.* New York: John Wiley and Sons, 1994.

[54] Quoted in Power. *Problem from Hell,* p. 34.

[55] Power. *Problem from Hell,* p. 37.

[56] The most detailed biography of Wallenberg in English is Harvey Rosenfeld. *Raoul Wallenberg,* 2nd ed. New York: Holmes and Meier, 1995. Wallenberg was arrested by the Soviet Union on January 17, 1945, and taken to Lubyanka prison. It is thought that he was executed in July 1947, although some former prisoners claimed to have seen him in another Soviet prison as late as 1987.

[57] As of 2002, the archive at Yad Vashem contained the names and biographies of nearly 20,000 "righteous Gentiles." Some of their stories are recounted in Martin Gilbert. *The Righteous: The Unsung Heroes of the Holocaust.* New York: Henry Holt and Company, 2003.

[58] Hitler is reported to have said on several occasions in 1939 that no one remembered the slaughter of the Armenians; hence he could arrange for the "resettlement" of the Jews without hindrance or eventual retribution. See Vahakn N. Dadrian. "The Comparative Aspects of the Armenian and Jewish Cases of Genocide: A Sociohistorical Perspective." In Alan S. Rosenbaum. *Is the Holocaust Unique?: Perspectives on Comparative Genocide.* Boulder, Colo.: Westview Press, 2001, p. 149.

[59] Charles Taylor. *Sources of the Self: The Making of the Modern Identity.* Cambridge, Mass.: Harvard University Press, 1989, p. 3–5.

[60] Grace Roosevelt. "A Brief History of the Quest for Peace: Pacifism and Just War Theory in Europe from the 16th to the 20th Centuries." Available online. URL: http://www.globalpolicy.org/reform/intro/1999jinx.htm. Accessed April 4, 2007.

[61] There is a time line of the events of April 29, 1945, and photographs of the camp and the executions available online. URL: http://www.humanitas-international.org/archive/dachau-liberation. Accessed September 9, 2008. One of the ironies of the massacre is that the executive officer of one of the rifle companies that machine-gunned the German soldiers was a full-blooded Cherokee from Oklahoma named Jack Bushyhead. Bushyhead was descended from one of the survivors of the Trail of Tears.

[62] The Japanese leaders identified as war criminals were tried in Tokyo before the International Military Tribunal for the Far East (IMTFE) between 1946 and 1948, with the seven defendants sentenced to death executed on December 22, 1948. A detailed account of the IMTFE can be found in Brackman. *The Other Nuremberg.* Brackman was a United Press staff correspondent who covered the trials as a reporter in 1946.

[63] Bormann left the bunker where Hitler was hiding under the ruins of Berlin on May 2, 1945, after which he disappeared. Bormann's remains were discovered in 1972 and confirmed as his by DNA analysis in 1998. It appears that Bormann became disoriented by the confusion around him after he left the bunker and committed suicide by swallowing a cyanide capsule to avoid capture by the Red Army.

[64] Shimon Samuels. "Applying the Lessons of the Holocaust." In Alan S. Rosenbaum, ed. *Is the Holocaust Unique? Perspectives on Comparative Genocide,* 2nd ed. Boulder, Colo.: Westview Press, 2001, p. 211.

[65] See Jones. *Genocide,* pp. 179–180, for a brief account of atrocities inflicted on German civilians and soldiers during World War II.

[66] David J. C. Irving. *Hitler's War.* New York: Avon Books, 1990. Irving minimizes the magnitude of the Holocaust, preferring to refer to Hitler's "atrocities" and maintaining that Hitler knew nothing of Heydrich's plans for the Final Solution until late in 1943.

[67] Arthur R. Butz. *The Hoax of the Twentieth Century: The Case against the Presumed Extermination of European Jewry,* 3rd ed. Chicago: Theses & Dissertations Press, 2003.

[68] Robert Faurisson. *Écrits révisionnistes, 1974–1998,* 4 vols. Pithiviers: Ed. privée, 1999.

[69] Associated Press. "Nobel Laureate Accosted at San Francisco Peace Forum." *San Francisco Examiner* (2/9/07). Available online. URL: http://www.examiner.com/a-556256~Nobel_laureate_accosted_at_peace_conference.html. Accessed February 9, 2007.

[70] Laura Clark. "Teachers Drop the Holocaust to Avoid Offending Muslims." *Daily Mail* (4/2/07). Available online. URL: http://www.dailymail.co.uk/pages/live/articles/news/news.html?in_article_id=445979&in_page_id=1770. Accessed April 4, 2007.

[71] Quoted in Weissmark. *Justice Matters,* p. 152.

[72] Roy F. Baumeister, Ph.D. *Evil: Inside Human Violence and Cruelty.* New York: W. H. Freeman and Company, p. 43.

[73] Lifton. *Destroying the World,* pp. 246–249.

2

Focus on the United States

The issue of genocide in the United States is significantly complicated for a number of reasons. To begin with, it is more accurate to speak of genocide in the general North American continent before the 19th century, rather than the United States in particular, because the present national boundaries of Canada, Mexico, and the United States did not yet exist. Some incidents of ethnocide (destruction of the language and culture of a people) or genocide took place across the present-day international borders.

Second, the lack of written historical records poses a greater difficulty in researching instances of mass killing in North America than in Europe or Asia. Not only were some written records destroyed (which also happened frequently elsewhere in the world), but a high proportion of the indigenous inhabitants of the continent had not developed written languages when Europeans arrived in the late 15th century. This fact requires historians to depend more heavily on archaeological evidence and folk memory (tribal legends, chants, and oral histories) as sources of information.

Third, the application of the term *genocide* to the rapid decrease of the native population in North America after 1500 is one of the most vexing and contentious fields in modern genocide scholarship. David E. Stannard's *American Holocaust,* published in 1992, set off a major controversy among scholars with comments such as that declaring, "The destruction of the Indians of the Americas was, far and away, the most massive act of genocide in the history of the world."[1] Stannard's book disturbed some historians because of its apparent minimization of Adolf Hitler's attempt to exterminate Jews, Roma, and other minorities in the 1940s. Maintaining the uniqueness of the Nazi Holocaust is a major concern to a number of historians. Steven Katz, a historian of the Holocaust, rejects the claim that the "subjugation and abuse" of the Indians of the Americas, though historically undeniable and morally tragic, is comparable to the Holocaust "for several fundamental reasons, the most basic of which is the role that disease has played in this [North American] history."[2] Katz also makes the point that the Holocaust was unique because it was a deliberate act on the part of a state to wipe out every child and adult belonging to a specific people.

The other aspect of Stannard's charge that made it controversial is the question of intent. This question is directly related to the impact of contagious diseases on the native population in that, as Steven Katz put it, "... the European invaders and settlers who were directly responsible for their (often unknowing) importation lacked the scientific knowledge to halt their deadly work once it had begun."[3] Intent is specified by the 1948 Convention on the Prevention and Punishment of the Crime of Genocide in its listing of "acts committed with intent to destroy" as an essential dimension of genocide. By that standard, the impact of European settlement in the New World does not qualify as genocide. On the other hand, some scholars reject the Convention's emphasis on intention, preferring instead to define genocide in terms of outcomes. If outcome is adopted as the standard "... there is nothing in recorded human experience to set alongside the genocide of the indigenous peoples in the Americas. It lasted longer, and destroyed a greater percentage and possibly a greater total number of victims, than any [other] genocide in history."[4] The definition of genocide in this chapter will, however, assume intent.

PRECOLONIAL AMERICA

Recent scholarship about the prehistoric American Southwest has turned away from the older view that warfare among tribes in North America was uncommon "with few fatalities and even fewer social consequences,"[5] or that it was the result of contact with Europeans. Steven A. LeBlanc, an expert on prehistoric warfare in the Americas, estimated that 20 to 30 percent of all males and 3 to 5 percent of all females died as a direct result of war. These deaths resulted from four basic types of warfare: formal battles, ambushes, surprise attacks, and massacres of entire communities. Moreover, such traditional explanations for prehistoric warfare as ecological stress, tribal vengeance, or ritual displays of masculinity have not been borne out; the primary motive for ethnocidal conflicts appears to have been simple competition.[6] Ethnocidal in this context refers to the destruction of an ethnic group or tribe rather than an entire nation or religion. Ethnocide is sometimes distinguished from genocide on the grounds that the harm done to the injured group is not always motivated by notions of racial or ethnic superiority. In addition, ethnocide may involve interference with the transmission of a group's culture and language as well as killing or kidnapping members of the group.

Ethnocidal warfare among Native Americans in the Southwest involved competition for land and other resources, but also ended in the disappearance of entire cultures, even though their obliteration may not have been the primary goal of the dominant tribes. Such practices as cannibalism and human sacrifice were part of ethnocidal conflicts in this region before the coming of Europeans, apparently as ways for some warrior tribes to terrorize and gain control over weaker groups or settlements. The most important point to keep in mind is that the Native Americans of precolonial North and Central America were as capable of mass killing and enslavement of smaller or weaker groups as were aggressive states in Europe or Asia during the same period.

The evidence for ethnocidal warfare among Native Americans in the Southwest comes from several sources. One is oral histories of massacres of entire settlements. The following comes from a traditional account of the destruction of Awat'ovi, a Hopi pueblo about nine miles southwest of Keams Canyon in Arizona.

> *There the warrior chief once again admonished his men: "Be sure you don't hold back now. . . . Don't show mercy to anyone." . . . They shot their arrows down on the men. The latter had been completely unsuspecting and had no weapons whatsoever. Now the raiders stormed into all the houses. Whenever they came across a man, no matter whether young or old, they killed him. . . . Not a single man or boy did they spare. . . . Whenever they found an old man, they cut him down. Old women they killed too, Younger women and girls they herded together at a place by the dump. . . . Anyone who attempted to escape was killed.*[7]

Other evidence comes from archaeological findings. Weapons, human remains showing evidence of violent treatment, and buildings that give evidence of destruction by burning have all been uncovered at many sites in present-day New Mexico, Arizona, and Utah. The most disturbing findings, however, are those that indicate that some southwestern Indians practiced cannibalism that was not starvation-induced in the period between 900 and 1200 C.E. The sites that have been studied yield an average of nine victims per site, a few as many as 35, with all age groups represented. "The examples do not look like ambushes. . . . Instead, they look very much like small communities that were attacked, and where everyone, or almost everyone, was killed and their remains processed."[8] Although some scholars argue that these small communities were attacked because other groups of Pueblo Indians thought the inhabitants were witches, they acknowledge that the entire community was in fact massacred.[9]

The Aztecs farther to the northwest in the valley of central Mexico weakened their empire by the wars they waged to obtain captives for human sacrifice to their gods. Although some scholars initially believed that the Aztecs ate the flesh of their victims, most now maintain that the most adequate explanation of Aztec sacrifice was political—to gain control over neighboring tribes through terror and intimidation. "For example, the Aztec king Ahuitzotl purportedly organized the butchery of 80,400 prisoners during a four-day blood sacrifice at the 1487 inauguration of the Great Temple ... in Tenochtitlán—an industrialized murder in its own right. Ahuitzotl's killing rate of 14 victims a minute over the 96-hour bloodbath far exceeded the daily murder record at either Auschwitz or Dachau."[10] Although, as Robert Jay Lifton, a psychiatrist who has written several studies of genocide, has noted, the Aztec practice of human sacrifice was rooted in a belief that the gods required periodic nourishment with human blood in order to continue sustaining the universe rather than the Nazi notion of scientific eugenics, what the two societies had in common was the concept that killing others was a way to preserve the "life power" of one's own group. "Both groups went on killing in the face of increasing evidence that the killing itself interfered with the survival of the state: with the conduct of the war, in the case of the Nazis; and with the entire social and economic existence of an exhausted empire, in the case of the Aztecs."[11]

Until the early 2000s, it was thought that the accounts of Aztec human sacrifice given by the Spanish conquistadores were biased in order to prejudice later readers against the indigenous cultures of Mexico. While it is possible that the Spaniards exaggerated the numbers of sacrificial victims, forensic archaeologists have found physical evidence that the methods recorded to sacrifice humans—cutting open the victim's chest to remove the heart, decapitation, stoning, crushing, shooting with arrows, burning alive, and burying alive—were indeed used by the Aztecs. Nor were captured warriors the only sacrificial victims; children were frequently sacrificed because the Aztecs considered them pure and unspoiled. In 2002 a Mexican archaeologist discovered the remains of 42 boys around the age of six who had been sacrificed on the site of an Aztec temple in Mexico City to appease the gods during a drought.[12]

COLONIAL AMERICA

When studying or discussing genocide in North America during the colonial period, the reader should keep in mind that three different empires—England, France, and Spain—sent colonists to the New World, and that these three European nations had very different approaches to conquest and settlement.

The Spanish Colonies of Central and South America

The extreme brutality of the Spanish conquistadores was in part a by-product of the relatively recent unification of Spain under Ferdinand and Isabella and the expulsion of the last of the Moorish rulers from Granada in 1492—only months before Columbus set foot on the island he named San Salvador. Part of the Spanish mind-set in this period was a fanatical version of Roman Catholicism that divided the world into absolute good and evil. "Jews, Moors, and Protestants were fair game, in addition to Catholics of dubious faith who were accused of anything from bathing daily to reading imported literature."[13] Translated into economic and political terms, the Spanish were concerned with aristocratic honor, preferably displayed in warfare, and the acquisition of gold, land, military titles, and Indian subjects. Although the Indians were defended by such missionary priests as Bartolomé de Las Casas (1484–1566), who tried to secure the protections of Spanish law for them, they were exploited and subjugated by aristocratic governors who knew that their king's bureaucracy was five weeks away by ship and notorious for its inaction. A typical case of the law's delay involved the audit of a former viceroy of Peru, which took 13 years and 50,000 sheets of paper to complete. By then the corrupt official was long since dead.[14] Las Casas himself was quite convinced that the Indians he encountered were not inferior to his compatriots; if anything, he clearly thought the conquerors could learn from the conquered about virtuous character.[15]

Few of the Spanish colonists paid much attention to Las Casas. Pedro de Cieza de León (1518–60), himself a conquistador who accompanied Francisco Pizarro (c. 1475–1541) in the conquest of Peru, believed that the Spanish had the right to extract forced labor from the Indians, but even he noted in his 1540 history of the Incas that the Spaniards slaughtered them "as though a fire had gone, destroying everything in its path." Cieza de León continued

> *I would not condemn the employment of Indian carriers . . . but if a man had need of one pig, he killed twenty; if four Indians were wanted, he took a dozen . . . and there were many Spaniards who made the poor Indians carry their whores in hammocks borne on their shoulders. Were one ordered to enumerate the great evils, injuries, robberies, oppression, and ill treatment inflicted on the natives during these operations . . . there would be no end of it . . . for they thought no more of killing Indians than if they were useless beasts.[16]*

Forced labor within the Spanish *encomienda* system (which was a trusteeship arrangement rather than direct ownership of land), as grueling as it was, was preferable to work on the coca plantations established by the Spanish on the edge of rain forests, or labor in the silver mines of the Andes. Between one-third and one-half of the coca workers died during their five months' required service in the fields; the life expectancy of a mine worker, forced to inhale the poisonous vapors of arsenic, mercury, and cinnabar 700 feet below the ground, was about three months—"about the same as that of someone working at slave labor in the synthetic rubber manufacturing plant at Auschwitz in the 1940s."[17]

The same harsh treatment characterized the Spanish treatment of the Indians living in what are now the states of Arizona and New Mexico. Pedro de Castañeda (dates unknown), the chronicler of the expedition led by Francisco Vásquez de Coronado (c. 1510–1554), tells of Coronado's exploitation of and cruelty toward the Tiguex Indians (living near present-day Bernalillo, northwest of Albuquerque) in the winter of 1540–41 in a chapter titled "Of how the people of Tiguex revolted, and how they were punished, without being to blame for it":

> ... The [Indians] were taken to the tent of Don Garcia, who ... as he had been ordered by the general not to take them alive, but to make an example of them so that the other natives would fear the Spaniards, he ordered 200 stakes to be prepared at once to burn them alive. Nobody told him about the peace that had been granted them, for the soldiers knew as little as he, and those who should have told him about it remained silent, not thinking that it was any of their business. Then when the enemies saw that the Spaniards were binding them and beginning to roast them, about a hundred men who were in the tent began to struggle and defend themselves with what there was there and with the stakes they could seize. Our men who were on foot attacked the tent on all sides, so that there was great confusion around it, and then the horsemen chased those who escaped. As the country was level, not a man of them remained alive, unless it was some who remained hidden in the village and escaped that night to spread throughout the country the news that the strangers did not respect the peace they had made, which afterward proved a great misfortune.[18]

This attitude toward the Indians continued into the next two centuries. Don Diego de Vargas (1643–1704), the governor of New Spain responsible for the reconquest of territory after the Pueblo revolt of 1680, is reported to have said in 1693, "You might as well try to convert Jews without the Inquisition as Indians without soldiers."[19]

The French Colonies of North America

Relations between the French settlers along the St. Lawrence and Hudson Rivers and the Indians of northeastern North America were less tense than those between their Spanish counterparts and the Indians of the Southwest. One reason is that France and England were relative latecomers to the colonization of the New World, almost a century later than the Spanish. Both countries were farther along the path to becoming nation-states than Spain, and both were more concerned with trade than with direct acquisition of precious metals through either plunder or mining. With regard to France in particular, the country's absolute monarchy was better able to formulate a unified colonial policy and to exercise centralized control over the settlers of New France. The Bourbon kings valued the lucrative fur trade along the St. Lawrence and therefore wanted to maintain good relations with the Indians. In addition, they sent a smaller number of settlers—in 1715 the French-speaking population of Canada stood at only 18,500 persons, compared to the 400,000 settlers in the English colonies farther south.[20] This smaller white population meant less friction with the native tribes.

An additional factor was the different character of French Catholic spirituality in the 17th century. The Jesuit missionaries who accompanied the French settlers had been schooled in a model of piety that emphasized human humility in the face of God's grandeur, patient endurance of hardship, and devotion to the sufferings of Christ[21] rather than the aggressive and triumphalistic form of Catholicism imported by the Spanish. Jean de Brébeuf (1593–1649), who was later killed by the Iroquois and canonized as the patron saint of Canada (1930), instructed his fellow missionaries among the Huron (Wyandot)[22] Indians in 1637 to "love these Hurons, ransomed by the blood of the Son of God, as brothers."[23]

The French, however, bear an indirect responsibility for the destruction of the Hurons at the hands of the Iroquois in 1649. The rivalry between the French fur traders and the Dutch for control of the trade in beaver pelts led the French to destroy any possibility of peaceful cooperation between the Hurons and their ancestral rivals. Although hostility between the two tribes predated the arrival of Europeans, the French encouraged the tension and inflamed it. On the Dutch side, the Dutch settlers helped to supply the Iroquois with guns, which gave them a distinctive military advantage over the Hurons.[24] Finally, on March 16, 1649, the Huron village of St. Ignace was attacked by 1,200 Iroquois while the defenders slept. The Iroquois then proceeded to attack the nearby village of St. Louis, which they also captured and burned. The inhabitants who were not taken as prisoners were massacred, including Jean de Brébeuf and his companion Gabriel Lalemant. The torture and execution of the Hurons and the missionaries in St. Louis has been described as quasi-genocidal; among other cruelties, the Iroquois practiced cannibalism on that occasion, as they had elsewhere during the so-called Beaver Wars.[25] By May 1649, the Huron confederacy had virtually ceased to exist, most of the survivors of the Iroquois attacks having been captured or forced to accept adoption into the Iroquois confederacy. By later standards, this forcible absorption of another tribe would be defined as ethnocidal.

The English Colonies of North America

Like the French settlements, the English colonies of North America were chartered by the Crown in the interests of trade. Unlike the French government, however, the English Parliament did not maintain a fixed and relatively unified policy toward the colonies but veered between strict enforcement of parliamentary trade regulations and periods of what might be termed benign neglect.[26] The variety of climatic conditions and other environmental features along the eastern seaboard south of Massachusetts posed an additional difficulty in regulating the trading activities of the English colonists. Moreover, the English colonists were more interested than the French fur traders in acquiring land for farming and permanent settlement; relatively few of them thought of eventually returning to England.

Another factor that differentiated the English colonists from their French and Spanish counterparts was their relationship to the state church of the mother country. Instead of being missionaries for the Church of England, many of the early settlers—particularly in New England and the Middle Atlantic colonies—were dissenters from Anglicanism who had their own ideas about the forms of worship and church order most conducive to godliness. The Puritans of Massachusetts and Connecticut, the Baptists in Rhode Island, the Presbyterians in New Jersey, and the Quakers in Pennsylvania were initially more concerned with establishing their own churches in the wilderness than with converting Indians. Moreover, the Puritan concept of the church as a select group of visibly purified saints bound together by a covenant tended to minimize their interest in the indigenous peoples.[27] It was not until the late 17th century that the Anglican Church and the various other Protestant groups began to send out missionaries to the Indians. In addition to the religious distinction, the ratio of men to women was more nearly equal among the English colonists than among either the French or the Spanish, which meant that there was less intermarriage between the English and the Native tribes.[28]

The first major episode of ethnocidal warfare against the Indians on the part of Puritans in New England was the Pequot War of 1637, which was motivated primarily by the colonists' desire to expand their territorial holdings. It was also the Native peoples' first encounter with the European style of total warfare, the use of all available resources (human, technological, etc.) to destroy the enemy's ability to keep fighting.[29] The Pequot Indians were a tribe

40

living in what is now southeastern Connecticut. They had already been weakened by a smallpox epidemic that began in 1634 and by their attempts to gain control over other tribes living in the area, the Narragansetts, the Mohegans, and some Algonquian tribes living on present-day Long Island. In the summer of 1636, the body of John Oldham—a trader sailing to Block Island off the coast of Rhode Island—was found near his looted vessel. It is still uncertain who was responsible for Oldham's death, but colonial officials spoiling for an excuse to go to war sent a force of soldiers from the Massachusetts Bay Colony, which attacked several Pequot villages near Block Island in the winter of 1636. The Massachusetts militiamen then went home, leaving the Connecticut settlers to deal with the enraged Pequots. The Pequots besieged Fort Saybrook in late 1636 and made raids on some other towns, killing about nine settlers in Wethersfield and stealing horses and cattle.

In response, in May 1636, the Connecticut General Court met in Hartford, declared war on the Pequots, and sent a militia under the command of an Englishman named John Mason (c. 1600–72). Forming an alliance with the Narragansett and Mohegan Indians, Mason led a force totaling 400 armed men to Misistuck (now Mystic), a Pequot village on the shoreline near the site of present-day New London. On May 26, 1637, Mason's force took the village in a surprise attack and burned it. Of the 600 to 700 inhabitants—mostly women, children, and the elderly, as the Pequot warriors had left the village a few days earlier—seven escaped into the forest and seven others were captured. The remaining inhabitants died in the attack. Writing of the massacre later, Mason considered it "the just Judgment of God" that about 150 Pequots from a nearby village had come to Misistuck the night before the attack "when this heavy Stroak came upon them where they perished with their Fellows":

> *Then were they now at their Wits End, who not many Hours before exalted themselves in their great Pride, threatening and resolving the utter Ruin and Destruction of all the English, Exulting and Rejoycing with Songs and Dances: But God was above them, who laughed his Enemies and the Enemies of his People to Scorn, making them as a fiery Oven: Thus were the Stout Hearted spoiled, having slept their last Sleep, and none of their Men could find their Hands: Thus did the Lord judge among the Heathen, filling the Place with dead Bodies!*[30]

In the aftermath of the massacre, the Narragansett and Mohegan joined with the settlers in pursuing and killing or capturing the remaining Pequot. At the Treaty of Hartford, signed on September 21, 1638, the captured Pequots were given to the other Indian tribes as slaves or sold into slavery in Bermuda and the West Indies.

There were a few exceptions among the Puritans to this attitude of contempt for the Indians. John Eliot (1604–90) was a minister in the Boston area who began a ministry to the Massachusett Indians in their own language. Eliot devised an alphabet for the tribe and translated the Bible into their language. Published in Boston in 1663, it was the first Bible printed in any language in North America. Eliot was a cross-cultural missionary; instead of demanding that the Massachusett tribes adopt the clothing and other customs of the settlers, he tried to help them preserve their culture by organizing towns where they could live by their own tribal rules as Christians, and he ordained a number of Indians to the ministry. By the early 1660s, there were 14 towns of "Praying Indians," one of which—Natick—has kept its original name.[31] Eliot succeeded in securing a grant of money from Parliament in 1649 that allowed him to build schools for the Indians; the fund was still able to support Jonathan Edwards (1703–58) in his missionary work among the Stockbridge Indians in the 1750s, over a century later.[32] Eliot's promising work, however, was virtually undone by the outbreak of King Philip's War in 1675. The settlers of the Bay Colony confined the Praying Indians to Deer Island in Boston Harbor and destroyed their villages.

The Role of Disease in the Depopulation of the Americas

The role of disease in the loss of the indigenous population after 1490 is an important aspect in the debate over the charge of genocide, and it rests in part on the accuracy of population estimates for the Americas prior to the coming of Europeans. The first academic attempt to estimate the size of the Native population in 1490 was made in the 1920s by an ethnographer at the Smithsonian Institution named James Mooney, who arrived at a figure of 1.15 million people. Mooney's figure was rarely questioned until 1966, when Henry F. Dobyns, an anthropologist who had been studying old archival records in Mexico and Peru, came to the conclusion that Mooney had based his estimate on figures recorded *after* the population had already been cut down by disease. Dobyns noted that smallpox, brought to the New World in December 1518, first appeared on the island of Hispaniola. It then spread to Puerto Rico and Cuba. In 1520, the smallpox virus was brought to Mexico by an infected African slave who accompanied Hernán Cortés on his journey of conquest. Cortés's soldiers were largely immune to the virus, but the Native population was not. The disease not only attacked the Aztecs and other tribes, but also spread southward through Central and South America, thus killing hundreds of thousands of people who had never seen a European. Dobyns recognized that many of the figures given by early European settlers were actually post-epidemic numbers and not reasonable approximations of population levels before 1490. In 1966, Dobyns published an article stating that the population of the Americas before contact with Europe was between 90 and 112 million people, or nearly 100 times larger than Mooney's estimate.[33] If Dobyns is correct, there were more people living in North and South America in 1490 than in Europe, and disease killed between 80 and 100 million Indians between 1500 and 1635.[34] Dobyns's work touched off a controversy among scholars that has not stopped, nearly four decades later.

Smallpox was not the only disease that entered the New World from Europe; there were others, carried by animals as well as human beings. Epidemiologists and anthropologists were originally puzzled by the fact that French explorers in the Mississippi Valley in 1682 found no traces of the populous settlements described by Hernando de Soto, who had visited the area in 1539. Eventually they came to the conclusion that the Native tribes had been wiped out by zoonoses—animal-borne infectious diseases—carried by the 300 pigs and horses that de Soto brought with him from Spain. Pigs alone can carry anthrax, brucellosis, trichinosis, and tuberculosis, among other potentially fatal illnesses; moreover, they breed rapidly and readily infect such forest animals as deer and wild turkeys. Even a few of de Soto's pigs wandering into the woods would have been enough to spread zoonotic diseases across southeastern North America from Florida to Texas.[35]

There have been several theories about the unusual susceptibility of Native Americans to European microbes. Prior to the 1960s, most epidemiologists attributed the high death toll among the Indians in the 16th century either to extremely powerful strains of smallpox and other viruses or to the fact that the Indians were "virgin soil"—that is, they had no acquired immunity built up over generations of exposure to the disease agent. In the late 1960s and early 1970s, however, Francis Black, a virologist at Yale's School of Public Health, came up with a third theory, namely that the Indians' vulnerability was related to their genetic profiles. Dr. Black had been testing the safety of a new and improved measles vaccine for South American Indians when he discovered that due to genetic homogeneity, Native Americans as a whole have a restricted range of human leukocyte antigen (HLA) profiles compared to Europeans. Dr. Black found that 28 percent of Native Americans have identical or near-identical patterns of disease resistance, compared to 2 percent among Europeans and less than 1 percent among Africans. The high percentage of similar HLA profiles among Native Americans would explain why epidemics spread among them so quickly and had such high death rates.[36]

CASE STUDY: THE MASSACRE OF THE CONESTOGA INDIANS

Background
Eighteenth-century massacres of Indians had less to do with a desire for land than with concern about the safety of the frontier. The massacre of a group of

Conestoga Indians in Lancaster, Pennsylvania, in December 1763 was committed by a group of Scots-Irish frontiersmen named the Paxton Boys (after the village of Paxton or Paxtang near present-day Harrisburg), who felt that the Quaker-dominated Pennsylvania Assembly and Governor John Penn had failed to protect them from the fighting in the western part of the state that had broken out in the spring. The war, known as Pontiac's Rebellion after the Ottawa chief who led it, was the first large-scale multi-tribal offensive against European colonists.

The rebellion began in May 1763 when the allied tribes attacked a number of British forts and settlements in the Great Lakes region. These forts had been taken from the French garrisons by British troops under Lord Jeffrey Amherst (1717–97) during the Seven Years' War, which officially ended with the Treaty of Paris in 1763. Most of the Indians who joined Pontiac's Rebellion were from tribes that had been allies of the French and resented the British for their arrogant attitude. Whereas the French fur traders had maintained cordial relations with the Indians by giving them knives, clothing, and other gifts, Amherst cut off the gift-giving, which he considered bribery. Another factor in fomenting the rebellion was the preaching of Neolin (dates unknown), also known as the Delaware Prophet, who had a vision in 1761 of an angry God who told him that God would punish the Indians unless they returned to their traditional ways. Pontiac was one of Neolin's converts.

In the spring and summer of 1763, the Indians not only succeeded in capturing the British forts around the Great Lakes, they butchered the garrisons, burning some of the soldiers at the stake and making a ritual cannibal meal of others. The single best-known episode of the uprising was Amherst's suggestion to Henry Bouquet, a British officer, to expose the Indians to smallpox by giving them some infected blankets. Bouquet agreed, telling Amherst in July, "I will try to inoculate the bastards with some blankets that may fall into their hands, and take care not to get the disease myself." Amherst was pleased: "You will do well to inoculate the Indians by means of blankets, as well as every other method that can serve to extirpate this execrable race."[37]

Course of Events
In September 1763, a group of about 300 Senecas, Ojibwas, and Ottawas attacked a wagon train near Niagara Falls, killing about 72 English soldiers and settlers. This incident, known as the Devil's Hole Massacre, appears to have been the event that set off the Paxton Boys. Determined to get even at the expense of the Indians—many of whom were Christians—living in the midst of white settlements in eastern Pennsylvania, the vigilantes attacked a group of six Susquehannocks living in the village of Conestoga on December

14, 1763. These Susquehannocks were a small remnant of a once-sizable tribe that had been reduced to a few thousand people by wars with the Iroquois in the 17th century. The survivors of these inter-Indian wars were further weakened by a smallpox epidemic in the early 18th century. After the massacre at Conestoga, the remaining 14 Indians were taken to nearby Lancaster and placed in the workhouse for their protection from the Paxton mob. On December 27, however, the Paxton Boys broke into the Lancaster workhouse and slaughtered the defenseless Susquehannocks. Benjamin Franklin described the butchery in a pamphlet he published in 1764:

> *When the poor Wretches saw they had no Protection nigh, nor could possibly escape, and being without the least Weapon for Defence, they divided into their little Families, the Children clinging to the Parents; they fell on their Knees, protested their Innocence, declared their Love to the English, and that, in their whole Lives, they had never done them Injury; and in this Posture they all received the Hatchet!—Men, Women and little Children—were every one inhumanly murdered!—in cold Blood!*[38]

Aftermath

Governor Penn sent out a warrant for the arrest of the perpetrators, who were never identified by anyone who knew them. In January 1764, several hundred Paxton Boys reassembled and marched on Philadelphia to massacre other eastern Pennsylvania Indians who had fled to the city for protection. The presence of British troops and the local militia, organized by Franklin, prevented further violence. Franklin also negotiated with the leader of the vigilantes, bringing an end to the immediate crisis. Violence along the frontier continued on the part of both Indians and settlers through 1764, however, leading the Pennsylvania Assembly to reintroduce the bounty paid during the Seven Years' War for the scalps of dead Indians—women included. Given that the Indians murdered at Lancaster were the last survivors of their tribe, it is not surprising that later historians have described the massacre of the Conestoga Indians as an instance of ethnic cleansing.[39]

THE NINETEENTH CENTURY

After the War of Independence, in which some Indians fought in the colonial militias, the new nation continued its westward push, displacing one tribe of Native Americans after another. By the early 19th century, Roman Catholic and Protestant missionaries had been sent to the tribes along the East Coast and many Indians had accepted Christianity within a few decades of the ratification of the Constitution. Steven Katz has called attention to the remarkable outpouring of money on the part of private individuals and mission societies as well as the federal government to open and staff mission schools for the Indians of the southeastern United States. The Indian Department reported to Congress in 1825 that $202,070.85[40] had been raised for the construction of schools among the so-called Five Civilized Tribes—the Cherokee, Choctaw, Chickasaw, Creek, and Seminole.[41] Although later writers have described the impact of missionary activity on Native cultures as paternalistic at best and destructive at worst, it was, in Katz's phrase, "contragenocidal in intent."[42] In addition, several missionaries to the Cherokee, especially Jeremiah Evarts (1781–1831), were leaders of the struggle to protect the Cherokees' rights in the 1830s.

Case Study: The Trail of Tears

BACKGROUND

The Trail of Tears is one of the best-known episodes of forced removal of Native Americans within the United States. The events that led up to the mass deportation of the Cherokees of Georgia in 1838 were a complex mix of economic pressure, changes in the population ratio between Indians and settlers, disagreements over the proper role of the federal government in the affairs of individual states, growing division between northern and southern states, and tension between the federal government's executive and judicial branches. By 1800, the Native American population in North America had dropped to about 600,000, against more than 5 million white settlers.[43] Henry Knox (1750–1806), George Washington's first secretary of war, was the member of the president's cabinet responsible for Indian affairs. Foreseeing the gradual displacement of the Indians by white settlers, Knox tried to set aside land for Indian farms, but was frustrated by federal policies that gave priority to white settlers. In addition, individual states routinely ignored federal laws in the 1790s; for example, the state of Georgia sold more than 25 million acres of Indian lands to speculators in spite of a law that required federal approval of such transactions.[44]

In 1802, Georgia signed an agreement with the federal government relinquishing its claims to its western territory, which eventually became the states of Alabama and Mississippi. In return, the federal government promised to make treaties with Indian tribes that would allow their eventual relocation. Two further developments sealed the Cherokees' fate. The first was the Cherokees' adoption of a written constitution on July 26, 1827. This constitution, modeled on the U.S. Constitution as well as ancestral tribal law, declared the Cherokees to be a sovereign and independent nation. The second event was the discovery of gold in Georgia in 1829, which touched off the first gold rush in American history. Hopeful prospectors began trespassing on Cherokee lands, which led to pressure on the Georgia state government for the removal of the Indians.

COURSE OF EVENTS

In 1830, President Andrew Jackson (1767–1845) signed the Indian Removal Act into law after a heated debate in Congress. When the state of Georgia then moved to extend its power over Cherokee tribal lands (including arrests of missionaries regarded as troublemakers), Jeremiah Evarts, who had written a number of essays on Indian rights under the pen name William Penn, helped the Cherokees take their case to the Supreme Court. In *Cherokee Nation v. Georgia* (1831), Chief Justice John Marshall (1755–1835) ruled that the case did not come under the Court's jurisdiction, but in 1832, the Court ruled in favor of the Cherokees in *Worcester v. State of Georgia.*

Jackson was reelected by a landslide in 1832, which led some of the Cherokee leaders to rethink their opposition to removal. The tribe split into two factions, one that thought the tribe should seek terms with the federal government before white settlers made matters worse. This group was known as the Ridge party after its primary spokesman, John Ridge (1792–1839). The other was a group led by John Ross (1790–1866), the elected chief of the Cherokees, who remained opposed to removal. Since 1824, Ross had traveled to Washington several times to petition Congress directly on behalf of his nation and had won support from such leaders as Daniel Webster (1782–1852), senator from Massachusetts, later secretary of state, and Henry Clay (1777–1852), speaker of the House of Representatives. Most of the supporters of Native Americans were northern statesmen and writers; the agrarian South generally favored Indian removal.

By 1835, however, the Ridge party was willing to sign a removal treaty. The Cherokee tribal council rejected the federal government's first offer in October 1835, but the Ridge party signed the Treaty of New Echota on December 29, 1835. The terms of the treaty gave the Cherokees $4.5 million for their lands in exchange for voluntary removal by May 23, 1838. Chief Ross circulated a petition to have the treaty invalidated, as no member of the tribal council had signed it, and Ralph Waldo Emerson (1803–82) sent a letter in April 1838 to President Martin van Buren (1782–1862) asking him to intervene, but to no avail. Van Buren assigned General Winfield Scott (1786–1866) to begin forcible removal of the Cherokees—including the black slaves owned by some of the wealthier members of the tribe.

Scott arrived in Georgia in early May, sending the Cherokee a formal declaration on May 10.[45] His 7,000 soldiers began the forcible removal of the Cherokees on May 26, 1838, ordering about 17,000 Cherokees and 2,000 black slaves to departure points at Ross's Landing (Chattanooga, Tennessee), Gunter's Landing (Guntersville, Alabama), and Charleston, Tennessee. Many were forced to leave at gunpoint with only the clothes on their backs. From the departure points they traveled westward on foot or by a combination of horse, wagon, and boat about 1,200 miles to what is now Tahlequah, Oklahoma.

The first three groups suffered so many losses from dysentery and other diseases that the Cherokees petitioned Scott to delay further departures until cooler weather. Scott consented not only to the delay but also to allowing Chief Ross to administer the removal of the remaining groups, about 13,000 persons.[46] Although this arrangement improved conditions somewhat for the Cherokee, many still fell sick along the way. Dr. Elizur Butler, a physician as well as a missionary, made the journey westward with the Cherokee and estimated that about 4,000 died, 2,000 in the camps awaiting transportation and 2,000 along the trail.[47] His is the figure most often cited for the death toll, but contemporary scholars suggest that as many as 8,000 perished during the removal. Meanwhile, the official government figure was 424.[48]

AFTERMATH

The turmoil that followed the Trail of Tears took several forms. One was political assassination. With one exception, the leaders of the Ridge Party were ambushed and killed within a few months of the removal, in June 1839. Another was division over taking sides in the Civil War. The slaveholding Cherokees generally supported the Confederacy, while most of the others were Union sympathizers. Chief Ross had initially asked the Confederacy to support the tribe, but traveled to Washington—again—in 1861 to seek help from President Abraham Lincoln when 3,000 Cherokees who had joined the Confederate army began raiding the homes and farms of Union supporters. The black slaves who had been taken to Oklahoma by their Cherokee masters fled to the Ozarks, where they hid until the Emancipation Proclamation. After news of the proclamation reached their hideouts, the adult males immediately volunteered to serve in the Union army.[49]

In Oklahoma, however, the Cherokees prospered and their population rebounded after the Civil War ended in 1865. Today, they are the largest Native American tribe in the United States. The former slaves were given their own portion of territory and began to intermarry with the Cherokees. In the 20th century, increasing recognition on the part of the general public as well as professional historians of the suffering inflicted on the Cherokees led to the designation of the Trail of Tears as a National Historic Trail in 1987. Maintained by the National Park Service, the trail covers 2,200 miles across nine southeastern states. On May 6, 2004, Senator Sam Brownback of Kansas introduced a joint resolution in the Senate "to acknowledge a long history of official depredations and ill-conceived policies by the United States Government regarding Indian Tribes and offer an apology to all Native Peoples on behalf of the United States."[50] The resolution was placed on the Senate calendar in July 2004 but no action has been taken as of 2009.

Case Study: The Sand Creek Massacre

The Sand Creek Massacre of 1864 is a useful case study in genocide less because of the number of its victims than because of the way in which they died. As a present-day scholar has observed, Sand Creek is "representative in its savagery of innumerable other events that differ from it only because they left behind less visible traces."[51]

BACKGROUND

The Sand Creek Massacre took place not only against the backdrop of the Civil War (1861–65), but also, like the forced removal of the Cherokee from Georgia, as the partial consequence of a gold rush. When gold was discovered in the Rocky Mountains near Pikes Peak in July 1858, more than 100,000 prospectors and other settlers poured into Colorado, eager to acquire land that had been confirmed as the property of the Cheyenne and Arapaho tribes by the Treaty of Fort Laramie in 1851. In 1861, the government of the newly organized Colorado Territory compelled the tribal chiefs to surrender most of their land in the Treaty of Fort Wise. The treaty did not, however, represent the consent of all the tribal members. In particular, a group of southern Cheyenne known as the Dog Soldiers refused to move to the new reservation in eastern Colorado.

In addition to the tensions within the two tribes, the situation was further complicated by fears of Confederate influence spreading to Colorado, as Texas had joined the Confederacy in February 1861 and Confederate sympathies were strong among the white population of what is now New Mexico and Arizona. Lastly, the Dakota uprising in Minnesota in August 1862 was frightening to many settlers in Colorado because of the number of Minnesota whites who were killed—between 300 and 800—even though the war lasted only six weeks and ended with the largest mass execution in American history.[52] The panic of the white miners and other settlers appears in hindsight to have been an overreaction, as the Cheyenne and Arapaho were among the least hostile of Native American tribes in the early 1860s.[53]

COURSE OF EVENTS

The short-term cause of the tragedy at Sand Creek was the ambition of the territorial governor John Evans (1814–97) to eliminate all the Indians from the plains of eastern Colorado in the wake of the Minnesota uprising. Evans wanted the transcontinental railroad, which had begun construction in 1863, to be routed through Denver so that travel and further white settlement could proceed smoothly. In order to consolidate his control over the tribes,

Evans invited the Cheyenne and Arapaho leaders to a council to be held near Denver in the fall of 1863. When the tribesmen refused to attend, the governor became convinced that they were planning war.

Evans also wanted Colorado to become a full state as soon as possible. Most of the settlers were opposed to this move, but the local newspaper, the *Rocky Mountain News,* which was also in favor of statehood, began to whip up hatred for the Indians in order to promote a change in the territory's constitution that would have speeded up the transition from territorial status to statehood. The editors of the *News* seemed to think that spreading fear of the Indians among the settlers would serve their political agenda by convincing voters that statehood was necessary in order to secure enough federal troops to control the Indians. Of 27 stories published about the Indians in 1863, the *News* urged the extermination of the Indians in 10. The newspaper stated in March 1863 that "[The Indians] are a dissolute, vagabondish, brutal, and ungrateful race, and ought to be wiped from the face of the earth."[54]

Evans had an ally in Colonel John Chivington (1821–92), a former Methodist minister who had acquired the nickname "The Fighting Parson" for his victories over Confederate forces at Apache Canyon and Glorieta Pass in New Mexico in 1862. One genuinely puzzling aspect of Chivington's role in the massacre at Sand Creek is his previous history as an opponent of racism. He had been a missionary among the Wyandot (Huron) Indians in Kansas in 1853 and had been transferred by the Methodist Church to Nebraska in 1856 when his outspoken abolitionist views resulted in threatening letters from pro-slavery members of the Kansas congregation. It is possible that Chivington's experiences of combat during the Civil War brought out the latent dark side of his personality. A Confederate chaplain taken prisoner by Chivington's troops in New Mexico reported later that Chivington had threatened to kill the prisoners. A recent historian Gregory F. Michno suggested that Chivington was caught in a political net not of his making—blamed for a situation that had escalated out of control by the head of the military tribunal, who disliked him personally, and by a group of dishonest white traders who stood to profit financially from the massacre by claiming damages from the army for their loss of property.[55]

In early 1864, both Evans and Chivington were worried by the departure of federal troops from the Colorado Territory to fight the Confederacy in Missouri and Kansas. The War Department in Washington, however, rejected Evans's appeals for a larger force in Colorado. In April 1864, a skirmish between soldiers of the First Colorado Cavalry and a group of Cheyenne Dog Soldiers led to a series of raids and counterattacks between federal troops and the Cheyenne; in retaliation, the Indians attacked and killed an entire family of white settlers in July at Box Creek, only 30 miles from Denver. By early fall, the citizens of Denver were close to panic, as the murder of the Hungate family was still unsolved and the constant fighting in eastern Colorado had interrupted overland deliveries of food and other goods. The *Rocky Mountain News* continued its inflammatory editorials, while Evans issued an emergency proclamation in August authorizing the settlers to form regiments of citizen-soldiers and "pursue, kill, and destroy" any Indians they found.[56] Chivington was given the responsibility of preparing the newly organized Third Colorado Regiment for field service. In mid-November he left Denver with the regiment and moved eastward along the Arkansas River to Fort Lyon, about 37 miles from the Cheyenne village at Sand Creek.

The Indians who were camped at Sand Creek in November 1864 were a mix of Cheyenne and Arapaho tribesmen led by a chief named Black Kettle (1801–68). Among other things, some of Black Kettle's tribesmen had killed about 50 settlers in August and taken seven captives, raping the adult women among the captives. Black Kettle then wrote a letter to the authorities at Fort Lyon at the end of August saying that he would like to trade the seven captives for "peace." He met with Governor Evans and Chivington in September 1864 at a council held near Denver and agreed to all the conditions that the two men told him were necessary for peace. He left the council for Sand Creek in early October thinking that all was well; however, according to Michno, his poor judgment in taking captives, allowing them to be mistreated, and then using them as bargaining chips was a factor in the disaster that occurred only a few weeks later.[57]

Chivington and the commanding officer at Fort Lyon had been ordered by Major General Samuel Curtis (1805–66), Chivington's superior, to punish the Indians, not make treaties with them. Some of the officers at the fort protested the proposed attack on Sand Creek, however, maintaining that Black Kettle had put his people under the protection of the federal government and that a military attack on the village would violate the government's promise. According to testimony given to Congress the next year by one of Chivington's soldiers, Chivington replied that it was "right and honorable to kill Indians that would kill women and children, and 'damn any man that was in sympathy with Indians.'"[58]

Chivington left Fort Lyon around 8 P.M. on November 28, arriving at Sand Creek around daybreak on November 29. His soldiers moved into a dry streambed that ran alongside the village, towing four howitzers and other artillery. They began shooting howitzer shells into the camp, followed by small-arms fire. Black Kettle raised a white flag and an American flag on a pole beside his lodge, but his gesture was ignored. Most of the men in the tribe were away hunting buffalo when Chivington's force arrived, but those who remained tried to shield the women, children, and elderly. Some of the inhabitants of the village ran into the streambed and tried to dig pits and trenches as shelter from the soldiers but were killed by shells from the howitzers. Others who had managed to flee the village on horseback when the shooting began were chased down and killed by Chivington's cavalry. By the time the massacre ended around 2 P.M., between 150 and 200 Indians lay dead in the streambed or elsewhere in the village. Surprisingly, most of the villagers, including many who were wounded, somehow escaped the blood-bath and made their way over the next few days to other Cheyenne camps lying to the northeast of Sand Creek.[59]

Perhaps the worst aspect of the Sand Creek Massacre was the desecra-tion of the bodies of the victims. Chivington's men roamed what was left of the village, scalping the bodies of the dead, cutting off their genitalia, ripping open the abdomens of pregnant women, and making trophies of the body parts—which they took back to Denver for public display. The *News* cel-ebrated the slaughter as a glorious victory:

> *A thousand incidents of individual daring and the passing events of the day might be told, but space forbids. We leave the task for eye-witnesses to chronicle. All acquitted themselves well, and Colorado soldiers have again covered themselves with glory.*[60]

AFTERMATH

The Sand Creek Massacre had both a short-term and a long-term aftermath. Within a few months, news of the atrocity traveled eastward and prompted calls for investigation. Most people in the East were sickened by the news. In the spring of 1865, three separate investigations were mounted, two con-gressional and one military. Senator James Doolittle of Wisconsin, chairman of the Senate Committee on Indian Affairs, spoke of the massacre as mak-ing "one's blood chill and freeze with horror."[61] Although the investigators determined that Chivington had "deliberately planned and executed a foul and dastardly massacre . . . to gratify the worst passions that ever cursed the heart of man,"[62] they could not prosecute him directly, as he had left military service by early 1865. Chivington's political career was ruined, however, as was Evans's. Evans was forced to resign his office, but the former governor became a successful businessman and later founded the University of Den-ver. Chivington moved back to Nebraska, where he was far less successful in business than Evans. He later returned to Denver, where he served as a deputy sheriff until his death from cancer in 1892.

In the years immediately following the massacre, public indignation resulted in a reform of the military that continued throughout the period of conflicts with the Indians after the Civil War. Generals Philip H. Sheridan and William T. Sherman, whose administrative responsibilities included the Great Plains region, instituted new policies intended to keep noncombatant casualties as low as possible. In spite of their efforts and the partial success of the new policies, however, Sand Creek became a symbol from 1865 through the 1880s of the government's inhumane treatment of the Indians.[63]

Another disastrous aftereffect of the Sand Creek Massacre was its impact on relations between Indians and white settlers. In addition to stirring up renewed warfare and long-lasting distrust on the part of other Plains tribes, Chivington's soldiers wiped out a generation of leaders among the Cheyenne and Arapaho who had counseled cooperation with the whites. The Cheyenne society, which had already begun to fracture with the formation of the Dog Soldiers, continued to fragment after 1864. Unlike the deported Cherokee of Oklahoma, the Cheyenne and Arapaho were not able to recover either their prewar population level or their tribal holdings. There are about 7,000 Arapaho in the United States as of the 2000 Census, but 99 percent of them live in Wyoming or Oklahoma; there are very few in present-day Colorado.[64] Although Black Kettle survived the massacre at Sand Creek, he was killed in November 1868 in a shootout with the Seventh Cavalry led by Colonel George Armstrong Custer.

It was not until the 1990s, more than a century later, that concerted efforts were made to locate the exact site of the massacre[65] as an act of reparation. Senator Ben Nighthorse Campbell of Colorado persuaded Congress to pass a study act in 1998. By 1999 a team of historians and archaeologists, who used oral histories taken from descendants of Sand Creek survivors and traditional tribal knowledge as well as contemporary methods of fieldwork and excavation, completed its study of the site for the National Park Service.[66] The location of the Sand Creek Massacre was made an official National Historic Site on August 2, 2005, by President George W. Bush, with a public ceremony that took place on April 28, 2007.[67]

GENOCIDE IN THE UNITED STATES: A SUMMARY OF THE DISCUSSION

Genocide in the United States is a complicated question that is likely to be disputed by archaeologists, historians, political scientists, and other analysts for the foreseeable future. The massacres and incidents of cannibalism or human sacrifice that occurred in Central America and the American Southwest before the coming of European colonists are better understood as ethnocide than genocide in the modern sense. Similarly, the destruction of the languages and cultures of Native Americans during the colonial period fits recent definitions of ethnocide better than genocide, particularly because intertribal warfare among Native Americans did not end with the coming of European settlers. Arguments over the role of disease in the depopulation of the Americas are likely to continue as experts in medicine and public health begin to use such modern techniques as DNA analysis to track the origins, spread, and magnitude of the epidemics that killed so many Native Americans after 1492.

With regard to massacres of Native Americans during the colonial period, more attention is being paid to the role of the alliances between Native American tribes and the different European powers that were competing for control of North America. The most common name of the 18th-century conflict between Great Britain and France—the French and Indian War (1756–63)—obscures the fact that there were Native Americans fighting on both sides and killing members of other Native tribes as well as European settlers.

In terms of government involvement in genocides, the role of the federal government in the removal of the Cherokees and in the Indian Wars of the 19th century is ambiguous. On one hand, there is little doubt that events such as the Trail of Tears and the Sand Creek Massacre would be considered genocide if they occurred today. On the other hand, there were missionaries, writers, and political leaders who protested the Cherokee removal at the time it took place, and there were several congressional as well as military investigations of the Sand Creek Massacre within months of the tragedy.

The United States was not considered a major international power until World War I (1914–18), and its delayed entry into that conflict resulted in part from the fact that it had significant numbers of recent immigrants from all the warring European states in 1914. As a result, its involvement with international justice between the two wars and after World War II took the form of ad hoc decisions based on specific situations rather than acceptance of such general principles as Woodrow Wilson's Fourteen Points.

THE UNITED STATES AND INTERNATIONAL JUSTICE

World War I and the League of Nations

Prior to the United States's involvement in World War I (1914–18), the nation had given relatively little attention to questions of international law—in part because it was not a major power until the early 20th century and in part because of a tradition of isolationism going back to George Washington himself. In his Farewell Address (1796), Washington urged the new nation to beware of long-term alliances with other countries, in part because of its advantageous geographic position:

> *The great rule of conduct for us in regard to foreign nations is in extending our commercial relations, to have with them as little political connection as possible. So far as we have already formed engagements, let them be fulfilled with perfect good faith. Here let us stop. Europe has a set of primary interests which to us have none; or a very remote relation. Hence she must be engaged in frequent controversies, the causes of which are essentially foreign to our concerns. Hence, therefore, it must be unwise in us to implicate ourselves by artificial ties in the ordinary vicissitudes of her politics, or the ordinary combinations and collisions of her friendships or enmities.*[68]

The United States, however, was less effectively isolated by geography by 1917, when it entered World War I on the side of the Allies. Although routine and affordable transatlantic air travel lay several decades in the future, the steamships of the early 20th century had cut the time of ocean travel between Europe and the United States to less than a week—a considerable advance over the nine weeks required for Columbus's ships in 1492 and the *Mayflower* in 1620. In addition, the telegraph speeded up intercontinental communication; primitive though it was by today's standards, it enabled the *New York Times* to publish accounts of the 1915 genocide of the Armenians within a few days of transmission.[69] Another factor that made isolationism increasingly difficult was the ethnic diversity of the United States. When war broke out in Europe in August 1914, there were American citizens linked by ethnicity to all the combatants, and feelings ran high. The large German-American population in particular was one reason why President Woodrow Wilson (1856–1924) tried to maintain the neutrality of the United States during the first three years of the war.

Preservation of neutrality was the major reason why Wilson was not inclined to interfere when Henry Morgenthau Sr. (1856–1946), the American ambassador to Turkey, began sending cables to Washington in July 1915 requesting intervention on behalf of the Armenians. Turkey was a war ally of the Central Powers, Germany and Austria-Hungary, and Wilson did not want to pick a quarrel with the Ottoman Empire.[70] The sinking of RMS *Lusitania* by a German U-boat on May 7, 1915, with 128 Americans among the 1,198 passengers who died that day, had drawn no more than a verbal protest from Wilson to the German government in spite of massive outrage in the United States. The two factors that finally forced Wilson to reconsider his position were the effects of British propaganda on the general American population and the Zimmermann Telegram. The propaganda consisted largely of atrocity stories about German soldiers raping nuns, murdering babies, and perpetrating similar crimes—many of which were complete fabrications.[71] But the propaganda did its work; one man who attended a New England town meeting reported that when one speaker demanded that the German kaiser should be boiled in oil when captured, "the entire audience stood on chairs to scream its hysterical approval. This was the mood we were in."[72]

The Zimmermann Telegram was an encrypted message sent by the recently appointed German foreign minister, Arthur Zimmermann, to the German ambassador in Washington proposing to delay or prevent American involvement in the war by a combination of unrestricted U-boat attacks on American civilian ships and an alliance between Mexico and Germany to be followed by a Mexican invasion of the Southwest. On January 18, 1917, the British intercepted the telegram, and a team of brilliant cryptographers deciphered it within a day. By February 23, the contents of the note were given to President Wilson, by February 27 they were released to the press, and by April 2, 1917, Wilson asked Congress to declare war on Germany. Although the Zimmermann Telegram was a minor incident in some respects, it also "killed the American illusion that we could go about our business happily separate from other nations."[73]

Wilson's contribution to the idea of an international law that would commit governments to act by certain moral standards began before the end of the war, when he addressed Congress on January 8, 1918, with his Fourteen Points speech. In that speech the president set forth the principles that he thought should guide any peace treaties drawn up after the war. Some of Wilson's points referred to the boundaries or status of specific nations, but the first five and the 14th point are significant for their enunciation of general moral principles that should guide the conduct of states rather than self-interest:

I. Open covenants of peace, openly arrived at, after which there shall be no private international understandings of any kind but diplomacy shall proceed always frankly and in the public view.

II. Absolute freedom of navigation upon the seas, outside territorial waters, alike in peace and in war, except as the seas may be closed in whole or in part by international action for the enforcement of international covenants.

III. The removal, so far as possible, of all economic barriers and the establishment of an equality of trade conditions among all the nations consenting to the peace and associating themselves for its maintenance.

IV. Adequate guarantees given and taken that national armaments will be reduced to the lowest point consistent with domestic safety.

V. A free, open-minded, and absolutely impartial adjustment of all colonial claims, based upon a strict observance of the principle that in determining all such questions of sovereignty the interests of the populations concerned must have equal weight with the equitable claims of the government whose title is to be determined. . . .

XIV. A general association of nations must be formed under specific covenants for the purpose of affording mutual guarantees of political independence and territorial integrity to great and small states alike.[74]

Although Wilson's Fourteen Points became the basis for the terms of Germany's surrender to the Allies in November 1918 and were incorporated in the Treaty of Versailles that officially ended the war in 1919, the Senate refused to ratify the treaty on March 19, 1920. It also refused to join the League of Nations that was proposed in Wilson's 14th point, and whose covenant Wilson had drafted in February 1919. The League's purposes included disarmament, settling disputes among nations through diplomacy, and providing for collective security. However, without an armed force of its own, the League could not enforce its resolutions or impose economic sanctions on offenders. The refusal of the United States to join the League resulted from a combination of domestic opposition, led by Senators Henry Cabot Lodge (1850–1924) of Massachusetts and William E. Borah (1865–1940) of Idaho, and Wilson's own unwillingness to compromise.

Although the League failed to deter the various acts of aggression by Germany and Italy in the 1930s that eventually led to World War II (1939–45), it did succeed in creating a number of international organizations that were inherited and restructured by the United Nations in 1945. Among these were a health organization, a disarmament commission, a labor organization, a commission for the care of refugees, and the Permanent Court of International Justice (PCIJ), founded in 1922 and sometimes called the World Court. The PCIJ, which was established on the basis of Article 14 of the Covenant of the League of Nations,[75] dealt with 29 cases between 1922 and 1946, when it was replaced by the present International Court of Justice (ICJ).

World War II and the War Crimes Trials

The Second Hague Convention of 1907 served as the underlying legal basis for the creation of an international court to try the surviving leaders of

Hitler's regime as war criminals.[76] The use of the Convention's definition of the laws of war, and hence labeling the German leaders war criminals, was controversial in that some of the belligerent nations of World War II had not signed the 1907 convention. The International Military Tribunal (IMT) maintained that this did not matter, arguing that ". . . by 1939 these rules [of land warfare] laid down in the Convention were recognised by all civilised nations, and were regarded as being declaratory of the laws and customs of war . . ."[77]

Not everyone agreed that the proceedings at Nuremberg represented impartial justice. Chief Justice Harlan Fiske Stone of the U.S. Supreme Court thought that Judge Robert H. Jackson, the U.S. prosecutor at the Nuremberg Trials, was "conducting a high-grade lynching party,"[78] while Associate Justice William Douglas opined that the defendants were judged according to ex post facto law; that is, they were charged according to a definition of a crime that did not exist at the time the offense was committed. Douglas said, ". . . the crime for which the Nazis were tried had never been formalized as a crime with the definiteness required by our legal standards, nor outlawed with a death penalty by the international community. By our standards that crime arose under an ex post facto law. Goering, et al., deserved severe punishment. But their guilt did not justify us in substituting power for principle."[79] In the case of the defendants at Nuremberg, the phrase "crime against humanity" had been used by the Allied governments in 1915 in reference to the Armenian genocide, but had not been explicitly defined as it was in the charter of the IMT.

In spite of objections to its validity, however, the IMT did have a significant impact on the subsequent development of international law. In 1947 the United Nations set up the International Law Commission (ILC), which meets annually to continue its work on the codification of international law. The ILC published a study in 1950 on the principles of international law as reflected in the work of the IMT. The second important result of the IMT was the adoption in 1948 of the genocide convention for which Raphael Lemkin had worked so hard. The third was the eventual creation of the International Criminal Court (ICC), established by the Rome Statute of 1998. Although ad hoc tribunals were set up to try war crimes in the former Yugoslavia in 1993 and in Rwanda in 1994, the need for a permanent international criminal court was evident. The ICC came into legal existence on July 1, 2002, and can prosecute only war crimes or crimes against humanity committed after that date. Unlike the International Court of Justice, the ICC is structurally independent of the United Nations, although the UN Security Council may refer cases to the ICC that would not ordinarily fall under its jurisdiction. As of late 2008, the chief prosecutor of the ICC, Luis Moreno-Ocampo, has opened four investigations: Uganda, the Democratic Republic of the Congo, Central African Republic, and Darfur.[80]

The International Criminal Court and the United States

The United States has not ratified the Rome Statute as of 2008. Although President Bill Clinton signed the statute, he later stated that he did not support ratification of the statute as it stood,[81] and signed it only to allow the United States to participate in discussions of the ICC's procedures.

American objections to ratification are based on constitutional principles as well as political considerations. Ratification of the Rome Statute would in effect create a court above the U.S. Supreme Court, which would require a constitutional amendment. Second, the Clinton administration as well as the Bush administration regarded ICC jurisdiction as a potential infringement on U.S. sovereignty.[82] Third, the ICC's structure lacks the separation of functions (the tasks of defining, adjudicating, and enforcing laws) characteristic of Anglo-American law; in addition, it has no system of checks and balances.[83] The ICC courts do not include juries; the same judges determine a defendant's guilt and impose the sentence. Fourth, the ICC lacks adequate provision for accountability, as the chief prosecutor is subject to review only by a panel of three unelected judges. This structural weakness allows for the possibility that the court could be politicized: "Definitions of the relevant crimes are vague and highly susceptible to politicized application. . . . Any signatory state has the right to trigger an investigation. As the U.S. experience with the special prosecutors investigating the executive branch shows, such a procedure is likely to develop its own momentum without time limits and can turn into an instrument of political warfare."[84]

The American response to the operational existence of the International Criminal Court has been twofold. The first was the passage of legislation. The American Service-Members' Protection Act of 2002 (ASPA) was passed by Congress with strong bipartisan agreement as an amendment to the National Defense Authorization Act. Its stated purpose is "to protect United States military personnel and other elected and appointed officials of the United States government against criminal prosecution by an international criminal court to which the United States is not party. In addition, ASPA authorizes the president "to use all means necessary and appropriate to bring about the release of any person [described in the following subsection as covered] who is being detained or imprisoned by, on behalf of, or at the request of the International Criminal Court."[85]

The second form of response has been the formation of bilateral immunity agreements between the United States and other countries. These agreements are sometimes called Article 98 agreements, named for Article 98 of the Rome Statute. That article provides that a country need not hand over a foreign national to the ICC if it is prohibited from doing so by an agreement with that national's country. In addition, ASPA prohibits military assistance to countries that have ratified the Rome Statute but not entered into Article 98 agreements with the United States.

U.S. Policies on International Genocide

U.S. policies on international genocide are difficult to summarize briefly. On one hand, there are many activist groups, research centers, and nongovernmental organizations in the United States that seek to educate the public about genocide and to contribute humanitarian assistance whenever possible to the victims of specific genocides. In addition, judges from the United States have served on such tribunals as the International Criminal Tribunal for the Former Yugoslavia (ICTY) as well as in the International Court of Justice (ICJ). At the diplomatic level, however, the United States still does not allow charges of genocide to be brought against it according to the Convention on the Prevention and Punishment of the Crime of Genocide, nor has it yet joined the International Criminal Court. It is possible that this position will change after 2009.

CONCLUSION

It is difficult to predict whether the United States will take a more active role in the future in preventing or intervening to stop future genocides. The economic crisis of late 2008 may have far-reaching effects on any major power's willingness or ability to get involved in events outside its own borders. Increasing disillusionment with the United Nations is another factor likely to affect the United States's participation in or funding of peacekeeping forces or other rescue efforts sponsored by the United Nations. Documented financial irregularities, bureaucratic inefficiency, and instances of rape and abuse of civilians on the part of UN peacekeepers have been widely reported in the United States and have had some impact on public opinion.

---

[1] David E. Stannard. *American Holocaust: The Conquest of the New World.* New York: Oxford University Press, 1992, prologue, p. x.

[2] Steven T. Katz. "The Uniqueness of the Holocaust: The Historical Dimension." In part II, "The Case of the Native Americans: Colonial America and the United States." In *Is the Holocaust Unique? Perspectives on Comparative Genocide.* Edited by Alan S. Rosenbaum. Boulder, Colo.: Westview Press, 2001, p. 50.

[3] Katz. "Uniqueness of the Holocaust," p. 50.

[4] Adam Jones. *Genocide: A Comprehensive Introduction.* New York: Routledge, 2006, p. 83.

[5] Steven A. LeBlanc. *Prehistoric Warfare in the American Southwest.* Salt Lake City: University of Utah Press, 1999, p. 3.

[6] LeBlanc. *Prehistoric Warfare,* p. 14.

[7] Ekkehart Malotki, collector, translator, and editor. "The Annihilation of Awat'ovi" in *Hopi Tales of Destruction.* Lincoln: University of Nebraska Press, 2002, pp. 186–187. The narrative goes on to describe the massacre of the women and girls following a disagreement among the invaders about dividing the captives among them. "If we kill them all, nobody can have them." (p. 188).

[8] LeBlanc. *Prehistoric Warfare,* p. 174. The evidence for cannibalism is presented in more detail in Christy G. Turner II and Jacqueline A. Turner. *Man Corn: Cannibalism and Violence in the Prehistoric American Southwest.* Salt Lake City: University of Utah Press, 1999.

[9] See, for example, J. Andrew Darling. "Mass Inhumation and the Execution of Witches in the American Southwest." In *American Anthropologist,* New Series, 100 (September 1998): pp. 732–752.

[10] Victor Davis Hanson. "Technology and the Wages of Reason." In *Carnage and Culture: Landmark Battles in the Rise of Western Power.* New York: Doubleday, 2001, pp. 194–195.

[11] Robert Jay Lifton. *The Nazi Doctors: Medical Killing and the Psychology of Genocide.* New York: Basic Books, 2000, p. 485.

[12] Mark Stevenson. "Evidence May Back Human Sacrifice Claims." Associated Press (1/23/05). Available online. URL: http://www.livescience.com/history/human_sacrifice_050123.html. Accessed April 12, 2007.

[13] Hanson. *Carnage and Culture.* p. 198.

[14] Hanson, *Carnage and Culture,* p. 202.

[15] See Bartolomé de Las Casas. *Apologetic History of the Indies.* Translated from *Apologética historia de las Indias* (Madrid 1909), for *Introduction to Contemporary Civilization in the West.* New York: Columbia University Press, 1961. Available online. URL: http://www.columbia.edu/acis/ets/CCREAD/lascasas.htm. Accessed April 1, 2007.

[16] Quoted in Stannard. *American Holocaust,* pp. 87–88.

[17] Stannard. *American Holocaust,* p. 89.

[18] Pedro de Castañeda. *The Journey of Coronado, 1540–1542.* Translated and edited by George Parker Winship, introduction by Donald C. Cutter. Golden, Colo.: Fulcrum Publishing, 1990. Part II, chapter XV. Available online. URL: http://www.pbs.org/weta/thewest/resources/archives/one/corona5.htm#ch18. Accessed April 2, 2007.

[19] Quoted in Nancy Wood, ed. *The Serpent's Tongue: Prose, Poetry, and Art of the New Mexico Pueblos.* New York: Dutton Books, 1997, p. x.

[20] Frank Chalk and Kurt Jonassohn. *The History and Sociology of Genocide.* New Haven, Conn.: Yale University Press, 1990, p. 174.

[21] Some of their writings have been compiled in François Roustang, S. J. *Jesuit Missionaries to North America: Spiritual Writings and Biographical Sketches.* Translated by Sr. M. Renelle. San Francisco: Ignatius Press, 2006.

[22] *Huron* was the French name for these tribes. They preferred to call themselves the Wyandots (or Wyandottes, particularly in Oklahoma).

[23] Jean de Brébeuf. *Instructions to the Missionaries* (1637). Available online. URL: http://www.wyandot.org/instruct.html. Accessed April 1, 2007.

[24] Peter Lowensteyn. "The Role of the Dutch in the Iroquois Wars." Available online. URL: http://www.lowensteyn.com/iroquois/index.html. Accessed April 4, 2007.

[25] Thomas S. Abler. "Iroquois Cannibalism: Fact Not Fiction." *Ethnohistory* 27 (Autumn 1980): pp. 309–316.

[26] Chalk and Jonassohn. *History and Sociology of Genocide*, p. 175.

[27] Sydney E. Ahlstrom. *A Religious History of the American People.* New Haven, Conn.: Yale University Press, p. 156.

[28] Chalk and Jonassohn. *History and Sociology of Genocide*, p. 175.

[29] Stannard, *American Holocaust*, pp. 112–114.

[30] John Mason. *A Brief History of the Pequot War: Especially of the Memorable Taking of Their Fort at Mistick in Connecticut in 1637.* Boston: S. Kneeland and T. Green, 1736, p. 30. Spelling in original.

[31] The Natick Praying Indians still exist as an organized tribe. They have revived the tradition of an annual powwow and maintain their own Web site at http://natickprayingindians.org/.

[32] Ahlstrom. *Religious History*, p. 157.

[33] Henry F. Dobyns. "Estimating Aboriginal American Population: An Appraisal of Techniques with a New Hemispheric Estimate." *Current Anthropology* 7 (1966): pp. 395–416.

[34] Charles C. Mann. "1491." *Atlantic Monthly* (March 2002): pp. 104–105. Available online. URL: http://cogweb.ucla.edu/Chumash/Population.html. Accessed February 26, 2007.

[35] Mann. "1491," pp. 41–53.

[36] Mann. "1491," pp. 112–118.

[37] Quoted in Fred Anderson. *Crucible of War: The Seven Years' War and the Fate of Empire in British North America, 1754–1766.* New York: Knopf, 2000, pp. 541–542. Interestingly, although some of the Indians surrounding Fort Pitt did contract smallpox, it was not from Amherst's blankets. The disease had already entered western Pennsylvania before July 1763; in addition, the two chiefs who received the blankets were still healthy a month later.

[38] Benjamin Franklin. *A Narrative of the Late Massacres, in Lancaster County, of a Number of Indians, Friends of this Province, by Persons Unknown With Some Observations on the Same.* Philadelphia: Anthony Armbruster, 1764, pp. 5–6. Spelling in original.

[39] See for example, Daniel K. Richter. *Facing East from Indian Country: A Native History of Early America.* Cambridge, Mass.: Harvard University Press, 2001, p. 190.

[40] Somewhere between $6 and $7 million in contemporary dollars.

[41] Katz. "Uniqueness of the Holocaust," p. 52.

[42] Katz. "Uniqueness of the Holocaust," p. 54.

[43] Chalk and Jonassohn. *History and Sociology of Genocide*, p. 196.

[44] Chalk and Jonassohn. *History and Sociology of Genocide*, p. 196.

[45] Text in Edward J. Cashin, ed. *A Wilderness Still the Cradle of Nature: Frontier Georgia.* Savannah, Ga.: Beehive Press, 1994, pp. 137–138; also in Vicki Rozema, ed. *Voices from the Trail of Tears.* Winston-Salem, N.C.: John F. Blair, 2003, pp. 183–184. Available online. URL: http://www.cviog.uga.edu/Projects/gainfo/scottadd.htm. Accessed March 27, 2007.

[46] Winfield Scott. Letter of July 25, 1838, to John Ross. In Rozema, ed. *Voices,* pp. 120–122.

[47] A discussion of Dr. Butler's statistics may be found in John Ehle. *Trail of Tears: The Rise and Fall of the Cherokee Nation.* New York: Anchor Books, 1988, p. 390. Butler's own seven-month-old daughter died of dysentery along the journey.

[48] Ehle, *Trail of Tears,* p. 391.

[49] Ehle, *Trail of Tears,* p. 388.

[50] Senate Joint Resolution 37. Available online. URL: http://thomas.loc.gov/cgi-bin/bdquery/z?d108:SJ00037:@@@X. Accessed March 15, 2007.

[51] Stannard. *American Holocaust,* p. 129.

[52] Thirty-eight Indians were hanged on December 26, 1862, for the rape and murder of civilians—not for waging war against the United States. President Lincoln personally reviewed the trial records and commuted the death sentences of 265 other prisoners in response to pleas for clemency from Henry Whipple (1822–1901), the first Episcopal bishop of Minnesota.

[53] Jerome A. Greene and Douglas A. Scott. *Finding Sand Creek: History, Archaeology, and the 1864 Massacre Site.* Norman: University of Oklahoma Press, 2004, p. 7.

[54] Quoted in Stannard. *American Holocaust,* pp. 129–130.

[55] Gregory F. Michno. "Sand Creek Massacre: The Real Villains." In *Wild West* (December 2003). Available online. URL: http://www.historynet.com/culture/wild_west/3025016.html. Accessed March 22, 2007. Michno has also written a book-length treatment of the military as well as civilian politics involved in the Sand Creek Massacre. See Michno. *Battle at Sand Creek: The Military Perspective.* El Segundo, Calif.: Upton and Sons, 2004.

[56] Quoted in Stannard, *American Holocaust,* p. 130.

[57] Michno is of the opinion that Black Kettle was not the visionary man of peace he is often made out to be. With regard to the captives taken in August 1864, Michno says, "Black Kettle freely allowed hostage-taking renegades into his camp, or he could not prevent it; in either case it shows poor judgment and inability to control the situation." Gregory F. Michno. "Cheyenne Chief Black Kettle." In *Wild West* (December 2005). Available online. URL: http://www.historynet.com/culture/wild_west/3418666.html. Accessed March 22, 2007.

[58] Quoted in Greene and Scott. *Finding Sand Creek,* p. 17. Lieutenant Joseph Cramer, who sent a letter to the military authorities in Washington in December 1864, attributed these words to Chivington: "I told the Col. [Chivington] That I thought it murder to jump them friendly Indians. He says in reply: Damn any man or men who are in sympathy with them." Joseph Cramer. Letter to Edward W. Wynkoop, December 19, 1864. Available online. URL: http://rebelcherokee.labdiva.com/cramerltr.html. Accessed March 22, 2007. Spelling in original.

[59] Greene and Scott. *Finding Sand Creek,* p. 20. Chivington is said to have boasted of having killed between 500 and 600 Indians at Sand Creek but neither the 1865 investigations nor later archaeological findings corroborated his figure.

[60] Editorial, "The Battle of Sand Creek." *Rocky Mountain News.* (December 1864). Available online. URL: http://www.pbs.org/weta/thewest/resources/archives/four/sandcrk.htm#editorial. Accessed February 15, 2007.

[61] Quoted in Greene and Scott. *Finding Sand Creek,* p. 21.

[62] Excerpts from the investigation are printed in the appendix to Stan Hoig. *The Sand Creek Massacre.* Norman: University of Oklahoma Press, 1961, pp. 177–192.

[63] Greene and Scott. *Finding Sand Creek,* p. 24.

[64] Judy Mattivi Morley. "Our People: Southern Arapahos Are Part of Boulder's Spirit." Available online. URL: http://www.getboulder.com/visitors/articles/southernarapahoe.html. Accessed April 3, 2007.

[65] Eastern Colorado is a largely undeveloped rural area, and the precise site of Black Kettle's village has been lost.

[66] Interestingly, some of the descendants of the survivors of the massacre were hesitant to talk to the historians and archaeologists because they feared punishment from the government, while others thought that the stories belonged to the families only and should not be told to outsiders. Christine Whitacre. "The Search for the Site of the Sand Creek Massacre." *Prologue* 33, no. 2 (Summer 2001). Available online. URL: http://www.archives.gov/publications/prologue/2001/summer/sand-creek-massacre-1.html. Accessed April 2, 2007.

[67] National Park Service. Sand Creek Massacre National Historic Site, Schedule of Events. Available online. URL: http://www.nps.gov/sand/planyourvisit/events.htm. Accessed March 15, 2007.

[68] George Washington. *Farewell Address* (1796). Available online. URL: http://www.yale.edu/lawweb/avalon/washing.htm. Accessed January 1, 2007.

[69] Samantha Power. *A Problem from Hell: America and the Age of Genocide.* New York: Basic Books, 2002, p. 505.

[70] Power. *Problem from Hell,* p. 6.

[71] The exposure of some of these stories as fabrications was one reason why Raphael Lemkin, Jan Karski, and other witnesses of Nazi atrocities during World War II were not believed at first. The "hangover of skepticism" meant that the early reports of the Einsatzgruppen and the death camps were dismissed as an Allied propaganda effort. Power. *Problem from Hell,* p. 36.

[72] James Duane Squires, quoted in John Terraine. *The Great War.* Ware, England: Wordsworth Editions Ltd., 1999, p. 268.

[73] Simon Singh. *The Code Book: The Science of Secrecy from Ancient Egypt to Quantum Cryptography.* New York: Anchor Books, 1999, p. 115.

[74] Woodrow Wilson. Speech before Congress (1/8/18). Available online. URL: http://usinfo.state.gov/usa/infousa/facts/democrac/51.htm. Accessed January 2, 2007.

[75] Covenant of the League of Nations, Article 14. "The Council shall formulate and submit to the Members of the League for adoption plans for the establishment of a Permanent Court of International Justice. The Court shall be competent to hear and determine any dispute of an international character which the parties thereto submit to it. The Court may also give an advisory opinion upon any dispute or question referred to it by the Council or by the Assembly." Full text of the Covenant available online. URL: http://www.yale.edu/lawweb/avalon/leagcov.htm. Accessed January 1, 2007.

[76] The United States became a signatory to the second Hague Convention on January 26, 1910.

[77] Judgment of the International Military Tribunal: The Law Relating to War Crimes and Crimes against Humanity. Available online. URL: http://www.yale.edu/lawweb/avalon/imt/proc/judlawre.htm. Accessed April 1, 2007.

[78] Quoted by Chief Justice William H. Rehnquist. Remarks of the Chief Justice, American Law Institute Annual Meeting, May 17, 2004. Available online. URL: http://www.supremecourtus.gov/publicinfo/speeches/sp_05-17-04a.html. Accessed April 12, 2007.

[79] William O. Douglas, quoted in John F. Kennedy. *Profiles in Courage*. New York: Harper & Row, 1964, p. 190.

[80] Luis Moreno-Ocampo. "Instrument of Justice: The ICC Prosecutor Reflects," *Jurist* (1/24/07). Available online. URL: http://jurist.law.pitt.edu/forumy/2007/01/instrument-of-justice-icc-prosecutor.php. Accessed April 12, 2007.

[81] Henry Kissinger. "The Pitfalls of Universal Jurisdiction: Risking Judicial Tyranny." *Foreign Affairs* (July/August 2001). Available online. URL: http://www.globalpolicy.org/intljustice/general/2001/07kiss.htm. Accessed April 12, 2007.

[82] Power. *Problem from Hell*, p. 493.

[83] John H. Bolton. "American Justice and the International Criminal Court." (11/3/03). Available online. URL: http://www.state.gov/t/us/rm/25818.htm. Accessed April 12, 2007.

[84] Kissinger. "Pitfalls of Universal Jurisdiction."

[85] American Service-Members' Protection Act of 2002, sec. 2008, subsection a. Available online. URL: http://vienna.usembassy.gov/en/download/pdf/aspa2002.pdf. Accessed April 12, 2007.

3

Global Perspectives

In this chapter, the reader will be introduced to five genocides that took place in parts of the world other than the United States, including Central Asia, the Middle East, Southeast Asia, and Africa. The first two case studies, the genocides associated with the Mongol invasions of the 13th and 14th centuries and the Armenian genocide of the early 20th century, took place before the term *genocide* was coined. These case studies help us consider whether genocide is an exclusively modern phenomenon or what factors might qualify massacres or mass killings from the past to be considered genocidal.

THE MONGOL GENOCIDES OF CENTRAL ASIA
Background

The Mongol Empire of the late Middle Ages was the largest land empire in world history. Although the British Empire at its height covered about 10 percent more land area, it was spread over six of the world's seven continents and its territories were separated from Great Britain itself by thousands of miles of ocean. The Mongol Empire, by contrast, was compact as well as extensive, covering more than 12 million square miles from China in the east to present-day Russia and Hungary in the west.

Frank Chalk and Kurt Jonassohn, directors of the Montreal Institute of Genocide Studies, have observed that the Mongols did not invent any new methods of mass killing, which had been recurrent in the ancient world since the establishment of the Assyrian Empire in 934 B.C.E. "[The Mongols'] genius was confined to doing what others did but doing it much better. This applies even to their genocides. Massacres, wanton cruelty, the destruction of cities, and the devastation of whole regions were commonplace events in Central Asia and Persia as well as in many other areas that they conquered. The Mongols simply killed on a greater scale and as a deliberate part of their policy. . . ."[1] It is this intentional use of terror to frighten entire peoples into surrendering without a fight that helps to explain both why the empire expanded so rapidly over such a vast expanse of land and why the conquests of Genghis Khan and his successors can be considered genocidal. Ian Frazier estimates the death toll from the Mongols' various campaigns to be 18.4 million people; however, this figure is probably too high.[2]

Genghis Khan is really the title rather than the given name of the warrior Temüjin, who founded the Mongol Empire in 1206. Temüjin (c. 1162–1227) was born into the Borjigid clan not far from the current capital of Mongolia, Ulaanbaatar. In 1206, he brought together a number of nomadic tribes, including the Tatars, Merkits, Naimans, Keraits, and Uighurs as well as the Mongols, and was given the title of Genghis Khan or "universal ruler." He was illiterate; as a result, historians have no documents from his own hand to shed light on his personality or motives for the cruelties attached to his name. The primary source for Genghis's life and the mind-set of his people is the *Secret History of the Mongols,* written by an anonymous author in Mongolian around 1240, shortly after the khan's death.[3] Most modern-day psychological theories about him are based on the notion that a series of personal tragedies in his early life (the death of his father from poisoning and the kidnapping and rape of his fiancée) led him to become increasingly suspicious of others as he grew older, possibly to the point of paranoia.

Genghis Khan's first campaign, from 1206 to 1209, was an eastward march against the Western Xia kingdom of China, followed by war against the Jin (or Chin) rulers of northern China in 1211. This war has been described by the historian J. J. Saunders in his 1972 landmark study on the Mongol Empire, "a national or race war, in which the Turco-Mongol peoples of the north were united against the Tungus-speaking occupants of the northern provinces of China."[4] Although nation-states in the modern sense did not exist in the 13th century, tribal loyalties and language divisions generated a kind of nationalistic sentiment. By 1215, the Mongol troops had captured Beijing—the first city to be sacked and destroyed by Genghis's soldiers—while the Jin rulers fled southward. The Chinese dynasty was not defeated until 1234, after Genghis's death, because the khan's attention was diverted by his campaigns of conquest to the west of Mongolia. The first westward conquest was that of a rival khanate, the Qara-Khitai, in 1218. The last legitimate ruler of this khanate, which was predominantly Buddhist in religion and occupied part of the territory of present-day Kyrgyzstan, had been overthrown in 1211 by Küchülüg. Küchülüg was the former chief of the Naimans, one of the tribes that had accepted Genghis's rule in 1206. He was not only an old political rival of Genghis but was hated by his Muslim subjects for his persecution of their minority religion. Appeals from Küchülüg's subjects gave Genghis the excuse he needed to add the khanate to his possessions in 1218.

Course of Events

Genghis's next westward move brought him to the borders of Khorazm in 1220. The Persian historian Ala'iddin Ata-Malik Juvaini (1226–83), who recorded Genghis's conquests as well as those of his grandson Hulagu, left behind one of the few surviving primary sources for the period.[5] The conquest of Khorazm was only the first of many Mongol attacks on Muslim countries by Genghis and his heirs, but its sheer brutality has made Genghis's name accursed to generations of Muslims as the destroyer of Islamic civilization.

The khan always maintained that he never invaded any territory without provocation. According to Christopher P. Atwood, editor in chief of *Mongolian Studies, The Journal of the Mongolia Society,* "For Chinggis Khan in particular, war was a personal vendetta against willfully defiant rulers. After his unification of Mongolia, all Chinggis Khan's campaigns were justified in one of three ways: 1) avenging past attacks by the enemy on Chinggis's ancestors; 2) punishing those who gave refuge to defeated enemies of the Mongols; and 3) punishing those who executed Mongol envoys."[6] In the case of Khorazm the incident that provoked the khan's wrath was the treacherous behavior of Muhammad Ala ad-Din (Muhammad II, d. 1220), the shah, or ruler, of the empire, who was resented by his Muslim subjects for having attempted to depose the caliph of Baghdad, the supreme religious authority of the Muslim world, in 1216. Genghis, who was interested in expanding his power by economic as well as military means, sent envoys to the shah asking for a commercial treaty, which was granted. Soon after the treaty was signed, the first Mongol caravan of 500 camels, led by a Mongol ambassador, arrived at the city of Otrar. The governor of the city, tempted by the precious metals, silks, and furs, seized the ambassador, the merchants, and the camel drivers and executed them as spies. Not only did the shah refuse to punish the governor of Otrar for overstepping his authority, he had Genghis's next emissary beheaded and the severed head sent back to the khan in his capital at Karakorum. Genghis regarded this act as an intolerable insult. In 1219, Genghis marched his army westward toward Khorazm. His army reached Otrar in the fall of 1219, and the city fell in early 1220. By March 1220, the Mongols had taken Bukhara and Samarkand, two of the richest cities in central Asia. Genghis then ordered his son-in-law and two other generals to track down the shah and destroy any city that offered him shelter. Ala ad-Din, knowing he was a marked man, fled from one refuge to another, finally reaching a small island named Abaskun, where he died of pneumonia in January 1221.

One aspect of the Mongols' campaign of terror was their harsh treatment of enemy soldiers who surrendered or were captured. It was not unusual for them to use captives as body shields. An Italian Franciscan friar later reported that "[the Mongols] place their captives in the front of the battle, and if they fight not courageously they put them to the sword."[7] Genghis's forces slaughtered civilians in the cities of central Asia on a massive scale as well as the troops defending them:

> *There is something indescribably revolting in the cold savagery with which the Mongols carried out their massacres. The inhabitants of a doomed town were obliged to assemble in a plain outside the walls, and each Mongol trooper, armed with a battle-axe, was told to kill so many people, ten, twenty, or fifty. As proof that orders had been properly obeyed, the killers were sometimes required to cut off an ear from each victim, collect the ears in sacks, and bring them to their officers to be counted. A few days after the massacre, troops were sent back into the ruined city to search for any poor wretches who might be hiding in holes or cellars; these were dragged out and slain.[8]*

In some cities the severed heads of men, women, and children were piled into separate pyramids; in others, people were disemboweled to make sure that they had not swallowed precious stones or gold coins.[9] According to Atwood, wholesale massacres were a recurrent feature of medieval warfare. Yet,

> *. . . Mongol massacres stood out for their systematic character. When a city was taken by storm, the regular Mongol precedent was to order all the inhabitants of the defeated city out into the surrounding plain and to assign a specified number to each Mongol soldier. Craftsmen, including physicians, astronomers, and sometimes actors and clergy, were separated out. While the inhabitants were outside the city, the Mongol army would enter the city and pillage it, killing all they found hiding there. Sometimes sympathetic clergy were allowed to use churches, mosques, or temples as places of refuge. Having numbered the defeated, the Mongol soldiers, if so ordered, would dispatch their victims with an ax. Even if the inhabitants were generally spared, each soldier would levy a number of able-bodied men to serve as cannon fodder against the next city. The craftsmen would almost always be spared and divided among the commanders and princes to be deported and serve as slaves. At Zhongdu (modern Beijing) in 1215 and Baghdad in 1251 the population seems to have been too large to move out into the plain, so the victors simply entered the city and massacred as they pleased for a week or so.[10]*

The Mongol campaigns were also marked by mass rape and kidnapping of women. The Mongols avoided intermarriage within their tribes and generally sought wives from outside the immediate clan. Their religion permitted polygamy, which meant that Genghis and other high-ranking Mongols could amass huge harems from the women captured during their raids. The large numbers of children sired by Genghis and his successors have left permanent traces in the Chinese and central Asian gene pool. Eight percent of the men in a region stretching from the Pacific Ocean to the Caspian Sea (about 0.5 percent of all the males in the world) carry a genetic marker attributed to Genghis Khan and his direct descendants. The geneticists state that the genetic marker could not have spread by chance; "We therefore propose that it has spread by a novel form of social selection resulting from [Genghis's descendants'] behavior."[11]

Genghis's successors would press further southward and westward into the Muslim states of present-day Syria and Iraq as well as northwestward into the Christian states of Europe.

One aspect that researchers of genocide study is that of intent. Some political scientists do not consider mass killings from the medieval time period genocide because there was no political ideology involved; the victims were not killed because of political opposition or racial (in the modern sense of race) or ethnic identity. Some of the theories for the Mongols' actions include:

- *Mongol religious beliefs and the practice of human sacrifice.* In the 13th century, the basic religion of the Mongols was a form of shamanism, a type of religion in which priests (shamans) serve as intermediaries between unseen gods or spirits and humans. The Mongols believed in a supreme being called Tenggeri who governed all human affairs and was believed to have given world rule to the Mongols.[12] In fact, when the papacy protested Mongol attacks on Catholic kingdoms in central Europe Genghis's grandson Guyuk (1246–48) countered, "From the rising of the sun to its setting, all the lands have been made subject to me. Who could do this contrary to the command of God?"[13]

- *Need for territorial expansion into grazing lands.* Genghis's messengers as well as his armies needed a large supply of horses for daily operations and most owned three or four horses. The horses in turn required ample supplies of grass for grazing. Denis Sinor attributes the Mongol withdrawal from Hungary in 1242 to the fact that the Hungarian range had been overgrazed and the Mongols preferred to return eastward to find fresh pastures for their mounts.[14]

- *Contempt for urban lifestyles.* The Mongols of the 12th and 13th centuries were completely nomadic and unaccustomed to settled ways of living. Saunders maintains that "as nomads roaming the steppes, [the Mongols] despised the inhabitants of cities and felt constrained and imprisoned within their walls."[15]

- *Plunder as the means of paying the army.* The Mongol army was a people's army in the full sense of the word. The soldiers did not receive wages like the Roman legionaries, nor were they drafted (the military draft was introduced in 1793 during the French Revolution); rather, every able-bodied male Mongol over the age of 15 (except for shamans) was automatically considered a soldier.[16] The soldiers were paid for their service by being allowed to loot the wealth of captured cities.[17]

- *Revenge.* The Mongol massacres were not planned by one leader or central organization, as in the case of the Holocaust. Genghis gave his individual commanders considerable freedom in the conduct of their campaigns, which meant, among other things, that the soldiers typically felt intense loyalty to their immediate commander. If a leader was killed in action during the siege of a town, the soldiers had no mercy on its people when it finally surrendered. Nishapur, which fell to the Mongols in April 1221, was the scene of a horrific bloodbath because Genghis's son-in-law Tokuchar had been killed by the defenders during the siege.[18]

It was not only Genghis Khan and his sons who were brutal warriors; the pattern of mass killing continued among the khan's descendants into the 15th century. Hulagu Khan (1217–65) was the son of Genghis Khan's youngest son Tolui (1190–1232). His mother and his wife were both Christians although he continued to follow the traditional Mongol religion. Hulagu was sent by his brother Möngke (1208–59), who was great khan from 1251 to 1259, to conquer the Muslim countries of southwestern Asia. Hulagu's mission included the destruction of the Assassins (also known as the Hashshashin), a secret society of militant Shi'a Muslims that conducted targeted assassinations of Muslim rulers they considered insufficiently devout,[19] as well as the defeat of Syria, the sultanate of Egypt, and the Abbasid Caliphate of Baghdad.

After subduing the last of the Assassin leaders in February 1257, Hulagu set out for Baghdad in the fall of that year with perhaps the largest Mongol army ever assembled.[20] Hulagu sent a warning to the caliph, al-Mustasim (1213–58), to submit, but the caliph, misled by the flattery of his vizier, neither strengthened the walls of Baghdad nor gathered his army. When the Mongols appeared at the gates of the city in November 1257, some of the caliph's forces rode out to meet them but were trapped and drowned when the Mongols broke the dikes of the Tigris and flooded the ground behind the caliph's army. On January 29 Hulagu's army began the siege of Baghdad. By the morning of February 6 the Mongols had captured the eastern wall; the caliph offered to negotiate at this point, but Hulagu refused. On the 10th the city surrendered. Hulagu told the Christians in the city to remain inside a church that he had put off limits to his soldiers. On the 13th, the soldiers began their looting of the city and the massacre of the Muslim inhabitants. Although it is thought that Muslim estimates of the number of dead (2 million) are most likely too high, historians agree that several hundred thousand people were in the city when it fell to the Mongols.

Aftermath

The aftermath of the siege and destruction of Baghdad saw the first civil war among Genghis's descendants and the first major defeat of a Mongol army by an enemy force. Hulagu had left his army in the command of one of his subordinate generals, Kitbuqa, when his brother Möngke died in 1259. Kitbuqa was ambushed by a force of Egyptian Mamluks at Ain Jalut on September 3, 1260. The Mongols suffered a second defeat at Hims in Syria on December 10, 1260, even though they outnumbered their opponents by a ratio of four to one.[21] In addition, Hulagu's cousin Berke had converted to Islam in 1252. Angered by Hulagu's execution of the caliph in Baghdad, an act that Berke considered sacrilege, he led an army to the northern Caucasus and defeated Hulagu there in 1263. Thereafter, Hulagu gave up his plans for any further conquests in the Near East. The open civil war between Berke and Hulagu shattered the tradition of family loyalty among Genghis's descendants and set a precedent for destructive infighting that eventually caused the collapse of the Mongol Empire.

After Hulagu's time, Timur the Lame (known as Tamerlane in the West; 1336–1405), a Mongol who married into Genghis Khan's family, continued the Mongol tradition of mass killing and devastation. Although Tamerlane was a Muslim, some of his worst atrocities were carried out against other Muslims during his invasion of Syria in 1400–01.[22]

Genghis Khan is one of the few perpetrators of genocide who has received a measure of partial approval in later generations, in part because his atrocities lie almost eight centuries in the past. Adolf Hitler admired him, remarking to his general staff before the invasion of Poland in 1939, "Genghis Khan had millions of women and men killed by his own will and with a gay heart. History sees in him only a great state builder."[23] In postcommunist Mongolia, Genghis Khan has become a national hero, regarded as "a combination of King Arthur and Sitting Bull."[24] Annual horse races are held in his honor, with breweries and nightclubs as well as a university (founded in 1994) named for him.[25]

Genghis's newfound recognition is not just a question of the national identity of a struggling country. Genghis Khan has also been praised for his introduction of the *yasa* (or *jasaq*, named from the Mongolian word for "command" or "decree"), a law code that was welcomed by many of the peoples that Genghis conquered because it was predictable and impartially administered and therefore superior to the arbitrary or capricious punishments handed out by most medieval rulers.[26] There are, however, no surviving texts of the *jasaq*, so that it is difficult to determine what it actually stated. Most of what is known of its contents has been pieced together from fragments that have survived in different sources.[27]

Last, Genghis Khan has been praised for establishing the so-called Pax Mongolica, a period of relatively stable social order that allowed the peoples conquered by the Mongols to rebuild their ruined cities and resume trade with the West and the Far East under the protection of the Mongol army. "Mongol military power, perhaps we may add Mongol terror, made the highways of Asia safer than they had ever been."[28] Whether the revival of commerce along the fabled Silk Road, the new luxuries carried from China to the Middle East, and the travels of such visitors from the West as Marco Polo (1254–1324) were worth the death of millions is a question that must still be asked, however.

Conclusion

The 1948 Convention on the Prevention and Punishment of the Crime of Genocide defines genocide as "acts committed with intent to destroy, in whole or in part, a national, ethnical, racial or religious group." Measured by this 20th-century definition, the mass killings of the Mongol conquerors are not genocides because they were not based on the national, racial, or religious identities of the conquered groups—especially since nation-states as we know them today did not exist in the 13th and 14th centuries. Moreover, the Mongol rulers did not leave behind official decrees or other written evidence that might shed light on the reasons for their policies. As the behavior of Alexander the Great, Julius Caesar, and other ancient military leaders indicates, the wholesale destruction of cities and the slaughter of large numbers of civilians were not necessarily intended to destroy entire peoples. What set the Mongols apart was the scale of their cruelty and their deliberate use of it as a form of psychological warfare to terrorize neighboring tribes or countries into surrendering without resistance. If desire for wealth and power over others is considered a precondition for genocide, and if the definition of genocide is widened to include any one-sided mass killing of people defined by a perpetrator as a target for destruction, then the Mongol empire of the 13th and 14th centuries was constructed on a foundation of genocide.

THE ARMENIAN GENOCIDE
Background

The Armenian genocide of 1915–23 is often considered the first of the modern genocides because of its scale and the centralized government planning that preceded it. It set several precedents: indignation in the West followed by attempts to publicize the atrocities and to intervene; the first major human rights movement in the history of the United States;[29] calls for the establishment of an international organization with the power to punish genocide; and war crimes trials during the aftermath. The Armenian genocide was also marked by four ideological characteristics that reappeared in the Holocaust of the 1940s and the Cambodian genocide of 1975–79: racism (Armenians were identified by their nationalist opponents as non-Turks); religious hatred (Armenians were Christians); a lengthy history of conflict with Russia (the Young Turks, a collection of various political groups seeking to reform the empire, wanted Turkey to expand into portions of southern Russia to form a Turkestan as early as 1904); and idealization of peasant farmers as the core of the true nation.[30] Although "Turkey" was commonly used by Westerners since the 17th century to describe the country now known by that name, it was not used by the Turks themselves until the late 19th century, when the sense of a Turkish identity or a Turkish nation distinct from the Ottoman Empire began to emerge. "Turk," in fact, would have been considered an insult by members of the Ottoman upper class, because it implied a country bumpkin, an illiterate and uncultured peasant.[31]

Three main factors contributed to the genocide of 1915: a widespread sense of humiliation among those who wanted to modernize Turkey; the impact of World War I, which included Allied attacks in the west at Gallipoli (a peninsula in northwestern Turkey) and another Russian invasion; and the marginal position of the Armenians within the Ottoman Empire.[32] These factors, however, were in existence long before 1915.

SENSE OF HUMILIATION

The Ottoman Empire, which at its height in the 16th century had stretched from Hungary to Yemen, from Algiers to the Crimea and Iraq, had been in the process of declining ever since the signing of the Treaty of Carlowitz in 1699, in which the Ottoman ruler surrendered some of his lands in Europe to Austria, Poland, and Venice. The Ottomans had built a multiethnic and multireligious empire that included members of various Islamic sects, Orthodox Christians, Armenians, and Jews; the empire's relative religious tolerance stood out in an age when most European monarchs tried to impose religious homogeneity upon their subjects. Although the empire had been conscientiously and competently administered through the end of the 16th century, corruption and incompetence set in as well as political and cultural deterioration. "Increasing weakness in the face of foreign invasion and internal rebellion often led to oppression and brutality and tyranny. Suspicion, hatred, fear—and sometimes, we may add, the example of Western intolerance—transformed the Turkish attitude toward the [Armenians and other] subject peoples."[33] In the early 19th century, non-Muslims accounted for almost 40 percent of the empire. By the early 1880s, after heavy territorial losses in the Balkans, the proportion of non-Muslims had decreased to around 20 percent.

In April 1909 the last Ottoman sultan, Abdul-Hamid II (1842–1918), was finally deposed by a group of Young Turks who called themselves the Committee of Union and Progress (CUP). The members of this group are sometimes called Ittihadists, after the Turkish name of the CUP, Ittihad ve Terakki Cemiyeti. Although the coup was initially intended to bring in a more liberal form of government, within a few years the CUP leaders adopted the ideology of pan-Turkism, a mixture of Turkish chauvinism and Muslim intolerance of other faiths, in response to nationalist movements in the Balkan states and among Armenians and Arabs as well as aggression on the part of the Western powers—between 1908 and 1912 the Ottoman Empire lost 40 percent of its territory to Russia, Austria, and other European states.[34] One of the leading intellectuals of pan-Turkism was Ziya Gökalp (1876–1924), a sociologist and newspaper columnist who maintained that nationalism based on Turkish and Muslim identity rather than loyalty to a pluralistic empire was "the modern religion." Gökalp urged the elimination of the Armenians on the ground that their cultural differences threatened the solidarity of the Turkish state.[35] He wrote a secret memorandum to the CUP demanding an end to "the illusion of Muslim-Christian equality" and published an editorial in his newspaper in 1911 in which he said, "Turks are the 'supermen' imagined by the German philosopher Nietzsche. . . . New life will be born from Turkishness."[36] Gökalp also admired Genghis Khan, whom he considered a "Turkish" conqueror.[37]

EFFECTS OF WORLD WAR I

The role of World War I in the Armenian genocide of 1915 concerned Turkey's decision to enter the war as an ally of the Central Powers, Germany and Austria-Hungary. The Young Turks in control of the government at that time, led by Enver Pasha (1881–1922), the minister of war, Cemal Pasha (1872–1922), the minister of the navy, and Talat Pasha (1874–1921), the minister of the interior, expected that an alliance with the Central Powers would allow them to regain territory lost to the Russians in the late 19th century.

ARMENIANS IN OTTOMAN SOCIETY

The vulnerable position of the Armenians as a minority within the Ottoman Empire derived from their legal subordination. The empire defined minority communities according to religion rather than ethnicity; the name for these groups was *millet*. In addition to the Armenian *millet*, there were Greek Orthodox, Roman Catholic, Jewish, and Samaritan *millets* within the empire in the 19th century. According to Islamic law, non-Muslims living in a *millet* under the Ottoman sultans were not full citizens; these *dhimmi*, as they were known, had to pay a tax known as the *jizya*. They were allowed freedom of worship provided they accepted subservience to Muslims (such as being required to wear special garb and to step aside for Muslims on the street) and the supremacy of Islamic law to their own legal codes. "In sum, the pluralist Islamic model rested on both humiliation and toleration. It was expected that non-Muslims would willingly accept this status; acting otherwise was violation of the *dhimma* agreement."[38] When the Armenians began to protest for political equality in the 1890s, their actions were considered a provocation, and much of the anger of the Muslim majority focused on the Armenians' religion, Christianity.

Armenian identification with Christianity went back to the fourth century, when the Kingdom of Armenia became the first sovereign state to make Christianity its official state religion—a full decade before the Roman Empire accorded the new faith simple toleration. The Kingdom of Armenia survived until the 11th century, when it fell to the Seljuk Turks. It did not regain its independence until 1918. By the late 19th century, Armenians were the largest *millet* within the Ottoman Empire. They were regarded with fear and suspicion not only on account of their numbers, but also because their accomplishments in spite of official discrimination produced envy. The Armenians, like all non-Muslims under Ottoman rule, were barred from government offices and the civil service. Forced to seek other alternatives, the Armenians placed great emphasis on education as a means of advancement and filled the learned professions out of proportion to their numbers in the general population. Many middle-class Armenians sent their children to schools opened in Turkey in the 19th century by missionaries from Europe and the United States or to universities abroad. By the late 19th century there was a network of Armenian schools, literary journals, and newspapers throughout Turkey.[39]

Some Armenians became affluent through trade and economic innovations. When the collapse of the Ottoman Empire led to economic hardship for many Muslims, the relative prosperity of the Armenians made them obvious scapegoats.[40] They were also considered disloyal to the empire because their success came partly from a willingness to use Western technology and to conduct business with Westerners.[41] In addition, the Armenians held fast to their identity as Christians. "The more the Armenians were degraded by the dominant Muslims for their Christian faith and debarred from many spheres of social and national life, the more they clung to their faith and to all that is implied by it."[42] And as Bernard Lewis has observed, "Religion may or may not be a source of hatred but it certainly provides an emotionally satisfying expression of hatred."[43] In addition, some Armenians had been involved in a nationalist resistance movement since the Russian defeat of the Ottoman Empire in the Russo-Turkish War of 1877–78. The final factor that intensified Muslim religious prejudice against the Armenians was interference by European powers, who often justified their meddling in Ottoman internal affairs on the grounds that the Armenians were fellow Christians.[44] Sultan Abdul-Hamid II is reported to have said in 1895 that his empire was faced with "the endless persecutions and hostilities of the Christian world."[45]

One result of what many Muslims in the empire perceived as their loss of status relative to the Armenians and other *millets* was a series of massacres in the late 19th century that set the stage for the bloodbath of 1915. The massacres took place between 1894 and 1896, under the rule of Sultan Abdul-Hamid II (r. 1876–1909) in response to the formation of Armenian nationalist groups. These Hamidian massacres, as they are known, worsened the plight of the Armenians because the participants, irregular mounted Kurdish soldiers known as Hamidye or Hamidieh, went unpunished. As a result, the Turkish authorities came to believe they could repeat and even escalate their actions in 1915 without fear of retaliation. They were attracted by "prospects of new levels of victimization,"[46] which occurred from 1894 through 1896. Although the Hamidian massacres took place in different towns on different dates, they were centrally planned. Muslims were instructed that the massacres were a religious duty. The killings generally took place after Friday prayers. Witnesses of a mass killing at Urfa in southeastern Turkey reported that after binding the local Armenians hand and foot, the Muslims recited passages from the Koran and said prayers before slaughtering their captives.[47] According to Richard G. Hovannisian, a scholar of modern Armenian history, the Hamidian massacres are estimated to have cost between 100,000 and 200,000 lives.[48] Fears of recurrence proved justified; as early as 1897 a British scholar named William Ramsey predicted that the Armenians would eventually "in all probability be exterminated except the remnant that escapes to other lands."[49]

In April 1909 riots broke out around Adana (the ancient city of Antioch in Cilicia) and quickly spread to Tarsus (the birthplace of Saint Paul) and Alexandretta. The riots appear to have been started by local Ottoman functionaries who resented the reforms of the CUP following the deposition of Abdul-Hamid II and saw the Armenians, who had supported the CUP coup in the hope it would mean the restoration of the Ottoman constitution, as threats to their privileged positions. In March 1909 the sultan attempted a return to power in a countercoup, promising a return to Islamic law and the historic privileges of Muslims. He was finally deposed on April 27. By April 14, however, a mob had attacked the Armenian quarter of Adana, killing several thousand people, and violence broke out in other towns across Cilicia. The death toll of the Adana massacre is estimated at 15,000 to 30,000.[50] (Taner Akçam, a leading authority on the Armenian genocide, cites a Turkish officer as saying that 30,000 were killed. Akçam himself thinks 15,000–20,000 is more accurate.

In the aftermath of the Adana massacre, the Armenians armed themselves. The political reforms of the Young Turks that had been instituted in 1908 allowed Christians to acquire weapons, which had been forbidden under the old *millet* system. After the spring of 1909, small groups of Armenians began to stockpile guns and ammunition in order to have some means of defense in the event of future killings. These stockpiles were to cause additional suffering for Armenian leaders in 1915, because their discovery at the beginning of the genocide was used as justification for physical torture of the prisoners. Henry Morgenthau, the American ambassador to Turkey in 1915, reported that the Turkish police even rummaged through the records of the Spanish Inquisition and other historic torturers in order to find new ways to torment their victims.[51]

Course of Events

The Armenian genocide of 1915 has been described as a horrific innovation in that it was part of history's first total war:

> *The fact that Turkey was not among the leading industrial nations [in 1915] is neither here nor there; the war Turkey joined on the side of the Central Powers soon became a new kind of war, to whose radical character Turkey contributed through carrying out the Armenian genocide. In effect, total war did not produce genocide; it created the military, political, and cultural space in which it could occur, and occur again. Another way of putting the central point is to see total war as both the context and the outcome of genocide. . . . Indeed, genocide helped create total war.[52]*

The archives of the Ottoman government indicate, however, that genocide was considered as a solution to "the Armenian question" as early as 1912. In October of that year the empire lost its southern Balkan territories (primarily Thrace and Macedonia) to a coalition led by Greece, Bulgaria, and Serbia. This humiliating outcome cast religious tensions between Christians and Muslims within the empire into sharp relief, as many Ottoman Greek and Bulgarian soldiers switched sides during the war to fight alongside their fellow Greek and Bulgarian coreligionists.[53] The leaders of the Ottoman army concluded that the best way to improve the fighting abilities of their forces was to rely on purely Muslim troops.

In January 1913 the so-called Three Pashas—Enver Pasha, Cemal Pasha, and Talat Pasha—took control of the Ottoman government in a coup that restored the CUP to power. The empire was in effect now ruled by a one-party dictatorship with the Three Pashas as a triumvirate. There is some question regarding the timing of actual preparations for the Armenian genocide prior to the empire's official entry into World War I. Although the war broke out in early August 1914 and the Ottoman Empire signed a secret alliance with Germany on August 2, it did not join the Central Powers officially until November 11. As early as January 1914, however, a series of secret meetings were held after Enver Pasha became minister of war to discuss ways to cleanse Anatolia (the Asiatic portion of modern Turkey) of its non-Muslim "tumors."[54] The CUP also set up what it called a Special Organization (Teskilati Mahsusa) to plan and carry out the Armenian genocide. What speeded up its timetable were two military events: The humiliating defeat of the Ottoman army by the Russians in the winter of 1914–15 and the Allied landing at Gallipoli in early 1915. The first disaster was the direct result of Enver Pasha's unwise decision to invade the Russian Caucasus in the dead of winter. At the battle of Sarikamish in December 1914, the Ottoman army lost more troops to desertion and the bitter weather than to the Russians. The Gallipoli landing, which was intended to lead to the capture of Constantinople (Istanbul) and knock Turkey out of the war, was unsuccessful; the Allied forces were eventually withdrawn in January 1916. After the battle of Sarikamish the Russian army moved into eastern Anatolia in the winter of 1915. The Ottoman government was convinced that Ottoman Armenians had aided the Russian advance. The two events intensified the CUP's intention to destroy the Armenians.[55] Although there were Armenians serving in the Turkish army when war broke out in August 1914, they were put in forced labor battalions in February 1915, where they were either killed outright or worked to death.[56]

The genocide began with an attack on the Armenians living in the city of Van. It was one of the few instances during the genocide of 1915 in which the Armenians defended themselves. On April 19 the governor of the province called for the extermination of all Armenians in the city. The defenders, who had armed themselves, held off the Ottoman army until the Russian army relieved them in mid-May; most of the Armenian population left the city with the Russians at the end of the summer.

Five days after the beginning of the attack on Van, the Ottoman government rounded up and imprisoned between 250 and 300 leading Armenian intellectuals; this act, which has been termed eliticide, is now commemorated by Armenians as their genocide memorial day.[57] The primary measures of genocide, however, were the mass deportations that took place from May 1915 through February 1916 and the massacres that accompanied them. On May 29, the CUP's central committee passed the Tehcir Law, or Temporary Law of Deportation, which gave the government authority to deport anyone it considered a threat to national security.[58] The Tehcir Law was quickly followed by legislation authorizing the seizure of the Armenians' goods and property.

The pattern of deportation and massacre was evidence of centralized planning, as it was consistent throughout the empire.[59] First, Armenians serving in the Ottoman army were separated from their units and murdered in batches. Next, Armenian households were disarmed and weapons confiscated. Third, schools were closed and such community leaders as teachers and priests were arrested. Fourth, Armenian civilians in the towns were summoned by town criers to central locations for assembly. There they were told that they had between a day and a week to gather clothes for their deportation and to sell the rest of their possessions. When the deportation caravans were formed, the adult and adolescent males were separated from the women and children. They were killed outright by CUP officials or by the *chétés*, who were groups of criminals released from prison to fight the Russians and then turned loose against the Armenians.[60] The *chétés* were organized by two physicians who were members of the CUP, Mehmet Nazim and Behaeddin Shakir. The separation of the men, and subsequent gendercide, was followed by systematic rape and bayoneting of the women and children as they were marched through mountain passes and away from Turkish population centers. The Turkish police often withheld water from the deportees or stole their meager possessions. The goal of the deportation caravans was Aleppo and the deserts of Syria; however, ". . . the more fundamental goal of the deportations appeared to be death from attrition. . . . Caravans that had started out with thousands arrived in Aleppo with hundreds, or even less."[61] Many of the women committed suicide after being gang-raped.[62] At the end of the journey were concentration camps (thought to number about 25) in the Syrian desert, in a triangle between Urfa, Mosul (in present-day Iraq), and Deir el-Zor. The deportees who survived to reach the camps died there by the hundreds in the fall of 1915 from typhus and other epidemic diseases.

Another form of mass murder was drowning. Armenians living in Trebizond (Trabzon) or other towns along the Black Sea were taken out on ships into deep water and thrown overboard. Similar mass drownings were conducted along the Euphrates River.[63] All in all, it is estimated that between 800,000 and 1.5 million Armenians died in the genocide—the latter number represents half the Armenian population of the Ottoman Empire and one-third of the Armenian population worldwide.[64]

Aftermath

The Armenian genocide was protested at the time it happened, as photography and the telegraph allowed images as well as written eyewitness accounts to be quickly transmitted outside Turkey. Armin Wegner (1886–1978), a German military physician, took photographs of the genocide contrary to orders from the German government and was able to smuggle some of his photographs to the West. Even though the United States was still a neutral power in 1915, the American ambassador Henry Morgenthau, Sr. (1856–1946) received horrifying reports from the American consuls in the major cities of Turkey and tried to intervene. He met with the Three Pashas, who justified the deportations and massacres on the basis of wartime necessity. Morgenthau and several consuls sent hundreds of reports to the State Department, which had little immediate result because of the Wilson administration's desire to continue to keep the United States out of World War I.[65] Frustrated by the diplomatic foot-dragging, Morgenthau turned to such organizations as the American Committee for Armenian and Syrian Relief (later renamed the American Committee for Relief in the Near East or ACRNE), which was founded in 1915 to send food, clothing, and medical assistance to the Armenians. By the end of 1919, nearly $20 million had been raised from American churches, individual donors, and the Rockefeller Foundation.[66] The resources were distributed by the American consuls and by missionaries without interference from the Ottoman government.

The ACRNE opened orphanages in Turkey after the end of World War I to care for children whose parents or other family members had died during the deportations and massacres of 1915, and other shelters were built by European nations. Although some survivors returned to their home areas after the war, many were killed in later outbreaks of genocidal violence in the early 1920s.[67] Others moved to Europe and the United States.

In terms of legal proceedings, the Armenian genocide set a precedent for war crimes trials, although the Turkish postwar trials were not conducted by an international court.[68] The trials began shortly after the Ottoman Empire signed an armistice with the Allies on October 30, 1918, 12 days before the armistice on the western front. In November 1918, Sultan Mehmed VI instituted domestic courts-martial in Istanbul to punish members of the CUP for their role in leading the empire into World War I. The CUP was dissolved, its assets confiscated by the state, and 130 of its members deported to prison in Malta, where they were held for three years while their actions were investigated. The Three Pashas were sentenced to death in absentia. Ziya Gökalp was also brought to trial for his involvement with the CUP even though he was a civilian. Gökalp was sent into exile in 1919 but returned to Istanbul in 1921. He died there in 1924.

Turkey was compelled to recognize an independent Armenia when it signed the Treaty of Sèvres on August 10, 1920. Article 230 of the treaty also required the Ottoman Empire to "hand over to the Allied Powers the persons whose surrender may be required by the latter as being responsible for the massacres committed during the continuance of the state of war on territory which formed part of the Ottoman Empire on August 1, 1914." The Three Pashas and the two physicians involved in the Special Operations group, however, had been released from Malta and were moving freely about Europe and the Near East. A group called the Armenian Revolutionary Federation decided to take matters into its own hands, setting up what it called Operation Nemesis, named for the ancient Greek goddess of vengeance. Members of the group carried out targeted assassinations: Talat Pasha was shot in Berlin in March 1921; Behaeddin Shakir was assassinated in Berlin on April 17, 1922; Cemal Pasha in Tbilisi on July 25, 1922; and Enver Pasha in Bukhara on August 4, 1922. The Armenian group was assisted in its vigilante justice by the British and Russian secret services, who informed the group's members of their targets' locations.

Although the Armenian genocide of 1915 did not lead directly to the establishment of an international tribunal for the identification and punishment of genocide, it prepared the way for later courts and bodies of international law through its impact on Raphael Lemkin. In his still-unpublished autobiography, Lemkin credited the Armenian genocide with awakening his resolve to prevent future episodes of genocide. When Lemkin died in 1959, he left behind more than 20,000 pages of letters and other documents, including a 139-page manuscript on the Armenian genocide and a shorter six-page summary. Lemkin divided the longer manuscript into seven subsections, which he titled "Armenians—Background," "Taxation," "Massacres of the 1890s," "Massacres of 1909—Adana," "Massacres and Deportations of 1915–1916," "Intent to Kill—Who Is Guilty?" and "Reactions Abroad."[69]

One of the most depressing legacies of the Armenian genocide, in addition to the lives lost and the suffering caused by family separations, cultural dislocation, and emigration, is its heritage of denial. Although 22 countries (and such organizations as the International Association of Genocide Scholars) have officially recognized the Armenian massacres of 1915–16 as genocide as of 2008, others including Israel, the United Kingdom, Sweden, and Denmark, refuse to do so. In April 2007, 53 Nobel laureates signed an open letter to the governments of Armenia and Turkey requesting the two states to open their borders and resolve their tensions. The scholars also asked the Turkish government to acknowledge that the deportations and mass killing of an estimated 1.5 million Ottoman Armenians fits the internationally accepted definition of genocide.[70] In early September 2006, members of the European parliament voted to require Turkey to acknowledge the Armenian genocide as a precondition of admission to the European Union. The proposal was dropped, however, on September 27, with the progress report on Turkey's accession tabled until November 2006.[71]

Conclusion

Recognition of the 1915 Armenian massacres as genocide is generally limited to scholars as of 2008, although 22 nations and 42 of the 50 U.S. states have issued proclamations recognizing the mass killings and deportations of the Armenians as genocide. Reluctance on the part of some nations—specifically Denmark and Israel—is based on the belief that terms like *genocide* should be defined by historians and other scholars rather than politicians. Although the United Kingdom has officially condemned the massacres, it does not think that they meet the criteria of the 1948 Convention on the Prevention and Punishment of the Crime of Genocide. The government of the United Kingdom also maintains that the 1948 convention cannot be applied retroactively. Last, many countries—including the United States—are concerned about the effects of official recognition on diplomatic relations with Turkey.

Most scholars, however, maintain that the events of 1915 qualify as genocide on the grounds of their scope and planning; the religious and economic motivations for targeting the Armenians; the systematic way in which the massacres and deportations were carried out; and the cruelty of the methods employed for killing the Armenians.

THE CAMBODIAN GENOCIDE

If the Armenian genocide of 1915 is considered a textbook instance of genocide conducted under the cover of international warfare, the Cambodian genocide of 1975–79 has been described as a model of genocide caused by political revolution.[72] It is also regarded as an example of autogenocide, or the mass killing of a country's citizens by its own government or people. The Cambodian genocide led to the deaths of 1.5 to 3 million people, or between a fifth and a third of the country's 1975 population of 7.5 to 8 million. In terms of the proportion of the population that was killed, one in four people, the Cambodian genocide was one of the deadliest in world history.

Background

Cambodia is a small country (about the size of Oklahoma) in southwestern Indochina, presently a constitutional monarchy. It is considered the successor state of the powerful Khmer Empire, the largest empire in Southeast Asia between the 11th and 15th centuries. The majority of the population (about 90 percent) is ethnic Khmer and almost completely Buddhist. The largest ethnic minority populations are the Chinese, the Cham (mostly Muslim), and the Vietnamese (largely Roman Catholic).

When the power of the Khmer Empire began to decline after 1400, it came under the control of the Thai monarchs, one of whom sacked the

Khmer capital at Angkor in 1432. During the next several centuries, the Khmer kings were involved in nearly constant warfare with either the Thai or the Vietnamese, and at one point the Vietnamese kings exercised nearly complete control over the Khmer kingdom. This occupation led to a long-standing sense of rivalry between Cambodia and Vietnam that persists into the 21st century.[73] From 1863 until 1953, Cambodia was a French protectorate, administered as part of the French colony of Indochina. Between 1941 and 1945, it was occupied by imperial Japan. After the Japanese surrender to the Allies in August 1945, Cambodia reverted to French rule until 1953, when it became an independent kingdom under Norodom Sihanouk (1922–), who later took the title of prince rather than king.

Sihanouk's regime invested heavily in educational programs for the newly independent country. Although these programs increased the number of children enrolled in school, they also contributed to the eventual overthrow of Sihanouk's rule. Prior to 1945, the French colonial government of Cambodia had sent talented students to Hanoi, the capital of Vietnam, for university-level study, but after 1950 these gifted students were given scholarships to study in Paris instead. There they encountered an intellectual milieu that has been described as "a persecution-free environment in which Third World revolution could gestate."[74] Paris in the early 1950s was home to many of the leaders of the French Communist Party, which had a strong influence on mainstream French politics at that time. The city was also the home of Frantz Fanon (1925–61), a radical Algerian psychiatrist who "argued that only violence and armed revolt could cleanse the minds of Third World peoples and rid them of their colonial mentalities."[75] Among the Cambodian students sent to Paris were such future leaders of the Khmer Rouge as Saloth Sar (1925–98), better known as Pol Pot; Khieu Samphan (1931–), who later became president when Cambodia was renamed Democratic Kampuchea; Son Sen (1930–97), minister of defense under the Khmer Rouge regime; and Ieng Sary (1925–), deputy prime minister in charge of foreign affairs. Unfortunately, their education in French radical politics led them to a serious misunderstanding of the Khmer farmers in their homeland. They expected the Cambodian peasantry to eagerly welcome an armed revolutionary movement—an expectation that was severely disappointed.

On their return to Cambodia the radicalized former students joined the Indochinese Communist Party, which quickly developed internal tensions between its Cambodian and Vietnamese members. The Cambodian intellectuals also became teachers in Cambodia's best schools, where their opposition to the corruption of Sihanouk's government earned them considerable respect from their colleagues. In 1966 the government cracked down on left-wing teachers, and Khieu Samphan and others were forced underground.

The leader of the crackdown was General Lon Nol (1913–85), then prime minister of Cambodia. Sihanouk himself was caught between the North Vietnamese Communist regime of Ho Chi Minh, who supported him rather than the Cambodian Communist Party, and the Cambodian Communists, who saw him as an ally of the United States.[76] Sihanouk was forced from power in March 1970 in a coup led by Nol, a fanatical Buddhist who believed that a combination of "Buddhist teaching, racial virtues, and modern science made the Khmers invincible."[77] Nol was an incompetent head of state; he secluded himself in his villa in Phnom Penh and listened only to the advice of a mystical Buddhist monk named Mam Prum Moni, or "Great Intellectual of Pure Glory." At one point in 1972 the general had sand blessed by Buddhist monks sprinkled from airplanes around the boundaries of Phnom Penh to foil his Communist opponents.[78]

Once ousted from power, Sihanouk joined forces with the Communist former teachers and their allies. This unlikely coalition won popular support because many Cambodians still trusted the prince and saw him as the leader who had gained them independence from France. During the next five years, the Cambodian Communists reorganized themselves under the name Khmer Rouge (French for "Red Khmer") or Angkar ("The Organization") and trained themselves to become first-class soldiers.[79] Meanwhile, General Lon Nol invited American forces to use Cambodian territory to launch bombing raids against the North Vietnamese border sanctuaries that Sihanouk had allowed to develop inside Cambodia. The resultant large-scale destruction of Cambodian agriculture has been cited as a major factor in leading the population to support the Khmer Rouge. Between 1970 and 1973, U.S. forces dropped three times the quantity of explosives on Cambodia that they had dropped on Japan during World War II. Chhit Do, a Khmer Rouge leader who later defected, described the political side effects of the American bombing:

> *Every time after there had been bombing, they would take the people to see the craters, to see how big and deep the craters were. . . . The ordinary people . . . sometimes literally shit in their pants when the big bombs and shells came. . . . Their minds just froze up and they would wander around mute for three or four days. Terrified and half-crazy, the people were ready to believe what they were told [by the Khmer Rouge] . . . It was because of their dissatisfaction with the bombing that they kept on cooperating with the Khmer Rouge, joining up with the Khmer Rouge, sending their children off to go with them.[80]*

Another reason for the Khmer Rouge's success in the years immediately following 1970 was their intimidating harshness and brutality. Elizabeth

Becker, who covered the civil war in Cambodia for the *Washington Post* from 1972 through 1975, reported that the discipline inside the Khmer Rouge was "savage," with people treated as replaceable commodities.[81] Another observer, an American foreign service officer who had worked in a Vietnamese province that bordered Cambodia, interviewed Cambodian refugees who had fled to Vietnam—including a defector from the Khmer Rouge. They told him of the Khmer Rouge's use of terror to intimidate the Cambodian peasants, forcing people to leave their homes and burning them so they would have nothing to return to; separating parents from children; attacking Buddhist monks; killing anyone who questioned their policies or disobeyed an order; and deporting the elderly to places unknown.[82] In addition to terrorizing the rural populations, the Khmer Rouge also began a purge of any Cambodian Communists who had spent time in Vietnam as well as any ethnic Vietnamese living in the parts of Cambodia they now controlled.[83]

By early 1975 it was obvious that the Khmer Rouge would take over all of Cambodia. General Lon Nol's army had been weakened by its clashes with the North Vietnamese and was no match for the tightly disciplined Khmer Rouge. In retrospect, observers at the time were unduly optimistic about the results of a Khmer Rouge victory. One explanation for the relative hopefulness of the Cambodians themselves was the high cost of the civil war: At least 1 million had been killed and another 3 million displaced; more than 1 million of these internal refugees had crowded into Phnom Penh, tripling the population of the capital. In addition, many of the Cambodians in the city thought that the stories leaking in from the countryside of Khmer Rouge brutality were by-products of battle stress rather than innate cruelty or ideological conviction; they therefore dismissed them as Lon Nol propaganda.[84] Sydney Schanberg, a reporter for the *New York Times,* was skeptical of the fears of a bloodbath voiced by Elizabeth Becker, who was concerned about the fate of two Japanese colleagues who tried to learn more about the mysterious Khmer Rouge and were never seen again. He chose to remain in Cambodia even after the U.S. embassy evacuated its personnel in April 1975 because of curiosity and hopefulness about the transition from civil war to restoration of order. Schanberg later said,

> We knew the KR had done some very brutal things. Many reporters went missing and never came back. But we all came to the conclusion—it wasn't a conclusion, it was more like wishful thinking—that when the Khmer Rouge marched into Phnom Penh, they'd have no need to be so brutal. There'd be some executions—of those on the Khmer Rouge's "Seven Traitors List"—but that was it. We were talking to . . . our Cambodian friends who want to believe the best. Nobody believes they will get slaughtered. It is unthinkable and you don't wrap your mind around it.[85]

The reader may be reminded of the similar wish to "believe the best" that Raphael Lemkin encountered in 1939 when he tried to convince his relatives and other Jews to flee Poland before the Germans occupied the entire country; none of them could "wrap their minds around" the coming horror either.

Course of Events

The Khmer Rouge entered Phnom Penh on April 17, 1975. Within hours they formed a new government, renamed Cambodia as Democratic Kampuchea, and declared that 1975 would thereafter be known as Year Zero in the Cambodian calendar.[86] They also began making announcements over loudspeakers that the city must be completely evacuated, telling the citizens that American bombers were about to "raze the city" and that prompt flight into the countryside was necessary to guarantee safety. By April 19, more than 2 million people had left the city. The Khmer Rouge had long viewed cities as capitalist redoubts. Intent on creating a model peasant society, the Khmer Rouge ideology consisted of five threads: idealization of the peasantry; anti-intellectualism and purge of the educated classes; distrust of cities; persecution of ethnic and religious minorities; and xenophobia, or hatred of foreigners.

KHMER ROUGE IDEOLOGY

Idealization of the Peasantry

The Khmer Rouge idealized the Cambodian peasantry as the "true" or "pure" Cambodians. The irony here is that none of the Khmer Rouge leaders came from peasant backgrounds; except for Ta Mok, they were all urban-born and urban-educated. François Ponchaud, a French priest who remained in Cambodia until the fall of the capital, noted that these men, with their citified backgrounds and higher education, were identical to those they proposed to destroy as "enemies of the people."[87] The distinction between urban and rural, however, was fundamental to the Khmer Rouge's division of Cambodian society into two basic groups: the "base people" (*neak moultanh*) or ethnic Khmer farmers; and the "new people" (*neak thmei*), the townspeople or urban working class. These two large categories were in turn subdivided into castes, with religious and ethnic minorities at the bottom along with the people deported from Phnom Penh; a few other groups of "new people" in a middle caste; and the "base people" as the only group having "full rights."[88] The former city dwellers who had been forcibly removed to the countryside found themselves on the receiving end of prejudice and selective mistreatment.

Although some of the rural peasants were initially pleased to be given better treatment than the urban deportees, the Khmer Rouge eventually lost the support of the peasants because they destroyed the three traditional bases of Cambodian peasant life: the family farm, the family unit, and the Buddhist religion.[89] Family farms and rice paddies were nationalized, and peasants and former city dwellers alike worked in shifts on remote work sites. Parents were separated from their children and compelled to eat in large mess halls rather than at their own tables. Children were taught to regard their parents as enemies and family relationships as a form of class exploitation. Instead, parents were instructed to honor their children, whose minds were pure and uncontaminated by their parents' previous lifestyles of corruption.[90] Dating or courtship between men and women was forbidden and replaced by mass marriages at communal assemblies.[91]

With regard to religion, even though Buddhism had been the official state religion of Cambodia, the Khmer Rouge labeled it "reactionary." The peasants were horrified to be denied their traditional religious practices, to see temples destroyed and Buddhist monks executed. Some other Buddhist temples were turned into prisons and execution chambers.[92] By the end of 1975, some Khmer Rouge leaders boasted that they had achieved 90 to 95 percent success in wiping out Buddhism in Cambodia. It is estimated that only 2,000 of Cambodia's 70,000 monks survived the genocide.[93]

Anti-Intellectualism

One of the more distinctive aspects of Khmer Rouge ideology was its primitivism and distrust of education. In addition to maintaining that parents could learn proper political values from their uncorrupted children, the Khmer Rouge—many of whose leaders had been schoolteachers—argued that the youth did not need a scientific or technical education. The idealization of the peasantry led to the notion that the workers and peasants "are the sources of all knowledge," according to a propaganda radio broadcast. Whereas becoming an airplane pilot had formerly required a minimum of a high school diploma, the revolutionary regime argued that education or specialized aviation training was unnecessary—"political consciousness is the decisive factor."[94] Primitivism allowed the Khmer Rouge leaders to go even further and declare all educated people (which in practice meant anyone with more than a seventh-grade education) automatically enemies of the state. What followed was a systematic purge of the Cambodian civil service, military, and those in the learned professions—medicine, law, and teaching. Libraries were looted and burned and the ability to speak a foreign language might bring a death sentence. Several observers reported that even wearing eyeglasses was considered proof of higher education and therefore was punishable by immediate execution.[95] It is estimated that 90 percent of all the school buildings in Cambodia were destroyed between 1975 and 1979 and that 75 percent of all schoolteachers and university professors were executed.[96]

Distrust of Cities

Some scholars contend that the evacuation of Phnom Penh in April 1975 constituted urbicide, "an attack on the very idea of a city, which was repugnant to the Khmer Rouge leadership."[97] The Khmer Rouge's hatred of cities appears to have been based on two factors, the first being a misunderstanding of the term *bourgeoisie,* the communist term for capitalists or property holders. Karl Marx regarded the bourgeoisie as a ruling class that exploited the mass of the population—the proletariat or working class. Pol Pot, however, seems to have interpreted *bourgeoisie* to mean "urbanites" or "city dwellers,"[98] as the modern French word was derived from *burgeis,* a medieval term for a townsman or burgher. He and the other Khmer Rouge leaders thus identified the citizens of Phnom Penh and other Cambodian cities with capitalist corruption and foreign decadence. They were considered parasites who were exploiting the farmers who produced the country's food and contributing to the underdevelopment of the rural areas.

The second factor underlying the Khmer Rouge leaders' punitive attitude toward cities may have been their own previous experience. Many of them had been forced underground during Sihanouk's repressive measures in 1966. "In the end, the leaders were forced to flee to remote rural areas. Why should not the urban population, 'unproductive' and politically suspect as it was, be forced to do the same in 1975?"[99]

Persecution of Minorities

While Buddhism was eradicated as a "reactionary" system, the situation was even worse for Cambodia's religious minorities, the Muslims (most of whom were members of the Cham ethnic minority) and the Christians. The Cham in Cambodia, descendants of the medieval kingdom of Champa, were living primarily in the eastern portion of the country near the Vietnamese border. As they represented an ethnic as well as a religious minority, they were singled out for intensive persecution and destruction. Only about half of the estimated 1 million Cham in Cambodia in 1975 escaped death. Entire villages were destroyed; the survivors were forced to speak Khmer and their children were taken away to be reared as Khmers. They were forced to eat pork and raise pigs, activities that violate Muslim beliefs, and their copies of the Koran were destroyed.[100] A Khmer Rouge order from 1976 stated that "the Cham nation no longer exists on Kampuchean soil belonging to the Khmers."[101] As for the Christians, most of whom were Vietnamese Roman Catholics, almost all died during the genocide.[102] The Khmer Rouge made plans to demolish the Roman Catholic cathedral in Phnom Penh; of the Christian clergy, only one pastor survived the bloodbath.[103]

Xenophobia

The ideological thread that tied together the idealization of the peasantry, the distrust of cities, the persecution of ethnic and religious minorities, and the purge of the educated classes was xenophobia, or hatred of foreigners. Cities were the favored locations of foreign traders, diplomats, and entertainers, all of them sources of corruption. The Cham, Chinese, and Vietnamese were by definition unwanted aliens, and both Islam and Christianity were foreign religions. Higher education meant automatic exposure to foreign influences. Although xenophobia had certainly existed in Asia before the Khmer Rouge,[104] the Cambodian genocide was one of the bloodiest episodes of xenophobia in Asian history.

The xenophobia of the Khmer Rouge required cutting off as much contact with the outside world as possible. This policy included economic transactions as well as a news blackout and breaking off diplomatic relations with most countries. The Khmer Rouge refused humanitarian aid from UNICEF and other organizations after April 1975. They abolished all money and private property within Cambodia and dynamited the national bank. Trade was limited to exporting raw materials to China, Yugoslavia, and North Korea in exchange for weapons and agricultural assistance.[105] Foreign embassies were closed; telephone, telegraph, and mail service to the outside were all shut down.[106] "The Khmer Rouge may well have run the most secretive regime of the twentieth century. They sealed the country completely."[107]

This blackout had several consequences. The first was that the outside world was skeptical of the first reports of Khmer Rouge massacres that began trickling back to the West from foreign service officers and such witnesses as François Ponchaud. Ponchaud himself was motivated by a wrongheaded editorial in the French newspaper *Le Monde* in February 1976 to tell about the savagery he had witnessed during the evacuation of Phnom Penh. After writing a three-page article for the newspaper, he published his book-length account in 1977.[108] *Cambodia: Year Zero* was credited with changing the minds of Noam Chomsky (who had attributed the early accounts of atrocities to cold war propaganda[109]) and others regarding the true nature of the Khmer Rouge.[110]

The second result of the Khmer Rouge's sealing of Cambodia was that Westerners could not identify either the leaders of the Khmer Rouge by name or their affiliation with communism. It was not until September 1977 that Pol Pot emerged as the formal leader of the Khmer Rouge and identified the mysterious Angkar or "The Organization" as a communist party.[111]

STAGES OF GENOCIDE

The genocide itself had several stages or phases. The first phase (roughly 1975 to 1977) was marked by the roundup and mass execution of educated professionals, religious and ethnic minorities, and Buddhist monks—and anyone else who was considered a threat to the "Year Zero" mind-set of the Khmer Rouge to build an entirely new society. Because the Khmer Rouge wanted to save military ammunition, most of the victims of the so-called killing fields were put to death by handheld tools, including pickaxes, hoes, and lengths of bamboo. A Cambodian who witnessed one mass execution later reported that "At the place of execution nothing was hidden. The bodies lay in open pits, rotting under the sun and monsoon rains."[112] In addition to summary executions, people died by the thousands as the result of harsh forced labor conditions in the countryside agricultural camps.

The second phase of the genocide began in 1977, when the Khmer Rouge's opposition to the use of pesticides and Western medical treatments led to crop failure, famine, and the rapid spread of malaria. Although the regime attempted to impose stringent new goals for agricultural production, these were impossible to meet. Food rations, already low, were cut drastically; each person was allotted 180 grams of rice every two days, when the minimum amount necessary to avoid malnutrition was about 500 grams per day.[113] As many as 200,000 Cambodians may have died from starvation alone.

The third phase of the genocide was marked by internal purges of the Khmer Rouge leadership and general paranoia. Among the 14,000 people who were murdered in Tuol Sleng (also known as S-21), one of the most notorious extermination centers, were more than 1,000 Khmer Rouge soldiers who had been accused of disloyalty to the regime.[114] No official was too highly placed to escape Pol Pot's suspicions. In May 1978, the dictator ordered a repressive extermination campaign within the Eastern Zone of Cambodia, which lies along the border with Vietnam. This 1978 purge of ethnic Vietnamese still living in Cambodia was led by Ta Mok, nicknamed "The Butcher," who was later held responsible for the deaths of 250,000 persons. Outsiders were not safe either. In December 1978, Pol Pot granted interviews to three Western journalists, the first to be permitted inside Cambodia since April 1975. On their last full day in the country, Malcolm Caldwell (1931–78), a leftist who sympathized with the Khmer Rouge and doubted the accounts of genocide, was shot and killed—most likely to deter other foreigners from visiting Cambodia.[115]

Another reason for fear on the part of the Khmer Rouge leadership was tension with Vietnam. The regime had attempted to extend the boundaries of Cambodia through border warfare with Vietnam, leading to hostility that escalated when Pol Pot ordered Cambodian troops to invade Vietnam in December 1978. Vietnam responded by launching a full-scale invasion of Cambodia on December 25, three days after Caldwell's murder. The Vietnamese army met little resistance from its Cambodian opponents and entered Phnom Penh less than two weeks later, on January 7, 1979. The

Khmer Rouge leadership fled to the northern part of Cambodia, which is mostly jungle, and escaped across the border into Thailand.

Aftermath

Vietnam essentially ruled Cambodia through a puppet government of former Khmer Rouge leaders from the Eastern Zone who had rebelled against Pol Pot in 1978. The new People's Republic of Kampuchea lasted from January 1979 until 1989, when the Vietnamese army finally left the country. Meanwhile, Pol Pot and the others who had fled with him staged an insurgency from their jungle hiding places, hoping to return to power. After the Vietnamese left Cambodia in 1989, the United Nations set up a provisional field operation to help restore peace to Cambodia, known as the UN Transitional Authority in Cambodia or UNTAC, which operated from 1991 to 1995. In the mid-1990s Pol Pot's insurgency became less active, not least because of ongoing internal purges. Son Sen, who was at one time the fourth-highest official in the Khmer Rouge and oversaw the mass killings at Tuol Sleng, was murdered (along with his entire family) on Pol Pot's orders in June 1997. Pol Pot himself died, apparently of a heart attack, in April 1998. He had been engaged in a power struggle with Ta Mok for control over what was left of the Khmer Rouge, and some observers maintain either that Ta Mok killed his former superior or that Pol Pot had a heart attack when he learned that Ta Mok was planning to hand him over to Cambodian authorities.[116]

Bringing the architects of the Cambodian genocide to justice was frustrated by the passage of time and by disagreements between the United Nations and the Cambodian government over the nature and composition of the international tribunal intended to punish the genocide. In 1997 the government of Cambodia set up a Khmer Rouge Trial Task Force to create a judicial structure to try the surviving Khmer Rouge leaders for war crimes and crimes against humanity. Progress was slow, however, because Hun Sen, the acting premier, had been a member of the Khmer Rouge in the Eastern Zone and did not want to bring former comrades to trial. Khieu Samphan and Ieng Sary, two of Pol Pot's closest associates, surrendered to the Hun Sen government in exchange for freedom from prosecution. In March 1999, Ta Mok was captured by the Cambodian army near the Thai border and put in a military prison. He was charged with crimes against humanity in 2002 but died in the prison hospital of natural causes in July 2006.

In June 2003, the UN and the Cambodian government came to an agreement about the proposed mixed or hybrid tribunal: International jurists and lawyers would be appointed as the co-prosecutor, the co-investigating judge, and two of the five trial court judges; the others would be named by the Cambodian government.[117] In March 2006, Kofi Annan, then secretary general of the United Nations, nominated seven judges for the genocide tribunal; in May 2006, the Cambodian minister of justice announced the names of 30 international and Cambodian jurists who would serve on the tribunal. A final obstacle to the trial of the former Khmer Rouge leaders was removed when the United Nations and the Cambodian government agreed in June 2007 on the legal procedures to be followed during the trial.[118]

Conclusion

There is less disagreement about the genocidal nature of the mass killings in Cambodia than is the case with Armenia. This consensus may be due partly to the fact that the Khmer Rouge regime came into power after the passage of the 1948 United Nations Convention on the Prevention and Punishment of the Crime of Genocide, so that referring to the regime's slaughter of its own people as genocide cannot be considered retroactive. In addition, the Khmer Rouge's explicit adoption of a political ideology that incorporated nationalism, hatred of foreigners, and a concept of racial purity based on class membership certainly fits the pattern of genocidal mentality. The distinctive features of the Cambodian genocide were the regime's focus on cities as particular targets for annihilation and its severing of contacts with the outside world between 1975 and 1979.

The aftereffects of the Cambodian genocide are not likely to be resolved in the near future. Although the Cambodian genocide tribunal handed down its first indictment in August 2008, and the United States agreed to help fund the tribunal the following month, the judges announced in October 2008 that the first trial will be postponed until 2009 due to legal appeals. Although five surviving Khmer Rouge leaders are awaiting trial, few observers expect justice to be served quickly. From this perspective, the slowness of judicial procedures underscores the limitations of legal measures in healing the scars of genocide.

THE RWANDAN GENOCIDE
Background

The Rwandan genocide of 1994 is an example of an atrocity that is often misunderstood. It has been described by journalists and the popular media as the outcome of age-old tribal enmity—in this case between Hutus and Tutsis, the primary groups in Rwanda. In fact, there was "very little that was traditional, primordial, or premodern in the Rwandan genocide. . . . [It] was the product of a postcolonial state, a racialist ideology, a revolution . . . and war—all manifestations of the modern world."[119] There is no evidence that the Hutus and Tutsis were enemies before the arrival of Europeans;[120] in addition, it is now known that foreign journalists were manipulated and encouraged to believe that the genocide was a "purely ethnic" matter by propagandists in the Rwandan media.[121] Sadly, the antagonism that had been fostered between the two groups led to the most rapid as well as one of the bloodiest 20th-century genocides. The Rwandan genocide also stands out from its predecessors by the sheer scale of popular participation in the massacres. Thousands of ordinary Hutu men, women, and even children obeyed government orders to slaughter their Tutsi neighbors at a rate five times that of the Holocaust.[122] Whereas Hitler's killers wore uniforms and took precautions to make sure that German civilians did not witness the massacres, the situation was very different in Rwanda, where the authorities turned the bulk of the civilian population into agents of genocide for the first time in modern history.[123] Although Western media commonly portrayed the genocide "as a spontaneous, uncontrollable outpouring of ethnic hatred which, as such, could not be stopped," the killings were actually carefully planned beforehand as early as 1990 by a small group of politicians—including the president's wife[124]—who openly discussed genocide at cabinet meetings.[125]

Rwanda is a small landlocked nation in east-central Africa, slightly larger than the state of New Hampshire. One of the most densely populated countries in Africa, it had a 1994 population of about 8 million. Rwanda was known as the "Land of a Thousand Hills" (*Pays des Mille Collines* in French) because of its fertile landscape of rolling hills. The soil of the hillsides has been depleted by subsistence agriculture, however, and the country has been troubled by recurrent crop failures and consequent malnutrition, with 60 percent of the population living below the poverty line. According to the UN World Food Programme (WFP), between 10 and 12 percent of Rwanda's people suffer from food insecurity each year, with infant mortality rates among the highest in the world. There are few industries or natural resources; 90 percent of the population is still involved in subsistence agriculture as of the early 2000s.[126]

The early history of Rwanda is still incompletely understood because the country had no written language prior to the arrival of European colonial powers in the 19th century. Modern geneticists and linguists believe that the medieval kingdom of Rwanda consisted of only one ethnic group speaking a common language, Kinyarwanda. The kingdom was a homogeneous society with its own religion. It was noted for having a well-organized army and successfully fought off invaders from nearby Burundi. Social distinctions were based on wealth (measured in cattle) rather than on race or religion; the Tutsis generally owned cattle while the Hutus, who comprised about 80 percent of the population, provided labor. There were some physical differences between the two groups; the Tutsis were generally taller and slenderer than the Hutu, and their facial features resembled those of Europeans more closely. Unfortunately, the European colonists attributed these physical differences to racial distinctions, a notion which eventually became a major factor in the massacres of 1994. A succession of German and Belgian anthropologists and colonial officials subscribed to the so-called Hamitic hypothesis or Hamitic myth,[127] which held that certain northern African tribes were more "advanced" and destined to rule over "inferior" Africans. The hypothesis originated with an English explorer, John Hanning Speke (1827–64), who visited Rwanda in the early 1860s looking for the source of the Nile River. The Hamitic hypothesis maintained that the Tutsi were originally a Hamitic group from Ethiopia and so had obviously conquered the "local" tribe, the Hutu. A Belgian colonial administrator said in the 1920s, "The Batutsi [Tutsi] were meant to reign. Their fine [racial] presence is in itself enough to give them a great prestige vis-à-vis the inferior races which surround [them]. . . . It is not surprising that these good Bahutu [Hutu], less intelligent, more simple, more spontaneous, more trusting have let themselves be enslaved without ever daring to revolt."[128]

Rwanda's political troubles, however, began even before the European powers came to control the country. The economic imbalance between the cattle-owning Tutsis and the farming Hutus gradually became a political imbalance, with the Tutsis forming a ruling class with a *mwami* or king at the top. Taxes imposed by the *mwami* were collected by Tutsi chiefs. The last independent king of Rwanda, Kigeri IV or Rwabugiri (1853–95), was an authoritarian ruler who intensified the social division between the Tutsis and Hutus by imposing forced labor on Hutu farmers in exchange for access to land while exempting Tutsis from this labor tax.[129] Rwabugiri also maintained that the differences between Tutsis and Hutus were based on ethnicity—a distinction that the Europeans accepted when they imposed their own colonial administrations on Rwanda.[130] In 1894 imperial Germany established a kind of indirect rule over Rwanda through treaties negotiated with the *mwami*. The Germans sent relatively few administrators to Rwanda; there were only six in the country when World War I broke out in 1914.[131] German rule came to an end in 1916, when Belgian troops occupied German East Africa. The League of Nations gave Belgium a mandate to administer Rwanda at the end of World War I; in 1946, Rwanda became a Belgian trust territory under the authority of the United Nations.

Like the Germans, the Belgians made use of the centralized government that Rwabugiri had instituted, but they made the class distinctions between Tutsi and Hutu more rigid and based them on supposed racial characteristics rather than economic status. Eugenicists from Europe visited Rwanda to verify that the Tutsis had larger skulls and lighter skins than the Hutus; thus the Tutsi were considered to be closer to Europeans and easier to work with than the Hutus. The Tutsis received preferential treatment in the schools administered by Belgian Roman Catholic priests; many converted to Roman Catholicism in order to be eligible to attend mission schools and gain the economic advantages that went along with education. The teaching of the Hamitic hypothesis within the schools meant that members of both groups came to believe the European version of their history and class structure. "Indeed, the more educated the Rwandan, the more likely he or she was to ... internalize European ethnic and racial categories. ... [while] the Hutu came to view all Tutsis as foreign conquerors and interlopers."[132] In 1931 the Belgian government issued racial identity cards to all Rwandans, similar to the cards issued by Nazi Germany a few years later.

In the 1950s the Belgian authorities began to accord greater power to the Hutu majority in Rwanda, in part because the Roman Catholic hierarchy had started to condemn discrimination against the Hutus. This move toward greater democratization was resisted by the Tutsis. In addition, when the Belgians introduced elections by secret ballot in the late 1950s, the Hutus began to make rapid political gains. By 1957 the Hutus had begun to form political parties that referred to the Tutsis as aliens, not as a native upper class. In November 1959, the Hutus revolted, overthrowing the last Tutsi *mwami*, who fled to neighboring Uganda. The Tutsis, angered by their loss of power, attempted to assassinate a Hutu leader. This act was followed by the Hutus' genocidal attack on the Tutsis, with 20,000 to 100,000 lives lost. Years later, a conference of Tutsi survivors of the 1994 genocide dated its origins to 1959, "when they were made second-class citizens in a racially polarized state."[133]

In 1960 a referendum was held following UN intervention, and Rwandans voted to replace the monarchy with a republic. When Belgium gave the country its independence in 1962, it was obvious that the Hutus would dominate the new government. Grégoire Kayibanda (1924–76), the first president, held office from 1961 to 1973, when he was overthrown by Juvénal Habyarimana (1937–94), a military leader.

Habyarimana governed Rwanda from 1973 until he died when his plane was shot down in 1994—the incident that triggered the genocide. The president projected a liberal image to the outside world, but in reality he governed through a mafialike group of Hutus from northern Rwanda known as the *akazu*, or little house.[134] His wife, Agathe Habyarimana (1942–), dominated the *akazu* and has since been accused of involvement in the 1994 genocide.[135] In 1987 a group of Tutsis who had fled to Uganda during the genocide of 1959 formed the Rwandan Patriotic Front, or RPF, which led a military invasion of Rwanda three years later. Habyarimana's government received support from France, including military advisers who trained his

Hutu-led army. Hutus who knew of massacres along the Rwandan border carried out by the invaders came to fear the RPF. Between 1990 and 1993 there were several small-scale killings of Tutsis in different parts of Rwanda, which are now thought to have been rehearsals for the genocide of 1994. Hatred of Tutsis and an ideology known as Hutu Power was inflamed by the Rwandan media, including *Kangura*, a radical Hutu bimonthly periodical established in May 1990[136] that printed such inflammatory articles as the "Hutu Ten Commandments."[137] The Tutsi were portrayed by the media as devils and "Black Khmer," a reference to the Khmer Rouge of Cambodia.[138] Another source of media-fed hatred was a radio station known as RTLM (*Radio-Télévision Libre des Mille Collines*), which began broadcasting in 1993. RTLM's broadcasters repeatedly referred to Tutsis as *inyenzi,* or cockroaches, and urged their complete extermination.[139] In August 1993, Habyarimana's government was persuaded through the mediation of France, the United States, and the Organization of African Unity to sign the Arusha Accords, a set of agreements that guaranteed a cease-fire and free elections in Rwanda within two years that would include the RPF. After the signing of the accords, the UN Assistance Mission for Rwanda, or UNAMIR, was formed by the Security Council in October 1993 to monitor the cease-fire and provide humanitarian assistance to refugees. When Roméo Dallaire, the Canadian commander of the UNAMIR force, arrived in Kigali, the capital of Rwanda, on October 22, the city was hysterical with rumors of a Tutsi takeover. The government of the neighboring state of Burundi had been overthrown by a Tutsi military coup only the day before and an ethnic bloodbath was already underway there.[140] Resentment on the part of the Hutu Power extremists boiled over; they imported over 580,000 machetes into the country between the end of 1993 and early 1994, or one for every third Hutu male.[141] These knives would become the symbol of the 1994 genocide.

Course of Events

The actual genocide began on April 7, 1994, the day after President Habyarimana's plane was shot down over the Kigali airport. The responsibility for the targeted assassination has never been completely determined; the French government maintained that Paul Kagame, the leader of the RPF, had masterminded the attack on the plane, while others thought that Hutu extremists within the president's own party had downed the plane in order to justify attacks on the Tutsis. Meanwhile, lists of prominent Tutsis had been prepared well ahead of time. Within hours of the plane crash, Hutu militiamen took over Kigali and killed the prime minister as well as 10 Belgian soldiers who were part of the UNAMIR peacekeeping mission.

The massacres of Tutsis began at once. In the cities and larger towns, Hutus went from house to house, dragging Tutsis out of their homes into the streets, where they were commonly raped and tortured before being killed. The militiamen also set up roadblocks along the streets where they demanded that all passersby must show their ID cards; having a Tutsi ID card meant instant death. "No other factor was more significant in facilitating the speed and magnitude of the 100 days of mass killing in Rwanda."[142] The rapidity as well as the scale of the massacres was horrifying; in one parish church, between 35,000 and 43,000 people were slaughtered in less than six hours (April 20, 1994), a record which "may stand as the most concentrated ground-level slaughter of the twentieth century."[143]

UNAMIR general Roméo Dallaire had tried to warn the UN in January that genocide had been planned; he had been contacted by an informant about arms caches and planned assassinations. In what became known as the "genocide fax,"[144] Dallaire relayed this information to UN headquarters in New York and requested permission to raid the arms caches. He was shocked to be told by Kofi Annan, at that time the head of the UN's peacekeeping operations, that his task was limited to monitoring the situation: "My failure to persuade New York to act on Jean-Pierre's information still haunts me. . . . They were tying my hands."[145] In addition to the UN's hands-off attitude, another aspect of the Rwandan genocide that both frightened and disgusted the UNAMIR troops was the extent of popular participation in the killings. The massacres were not characterized by mob violence but rather by orderly, almost assembly-line, rhythm. "Killers arrived for their duties at a designated hour, and broke off their murderous activities at five in the afternoon, as though clocking off."[146] Tragically, the groups of Hutu killers included women and children. The third aspect of the Rwandan genocide that was profoundly disturbing was the inaction on the part of the major powers after the killing began. The Hutu extremists had in fact counted on a sluggish Western response to the massacres. No Western high-level diplomat, including U.S. ambassador to the United Nations Madeleine Albright and her British counterpart, wanted to use the g word.[147] General Dallaire began to use the term genocide on April 30, 1994, after having borrowed a book on international law from the Red Cross mission in Rwanda and talking with representatives from Oxfam. "Little did I realize the storm of controversy this term would invoke in New York and in the capitals of the world. To me it seemed an accurate label at last."[148] Journalists avoided the word because they had accepted the RTLM's version of the violence as typical "African tribal hostility" or "ancient tribal hatreds."[149] With regard to the United States, there was a widespread weariness with "what had come to feel like an insatiable global appetite for mischief and an equally insatiable UN appetite for [peacekeeping] missions. . . . It is shocking to note that during the entire three months of the genocide, [President] Clinton never assembled his top policy advisers to discuss the killings."[150] Meanwhile Dallaire was constantly frustrated by his inability to obtain a larger armed force or necessary supplies for the soldiers under his command through the UN bureaucracy. Although the UN redefined UNAMIR's mission several times between October 1993 and the official closure of the mission in March 1996, the Security Council doomed any chance of even partial success by voting on April 21, 1994, to slash Dallaire's force size to only 270 soldiers. Most of the UNAMIR troops were evacuated by April 25.

The genocide in Rwanda came to an end in late June and early July 1994, not because of a French intervention codenamed Operation Turquoise but because Paul Kagame's RPF forces gained control of Kigali and quickly established a new provisional government. Meanwhile the presence of the French troops in western Rwanda allowed for the evacuation of 2 million Hutus to refugee camps in neighboring Zaïre. A second humanitarian crisis developed in short order, when an epidemic of cholera broke out that killed thousands of refugees. This time the world community was quick to send help. American troops arrived within days to distribute food, water, and medicines in the refugee camps.[151]

Aftermath

The survivors of the Rwandan genocide have tried to learn from the experiences of those who survived previous genocides. It is significant that the leaders of the Rwandan unity government sought advice from three Jewish experts on the Holocaust in regard to helping survivors to recover, bringing the perpetrators to justice, and setting up means for commemorating the dead and educating future generations. "The Holocaust has taught us that no closure can be possible without serving rehabilitation, justice, and memory."[152] Some survivors have been followed in long-term psychiatric studies for more than a decade to determine the effects of genocide on people's attitudes toward reconciliation as well as their mental and emotional difficulties. An article in the *Journal of the American Medical Association (JAMA)* reported in 2004 that survivors who did not meet the criteria for post-traumatic stress disorder (PTSD) were more likely to believe in the possibility of reconciliation between Tutsis and Hutus and to favor the international courts over either local or national Rwandan courtroom proceedings, while those who met criteria for PTSD were less likely to have a positive impression of the national trials and also less likely to believe in the possibility of communal healing.[153]

As the *JAMA* article indicates, as of mid-2008, Rwanda has three types of judicial proceedings for dealing with the aftermath of the 1994 genocide.

As early as November 1994, the UN Security Council set up the International Criminal Tribunal for Rwanda (ICTR) in Arusha in Tanzania, for the prosecution of genocide, crimes against humanity, and war crimes committed between January 1 and December 31, 1994. The ICTR has proceeded very slowly, however, not hearing its first case until 1997. By 2004 it had convicted only 18 defendants of genocide and crimes against humanity.[154] As of October 2008, the ICTR had completed 28 trials, with another 30 in progress, and seven people in jail awaiting trial. Eighteen other fugitives are still at large; some may have died in the interim.[155] On December 18, 2008, the ICTR sentenced Colonel Théoneste Bagosara, the alleged mastermind of the massacre, to life imprisonment for genocide, crimes against humanity, and war crimes. It also sentenced two of his codefendents to life in prison. According to Security Council Resolution 1503, the ICTR is expected to complete its work in 2010 and disband, but this expectation is widely considered unrealistic.

The second level of prosecution for genocide is the national courts of Rwanda. These quickly became overwhelmed with cases in the mid-1990s. By 2000, there were about 120,000 people accused of genocide and crimes against humanity in Rwandan prisons; about 10,000 of these had been tried by December 2006. In order to speed up the judicial process, about 50,000 prisoners were released in 2004 and 2005,[156] with an additional 8000 in January 2007.

The third type of court is unique to Rwanda and is based on a traditional system of community justice. These *gacaca* (pronounced "ga-cha-cha") courts were instituted by the government of Rwanda in 2001 in order to punish the perpetrators of genocide as swiftly as possible and speed the process of reconciliation between Tutsis and Hutus. *Gacaca* means "grass" or "hilltop" in Kinyarwanda, and the *gacaca* courts can be roughly translated as "justice on the grass" or "grassroots justice." In the traditional Rwandan system, the village elders would summon the parties to a crime to a village assembly and mediate by imposing a fine or act of contrition on the guilty party. In the present Rwandan *gacaca* courts, the trials are interactive, involving plaintiffs and witnesses as well as defendants. The defendants do not have lawyers, but anyone in the village can speak either in favor of or against the defendant. The 250,000 judges who presently serve in the *gacaca* courts were elected directly by Rwandan citizens and have been given basic legal training. The *gacaca* courts, however, do not have authority over high officials or those accused of planning genocide; their jurisdiction covers cases of murder not involving rape or sexual abuse; severe bodily injury not leading to death; and property damage. The goal of the *gacaca* courts is restorative justice; typical sentences involve restitution through service—helping to build houses, repairing schools or hospitals, or doing farm labor.[157] The judges hope to try 110,000 cases by the end of 2008.[158]

Conclusion

The Rwandan genocide has become a case study in evaluating the role of bystanders (corporate as well as individual) in genocide. One expert on the psychological dimension of genocide has remarked, "The roles and responsibilities of bystanders is one of the more thorny and vexing aspects of the dilemma of evil. . . . It is appealing but misleading to sort history into perpetrators and victims. Often there are more bystanders present than either perpetrators or victims, and the bystanders have the power to alter the outcome, whether they realize it or not."[159] It was far easier for the international community to assist with medical assistance after the fact than to intervene during the killing.

As in the case of Cambodia, the massacres in Rwanda in 1994 are generally acknowledged as genocide according to the 1948 United Nations convention; the UN itself admitted in May 1994 that the mass killings were genocidal. What is unique about the case of Rwanda was the speed of the killing—12 weeks—and the participation of ordinary citizens, women and children as well as men, in the massacres. What was not unique was the passive role played by the UN assistance mission, or UNAMIR. That same ineffectiveness characterizes the present UN peacekeeping force in Darfur, the United Nations African Mission in Darfur (UNAMID). Moreover, the international community has basically adopted the same position of outside observer or bystander in regard to Darfur as it did with Rwanda. It is possible from this angle to regard Rwanda as a sinister precedent for the ongoing tragedy in Darfur. Bashir and other Sudanese leaders seem to have learned from the Rwandan genocide that they can do as they please in Darfur without any serious concerns about international intervention.

DARFUR: A CONTEMPORARY INSTANCE OF GENOCIDE

Background

Darfur is an impoverished part of Africa that was nearly unknown to most Americans prior to the outbreak of the present conflict in 2003. A landlocked area of about 150,000 square miles, or approximately the size of Texas, the region was an independent sultanate until 1916, when it was taken over by the British and incorporated into the Sudan. Most of the population became Muslim shortly after the establishment of the sultanate in the early 15th century,[160] although about 5 percent of the people (mostly in the south) are Christian and another 20 percent follow indigenous religions. Only 60 percent of the present-day population is literate, with an average life expectancy of only 55 years. Forty-seven percent of Darfur's people are 14 years old or younger; the median age is only 18.[161] When Sudan became an independent republic in 1956, Darfur became a state within the new nation, divided into three smaller states: North Darfur (Shamal Darfur), South Darfur (Janub Darfur), and West Darfur (Gharb Darfur).

With regard to geography, Darfur can be roughly divided into three climatic zones: a dry belt in the north on the edge of a desert populated primarily by nomadic herders; a central semifertile area in which corn, tomatoes, and a few other crops can be grown; and a semimoist region in the south that allows farmers to cultivate fruit and nut trees along with small amounts of cotton. The region's economy is based on subsistence agriculture. Although Darfur's population is estimated to be between 6.5 and 7.4 million as of 2008, there are no large cities.

The current distress can be traced back to the 1980s, when competition for land increased within Sudan. The population of Darfur is a mosaic of about 90 different tribes and hundreds of subclans, with a long tradition of intermarriage. This pattern of population mixing began to break down, however, when a drought in the early 1980s led the largely Arab herders of northern Darfur to move farther south in search of grazing lands for their animals, while the farmers in the middle and southern portions of Darfur—largely of African descent—resented the damage done to their farms by the Arab horsemen. By 1983 a civil war that had ended in 1972 broke out again and by 1984 there was also a full-blown famine in Darfur.

The civil war that was revived in 1983 had a religious dimension too, as the central government in Khartoum, the country's capital, promulgated a series of strict laws based on sharia, or Islamic religious law. The non-Muslim groups in the south rebelled. Their hopes for greater freedom were dashed in 1989, when Omar al-Bashir (1944–   ), the current ruler of Sudan, took power in a military coup and proceeded to impose a fundamentalist form of Islam on the country. Even though the people of Darfur were almost all Muslim, Bashir's regime regarded them as "hypocrites and apostates" because they follow the Sufi form of Islam, which is less legalistic and more mystically inclined, and because they doubt "the Islamic justification of jihad,"[162] or holy war.

The economic tensions between the farmers and herders in Darfur itself escalated because the tribal administration system that had worked reasonably well under British rule had been weakened by Sudan's central government in Khartoum. Polarization between the Arab herders and the African farmers intensified to the point that open fighting broke out in 1987, continuing until 1989. About 500 Arab herders were killed along with 2,500 farmers; 400 villages were burned as well as hundreds of the herders' tents. A local intertribal conference was called to stop the fighting, but its recommendations regarding compensation and punishment were not implemented. The conflict that began in April 2003 is in part the result of old grievances that had never been resolved.[163]

Course of Events

The present crisis in Darfur began in February 2003, when a group of men who considered themselves ethnically African formed the Sudanese Liberation Army (SLA) in reaction to what they considered the central government's neglect of Darfur and its favoritism toward Arabs. Following earlier incidents by other groups, on April 25, 2003, the SLA attacked and took over a military outpost at El Fasher (or Al Fashir). In Bashir's response to the raid on El Fasher, he relied not only on the Sudanese army and air force but also on local Arab militias. The militiamen, known as Janjaweed, were armed and supplied with horses by the government. Janjaweed can be translated roughly as "evil men on horseback." The attacks on the villages of Darfur that followed reminded some observers of Hitler's Einsatzgruppen. Cluster bombs were dropped by Bashir's air force, followed by combat helicopters and fighter bombers that attacked such larger structures as schools and warehouses. After the air attacks, regular army units and groups of Janjaweed moved in, setting houses on fire, raping women and girls, shooting the men, often throwing small children back into the burning houses, poisoning wells, and stealing cattle. The systematic nature of these attacks was documented by Brian Seidle, a former U.S. Marine captain who worked with the African Union (AU), an organization of 53 African states formed in 2001. The AU deployed a force of about 7,000 peacekeepers known as the African Union Mission (AMIS), most of them from Rwanda, to Darfur in 2005, with a mandate that was set to expire at the end of 2006. During his work alongside the AU peacekeepers, Seidle noted that one sign of an imminent attack was loss of cell phone service; the authorities would shut down local cell phone systems to prevent villages from warning one another. Seidle reported in his testimony to Congress that ". . . we saw villages of up to 20,000 inhabitants burned to the ground with nothing left but ash frames. . . . We witnessed scores of dead bodies providing evidence of torture—arms bound, ears cut off, eyes plucked, males castrated and left to bleed to death, children beaten to a pulp, people locked in their huts before being burned alive, and apparent executions."[164]

Without reliable sources of food or water, the survivors of these attacks fled over the border into neighboring Chad or sought refuge in camps for displaced persons inside Sudan. As of late 2008, the casualty figures given by the Central Intelligence Agency's *World Factbook* indicate that more than 400,000 people have been killed and at least 2 million displaced from their homes.[165] In April 2008 the United Nations admitted that it may have underestimated the deaths in Darfur by 50 percent. The actual death toll may well be considerably higher, as many of the refugees are susceptible to death from malnutrition, exposure to the elements, and the disease epidemics that ravage the camps. Humanitarian workers were barred by Bashir's troops from delivering food supplies and medicines to the camps. The UN's Special Inter Agency Team reported that in other camps the refugees were fearful of accepting the supplies because they feared being raped or massacred by the Janjaweed who surrounded the camps.[166]

International Response

International response to the killing in Darfur has varied. The response of the United States was slow but more generous than that of most other nations. By April 2004, the United States had given $28 million to the UN's relief program for Darfur, Germany had contributed $1 million, but France had given nothing.[167] Part of the impetus in the United States came from religious communities, both Jewish and Christian. The Holocaust Memorial Museum in Washington, D.C., issued a "genocide warning" for Sudan as early as 2001,[168] while a group of 51 evangelical Christian leaders called on President George W. Bush to send troops to Darfur in August 2004 to "stop the genocide."[169] Most of the food and medical supplies sent to the camps came from the United States. Finally, Secretary of State Colin Powell referred to the killings in Sudan as "genocide" in a statement to the Senate Foreign Relations Committee.[170]

Europeans have generally preferred to minimize the massacres in Darfur as a "humanitarian crisis," a "counter-insurgency," or "ethnic cleansing" and to accuse the United States of overreacting. Renaud Muselier, the French secretary of state for foreign affairs, quoted Kofi Annan, then secretary general of the UN, to the effect that the events in Darfur are not genocide. "Kofi Annan, who is very careful in his choice of words . . . has said very clearly that this is not genocide. That is what I also believe. . . . It is [not genocide but] a civil war."[171] According to Gérard Prunier, a researcher at the National Center for Scientific Research (CNRS) in Paris and director of the French Centre for Ethiopian Studies in Addis Ababa, the reasons for indifference on the part of European governments include a reflex anti-Americanism; economic interest in the oil reserves of the Sudan; and a long-standing tendency to react to mass killing in Africa as "the quintessential 'African crisis': distant, esoteric, extremely violent, rooted in complex ethnic and historical factors which few understood, and devoid of any identifiable practical interest for the rich countries."[172] An additional factor is the unexpected and confusing outbreak of Muslim-on-Muslim violence in Darfur, which does not fit the usual pattern of religious hatred.[173]

Darfur largely slipped off the developed world's collective radar screen after December 2004, when the natural disaster of the Asian tsunami took the attention of the mass media. Although AMIS was expanded to 7,000 soldiers in mid-2005 (up from 150 in 2004), the force has been underfunded. It was the only external military force in Darfur until it was replaced by the United Nations African Union Mission in Darfur (UNAMID) on December 31, 2007. On August 31, 2006, the UN Security Council passed Resolution 1706, to send a UN peacekeeping force of 20,000 soldiers to Darfur. Since the resolution was opposed by the government of Sudan, the AU extended the mandate of AMIS through June 30, 2007. In the opinion of some knowledgeable Western observers, AMIS has had no greater success than previous attempts to improve the situation in Darfur. It "is clearly overwhelmed. . . . [T]his stopgap mission will fail not only those in need of protection but all the other interested parties as well."[174] On April 2, 2007, five of the AU's peacekeepers were killed while guarding a water hole near the border with Chad.[175]

One reason for the relative inaction of the UN since the defeat of Resolution 1706 has been the discovery of the UN's humanitarian agencies that "non-Western powers care even less about Darfur than the Western powers do. Arab governments stand behind the Sudanese regime."[176] On July 31, 2007, the Security Council passed Resolution 1769, establishing UNAMID, which has a mandate to operate until July 31, 2009. The African Union peacekeepers presently in Darfur were merged into UNAMID on December 31, 2007. The new mission will eventually have about 19,500 peacekeepers and 3,700 police.[177]

Is Darfur an Instance of Genocide?

Although there have been a few articles in medical journals regarding the "diagnosis" of Darfur as an instance of genocide,[178] the most extensive discussion to date of the applicability of the term *genocide* to the massacres in Darfur is found in Gérard Prunier's book on Darfur, published in 2005. Prunier notes that the killings in Darfur fit the definition of the 1948 UN Convention on Genocide, and that Colin Powell based his remarks in September 2004 on that definition.[179] At the same time, the UN's Commission of Inquiry decided that the situation in Darfur does not constitute an act of genocide because a genocidal intent is lacking. ". . . [There was] not sufficient evidence to indicate that Khartoum had a state policy intended to exterminate a particular racial or ethnic group."[180] What eventually happened instead was an indictment handed down by the International Criminal Court (ICC) against a high-ranking Sudanese minister of the interior and a leader of the Janjaweed in February 2007. The ICC charged Ahmed Haroun and Ali Kushayb with 51 counts of war crimes and crimes against humanity.[181]

Whether the terminology will make any difference in the resolution of the disaster remains to be seen. The chief prosecutor of the ICC, Luis Moreno-Ocampo, has noted the difficulties in conducting its ongoing investigation: providing adequate protection for witnesses in situations of persistent violence; widespread prevalence of contagious disease, which affects investigators as well as witnesses; executing arrest warrants; and finding qualified translators for languages that "have no corresponding words for the legal terminology required for the interview."[182] As of late 2008, the United Nations has still stopped short of referring to the killing in Darfur as genocide, although Moreno-Ocampo filed 10 charges of war crimes and three of genocide against al-Bashir on July 14, 2008.

[1] Frank Chalk and Kurt Jonassohn. "The Empire of the Mongols." In *The History and Sociology of Genocide: Analyses and Case Studies.* New Haven, Conn.: Yale University Press, 1990, p. 95.

[2] Ian Frazier. "Annals of History: Invaders." *New Yorker* (4/25/05). Available online. URL: http://www.newyorker.com/archive/2005/04/25/050425fa_fact4. Accessed October 20, 2006. Christopher Atwood in *Encyclopedia of Mongolia and the Mongol Empire* states, "The death toll of Mongol massacres is difficult to estimate. Persian historians estimate the death toll in cities such as Herat and Nishapur (Neyshabur) at more than 1.5 million, but these estimates seem to exceed considerably the possible populations of these cities. Hüle'ü claimed that his Mongol soldiers killed 200,000 people in Baghdad (1258). In North China, under the previous Jin dynasty (1115–1234), a census of 1207 found 7.68 million households, while the Mongol census of the same territory in 1236 found only 1.83 million households. While the Mongol census certainly involved a major undercount, the figures plainly demonstrate a demographic catastrophe." *Encyclopedia of Mongolia and the Mongol Empire.* New York: Facts On File, 2004, p. 344.

[3] The text was not available in any European languages until 1941, when Erich Haenisch published a German translation. English translations include Francis Woodman Cleaves. *The Secret History of the Mongols.* Cambridge, Mass.: Harvard University Press for the Harvard-Yenching Institute, 1982 and Igor de Rachewiltz. *The Secret History of the Mongols: A Mongolian Epic Chronicle of the Thirteenth Century.* Boston and Leiden: Brill, 2004, 2006. A short excerpt from de Rachewiltz's translation is available online. URL: http://www.mongolianculture.com/TheSecretHist.htm. Accessed July 7, 2007.

[4] J. J. Saunders. *The History of the Mongol Conquests.* Philadelphia: University of Pennsylvania Press, 2001, p. 45.

[5] Ala'iddin Ata-Malik Juvayni. *The History of the World-conqueror.* Translated by John Andrew Boyle. Manchester, England: Manchester University Press, 1958.

[6] Atwood, Christopher P. *Encyclopedia of Mongolia and the Mongol Empire.* New York: Facts On File, Inc., 2004, p. 349.

[7] Friar John of Plano Carpini. *History of the Mongols,* chapter 16. Available online. URL: http://www.deremilitari.org/resources/sources/carpini.htm. Accessed June 2, 2007.

[8] Saunders. *Mongol Conquests,* p. 62.

[9] Saunders. *Mongol Conquests,* p. 59.

[10] Atwood. *Encyclopedia of Mongolia and the Mongol Empire*, p. 343.

[11] T. Zerjal, Y. Xue, G. Bertorelle, et al. "The Genetic Legacy of the Mongols." *American Journal of Human Genetics* 72 (March 2003): pp. 717–721.

[12] Atwood. *Encyclopedia of Mongolia and the Mongol Empire*, p. 469.

[13] Quoted in Atwood. *Encyclopedia of Mongolia and the Mongol Empire*, p. 349.

[14] Denis Sinor. "The Mongols in the West." *Journal of Asian History* 33 (1999). Available online. URL: http://www.deremilitari.org/resources/articles/sinor1.htm. Accessed July 22, 2007.

[15] Saunders. *Mongol Conquests*, p. 54.

[16] Atwood. *Encyclopedia of Mongolia and the Mongol Empire*, p. 350.

[17] Atwood. *Encyclopedia of Mongolia and the Mongol Empire*, p. 350.

[18] Saunders. *Mongol Conquests*, p. 53.

[19] Bernard Lewis. *The Assassins: A Radical Sect in Islam.* New York: Basic Books, 2002.

[20] L. Venegoni. "Hülägü's Campaign in the West—(1258–1260)." *Transoxiana: Journal Libre de Estudios Orientales*, Webfestschrift Marshak, 2003. Available online. URL: http://www. transoxiana.org/Eran/Articles/venegoni.html. Accessed July 25, 2007.

[21] Venegoni. "Hülägü's Campaign in the West."

[22] A contemporary account of Tamerlane's destruction of the cities of Aleppo and Damascus may be found in chapter 5 of Yusuf ibn Taghri Birdi's *Tamerlane's Invasion of Syria*.

[23] Quoted in Adam Jones. *Genocide: A Comprehensive Introduction.* New York: Routledge, 2006, p. 101.

[24] Robert Marquand. "Mongolia's Marauding Son Gets a Makeover." *Christian Science Monitor* (5/10/02). Available online. URL: http://www.csmonitor.com/2002/0510/p01s04-woap. html. Accessed July 1, 2007.

[25] Rupert Wingfield-Hayes. "Mongolia's Cult of the Great Khan." *BBC News* (8/12/03). Available online. URL: http://news.bbc.co.uk/2/hi/programmes/from_our_own_correspondent/3144099. stm. Accessed July 15, 2007.

[26] Chalk and Jonassohn, "Empire of the Mongols," p. 95.

[27] Some of these have been assembled (with academic commentary) by Per Inge Oestmoen. "The Yasa of Chingis Khan: A Code of Honor, Dignity and Excellence." Available online. URL: http://www.coldsiberia.org/webdoc9.htm. Accessed July 2, 2007.

[28] Saunders. *Mongol Conquests*, p. 69.

[29] Peter Balakian. *The Burning Tigris: The Armenian Genocide and America's Response.* New York: HarperCollins, 2003, p. xii.

[30] Ben Kiernan. "Twentieth-Century Genocides: Underlying Ideological Themes from Armenia to East Timor." In *The Specter of Genocide: Mass Murder in Historical Perspective*, edited by Robert Gellately and Ben Kiernan. New York: Cambridge University Press, 2003, pp. 29–40.

[31] Bernard Lewis. "History Writing and National Revival in Turkey." *Middle Eastern Affairs* 4 (1953), p. 221.

[32] Jones. *Genocide*, p. 102.

[33] Bernard Lewis. "Europe and the Turks: The Civilization of the Ottoman Empire." *History Today* (October 1953), p. 678.

[34] Robert F. Melson. "The Armenian Genocide as Precursor and Prototype." In *Is the Holocaust Unique? Perspectives on Comparative Genocide*, edited by Alan S. Rosenbaum. Boulder, Colo.: Westview Press, 2001, pp. 120–121.

[35] Donald E. Miller and Lorna Touryan Miller. *Survivors: An Oral History of the Armenian Genocide*. Berkeley, Calif.: University of California Press, 1999, pp. 47–48.

[36] Quoted in Taner Akçam. *A Shameful Act: The Armenian Genocide and the Question of Turkish Responsibility*. Translated by Paul Bessemer. New York: Henry Holt and Company, 2006, p. 88.

[37] Robert F. Melson. "Provocation or Nationalism? A Critical Inquiry into the Armenian Genocide of 1915." In *The Armenian Genocide in Perspective*, edited by Richard G. Hovannisian. New Brunswick, N.J.: Transaction Publishers, 1986, p. 78.

[38] Akçam. *A Shameful Act*, pp. 24–25.

[39] Richard G. Hovannisian, ed. *The Armenian Genocide in Perspective*. New Brunswick, N.J.: Transaction Publishers, 1986, p. 23.

[40] Jones. *Genocide*, p. 102.

[41] Donald Bloxham. "Determinants of the Armenian Genocide." In *Looking Backward, Moving Forward: Confronting the Armenian Genocide*, edited by Richard G. Hovannisian. New Brunswick, N.J.: Transaction Publishers, 2003, p. 28.

[42] Vahakn N. Dadrian. "The Comparative Aspects of the Armenian and Jewish Cases of Genocide: A Sociohistorical Perspective." In *Is the Holocaust Unique? Perspectives on Comparative Genocide*, edited by Alan S. Rosenbaum. Boulder, Colo.: Westview Press, 2001, p. 145.

[43] Bernard Lewis. "A Taxonomy of Group Hatred." *Transit* 16 (Winter 1998–1999), p. 6.

[44] Akçam. *A Shameful Act*, p. 35.

[45] Quoted in Akçam. *A Shameful Act*, p. 43.

[46] Dadrian. "Comparative Aspects," p. 146.

[47] Akçam. *A Shameful Act*, p. 46.

[48] Hovannisian. *Armenian Genocide in Perspective*, p. 27.

[49] Quoted in Dadrian. "Comparative Aspects," p. 146.

[50] Akçam. *A Shameful Act*, pp. 69–70.

[51] Dadrian. "Comparative Aspects," p. 136. Morgenthau related that a prize was given to an official who came up with the idea of nailing horseshoes to the feet of his Armenian victims.

[52] J. M. Winter. *The Experience of World War I*. New York: Oxford University Press, 1989, p. 191.

[53] Bloxham. "Determinants of the Armenian Genocide," p. 32.

[54] Bloxham. "Determinants of the Armenian Genocide," p. 33.

[55] Akçam. *A Shameful Act*, p. 126.

[56] Melson. "Provocation or Nationalism?" p. 121.

[57] Jones. *Genocide*, p. 106.

[58] Balakian. *Burning Tigris*, pp. 186–188.

[59] Richard G. Hovannisian. "Bitter-Sweet Memories: The Last Generation of Ottoman Armenians." In *Looking Backward, Moving Forward: Confronting the Armenian Genocide*, edited by Richard G. Hovannisian. New Brunswick, N.J.: Transaction Publishers, 2003, pp. 118–119.

[60] Hovannisian. *Armenian Genocide in Perspective*, p. 38.

[61] Miller and Miller. *Survivors*, pp. 43–44. The American ambassador reported to the State Department that one caravan left Anatolia with 18,000 people and arrived at Aleppo with 150.

[62] Hovannisian. *Armenian Genocide in Perspective*, p. 39.

[63] Dadrian. "Comparative Aspects," p. 137.

[64] Miller and Miller. *Survivors*, p. 44.

[65] Simon Payaslian. "The United States Response to the Armenian Genocide." In *Looking Backward, Moving Forward: Confronting the Armenian Genocide*, edited by Richard G. Hovannisian. New Brunswick, N.J.: Transaction Publishers, 2003, pp. 64–65.

[66] Miller and Miller. *Survivors*, p. 120.

[67] Miller and Miller. *Survivors*, pp. 138–140.

[68] Joe Verhoeven. "The Armenian Genocide and International Law." In *Looking Backward, Moving Forward: Confronting the Armenian Genocide*, edited by Richard G. Hovannisian. New Brunswick, N.J.: Transaction Publishers, 2003, p. 137.

[69] Steven L. Jacobs. "Raphael Lemkin and the Armenian Genocide." In *Looking Backward, Moving Forward: Confronting the Armenian Genocide*, edited by Richard G. Hovannisian. New Brunswick, N.J.: Transaction Publishers, 2003, p. 129. Lemkin is thought to have written the two manuscripts in the early 1950s, after the United Nations had adopted the Convention on the Prevention and Punishment of the Crime of Genocide in 1948.

[70] Emil Danielyan. "Nobel Laureates Call for Armenian-Turkish Reconciliation." *Radio Free Europe* (4/10/07). Available online. URL: http://www.rferl.org/featuresarticle/2007/4/F1CACD86-B6BF-413F-B6AD-6C423454F845.html. Accessed July 28, 2007.

[71] *EurActiv.* "Parliament Faces Crucial Enlargement Decisions." (9/25/06). Available online. URL: http://www.euractiv.com/en/enlargement/parliament-faces-crucial-enlargement-decisions/article-158105. Accessed July 28, 2007.

[72] Edward Kissi. "Genocide in Cambodia and Ethiopia." In *The Specter of Genocide: Mass Murder in Historical Perspective*, edited by Robert Gellately and Ben Kiernan. New York: Cambridge University Press, 2003, p. 307.

[73] Chalk and Jonassohn. "Cambodia." In *History and Sociology of Genocide*, p. 399.

[74] Jones. *Genocide*, p. 186.

[75] Chalk and Jonassohn. "Cambodia." In *History and Sociology of Genocide*, p. 400.

[76] Jones. *Genocide*, p. 188.

[77] David P. Chandler. *The Tragedy of Cambodian History: Politics, War, and Revolution Since 1945.* New Haven, Conn.: Yale University Press, 1991, p. 205.

[78] Samantha Power. *A Problem from Hell: America and the Age of Genocide.* New York: HarperCollins, 2002, pp. 92–93.

[79] Chalk and Jonassohn. "Cambodia." In *History and Sociology of Genocide,* p. 401.

[80] Quoted in Power. *Problem from Hell,* pp. 94–95.

[81] Elizabeth Becker. *When the War Was Over: The Voices of Cambodia's Revolution and Its People.* New York: Simon and Schuster, 1986, pp. 171–172.

[82] Power. *Problem from Hell,* pp. 96–97.

[83] Ben Kiernan. *The Pol Pot Regime: Race, Power and Genocide in Cambodia under the Khmer Rouge, 1975–1979,* 2nd ed. New Haven, Conn.: Yale University Press, 2002, pp. 296–298.

[84] Power. *Problem from Hell,* p. 101.

[85] Quoted in Power. *Problem from Hell,* p. 102.

[86] The Khmer Rouge are thought to have borrowed the concept of a Year Zero from the French Revolution. After the abolition of the French monarchy in September 1792, the National Convention introduced a new calendar, with 1792 as Year One.

[87] François Ponchaud. *Cambodia Year Zero.* Translated by Nancy Amphoux. London: Allen Lane, 1978, pp. 62–63.

[88] Ben Kiernan. "Sources of Khmer Rouge Ideology." In *The Third Indochine War.* Ed. by Odd Arne Westal and Sophie Quinn-Judge. Florence, Ky.: Routledge, 2006, p. 192.

[89] Kiernan. "Sources of Khmer Rouge Ideology," p. 191.

[90] Ponchaud. *Year Zero,* p. 143.

[91] Power. *Problem from Hell,* p. 117.

[92] Power. *Problem from Hell,* p. 119.

[93] Kissi. "Genocide in Cambodia and Ethiopia," p. 312.

[94] Cited in Jones. *Genocide,* p. 191.

[95] Power. *Problem from Hell,* p. 117.

[96] Thomas Clayton. "Education under Occupation: Political Violence, Schooling, and Response in Cambodia, 1979–1989." *Current Issues in Comparative Education* 2 (11/15/99), p. 7.

[97] Chalk and Jonassohn. "Cambodia." In *History and Sociology of Genocide,* p. 404.

[98] Charles Burton. Book review of *Revolution and Its Aftermath in Kampuchea,* edited by David Chandler and Ben Kiernan. In *Pacific Affairs* 57 (Fall 1984): p. 532.

[99] Jones. *Genocide,* p. 193.

[100] Kissi. "Genocide in Cambodia and Ethiopia," p. 314.

[101] Gregory H. Stanton. "The Cambodian Genocide and International Law." Lecture delivered at Yale Law School. (2/22/92). Available online. URL: http://www.genocidewatch.

org/THE%20CAMBODIAN%20GENOCIDE%20AND%20INTERNATIONAL%20LAW. htm. Accessed March 2, 2007.

[102] Kiernan. "Sources of Khmer Rouge Ideology," p. 192.

[103] Stanton. "Cambodian Genocide and International Law."

[104] Japan under the Tokugawa shoguns (1603–1868) offers an earlier case study of Asian xenophobia.

[105] Kiernan. "Sources of Khmer Rouge Ideology," p. 194.

[106] Power. *Problem from Hell*, p. 118.

[107] Power. *Problem from Hell*, p. 109.

[108] Alan Channer. "Priest of Many Frontiers: Alan Channer Meets François Ponchaud, the Catholic Priest Who Brought the Cambodian Genocide to the Attention of the World." *For a Change* (December–January 1999). Available online. URL: http://findarticles.com/p/articles/ mi_m0KZH/is_6_12/ai_30125891. Accessed July 7, 2007.

[109] Power. *Problem from Hell*, p. 112.

[110] Phelim Kyne. "François Ponchaud: The Priest Who Exposed Pol Pot to the World." *Taipei Times* (4/16/00), p. 5. Available online. URL: http://www.taipeitimes.com/News/ asia/archives/2000/04/16/32499. Accessed July 5, 2007.

[111] Power. *Problem from Hell*, pp. 109–110.

[112] Quoted in Jones. *Genocide*, p. 198.

[113] Ponchaud. *Year Zero*, pp. 81–82.

[114] Chalk and Jonassohn. "Cambodia." In *History and Sociology of Genocide*, p. 407.

[115] Power. *Problem from Hell*, pp. 139–140.

[116] Nate Thayer. "Dying Breath: The Inside Story of Pol Pot's Last Days and the Disintegration of the Movement He Created." *Far Eastern Economic Review* (4/30/98). Available online. URL: http://www.cybercambodia.com/dachs/killing/polpot.html. Accessed July 30, 2007.

[117] Jones. *Genocide*, pp. 201–202.

[118] "How the Mighty Are Falling: The Beginning of the End of Impunity for the World's Once All-Powerful Thugs." *Economist* (7/5/07). Available online. URL: http://www.economist. com/world/international/displaystory.cfm?story_id=9441341. Accessed August 12, 2007.

[119] Robert Melson. "Modern Genocide in Rwanda: Ideology, Revolution, War, and Mass Murder in an African State." In *The Specter of Genocide: Mass Murder in Historical Perspective*, edited by Robert Gellately and Ben Kiernan. New York: Cambridge University Press, 2003, p. 326.

[120] Gérard Prunier. *The Rwanda Crisis: History of a Genocide*. New York: Columbia University Press, 1997, p. 39.

[121] Jean-Pierre Chrétien. "RTLM Propaganda: The Democratic Alibi." In *The Media and the Rwandan Genocide*, edited by Allan Thompson. London: Pluto Press and Fountain Publishers, 2007. Available online. URL: http://www.idrc.ca/en/ev-108180-201-1-DO_TOPIC.html. Accessed August 22, 2007.

[122] Christian P. Scherrer. *Genocide and Crisis in Central Africa.* Westport, Conn.: Praeger, 2002, p. 125.

[123] Jones. *Genocide,* p. 232.

[124] Linda Melvern. *Conspiracy to Murder: The Rwandan Genocide.* New York: Verso, 2004, pp. 12–19.

[125] Mark Doyle. "Ex-Rwandan PM Reveals Genocide Planning." *BBC News* (3/26/04). Available online. URL: http://news.bbc.co.uk/1/hi/world/africa/3572887.stm. Accessed August 5, 2007.

[126] World Food Programme. "Where We Work—Rwanda." Available online. URL: http://www.wfp.org/country_brief/indexcountry.asp?country=646. Accessed August 2, 2007.

[127] The term *Hamitic* is derived from Ham, one of the four sons of the biblical patriarch Noah listed in Genesis 10:6. Ham was considered the ancestor of the Egyptians and the Cushites, or Ethiopians.

[128] Cited in Melson. "Modern Genocide in Rwanda," p. 328.

[129] Tor Sellström and Lennart Wohlgemuth. *The International Response to Conflict and Genocide: Lessons from the Rwanda Experience,* Study 1: Historical Perspective: Some Explanatory Factors. Uppsala, Sweden: Nordic Africa Institute, 1996, chapter 2, Pre-Colonial Period. Available online. URL: http://www.reliefweb.int/library/nordic/book1/pb020d.html. Accessed August 5, 2007.

[130] Mahmood Mamdani. *When Victims Become Killers: Colonialism, Nativism, and the Genocide in Rwanda.* Princeton, N.J.: Princeton University Press, 2001, pp. 41–66.

[131] Sellström and Wohlgemuth. Historical Perspective, chapter 3, Colonial Period and Independence. Available online. URL: http://www.reliefweb.int/library/nordic/book1/pb020e.html. Accessed August 5, 2007.

[132] Melson. "Modern Genocide in Rwanda," p. 329.

[133] Melson. "Modern Genocide in Rwanda," p. 331.

[134] Jones. *Genocide,* p. 236.

[135] Falila Gbadamassi. "Kigali accuse Agathe Habyarimana de génocide: L'ancienne Première Dame du Rwanda menacée de poursuites judiciares." *Afrik.com* (4/1/04). Available online. URL: http://www.afrik.com/article7171.html. Accessed August 10, 2007.

[136] Marcel Kabanda. "*Kangura*: The Triumph of Propaganda Refined." In *The Media and the Rwandan Genocide.* Edited by Allan Thompson. London: Pluto Press and Fountain Publishers, 2007. Available online. URL: http://www.idrc.ca/en/ev-108184-201-1-DO_TOPIC.html. Accessed August 22, 2007.

[137] See chapter 5, "International Documents."

[138] Power. *Problem from Hell,* p. 340.

[139] Linda Melvern. *A People Betrayed: The Role of the West in Rwanda's Genocide.* London: Zed Books, 2000, p. 155.

[140] Roméo Dallaire. *Shake Hands with the Devil: The Failure of Humanity in Rwanda.* Toronto: Vintage Canada, 2003, pp. 96–98.

[141] Power. *Problem from Hell,* p. 337.

142 Jim Fussell. "Group Classification on National ID Cards as a Factor in Genocide and Ethnic Cleansing." Seminar presentation, Yale University Genocide Studies Program (11/15/01). Available online. URL: http://www.preventgenocide.org/prevent/removing-facilitating-factors/IDcards/. Accessed August 15, 2007.

143 Jones. *Genocide,* p. 239.

144 See chapter 5, "International Documents."

145 Dallaire. *Shake Hands with the Devil,* pp. 147, 167.

146 Jones. *Genocide,* p. 243.

147 Power. *Problem from Hell,* p. 355.

148 Dallaire. *Shake Hands with the Devil,* p. 333.

149 Power. *Problem from Hell,* p. 355.

150 Power. *Problem from Hell,* pp. 341, 366.

151 Jones. *Genocide,* p. 245.

152 Shimon Samuels. "Applying the Lessons of the Holocaust." In *Is the Holocaust Unique? Perspectives on Comparative Genocide,* edited by Alan S. Rosenbaum. Boulder, Colo.: Westview Press, 2001, p. 219.

153 P. N. Pham, H. M. Weinstein, and T. Longman. "Trauma and PTSD Symptoms in Rwanda: Implications for Attitudes toward Justice and Reconciliation." *Journal of the American Medical Association* 292 (August 4, 2004): pp. 602–612.

154 Jones. *Genocide,* p. 245.

155 International Criminal Tribunal for Rwanda. *Status of Cases.* Available online. URL: http://69.94.11.53/ENGLISH/cases/status.htm. Accessed July 27, 2007.

156 "Rwanda Starts Prisoner Releases." *BBC News* (7/29/05). Available online. URL: http://news.bbc.co.uk/2/hi/africa/4726969.stm. Accessed August 2, 2007.

157 Lyn S. Graybill. "Ten Years After, Rwanda Tries Reconciliation." *Current History* (May 2004), pp. 203–204.

158 Jones. *Genocide,* p. 371.

159 Roy F. Baumeister. *Evil: Inside Human Cruelty and Violence.* New York: W. H. Freeman and Company, 1999, p. 344.

160 Gérard Prunier. *Darfur: The Ambiguous Genocide.* Ithaca, N.Y.: Cornell University Press, 2005, pp. 8–9.

161 Central Intelligence Agency. *The World Factbook 2007.* Available online. URL: https://www.cia.gov/cia/publications/factbook/geos/su.html. Accessed March 1, 2007.

162 Allen D. Hertzke. "The Shame of Darfur." *First Things* 156 (October 2005): pp. 16–22. Available online. URL: http://www.firstthings.com/article.php3?id_article=239. Accessed October 5, 2006.

163 Samantha Power. "Dying in Darfur: Can the Ethnic Cleansing in Sudan Be Stopped?" *New Yorker* (8/30/04). Available online. URL: http://www.newyorker.com/archive/2004/08/30/040830fa_fact1. Accessed April 9, 2007.

[164] Quoted in Hertzke. "Shame of Darfur," p. 19.

[165] CIA. *World Factbook 2007.* Available online. URL: https://www.cia.gov/cia/publications/factbook/geos/su.html. Accessed March 1, 2007.

[166] Prunier. *Darfur,* pp. 112–113.

[167] Power. "Dying in Darfur."

[168] Hertzke. "Shame of Darfur," p. 18.

[169] Power. "Dying in Darfur."

[170] Glenn Kessler and Colum Lynch. "U.S. Calls Killings in Sudan Genocide." *Washington Post* (9/10/04), p. A1.

[171] Quoted in Power. "Dying in Darfur." Annan was booed by a crowd of demonstrators in Harvard Square in June 2004 for refusing to call Darfur a genocide; see Prunier, *Darfur,* p. 142.

[172] Prunier. *Darfur,* p. 124.

[173] Prunier. *Darfur,* p. 129.

[174] Samantha Power. "Missions." *New Yorker* (11/28/05). Available online. URL: http://www.newyorker.com/archive/2005/11/28/051128ta_talk_power. Accessed August 12, 2007.

[175] "African Troops Killed in Darfur." *BBC News* (4/02/07). Available online. URL: http://news.bbc.co.uk/2/hi/africa/6517791.stm. Accessed September 10, 2007.

[176] George Packer. "International Inaction." *New Yorker* (10/9/06). Available online. URL: http://www.newyorker.com/archive/2006/10/09/061009ta_talk_packer. Accessed August 9, 2007.

[177] "UN Backs New Darfur Peace Force." *BBC News* (8/1/07). Available online. URL: http://news.bbc.co.uk/2/hi/africa/6925187.stm. Accessed August 18, 2007.

[178] See, for example, J. Leaning. "Diagnosing Genocide—The Case of Darfur." *New England Journal of Medicine* 351 (August 19, 2004), pp. 735–738.

[179] Prunier. *Darfur,* pp. 156–157.

[180] Quoted in Prunier. *Darfur,* pp. 157–158.

[181] Robert Marquand. "World Court's Big Move on Darfur." *Christian Science Monitor* (2/28/07). Available online. URL: http://www.csmonitor.com/2007/0228/p01s02-woaf.html. Accessed February 28, 2007.

[182] Luis Moreno-Ocampo. "Instrument of Justice: The ICC Prosecutor Reflects." *Jurist* (1/24/07). Available online. URL: http://jurist.law.pitt.edu/forumy/2007/01/instrument-of-justice-icc-prosecutor.php. Accessed April 12, 2007.

PART II

Primary Sources

4

United States Documents

The primary sources in this chapter are divided into three sections—documents relating to the colonial period, to the postindependence period, and to international relations. The documents are arranged in chronological order within each section. Documents that have been excerpted are identified as such; all others are reproduced in full.

COLONIAL PERIOD

Bartolomé de Las Casas, *A Brief Account of the Destruction of the Indies* (1552) (excerpt)

Las Casas's Brief Account is a report by a Dominican missionary of the atrocities committed by the Spanish in Cuba, Central America, and Mexico. He witnessed some of the incidents he reports and reprinted material from others' eyewitness accounts. The Brief Account was originally published in Seville, Spain, in 1552 and dedicated to King Philip II of Spain (1527–98). The following excerpt is from the earliest (1689) English translation of Las Casas's work.

Now this infinite multitude of [the Indians] are by the Creation of God innocently simple, altogether void of and averse to all manner of Craft, Subtlety and Malice, and most Obedient and Loyal Subjects to their Native Sovereigns; and behave themselves very patiently, submissively and quietly towards the Spaniards, to whom they are subservient and subject; so that finally they live without the least thirst after revenge, laying aside all litigiousness, Commotion and hatred. . . .

The natives [are] tractable, and capable of Morality or Goodness, very apt to receive the instill'd principles of Catholick Religion; nor are they averse to Civility and good Manners, being not so much discompos'd by variety of Obstructions as the rest of Mankind; insomuch, that having suckt in (if I may so express my self) the very first Rudiments of the Christian

117

Faith, they are so transported with Zeal and Fervor in the exercise of Eccle-siastical Sacraments, and Divine Service, that the very [members of religious orders] themselves, stand in need of the greatest and most signal patience to undergo such extreme Transports. And to conclude, I myself have heard the Spaniards themselves (who dare not assume the Confidence to deny the good Nature predominant in them) declare, that there was nothing wanting in them for the acquisition of Eternal Beatitude, but the sole Knowledge and Understanding of the Deity.

The Spaniards first assaulted the innocent Sheep so qualified by the Almighty, as is premention'd, like most cruel Tygers, Wolves and Lions hunger-starv'd, studying nothing, for the space of Forty Years, after their first landing, but the Massacre of these Wretches, whom they have so inhumanely and barbarously butcher'd and harass'd with several kinds of Torments, never before known, or heard (of which you shall have some account in the following Discourse) that of Three Millions of Persons, which lived in Hispaniola itself, there is at present but the inconsiderable remnant of scarce Three Hundred. Nay the Isle of Cuba, which extends as far as Valledolid in Spain is distant from Rome, lies now uncultivated, like a Desert, and intomb'd in its own Ruins. You may also find the Isles of St. John, and Jamaica, both large and fruitful places, unpeopled and desolate . . . A most Healthful and pleasant Climate is now laid waste and uninhabited; and whereas, when the Spaniards first arriv'd here, about Five Hundred Thousand Men dwelt in it, they are now cut off, some by slaughter, and others ravished away by Force and Violence, to work in the Mines of His-paniola. . . . There are other Islands Thirty in number, and upward bordering upon the Isle of St. John, totally unpeopled; all which are above Two Thou-sand miles in Length, and yet remain without Inhabitants. . . .

As to the mainland, we are certainly satisfied, and assur'd, that the Spaniards by their barbarous and execrable Actions have absolutely depopulated Ten Kingdoms, of greater extent than all Spain, together with the Kingdoms of Arragon and Portugal, that is to say, above One Thousand Miles, which now lye waste and desolate, and are absolutely ruined, when as formerly no other Country whatsoever was more populous. Nay we dare boldly affirm that during the Forty Years space, wherein they exercised their sanguinary and detestable Tyranny in these Regions, above Twelve Millions (computing Men, Women, and Children) have undeservedly perished; nor do I conceive that I should deviate from the Truth by saying that above Fifty Millions in all paid their last Debt to Nature. . . .

[When the Spaniards perceived that the Indians were planning a revolt] they, mounted on generous Steeds, well weapon'd with Lances and Swords, begin to exercise their bloody Butcheries and Strategems, and overrunning their Cities and Towns, spar'd no Age, or Sex, nay not so much as Women with Child, but ripping up their Bellies, tore them alive in pieces. They laid Wagers among themselves, who should with a Sword at one blow cut, or divide a Man in two; or which of them should decollate or behead a Man, with the greatest dexterity. . . .

They snatcht young Babes from the Mothers Breasts, and then dasht out the brains of those innocents against the Rocks; others they cast into Rivers scoffing and jeering them . . . and inhumanely exposing others to their Merciless Swords, together with the Mothers that gave them Life.

They erected certain Gibbets, large, but low made, so that their feet almost reacht the ground, every one of which was so order'd as to bear Thirteen Persons in Honour and Reverence (as they said blasphemously) of our Redeemer and his Twelve Apostles, under which they made a Fire to burn them to Ashes whilst hanging on them. . . .

The Lords and Persons of Noble Extract were usually expos'd to this kind of Death; they order'd Gridirons to be placed and supported with wooden Forks, and putting a small Fire under them, these miserable Wretches by degrees and with loud Shrieks and exquisite Torments, at last Expir'd. I once saw Four or Five of their most Powerful Lords laid on these Gridirons, and thereon roasted . . . but the shrill Clamours which were heard there being offensive to the Captain, by hindring his Repose, he commanded them to be strangled with a Halter. The Executioner (whose Name and Parents at Seville are not unknown to me) prohibited the doing of it; but stopt Gags into their Mouths to prevent the hearing of the noise (he himself making the Fire) till that they dyed, when they had been roasted as long as he thought convenient. I was an Eye-Witness of these and an innumerable Number of other Cruelties. . . .

Source: Bartolomé de Las Casas. *A Brief Account of the Destruction of the Indies.* Available online. URL: http://www.gutenberg.org/2/0/3/2/20321/. Accessed March 12, 2007.

John Eliot, *The Day-Breaking If Not the Sun-Rising of the Gospell with the Indians in New-England* (1647) (excerpt)

Eliot's book was published in London in 1647 as an account of his missionary work among the Indians. He discovered that he had a gift for learning languages as an undergraduate at Cambridge University in England before coming to the Massachusetts Bay Colony in 1631. Eliot is said to have learned Algonquian, the language of the Native Americans living in the Boston area, from a servant who had been captured during the Pequot War. He had already become interested in preaching to the Indians after settling in Roxbury as the town minister in the early 1640s. His first sermons to the Indians, which he relates in The Day-Breaking, *were in English, but by early 1647 he had become fluent enough in Algonquian to preach to his hearers in their own language. Eliot generally emphasized the positive aspects of Christian belief in his sermons to the Indians. His last words on his deathbed in 1690 were "Welcome joy!"*

For about an houre and a quarter the Sermon continued, wherein one of our company ran thorough all the principall matter of religion, beginning first with a repetition of the ten Commandements, and a briefe explication of them, then shewing the curse and dreadfull wrath of God against all those who brake them, or any one of them, or the least tittle of them [Matthew 5:18], and so applyed it unto the condition of the Indians present, with much sweet affection; and then preached Jesus Christ to them the onely meanes of recovery from sinne and wrath and eternall death, and what Christ was, and whither he was now gone, and how hee will one day come againe to judge the world in flaming fire; and of the blessed estate of all those that by faith beleeve in Christ, and know him feelingly: he spake to them also (observing his owne method as he saw most fit to edifie them) about the creation and fall of man, about the greatnesse and infinite being of God, the maker of all things, about the joyes of heaven, and the terrours and horrours of wicked men in hell, perswading them to repentance for severall sins which they live in, and many things of the like nature; not meddling with any matters more difficult, and which to such weake ones might at first seeme ridiculous, untill they had tasted and beleeved more plaine and familiar truths.

Having thus in a set speech familiarly opened the principal matters of Salvation to them, the next thing wee intended was discourse with them by propounding certaine questions to see what they would say to them, that so wee might skrue [impart] by variety of meanes something or other of God into them; but before wee did this we asked them if they understood all that was already spoken, and whether all of them in the Wigwam did understand or onely some few? And they answered to this question with a multitude of voyces, that they all of them did understand all that which was then spoken to them. . . .

One of them after this answer replyed to us that hee was a little while since praying in his Wigwam, unto God and Jesus Christ, that God would give him a good heart, and that while hee was praying, one of his fellow Indians interrupted him, and told him, that hee prayed in vaine, because

Jesus Christ understood not what Indians speake in prayer, he had bin used to heare English men pray and so could well enough understand them, but Indian language in prayer, hee thought hee was not acquainted with it, but was a stranger to it, and therefore could not understand them. His question therefore was, whether Jesus Christ did understand, or God did understand Indian prayers.

This question sounding just like themselves wee studied to give as familiar an answer as wee could, and therefore in this as in all other our answers, we endeavoured to speake nothing without clearing of it up by some familiar similitude; our answer summarily was therefore this, that Jesus Christ and God by him made all things [John 1: 2], and makes all men, not onely English but Indian men, and if hee made them both (which wee know the light of nature would readily teach as they had been also instructed by us) then hee knew all that was within man and came from man, all his desires, and all his thoughts, and all his speeches, and so all his prayers; and if hee made Indian men, then hee knowes all Indian prayers also: and therefore wee bid them looke upon that Indian Basket that was before them, there was black and white strawes, and many other things they made it of, now though others did not know what those things were who made not the Basket, yet hee that made it must needs tell all the things in it, so (wee said) it was here.

Another propounded this question after this answer, Whether English men were ever at any time so ignorant of God and Jesus Christ as themselves?

When wee perceived the root and reach of this question, wee gave them this answer, that there are two sorts of Englishmen, some are bad and naught, and live wickedly and loosely, (describing them) and these kind of Englishmen, wee told them, were in a manner as ignorant of Jesus Christ as the Indians now are; but there are a second sort of Englishmen, who though for a time they lived wickedly also like other prophane and ignorant English, yet repenting of their sinnes, and seeking after God and Jesus Christ, they are good men now, and now know Christ, and love Christ, and pray to Christ, and are thankfull for all they have to Christ, and shall at last when they dye, goe up to heaven to Christ; and we told them all these also were once as ignorant of God and Jesus Christ as the Indians are, but by seeking to know him by reading his booke, and hearing his word, and praying to him, &c. they now know Jesus Christ and just so shall the Indians know him if they so seeke him also, although at the present they bee extremely ignorant of him. . . .

Source: John Eliot. *The Day-Breaking.* Available online. URL: http://digilib.bu.edu/dspace/bitstream/2144/1081/3/ daybreakingif00wilsrich.txt. Accessed April 22, 2007.

Benjamin Franklin, *A Narrative of the Late Massacres in Lancaster County* (1764) (excerpt)

Franklin's account of the Paxton Boys' massacre of the Conestoga Indians in December 1763 is one of his better-known writings. Franklin had contacts in Lancaster, as he had started the borough's first print shop in 1751 and sold it in 1757, when he moved to England temporarily. Following the massacre at Conestoga, the Paxton Boys marched toward Philadelphia, threatening to kill the 140 remaining Conestoga who had taken refuge there. At the request of Governor John Penn, Franklin and three other men met with the Paxton Boys and persuaded them to return home. Franklin lost his seat in the Pennsylvania General Assembly in the next election because of his support of the Indians.

These *Indians* were the Remains of a Tribe of the *Six Nations*, settled at *Conestogoe*, and thence called *Conestogoe Indians*. On the first Arrival of the *English* in *Pennsylvania*, Messengers from this Tribe came to welcome them, with Presents of Venison, Corn and Skins; and the whole Tribe entered into a Treaty of Friendship with the first Proprietor, WILLIAM PENN, which was to last "as long as the Sun should shine, or the Waters run in the Rivers."

This Treaty has been since frequently renewed, and the *Chain brightened*, as they express it, from time to time. It has never been violated, on their Part or ours, till now. As their Lands by Degrees were mostly purchased, and the Settlements of the White People began to surround them, the Proprietor assigned them Lands on the Manor of *Conestogoe*, which they might not part with; there they have lived many Years in Friendship with their White Neighbours, who loved them for their peaceable inoffensive Behaviour.

It has always been observed, that *Indians*, settled in the Neighbourhood of White People, do not increase, but diminish continually. This Tribe accordingly went on diminishing, till there remained in their Town on the Manor, but 20 Persons, *viz.* 7 Men, 5 Women, and 8 Children, Boys and Girls.

On *Wednesday*, the 14th of *December*, 1763, Fifty-seven Men, from some of our Frontier Townships, who had projected the Destruction of this little Common-wealth, came, all well-mounted, and armed with Firelocks, Hangers and Hatchets, having travelled through the Country in the Night, to *Conestogoe* Manor. There they surrounded the small Village of *Indian* Huts, and just at Break of Day broke into them all at once. Only three Men, two Women, and a young Boy, were found at home, the rest being out among the neighbouring White People, some to sell the Baskets, Brooms and Bowls they manufactured, and others on other Occasions. These poor defenceless Creatures were immediately fired upon, stabbed and hatcheted to Death! The good *Shehaes*, among the rest, cut to Pieces in his Bed. All of them were scalped, and otherwise horribly mangled. Then their Huts were set on Fire, and most of them burnt down. When the Troop, pleased with their own Conduct and Bravery, but enraged that any of the poor *Indians* had escaped the Massacre, rode off, and in small Parties, by different Roads, went home. The universal Concern of the neighbouring White People on hearing of this Event, and the Lamentations of the younger *Indians*, when they returned and saw the Desolation, and the butchered half-burnt Bodies of their murdered Parents, and other Relations, cannot well be expressed.

The Magistrates of *Lancaster* sent out to collect the remaining *Indians*, brought them into the Town for their better Security against any farther Attempt; and it is said condoled with them on the Misfortune that had happened, took them by the Hand, comforted and *promised them Protection.*—They were all put into the Workhouse, a strong Building, as the Place of greatest Safety. . . .

If an *Indian* injures me, does it follow that I may revenge that Injury on all *Indians*? It is well known that Indians are of different Tribes, Nations and Languages, as well as the White People. In *Europe*, if the *French*, who are White People, should injure the *Dutch*, are they to revenge it on the *English*, because they too are White People? The only Crime of these poor Wretches seems to have been, that they had a reddish brown Skin, and black Hair; and some People of that Sort, it seems, had murdered some of our Relations. If it be right to kill Men for such a Reason, then, should any Man, with a freckled Face and red Hair, kill a Wife or Child of mine, it would be right for me to revenge it, by killing all the freckled red-haired Men, Women and Children, I could afterwards any where meet with.

But it seems these People think they have a better Justification; nothing less than the *Word of God*. With the Scriptures in their Hands and Mouths, they can set at nought that express Command, *Thou shalt do no Murder*; and justify their Wickedness, by the Command given *Joshua* to destroy the Heathen. Horrid Perversion of Scripture and of Religion! to father the worst of Crimes on the God of Peace and Love!—Even the *Jews*, to whom that particular Commission was directed, spared the *Gibeonites*, on Account of their Faith once given. The Faith of this Government has been frequently given to those *Indians*;—but that did not avail them with People who despise Government. . . .

What had little Boys and Girls done; what could Children of a Year old, Babes at the Breast, what could they do, that they too must be shot and hatcheted?—Horrid to relate!—and in their Parents Arms! This is done by no civilized Nation in *Europe*. Do we come to *America* to learn and practise the Manners of *Barbarians*? But this, *Barbarians* as they are, they practise against their Enemies only, not against their Friends.—

These poor People have been always our Friends. Their Fathers received ours, when Strangers here, with Kindness and Hospitality. Behold the Return we have made them!—When we grew more numerous and powerful, they put themselves under our *Protection*. See, in the mangled Corpses of the last Remains of the Tribe, how effectually we have afforded it to them!

Source: Benjamin Franklin. *A Narrative of the Late Massacres.* Available online. URL: http://www.historycarper. com/resources/twobf3/massacre.htm. Accessed January 1, 2007.

DOCUMENTS AND TREATIES AFTER 1789

Indian Removal Act (May 28, 1830)

President Andrew Jackson's signing of the Indian Removal Act has been called one of the most shameful acts in American history. Passage of the act was important primarily to the Southern states, which wanted their white populations to be able to move westward into lands held by the Cherokee and Choctaw tribes. The act had little support in the North, where such members of Congress as Henry Clay, Theodore Freylinghuysen, and Daniel Webster spoke out in opposition to it; in addition, such missionaries as Jeremiah Evarts tried to persuade Congress to vote against the act. It was passed only after bitter debate in Congress; its passage led to the forced removal of the Cherokee eight years later.

**An Act to provide for an exchange of lands with the Indians
residing in any of the states or territories,
and for their removal west of the river Mississippi.**

Be it enacted by the Senate and House of Representatives of the United States of America, in Congress assembled, That it shall and may be lawful for the President of the United States to cause so much of any territory belonging to the United States, west of the river Mississippi, not included in any state or organized territory, and to which the Indian title has been extinguished, as he may judge necessary, to be divided into a suitable number of districts, for the reception of such tribes or nations of Indians as may choose to exchange the lands where they now reside, and remove there; and to cause each of said districts to be so described by natural or artificial marks, as to be easily distinguished from every other.

And be it further enacted, That it shall and may be lawful for the President to exchange any or all of such districts, so to be laid off and described, with any tribe or nation of Indians now residing within the limits of any of the states or territories, and with which the United States have existing treaties, for the whole or any part or portion of the territory claimed and occupied by such tribe or nation, within the bounds of any one or more of the states or territories, where the land claimed and occupied by the Indians, is owned by the United States, or the United States are bound to the state within which it lies to extinguish the Indian claim thereto.

And be it further enacted, That in the making of any such exchange or exchanges, it shall and may be lawful for the President solemnly to assure the tribe or nation with which the exchange is made, that the United States will forever secure and guaranty to them, and their heirs or successors, the country so exchanged with them; and if they prefer it, that the United States will cause a patent or grant to be made and executed to them for the same: *Provided always,* That such lands shall revert to the United States, if the Indians become extinct, or abandon the same.

And be it further enacted, That if, upon any of the lands now occupied by the Indians, and to be exchanged for, there should be such improvements as add value to the land claimed by any individual or individuals of such tribes or nations, it shall and may be lawful for the President to cause such value to be ascertained by appraisement or otherwise, and to cause such ascertained value to be paid to the person or persons rightfully claiming such improvements. And upon the payment of such valuation, the improvements so valued and paid for, shall pass to the United States, and possession shall not afterwards be permitted to any of the same tribe.

And be it further enacted, That upon the making of any such exchange as is contemplated by this act, it shall and may be lawful for the President to cause such aid and assistance to be furnished to the emigrants as may be necessary and proper to enable them to remove to, and settle in, the country for which they may have exchanged; and also, to give them such aid and assistance as may be necessary for their support and subsistence for the first year after their removal.

And be it further enacted, That it shall and may be lawful for the President to cause such tribe or nation to be protected, at their new residence, against all interruption or disturbance from any other tribe or nation of Indians, or from any other person or persons whatever.

And be it further enacted, That it shall and may be lawful for the President to have the same superintendence and care over any tribe or nation in the country to which they may remove, as contemplated by this act, that he is now authorized to have over them at their present places of residence: *Provided,* That nothing in this act contained shall be construed as authorizing or directing the violation of any existing treaty between the United States and any of the Indian tribes.

And be it further enacted, That for the purpose of giving effect to the Provisions of this act, the sum of five hundred thousand dollars is hereby appropriated, to be paid out of any money in the treasury, not otherwise appropriated.

Source: Indian Removal Act. Available online. URL: http://www.mtholyoke.edu/acad/intrel/removal.htm. Accessed January 12, 2007.

Treaty of New Echota (1835) (excerpt)

The Treaty of New Echota was signed on December 29, 1835, between representatives of the federal government and members of the so-called Ridge party within the Cherokee nation. The Ridge party opposed Chief John Ross's attempts to retain their tribal lands; they thought that the Cherokee would eventually lose these lands and that accepting removal to the West was the only way to preserve the Cherokee nation. The terms of the treaty committed the United States to pay the Cherokee people $4.5 million for their lands, cover the costs of relocation, and give them equivalent land in present-day Oklahoma in exchange for all Cherokee land east of the Mississippi River. After the treaty had been signed, the Cherokee refused to recognize it on the grounds that the Ridge party did not represent them. Chief Ross tried to persuade the Senate to invalidate the treaty, a move that failed by a single vote. The treaty was enforced by President Martin Van Buren in 1838, leading to the tragedy now known as the Trail of Tears. Members of the Ridge party who signed the treaty were assassinated after the forced removal westward had been completed.

ARTICLE 1.

The Cherokee nation hereby cede relinquish and convey to the United States all the lands owned claimed or possessed by them east of the Mississippi river, and hereby release all their claims upon the United States for spoliations of every kind for and in consideration of the sum of five millions of dollars to be expended paid and invested in the manner stipulated and agreed upon in the following articles. But as a question has arisen between the commissioners and the Cherokees whether the Senate in their resolution by which they advised "that a sum not exceeding five millions of dollars be paid to the Cherokee Indians for all their lands and possessions east of the Mississippi river" have included and made any allowance or consideration for claims for spoliations it is therefore agreed on the part of the United States that this question shall be again submitted to the Senate for their consideration and decision and if no allowance was made for spoliations that then an additional sum of three hundred thousand dollars be allowed for the same. . . .

ARTICLE 6.

Perpetual peace and friendship shall exist between the citizens of the United States and the Cherokee Indians. The United States agree to protect the Cherokee nation from domestic strife and foreign enemies and against intestine wars between the several tribes. The Cherokees shall endeavor to preserve and maintain the peace of the country and not make war upon their neighbors; they shall also be protected against interruption and intrusion from citizens of the United States, who may attempt to settle in the country without their consent; and all such persons shall be removed from the same by order of the President of the United States. But this is not intended to prevent the residence among them of useful farmers, mechanics and teachers for the instruction of Indians according to treaty stipulations.

ARTICLE 7.

The Cherokee nation having already made great progress in civilization and deeming it important that every proper and laudable inducement should be offered to their people to improve their condition as well as to guard and secure in the most effectual manner the rights guarantied to them in this treaty, and with a view to illustrate the liberal and enlarged policy of the Government of the United States towards the Indians in their removal beyond the territorial limits of the States, it is stipulated that they shall be entitled to a delegate in the House of Representatives of the United States whenever Congress shall make provision for the same.

ARTICLE 8.

The United States also agree and stipulate to remove the Cherokees to their new homes and to subsist them one year after their arrival there and that a sufficient number of steamboats and baggage-wagons shall be furnished to remove them comfortably, and so as not to endanger their health, and that a physician well supplied with medicines shall accompany each detachment of emigrants removed by the Government. Such persons and families as in the opinion of the emigrating agent are capable of subsisting and removing themselves shall be permitted to do so; and they shall be allowed in full for all claims for the same twenty dollars for each member of their family; and in lieu of their one year's rations they shall be paid the sum of thirty-three dollars and thirty-three cents if they prefer it.

Such Cherokees also as reside at present out of the nation and shall remove with them in two years west of the Mississippi shall be entitled to allowance for removal and subsistence as above provided.

ARTICLE 16.

It is hereby stipulated and agreed by the Cherokees that they shall remove to their new homes within two years from the ratification of this treaty and that during such time the United States shall protect and defend them in their possessions and property and free use and occupation of the same and such persons as have been dispossessed of their improvements and houses; and for which no grant has actually issued previously to the enactment of the law of the State of Georgia, of December 1835 to regulate Indian occupancy shall be again put in possession and placed in the same situation and condition, in reference to the laws of the State of Georgia, as the Indians that have not been dispossessed; and if this is not done, and the people are left unprotected, then the United States shall pay the several Cherokees for their losses and damages sustained by them in consequence thereof. And it is also stipulated and agreed that the public buildings and improvements on which they are situated at New Echota for which no grant has been actually made previous to the passage of the above recited act if not occupied by the Cherokee people shall be reserved for the public and free use of the United States and the Cherokee Indians for the purpose of settling and closing all the Indian business arising under this treaty between the commissioners of claims and the Indians. . . .

Source: Treaty of New Echota. Available online. URL: http://digital.library.okstate.edu/kappler/. Accessed January 1, 2007.

Letter from Ralph Waldo Emerson to President Martin Van Buren (April 23, 1838)

Ralph Waldo Emerson (1803–82) is better known as a poet and essayist than a political figure. Even before his opposition to Indian removal he had become controversial in New England for resigning from the Unitarian ministry on grounds of belief in 1832. His views on religion as expressed in the commencement address he gave at the Harvard Divinity School in July 1838, three months after the letter to President Van Buren, were shocking to many Protestant New Englanders and led to his being considered an atheist. Emerson's support of the Cherokees prefigured his strong support of the abolitionist movement to end slavery in the South before the Civil War.

SIR: The seat you fill places you in a relation of credit and nearness to every citizen. By right and natural position, every citizen is your friend. Before any acts contrary to his own judgment or interest have repelled the affections of any man, each may look with trust and living anticipation to your government. Each has the highest right to call your attention to such subjects as are of a public nature, and properly belong to the chief magistrate; and the good magistrate will feel a joy in meeting such confidence. In this belief and at the instance of a few of my friends and neighbors, I crave of your patience a short hearing for their sentiments and my own: and the circumstance that my name will be utterly unknown to you will only give the fairer chance to your equitable construction of what I have to say.

Sir, my communication respects the sinister rumors that fill this part of the country concerning the Cherokee people. The interest always felt in the aboriginal population—an interest naturally growing as that decays—has been heightened in regard to this tribe. Even in our distant State some good rumor of their worth and civility has arrived. We have learned with joy their improvement in the social arts. We have read their newspapers. We have seen some of them in our schools and colleges. In common with the great body of the American people, we have witnessed with sympathy the painful labors of these red men to redeem their own race from the doom of eternal inferiority, and to borrow and domesticate in the tribe the arts and customs of the Caucasian race. And notwithstanding the unaccountable apathy with which of late years the Indians have been some-times abandoned to their enemies, it is not to be doubted that it is the good pleasure and the understanding of all humane persons in the Republic, of the men and the matrons sitting in the thriving independent families all over the land, that they shall be duly cared for; that they shall taste justice and love from all to whom we have delegated the office of dealing with them.

The newspapers now inform us that, in December, 1835, a treaty contracting for the exchange of all the Cherokee territory was pre-tended to be made by an agent on the part of the United States with some persons appearing on the part of the Cherokees; that the fact afterwards transpired that these deputies did by no means represent the will of the nation; and that, out of eighteen thousand souls composing the nation, fifteen thousand six hundred and sixty-eight have protested against the so-called treaty. It now appears that the government of the United States choose to hold the Cherokees to this sham treaty, and are proceeding to execute the same. Almost the entire Cherokee Nation stand up and say, "This is not our act. Behold us. Here are we. Do not mistake that handful of deserters for us;" and the American President and the Cabinet, the Senate and the House of Representatives, neither hear these men nor see them, and are contracting to put this active nation into carts and boats, and to drag them over mountains and rivers to a wilderness at a vast distance beyond the Mississippi. And a paper purporting to be an army order fixes a month from this day as the hour for this doleful removal.

In the name of God, sir, we ask you if this be so. Do the newspapers rightly inform us? Men and women with pale and perplexed faces meet one another in the streets and churches here, and ask if this be so. We have inquired if this be a gross misrepresentation from the party opposed to the government and anxious to blacken it with the people. We have looked in the newspapers of different parties and find a horrid confirmation of the tale. We are slow to believe it. We hoped the Indians were misinformed, and that their remonstrance was pre-mature, and will turn out to be a needless act of terror.

The piety, the principle that is left in the United States, if only in its coarsest form, a regard to the speech of men, forbid us to entertain it as a fact. Such a dereliction of all faith and virtue, such a denial of justice, and such deafness to screams for mercy were never heard of in times of peace and in the dealing of a nation with its own allies and wards, since the earth was made. Sir, does this government think that the people of the United States are become savage and mad? From their mind are the sentiments of love and a good nature wiped clean out? The soul of man, the justice, the mercy that is the heart's heart in all men, from Maine to Georgia, does abhor this business.

In speaking thus the sentiments of my neighbors and my own, perhaps I overstep the bounds of decorum. But would it not be a higher indecorum coldly to argue a matter like this? We only state the fact that a crime is projected that confounds our understandings by its magnitude,—a crime that really deprives us as well as the Cherokees of a country? For how could we call the conspiracy that should crush these poor Indians our government, or the land that was cursed by their parting and dying imprecations our country, any more? You, sir, will bring down that renowned chair in which you sit into infamy if your seal is set to this instrument of perfidy; and the name of this nation, hitherto the sweet omen of religion and liberty, will stink to the world.

You will not do us the injustice of connecting this remonstrance with any sectional and party feeling. It is in our hearts the simplest commandment of brotherly love. We will not have this great and solemn claim upon national and human justice huddled aside under the flimsy plea of its being a party act. Sir, to us the questions upon which the government and the people have been agitated during the past year, touching the prostration of the currency and of trade, seem but motes in comparison. These hard times, it is true, have brought the discussion home to every farmhouse and poor man's house in this town; but it is the chirping of grasshoppers beside the immortal question whether justice shall be done by the race of civilized to the race of savage man,—whether all the attributes of reason, of civility, of justice, and even of mercy, shall be put off by the American people, and so vast an outrage upon the Cherokee Nation and upon human nature shall be consummated.

One circumstance lessens the reluctance with which I intrude at this time on your attention my conviction that the government ought to be admonished of a new historical fact, which the discussion of this question has disclosed, namely, that there exists in a great part of the Northern people a gloomy diffidence in the moral character of the government.

On the broaching of this question, a general expression of despondency, of disbelief that any good will accrue from a remonstrance on an act of fraud and robbery, appeared in those men to whom we naturally turn for aid and counsel. Will the American government steal? Will it lie? Will it kill?—We ask triumphantly. Our counsellors and old statesmen here say that ten years ago they would have staked their lives on the affirmation that the proposed Indian measures could not be executed; that the unanimous country would put them down. And now the steps of this crime follow each other so fast, at such fatally quick time, that the millions of virtuous citizens, whose agents the government are, have no place to interpose, and must shut their eyes until the last howl and wailing of these tormented villages and tribes shall afflict the ear of the world.

I will not hide from you, as an indication of the alarming distrust, that a letter addressed as mine is, and suggesting to the mind of the Executive the plain obligations of man, has a burlesque character in the apprehensions of some of my friends. I, sir, will not beforehand treat you with the contumely of this distrust. I will at least state to you this fact, and show you how plain and humane people, whose love would be honor, regard the policy of the government, and what injurious inferences they draw as to the minds of the governors. A man with your experience in affairs must have seen cause to appreciate the futility of opposition to the moral sentiment. However feeble the sufferer and however great the oppressor, it is in the nature of things that the blow should recoil upon the aggressor. For God is in the sentiment, and it cannot be withstood. The potentate and the people perish before it; but with it, and as its executor, they are omnipotent.

I write thus, sir, to inform you of the state of mind these Indian tidings have awakened here, and to pray with one voice more that you, whose hands are strong with the delegated power of fifteen millions of men, will avert with that might the terrific injury which threatens the Cherokee tribe.

> With great respect, sir, I am your fellow citizen,
> RALPH WALDO EMERSON.

Source: Letter from Ralph Waldo Emerson to President Martin Van Buren. Available online. URL: http://www.rwe.org/comm/index.php?option=com_content&task=view&id=79&Itemid=252. Accessed January 12, 2007.

John G. Burnett, *Cherokee Indian Removal, 1838–1839* (1890) (excerpt)

John Burnett (1810–?), a soldier who accompanied one group of Indians on their journey in the fall of 1838, recorded his memories in 1890. Burnett was a private

under the command of Captain Abraham McClellan. He served as an inter-
preter between the Cherokee and the army officers. Burnett wrote his memories of
the Trail of Tears in a letter to his grandchildren on his 80th birthday in 1890.

. . . until we reached the end of the fateful journey on March the 26th, 1839, the sufferings of the Cherokees were awful. The trail of the exiles was a trail of death. They had to sleep in the wagons and on the ground without fire. And I have known as many as twenty-two of them to die in one night of pneumonia due to ill treatment, cold, and exposure. Among this number was the beautiful Christian wife of Chief John Ross. This noble hearted woman died a martyr to childhood, giving her only blanket for the protection of a sick child. She rode thinly clad through a blinding sleet and snow storm, developed pneumonia and died in the still hours of a bleak winter night, with her head resting on Lieutenant Gregg's saddle blanket.

I made the long journey to the west with the Cherokees and did all that a Private soldier could do to alleviate their sufferings. When on guard duty at night I have many times walked my beat in my blouse in order that some sick child might have the warmth of my overcoat. I was on guard duty the night Mrs. Ross died. When relieved at midnight I did not retire, but remained around the wagon out of sympathy for Chief Ross, and at daylight was detailed by Captain McClellan to assist in the burial like the other unfortunates who died on the way. Her unconfined body was buried in a shallow grave by the roadside far from her native home, and the sorrowing Cavalcade moved on . . .

Somebody must explain the streams of blood that flowed in the Indian country in the summer of 1838. Somebody must explain the 4,000 silent graves that mark the trail of the Cherokees to their exile. I wish I could forget it all, but the picture of 645 wagons lumbering over the frozen ground with their cargo of suffering humanity still lingers in my memory. Let the historian of a future day tell the sad story with its sighs, its tears and dying groans. Let the great Judge of all the earth weigh our actions and reward us according to our work.

Source: John G. Burnett. *Cherokee Indian Removal.* Available online. URL: http://www.cherokee.org/home.aspx? section=culture&culture=culinfo&cat=I1i8o3ObxSpalG9xUqZT7g==&ID=JY45S/LKJQ0=. Accessed March 5, 2007.

Testimony of John S. Smith before Congress (March 14, 1865) (excerpts)

The following excerpts are taken from a transcript of the 1865 congressional
investigation of the Sand Creek Massacre in November 1864. This investigation
was carried out by the Joint Committee on the Conduct of the War, which was
created in 1861 to look into issues surrounding the conduct of Union soldiers

during the Civil War, and followed two military investigations of the massacre. The Joint Committee's work has been called into question by later historians; its members had little understanding of the military, it permitted secret testimony, and its members often leaked inappropriate information to the press. With regard to the Sand Creek Massacre in particular, the Committee was unduly influenced by its preconceived notions of what had happened at Sand Creek. In the words of Gregory Michno, a contemporary specialist in frontier history, the Committee "chose the testimony it wanted to hear as truth, and condemning the testimony that did not fit with its preconceived notions as false. The summary of the proceedings concluded that the soldiers were barbarians, while the Indians 'in every way conducted themselves properly and peaceably.'" John Smith, whose testimony follows this introduction, was a trader who had cheated the Indians in his dealings with them and used the Sand Creek investigation as an opportunity to collect damages from the federal government for his loss of goods and property.

I then left my own camp and started for that portion of the troops that was nearest the village, supposing I could go up to them. I did not know but they might be strange troops, and thought my presence and explanations could reconcile matters. Lieutenant Wilson was in command of the detachment to which I tried to make my approach; but they fired several volleys at me, and I returned back to my camp and entered my lodge. . . .

After I had left my lodge to go out and see what was going on, Colonel Chivington rode up to within fifty or sixty yards of where I was camped; he recognized me at once. They all call me Uncle John in that country. He said, "Run here, Uncle John; you are all right." I went to him as fast as I could. He told me to get in between him and his troops, who were then coming up very fast; I did so; directly another officer who knew me—Lieutenant Baldwin, in command of a battery—tried to assist me to get a horse; but there was no loose horse there at the time. He said, "Catch hold of the caisson, and keep up with us." By this time the Indians had fled; had scattered in every direction. The troops were some on one side of the river and some on the other, following up the Indians. We had been encamped on the north side of the river; I followed along, holding on the caisson, sometimes running, sometimes walking. Finally, about a mile above the village, the troops had got a parcel of the Indians hemmed in under the bank of the river; as soon as the troops overtook them, they commenced firing on them; some troops had got above them, so that they were completely surrounded. There were probably a hundred Indians hemmed in there, men, women, and children; the most of the men in the village escaped.

By the time I got up with the battery to the place where these Indians were surrounded there had been some considerable firing. Four or five soldiers had been killed, some with arrows and some with bullets. The soldiers continued firing on these Indians, who numbered about a hundred, until they had almost completely destroyed them. I think I saw altogether some seventy dead bodies lying there; the greater portion women and children. There may have been thirty warriors, old and young; the rest were women and small children of different ages and sizes.

The troops at that time were very much scattered. There were not over two hundred troops in the main fight, engaged in killing this body of Indians under the bank. The balance of the troops were scattered in different directions, running after small parties of Indians who were trying to make their escape. I did not go to see how many they might have killed outside of this party under the bank of the river. Being still quite weak from my last sickness, I returned with the first body of troops that went back to the camp.

The Indians had left their lodges and property; everything they owned. I do not think more than one-half of the Indians left their lodges with their arms. I think there were between 800 and 1,000 men in this command of United States troops. There was a part of three companies of the lst Colorado, and the balance were what were called 100 days men of the 3rd regiment. I am not able to say which party did the most execution on the Indians, because it was very much mixed up at the time.

We remained there that day after the fight. By 11 o'clock, I think, the entire number of soldiers had returned back to the camp where Colonel Chivington had returned. On their return, he ordered the soldiers to destroy all the Indian property there, which they did, with the exception of what plunder they took away with them, which was considerable.

Question. How many Indians were there?

Answer. There were 100 families of Cheyennes, and some six or eight lodges of Arapahoes.

Question. How many persons in all, should you say?

Answer. About 500; we estimate them at five to a lodge.

Question. 500 men, women, and children?

Answer. Yes, sir.

Question. Do you know the reason for that attack on the Indians?

Answer. I do not know any exact reason. I have heard a great many reasons given. I have heard that that whole Indian war had been brought on for self-ish purposes. Colonel Chivington was running for Congress in Colorado, and there were other things of that kind; and last spring a year ago he was looking for an order to go to the front, and I understand he had this Indian war in view to retain himself and his troops in that country, to carry out his electioneering purposes. . . .

Question. When did you talk with [Colonel Chivington]?

Answer. On the day of the attack. He asked me many questions about the chiefs who were there, and if I could recognize them if I saw them. I told him it was possible I might recollect the principal chiefs. They were terribly mutilated, lying there in the water and sand; most of them in the bed of the creek, dead and dying, making many struggles. They were so badly mutilated and covered with sand and water that it was very hard for me to tell one from another. However, I recognized some of them—among them the chief One Eye, who was employed by our government at $125 a month and rations to remain in the village as a spy. There was another called War Bonnet, who was here two years ago with me. There was another by the name of Standing-in-the-Water, and I supposed Black Kettle was among them, but it was not Black Kettle. There was one there of his size and dimensions in every way, but so tremendously mutilated that I was mistaken in him. I went out with Lieutenant Colonel Bowen, to see how many I could recognize.

By Mr. Gooch:

Question: Did you tell Colonel Chivington the character and disposition of these Indians at any time during your interviews on this day?

Answer. Yes, sir.

Question. What did he say in reply?

Answer. He said he could not help it; that his orders were positive to attack the Indians.

Question. From whom did he receive these orders?

Answer. I do not know; I presume from General Curtis . . .

Question. Who called on you to designate the bodies of those who were killed?

Answer. Colonel Chivington himself asked me if I would ride out with Lieutenant Colonel Bowen, and see how many chiefs or principal men I could recognize.

Question. Can you state how many Indians were killed—how many women and how many children?

Answer. Perhaps one-half were men, and the balance were women and children. I do not think that I saw more than 70 lying dead then, as far as I went. But I saw parties of men scattered in every direction, pursuing little bands of Indians.

Question. What time of day or night was this attack made?

Answer. The attack commenced about sunrise, and lasted until between 10 and 11 o'clock.

Question. How large a body of troops?

Answer. I think that probably there may have been about 60 or 70 warriors who were armed and stood their ground and fought. Those that were unarmed got out of the way as they best could.

Question. How many of our troops were killed and how many wounded?

Answer. There were ten killed on the ground, and thirty-eight wounded; four of the wounded died at Fort Lyon before I came on east.

Question. Were there any other barbarities or atrocities committed there other than those you have mentioned, that you saw?

Answer. Yes, sir; I had a half-breed son there, who gave himself up. He started at the time the Indians fled; being a half-breed he had but little hope of being spared, and seeing them fire at me, he ran away with the Indians for the distance of about a mile. During the fight up there he walked back to my camp and went into the lodge. It was surrounded by soldiers at the time. He came in quietly and sat down; he remained there that day, that night, and the next day in the afternoon; about four o'clock in the evening, as I was sitting inside the camp, a soldier came up outside of the lodge and called me by name. I got up and went out; he took me by the arm and walked towards Colonel Chivington's camp, which was about sixty yards from my camp. Said he, "I am sorry to tell you, but they are going to kill your son Jack." I knew the feeling towards the whole camp of Indians, and that there was no use to make any resistance. I said, "I can't help it." I then walked on towards where Colonel Chivington was standing by his camp-fire; when I had got within a few feet of him I heard a gun fired, and saw a crowd run to my lodge, and they told me that Jack was dead. . . .

Source: Testimony of John Smith before Congress. Available online. URL: http://www.pbs.org/weta/thewest/resources/archives/four/sandcrk.htm#smith. Accessed March 3, 2007.

INTERNATIONAL RELATIONS

Senate Resolution on Armenia (May 11, 1920)

The following is the full text of Senate Resolution 359, recognizing the independence of the Republic of Armenia after World War I and indicating acceptance of the "report[s of] massacres and other atrocities" committed by the government of the Ottoman Empire in 1915. Although the resolution does not contain the term genocide, *the present government of Armenia considers it an acknowledgment of the genocide on the part of the government of the United States. (See the official Web site of the Ministry of Foreign Affairs of the Republic of Armenia. Available online. URL: http://www.armeniaforeignministry. com/fr/genocide/current_status.html. Accessed August 22, 2007.*

66th Congress
2nd Session
S. RES. 359. [Senate Resolution 359]
In the Senate of the United States.

May 11, 1920

Mr. Harding, from the Committee on Foreign Relations, reported the following resolution; which was ordered to be placed on the calendar.

May 11 (calendar day, May 13), 1920.

Considered and agreed to.

Resolution
Whereas the testimony adduced at the hearings conducted by the subcommittee of the Senate Committee on Foreign Relations have clearly established

the truth of the reported massacres and other atrocities from which the Armenian people have suffered; and

Whereas the people of the United States are deeply impressed by the deplorable conditions of insecurity, starvation, and misery now prevalent in Armenia; and

Whereas the independence of the Republic of Armenia has been duly recognized by the supreme council of the peace conference and by the Government of the United States of America: Therefore be it

Resolved, That a sincere congratulations of the Senate of the United States are hereby extended to the people of Armenia on the recognition of the independence of the Republic of Armenia, without prejudice respecting the territorial boundaries involved; and be it further

Resolved, That the Senate of the United States hereby expresses the hope that stable government, proper protection of individual liberties and rights, and the full realization of nationalistic aspirations may soon be attained by the Armenian people; and be it further

Resolved, That in order to afford necessary protection for the lives and property of citizens of the United States at the port of Batum and along the line of the railroad leading to Baku, the President is hereby requested, if not incompatible with the public interest, to cause a United States warship and a force of marines to be dispatched to such port with instructions to such marines to disembark and to protect American lives and property.

May 11 (calendar day, May 13), 1920.—Considered and agreed to.

Source: Senate Resolution on Armenia. Available online. URL: http://www.armenian-genocide.org/Affirmation.164/ current_category.7/affirmation_detail.html. Accessed March 3, 2007.

Testimony by Senator William Proxmire before the Senate Foreign Relations Committee (May 24, 1977) (excerpts)

The following excerpts are taken from one of the 3,211 speeches that Senator Proxmire delivered on the floor of the Senate between 1967 and 1986 urging ratification of the Convention on the Prevention and Punishment of the Crime of Genocide. The United States finally ratified the Convention on February 11, 1986.

Thank you, Mr. Chairman. Mr. Chairman, first I would like to congratulate you on scheduling these hearings. This is an extremely important subject. One which I care deeply about. And I am very grateful for this opportunity to be your first witness.

As you pointed out, the Genocide Convention has been pending before the Senate since President Truman first submitted it for ratification in 1949.

Think about that for a moment. 1949 to 1977. That's a full quarter century. An entire generation has been born and grown to adulthood during those years, and still the Senate has not acted . . .

This morning I would like to briefly outline why I believe this Convention is so terribly important, why I have voiced my support for it almost every day on the floor of the Senate since our opening session in 1967, and review the further developments since your last hearings that make ratification this year urgent.

The Purpose of the Genocide Convention

Mr. Chairman, there is no human rights treaty that has been subjected to more detailed scrutiny and engendered more controversy than the Genocide Convention. Every line, every phrase, every syllable has been studied over and over.

What then is this treaty about that it warrants such attention?

Its purpose is quite clear. The Genocide Convention attempts to safeguard under international law the most fundamental human principle—the right to live.

It is that simple. It is that complex.

The treaty language attempts to prevent the destruction of a national, ethnic, racial or religious group by defining genocide, outlawing it, and establishing procedures for trying and punishing violators.

These are nice phrases. Grand abstract principles.

But let's face it: we are talking about the planned, premeditated murder or extermination of an entire group of people—the most vicious crime mankind can commit.

The Origins of the Genocide Convention

None of us can envision the monstrosity of 6 million Jews put to death in concentration camps—the most hideous genocide committed in our lifetime. But it is in this context that this human rights document was conceived. . . .

What is not widely recognized is that important role played by the United States in the drafting of the Convention during those years and our instrumental role in securing the unanimous vote within the General Assembly for this Convention. Critics who portray this treaty as some sort of Communist plot simply ignore the historical record. . . . The United States signed the Genocide Convention two days after its approval by the General Assembly, and it was transmitted to the Senate on June 16, 1949.

Growing Political Support for the Genocide Convention

Mr. Chairman, few treaties have enjoyed broader political support. In submitting this treaty for ratification, President Truman supported it in the strongest possible terms. Subsequent Administrations, Republican and Democratic alike, have renewed that endorsement. . . .

Of course, we all know how intensely—how deeply—the Jewish groups feel about the Convention, and rightly so. But I think few members of the Senate recognize how deeply this matter is felt by all denominations. This is not solely a "Jewish issue." Catholic and Protestant groups, most notably the National Council of Churches, have been outspoken in their support . . .

Why the Genocide Convention Deserves Ratification

The list of supporters goes on and on. Why do so many groups support ratification?

First and foremost, on moral grounds. The United States is the only major nation, except the People's Republic of China, that has not joined in condemning this heinous crime. In fact, all of our major NATO and SEATO allies have acceded to the treaty. We stand alone among free Western nations.

Second, our failure to ratify this treaty has been a constant source of embarrassment to us diplomatically that has puzzled our allies and delighted our enemies. . . . There is no logic in continuing to provide others with a club with which to hit us.

Third, our ratification will strengthen the development of international law in this crucial area of human rights. As you know, Mr. Chairman, the development of international law is a slow and tedious process, requiring the concurrence of all the major powers. Our inaction impeded the development of these fundamental moral principles.

Fourth, as a party to the Convention we would be in a better position to use our moral influence to bear in specific cases where genocide is alleged. . . .

Fifth, U.S. ratification at this time will help to spur renewed interest in the treaty among the newly emergent nations of the world. . . .

Conclusion

Mr. Chairman, it is clear that the Genocide Convention is a moral document. It is a call for a higher standard of human conduct. It is not a panacea for injustice.

But in the same way that the Geneva Conventions for the Treatment of Prisoners of War have improved the treatment of prisoners of war, the Genocide Convention will also make an important step toward civilizing the affairs of nations.

In closing my testimony in 1970 I recalled the words of the late Chief Justice Earl Warren, who said, "We as a nation should have been the first to ratify the Genocide Convention." My plea to this Committee and my colleagues in the Senate is: let us not be the last!

Source: Testimony by Senator Proxmire. Available online. URL: http://content.wisconsinhistory.org/cdm4/document.php?CISOROOT=/tp&CISOPTR=15027. Accessed April 15, 2007.

Ronald Reagan: Remarks on Signing the Genocide Convention Implementation Act of 1987 (the Proxmire Act) in Chicago, Illinois (November 4, 1988)

The following document is the complete text of former president Reagan's remarks on the signing of the Genocide Convention Implementation Act of 1987, also known as the Proxmire Act in honor of the senator who spoke in favor of ratifying the Convention more than 3,000 times between 1967 and 1986. Proxmire was still a member of the Senate when the implementation act was signed.

Well, good morning. We gather today to bear witness to the past and learn from its awful example, and to make sure that we're not condemned to relive its crimes. I am today signing the Genocide Convention Implementation Act of 1987, which will permit the United States to become party to the International Convention on the Prevention and Punishment of the Crime of Genocide that was approved by the United Nations General Assembly in 1948.

During the Second World War, mankind witnessed the most heinous of crimes: the Holocaust. And after the war, the nations of the world came together and drafted the genocide convention as a howl of anguish and an effort to prevent and punish future acts of genocide. The United States signed the convention, and in 1949 President Truman requested the Senate's advice and consent to ratification. In 1986 the Senate gave its consent, conditioned upon enactment of implementing legislation. We finally close the circles today by signing the implementing legislation that will permit the United States to ratify the convention and formally join 97 nations of the world in condemning genocide and treating it as a crime.

GENOCIDE AND INTERNATIONAL JUSTICE

I'm delighted to fulfill the promise made by Harry Truman to all the peoples of the world, and especially the Jewish people. I remember what the Holocaust meant to me as I watched the films of the death camps after the Nazi defeat in World War II. Slavs, Gypsies, and others died in the fires, as well. And we've seen other horrors this century—in the Ukraine, in Cambodia, in Ethiopia. They only renew our rage and righteous fury, and make this moment all the more significant for me and all Americans.

Under this legislation, any U.S. national or any person in the United States who kills members of a national, ethnic, racial, or religious group with the specific intent of destroying that group in whole or in substantial part may spend his or her life in prison. Lesser acts of violence are punishable by as much as 20 years in prison and a fine of up to $1 million. While I would have preferred that Congress had adopted the administration's proposal to permit the death penalty for those convicted of genocidal murders, this legislation still represents a strong and clear statement by the United States that it will punish acts of genocide with the force of law and the righteousness of justice.

The timing of the enactment is particularly fitting, for we're commemorating a week of remembrance of the Kristallnacht, the infamous "night of broken glass," which occurred 50 years ago on November 9, 1938. That night, Nazis in Germany and Austria conducted a pogrom against the Jewish people. By the morning of November 10th, scores of Jews were dead, hundreds bleeding, shops and homes in ruins, and synagogues defiled and debased. And that was the night that began the Holocaust, the night that should have alerted the world of the gruesome design of the Final Solution.

This legislation resulted from the cooperation of our administration and many in Congress, such as Congressmen Henry Hyde and Jack Davis and John Porter and Senator Bill Proxmire, to ensure that the United States redoubles its efforts to gain universal observance of human rights.

We pay tribute to those who suffered that night and all the nights that followed upon it with our action today.

So, I thank you, and God bless you all. And now I will sign the proclamation and the bill.

Note: The president spoke at 10:15 A.M. in the Air Force Reserve Building at O'Hare International Airport. S. 1851, approved November 4, was assigned Public Law No. 100-606.

Source: Ronald Reagan. Remarks on Signing the Genocide Convention Act. Available online. URL: http://www.reagan.utexas.edu/archives/speeches/1988/88nov.htm. Accessed April 15, 2007.

President Clinton's Statement on Signature of the International Criminal Court (ICC) Treaty, December 21, 2000

This is the complete text of the former president's statement on signing the treaty that established the ICC, just hours before the deadline for signing expired.

The United States is today signing the 1998 Rome Treaty on the International Criminal Court. In taking this action, we join more than 130 other countries that have signed by the December 31, 2000 deadline established in the Treaty. We do so to reaffirm our strong support for international accountability and for bringing to justice perpetrators of genocide, war crimes, and crimes against humanity. We do so as well because we wish to remain engaged in making the ICC an instrument of impartial and effective justice in the years to come.

The United States has a long history of commitment to the principle of accountability, from our involvement in the Nuremberg tribunals that brought Nazi war criminals to justice, to our leadership in the effort to establish the International Criminal Tribunals for the Former Yugoslavia and Rwanda. Our action today sustains that tradition of moral leadership.

Under the Rome Treaty, the International Criminal Court (ICC) will come into being with the ratification of 60 governments, and will have jurisdiction over the most heinous abuses that result from international conflict, such as war crimes, crimes against humanity and genocide. The Treaty requires that the ICC not supercede [*sic*] or interfere with functioning national judicial systems; that is, the ICC Prosecutor is authorized to take action against a suspect only if the country of nationality is unwilling or unable to investigate allegations of egregious crimes by their national, [*sic*] The U.S. delegation to the Rome Conference worked hard to achieve these limitation, [*sic*] which we believe are essential to the international credibility and success of the ICC.

In signing, however, we are not abandoning our concerns about significant flaws in the treaty. In particular, we are concerned that when the court comes into existence, it will not only exercise authority over personnel of states that have ratified the treaty, but also claim jurisdiction over personnel of states that have not. With signature, however, we will be in signature, we will not. [*sic*]

Signature will enhance our ability to further protect U.S. officials from unfounded charges and to achieve the human rights and accountability objectives of the ICC. In fact, in negotiations following the Rome Conference, we have worked effectively to develop procedures that limit the likelihood of politicized prosecutions. For example, U.S. civilian and military negotiators helped to ensure greater precision in the definitions of crimes within the Court's jurisdiction.

But more must be done. Court jurisdiction over U.S. personnel should come only with U.S. ratification of the treaty. The United States should have the chance to observe and assess the functioning of the Court, over time, before choosing to become subject to its jurisdiction. Given these concerns, I will not, and do not recommend that my successor submit the Treaty to the Senate for advice and consent until our fundamental concerns are satisfied.

Nonetheless, signature is the right action to take at this point. I believe that a properly constituted and structured International Criminal Court would make a profound contribution in deterring egregious human rights abuses worldwide, and that signature increases the chances for productive discussions with other governments to advance these goals in the months and years ahead.

Source: Clinton statement on signature of ICC Treaty. Available online. URL: http://www.amicc.org/docs/ Clinton_sign.pdf. Accessed August 22, 2007.

5

International Documents

The documents in this chapter are divided into four sections: the Laws of War, the Genocide Convention of 1948, International Courts, and Specific Genocides. Documents in the first three sections are organized chronologically; documents in the fourth section are grouped by event. Documents that have been excerpted are identified as such; all others are reproduced in full.

DOCUMENTS RELATED TO THE LAWS OF WAR

Immanuel Kant, *On Perpetual Peace: A Philosophical Sketch* Section I (1795)

Immanuel Kant (1724–1804), the leading philosopher of the German Enlightenment, published On Perpetual Peace *toward the end of his active teaching career at the University of Königsberg in East Prussia. The treatise is considered the foundational document of what has been called the democratic peace theory; that is, the notion that democracies rarely go to war with one another. Some contemporary political scientists have extended the democratic peace theory. They maintain that minor conflicts as well as major wars are also rare between democracies, and that democracies are also less likely to suffer from internal violence. The reader may recall that scholars of genocide have noted that war and revolution are common breeding grounds for genocide.*

THE PRELIMINARY ARTICLES FOR
PERPETUAL PEACE AMONG STATES

1. "No Treaty of Peace Shall Be Held Valid in Which There Is Tacitly Reserved Matter for a Future War";

Otherwise a treaty would be only a truce, a suspension of hostilities but not peace, which means the end of all hostilities—so much so that even to attach the word "perpetual" to it is a dubious pleonasm. The causes for making future wars (which are perhaps unknown to the contracting parties) are without exception annihilated by the treaty of peace, even if they should be dug out of dusty documents by acute sleuthing. When one or both parties to a treaty of peace, being too exhausted to continue warring with each other, make a tacit reservation *(reservatio mentalis)* in regard to old claims to be elaborated only at some more favorable opportunity in the future, the treaty is made in bad faith, and we have an artifice worthy of the casuistry of a Jesuit. Considered by itself, it is beneath the dignity of a sovereign, just as the readiness to indulge in this kind of reasoning is unworthy of the dignity of his minister. But if, in consequence of enlightened concepts of statecraft, the glory of the state is placed in its continual aggrandizement by whatever means, my conclusion will appear merely academic and pedantic.

2. "No Independent States, Large or Small, Shall Come under the Dominion of Another State by Inheritance, Exchange, Purchase, or Donation"

A state is not, like the ground which it occupies, a piece of property *(patrimonium)*. It is a society of men whom no one else has any right to command or to dispose except the state itself. It is a trunk with its own roots. But to incorporate it into another state, like a graft, is to destroy its existence as a moral person, reducing it to a thing; such incorporation thus contradicts the idea of the original contract without which no right over a people can be conceived.

Everyone knows to what dangers Europe, the only part of the world where this manner of acquisition is known, has been brought, even down to the most recent times, by the presumption that states could espouse one another; it is in part a new kind of industry for gaining ascendancy by means of family alliances and without expenditure of forces, and in part a way of extending one's domain. Also the hiring-out of troops by one state to another, so that they can be used against an enemy not common to both, is to be counted under this principle; for in this manner the subjects, as though they were things to be manipulated at pleasure, are used and also used up.

5. "No State Shall by Force Interfere with the Constitution or Government of Another State";

For what is there to authorize it to do so? The offense, perhaps, which a state gives to the subjects of another state? Rather the example of the evil into which a state has fallen because of its lawlessness should serve as a warning. Moreover, the bad example which one free person affords another as a *scandalum acceptum* is not an infringement of his rights. But it would be quite different if a state, by internal rebellion, should fall into two parts, each of which pretended to be a separate state making claim to the whole. To lend assistance to one of these cannot be considered an interference in the constitution of the other state (for it is then in a state of anarchy).

But so long as the internal dissension has not come to this critical point, such interference by foreign powers would infringe on the rights of an independent people struggling with its internal disease; hence it would itself be an offense and would render the autonomy of all states insecure.

6. "No State Shall, during War, Permit Such Acts of Hostility Which Would Make Mutual Confidence in the Subsequent Peace Impossible: Such Are the Employment of Assassins *(percussores)*, Poisoners *(venefici)*, Breach of Capitulation, and Incitement to Treason *(perduellio)* in the Opposing State";

These are dishonorable stratagems. For some confidence in the character of the enemy must remain even in the midst of war, as otherwise no peace could be concluded and the hostilities would degenerate into a war of extermination *(bellum internecinum)*. War, however, is only the sad recourse in the state of nature (where there is no tribunal which could judge with the force of law) by which each state asserts its right by violence and in which neither party can be adjudged unjust (for that would presuppose a juridical decision); in lieu of such a decision, the issue of the conflict (as if given by a so-called "judgment of God") decides on which side justice lies. But between states no punitive war *(bellum punitivum)* is conceivable, because there is no relation between them of master and servant.

It follows that a war of extermination, in which the destruction of both parties and of all justice can result, would permit perpetual peace only in the vast burial ground of the human race. Therefore, such a war and the use of all means leading to it must be absolutely forbidden. But that the means cited do inevitably lead to it is clear from the fact that these infernal arts, vile in themselves, when once used would not long be confined to the sphere of war. Take, for instance, the use of spies *(uti exploratoribus)*. In this, one employs the infamy of others (which can never be entirely eradicated) only to encourage its persistence even into the state of peace, to the undoing of the very spirit of peace.

Source: Immanuel Kant. *On Perpetual Peace.* Available online. URL: http://www.constitution.org/kant/perpeace. txt. Accessed March 13, 2007.

Convention Respecting the Laws and Customs of War on Land (Second Hague Conference, October 18, 1907) (excerpts)

The Hague Convention Respecting the Laws and Customs of War on Land was an attempt to minimize the damage of war by regulating the conduct of nations that had openly declared war toward one another and toward neutral nations. The convention represented a codification of the unwritten rules of warfare that went back to the late medieval period and are sometimes referred to by the Latin phrase jus in bello. *The laws of war in theory apply only to nations that have agreed to be bound by them, either through signing such documents as the 1907 Hague Convention, or through membership in such international organizations as the United Nations. In practice, however, the laws of war are considered to apply to all nations as of the early 2000s. In addition to its attempt to regulate the conduct of open warfare, the Hague Convention is significant because it served as the legal justification for trying the Nazi leaders for war crimes at the end of World War II.*

ENTERED INTO FORCE: 26 January 1910

REGULATIONS RESPECTING THE LAWS AND CUSTOMS OF
WAR ON LAND

SECTION I: ON BELLIGERENTS

CHAPTER I: The Qualifications of Belligerents

Art. 1. The laws, rights, and duties of war apply not only to armies, but also to militia and volunteer corps fulfilling the following conditions:

To be commanded by a person responsible for his subordinates;

To have a fixed distinctive emblem recognizable at a distance;

To carry arms openly; and

To conduct their operations in accordance with the laws and customs of war.

In countries where militia or volunteer corps constitute the army, or form part of it, they are included under the denomination "army."

Art. 2. The inhabitants of a territory which has not been occupied, who, on the approach of the enemy, spontaneously take up arms to resist the invading troops without having had time to organize themselves in accordance with Article 1, shall be regarded as belligerents if they carry arms openly and if they respect the laws and customs of war.

148

Art. 3. The armed forces of the belligerent parties may consist of combatants and non-combatants. In the case of capture by the enemy, both have a right to be treated as prisoners of war.

CHAPTER II: Prisoners of War

Art. 4. Prisoners of war are in the power of the hostile Government, but not of the individuals or corps who capture them. They must be humanely treated. All their personal belongings, except arms, horses, and military papers, remain their property. . . .

Art. 6. The State may utilize the labour of prisoners of war according to their rank and aptitude, officers excepted. The tasks shall not be excessive and shall have no connection with the operations of the war. Prisoners may be authorized to work for the public service, for private persons, or on their own account. Work done for the State is paid for at the rates in force for work of a similar kind done by soldiers of the national army, or, if there are none in force, at a rate according to the work executed. . . .

Art. 9. Every prisoner of war is bound to give, if he is questioned on the subject, his true name and rank, and if he infringes this rule, he is liable to have the advantages given to prisoners of his class curtailed. . . .

Art. 13. Individuals who follow an army without directly belonging to it, such as newspaper correspondents and reporters, sutlers and contractors, who fall into the enemy's hands and whom the latter thinks expedient to detain, are entitled to be treated as prisoners of war, provided they are in possession of a certificate from the military authorities of the army which they were accompanying. . . .

Art. 15. Relief societies for prisoners of war, which are properly constituted in accordance with the laws of their country and with the object of serving as the channel for charitable effort shall receive from the belligerents, for themselves and their duly accredited agents every facility for the efficient performance of their humane task within the bounds imposed by military necessities and administrative regulations. Agents of these societies may be admitted to the places of internment for the purpose of distributing relief, as also to the halting places of repatriated prisoners, if furnished with a personal permit by the military authorities, and on giving an undertaking in writing to comply with all measures of order and police which the latter may issue. . . .

Art. 18. Prisoners of war shall enjoy complete liberty in the exercise of their religion, including attendance at the services of whatever church they may belong to, on the sole condition that they comply with the measures of order and police issued by the military authorities. . . .

CHAPTER III: The Sick and Wounded

Art. 21. The obligations of belligerents with regard to the sick and wounded are governed by the Geneva Convention.

SECTION II: HOSTILITIES

CHAPTER I: Means of Injuring the Enemy, Sieges, and Bombardments

Art. 22. The right of belligerents to adopt means of injuring the enemy is not unlimited.

Art. 23. In addition to the prohibitions provided by special Conventions, it is especially forbidden—

To employ poison or poisoned weapons;

To kill or wound treacherously individuals belonging to the hostile nation or army;

To kill or wound an enemy who, having laid down his arms, or having no longer means of defence, has surrendered at discretion;

To declare that no quarter will be given;

To employ arms, projectiles, or material calculated to cause unnecessary suffering;

To make improper use of a flag of truce, of the national flag or of the military insignia and uniform of the enemy, as well as the distinctive badges of the Geneva Convention;

To destroy or seize the enemy's property, unless such destruction or seizure be imperatively demanded by the necessities of war;

To declare abolished, suspended, or inadmissible in a court of law the rights and actions of the nationals of the hostile party. A belligerent is likewise forbidden to compel the nationals of the hostile party to take part in the operations of war directed against their own country, even if they were in the belligerent's service before the commencement of the war. . . .

Art. 25. The attack or bombardment, by whatever means, of towns, villages, dwellings, or buildings which are undefended is prohibited. . . .

Art. 27. In sieges and bombardments all necessary steps must be taken to spare, as far as possible, buildings dedicated to religion, art, science, or charitable purposes, historic monuments, hospitals, and places where the sick and wounded are collected, provided they are not being used at the time for military purposes. . . .

Art. 28. The pillage of a town or place, even when taken by assault, is prohibited.

Source: Convention Respecting the Laws of War. Available online. URL: http://www.yale.edu/lawweb/avalon/ lawofwar/hague04.htm. Accessed April 1, 2007.

Covenant of the League of Nations (initial draft February 14, 1919; amended December 1924) (excerpts)

The Covenant of the League of Nations was written in 1919 by President Woodrow Wilson and amended by a special commission of the League in 1924. Article 10 was considered the most objectionable part of the Covenant by the members of the U.S. Senate who voted against joining the League. Wilson did, however, succeed in adding his proposal to create the League of Nations to the text of the Treaty of Versailles.

THE HIGH CONTRACTING PARTIES,

In order to promote international co-operation and to achieve international peace and security by the acceptance of obligations not to resort to war, by the prescription of open, just and honourable relations between nations, by the firm establishment of the understandings of international law as the actual rule of conduct among Governments, and by the maintenance of justice and a scrupulous respect for all treaty obligations in the dealings of organised peoples with one another,

Agree to this Covenant of the League of Nations.

ARTICLE 8.

The Members of the League recognise that the maintenance of peace requires the reduction of national armaments to the lowest point consistent with national safety and the enforcement by common action of international obligations. . . .

The Members of the League agree that the manufacture by private enterprise of munitions and implements of war is open to grave objections. The Council shall advise how the evil effects attendant upon such manufacture can be prevented, due regard being had to the necessities of those Members of the League which are not able to manufacture the munitions and implements of war necessary for their safety.

The Members of the League undertake to interchange full and frank information as to the scale of their armaments, their military, naval and air programmes and the condition of such of their industries as are adaptable to war-like purposes. . . .

ARTICLE 10.

The Members of the League undertake to respect and preserve as against external aggression the territorial integrity and existing political independence of all Members of the League. In case of any such aggression or in case of any threat or danger of such aggression the Council shall advise upon the means by which this obligation shall be fulfilled.

ARTICLE 11.

Any war or threat of war, whether immediately affecting any of the Members of the League or not, is hereby declared a matter of concern to the whole League, and the League shall take any action that may be deemed wise and effectual to safeguard the peace of nations. In case any such emergency should arise the Secretary General shall on the request of any Member of the League forthwith summon a meeting of the Council.

It is also declared to be the friendly right of each Member of the League to bring to the attention of the Assembly or of the Council any circumstance whatever affecting international relations which threatens to disturb international peace or the good understanding between nations upon which peace depends.

ARTICLE 12.

The Members of the League agree that, if there should arise between them any dispute likely to lead to a rupture they will submit the matter either to arbitration or judicial settlement or to enquiry by the Council, and they agree in no case to resort to war until three months after the award by the arbitrators or the judicial decision, or the report by the Council. In any case under this Article the award of the arbitrators or the judicial decision shall be made within a reasonable time, and the report of the Council shall be made within six months after the submission of the dispute.

ARTICLE 13.

The Members of the League agree that whenever any dispute shall arise between them which they recognise to be suitable for submission to arbitration or judicial settlement and which cannot be satisfactorily settled by diplomacy, they will submit the whole subject-matter to arbitration or judicial settlement. . . .

For the consideration of any such dispute, the court to which the case is referred shall be the Permanent Court of International Justice, established in accordance with Article 14, or any tribunal agreed on by the parties to the dispute or stipulated in any convention existing between them. . . .

ARTICLE 14.

The Council shall formulate and submit to the Members of the League for adoption plans for the establishment of a Permanent Court of International Justice. The Court shall be competent to hear and determine any dispute of an international character which the parties thereto submit to it. The Court may also give an advisory opinion upon any dispute or question referred to it by the Council or by the Assembly. . . .

Source: Covenant of the League of Nations. Available online. URL: http://www.yale.edu/lawweb/avalon/leagcov. htm. Accessed January 1, 2007.

DOCUMENTS RELATED TO THE GENOCIDE CONVENTION (1948)

Nazi Sterilization Law (July 14, 1933)

The Reich Sterilization Law of 1933, also known as the Law for Prevention of Hereditarily Diseased Offspring (Gesetz zur Verhütung erbkranken Nachwuchses), was signed into law by Hitler himself as part of the Nazi Party's eugenics program. Over 200 special courts were set up to administer the law. By 1945, over 400,000 persons had been forcibly sterilized. Article 2 of the Genocide Convention of 1948 was intended to cover this type of legislation as well as other practices intended to bring about the destruction of entire groups.

LAW FOR THE PREVENTION OF
HEREDITARILY DISEASED OFFSPRING

The Government of the German Reich has passed the following law which is promulgated herewith.

1. Whoever suffers from hereditary disease can be sterilized if, according to the finding of medical science, a great probability exists that his (or her) offspring will suffer from severe bodily or mental hereditary disease. An

hereditarily diseased person in the sense of the law is one who suffers from one of the following disease:

a. Innate mental deficiency,

b. Schizophrenia,

c. Recurrent (manic-depressive) insanity,

d. Hereditary epilepsy,

e. Hereditary St. Vitus' Dance (Huntingdon's chorea),

f. Hereditary blindness,

g. Hereditary deafness,

h. Severe hereditary bodily deformity,

Furthermore a person suffering from severe and chronic alcoholism is liable to be sterilized. A person thus liable to be sterilized is entitled to file a petition. If such a person is incapable of transacting business or is under tutelage on account of mental deficiency or if he is under eighteen years of age, his legal representative is entitled to file a petition in his stead, must first seek the authorization of the Court of Chancery. If the person has come of age and has been placed in the care of a guardian, the latter's consent is required.

2. A certificate required from a medical officer approved by the German Government that the person to be sterilized is fully aware of the consequences of the operation, is to accompany the petition.

3. The petition may be withdrawn.

The following persons may also present petitions for sterilization:
    a. Medical Officer.
    b. Director of hospital, mental institution, nursing home or prison for the inmates of the institution concerned.

The petition is to be made out in writing and sent to the offices of the competent Heredity Health Court. The facts supporting the claim are to be certified by medical experts. The Court is obliged to inform the M.O. concerning the petition. The decision rests with the Heredity Health Court within whose jurisdiction the domicile of the person to be sterilized is situated.

    These Heredity Health Courts form a branch of the district Courts. Each consists of a district judge, a medical officer and another doctor qualified for practice within the German Reich and a specialist in matters of heredity. For each of these members a representative must be appointed.

No one who has sought authorization from the Court of Chancery according to P. 2, I can be president of an Heredity Health Court. If the M.O. himself has filed the petition with the Heredity Health Court he may not vote in the Court.

Proceedings of the Heredity Health Court are not public.

It is the duty of the Heredity Health Court to make inquiries. It is authorized to examine the witnesses and experts, to summon the candidate for sterilization, to order his medical examination and in case of unjustifiable absence to apprehend him. The rules of Civil Courts are to be applied to the examination and swearing-in of witnesses and experts as well as to the exclusion of particular judges. Doctors examined as witnesses or as experts are strictly bound to give evidence. Law Courts, administrative Authorities, hospitals are bound to answer inquiries made by the Heredity Health Courts.

The Court must give judgment based on the result of the examination and evidence and according to its own unbiased conviction. The verdict is given after oral consultation and in accordance with the vote of the majority. It must be set down in writing and signed by the voters. The reasons for deciding on or refusing, sterilization must be stated. The verdict must be communicated to the petitioner, the M.O., and the subject for sterilization, or in the case of his legal inability to file a petition, to his legal representative.

The petitioner, the M.O., and the subject for sterilization may appeal in writing to the offices of the competent Court within one month after the receipt of the verdict. (The period for appeal has been shortened by a change in the law to a fortnight.) If the period during which appeal may be made has elapsed, the case may be reopened again in accordance with the rules for civil actions.

The higher Heredity Health Court forms part of a higher provincial Court and its competence extends as far as the jurisdiction of the latter. It consists of a member of a higher provincial Court, a M.O., and another doctor qualified for practice within the German Reich and a specialist in matters of heredity. For each of these members a representative must be appointed. Paragraph 6, 2 must be applied here also.

The proceedings of the higher Heredity Health Court are ruled by Paragraphs 7 and 8.

The surgical operation necessary for sterilization may be carried out only in a hospital and by a doctor qualified for practice within the German Reich. This doctor may not undertake the operation before the verdict has been finally given. The appointment of doctors and hospitals qualified for the performance of the operation is made by the supreme provincial Authorities, within their own territory. The operation may not be carried out by a doctor who filed the petition or took part in the Court as a member thereof.

The doctor who performs the operation has to submit to the M.O. a written report as to the carrying out of the sterilization, informing the M.O. of the method used in each particular case.

The final verdict of the Court having been given, the Sterilization is to be carried out, even if necessary, against the will of the person to be sterilized, unless this person be the one who also filed the petition. The M.O. has to apply to the police in order that necessary measures be taken. Physical force is admissible should other measures remain insufficient and ineffective.

Should circumstances arise which demand re-examination of the case, the Heredity Health Court is required to reconsider the case, in the meantime staying the execution of the sterilization order. Should the petition for sterilization have been refused by the Court, the case may not be re-opened unless new circumstances arise which would justify sterilization.

The costs of the action are borne by the state. The costs of the operation by the health insurance companies, in the case of a person insured; in the case of non-insured and indigent persons, by the public welfare department. In all other cases the state defrays the doctor's fees according to the minimum scale set down in official tariffs and the average hospital fees. The remainder has to be paid by the person to be sterilized.

Sterilizations performed beyond the prescriptions of this law, as also castrations, may be permitted only when carried out in accordance with sound medical practice, so that serious danger to the life or health of the person to be sterilized or castrated, whose consent must first be obtained, may be avoided. (This paragraph has recently been extended by a subsequent law. "Castration of a male is also allowed with his consent if the M.O. or doctor of the Court consider it to be necessary in order to relieve the person of a perverse sexual impulse which is likely to be the cause of further offences in the sense of PP. 175 to 178, 183, 223 to 226 of the Penal Code.") All persons taking part in the proceedings of the Courts or in the operation of sterilization are bound to professional secrecy. Those guilty of unjust violation of professional secrecy are liable for punishment by imprisonment, not exceeding one year, or by a fine. Prosecution cannot be made except by petition, which petition may also be lodged by the president.

The execution of this law is entrusted to the Governments of the German States.

The supreme provincial Authorities appoint the seats and areas of jurisdiction of the Courts, notwithstanding the prescriptions of Paragraph 6, 1 Sentence 1, and of Paragraph 10, 1, Sentence 1. They nominate the members of these Courts and their representatives.

The Minister of the Interior with the consent of the Minister of Justice issues the judicial and administrative regulations necessary for the execution of this law.

This law comes into force on January the first, 1934.

The Chancellor of the Reich,
The Minister of the Interior,
The Minister of Justice.

Source: Nazi Sterilization Law. Available online. URL: http://www.catholicculture.org/docs/doc_view.cfm?recnum=615. Accessed April 1, 2007.

Nuremberg Laws (1935)

The Nuremberg Laws of 1935 derived in part from social Darwinism, which is the notion that Darwin's biological concept of survival of the fittest can be applied to human societies. This pseudoscientific theory of the origin of racial differences among humans was exploited by the Nazis to draft legislation preventing marriages (or extramarital relations) between Aryans and Jews and to strip German Jews of their status as citizens. As with forced sterilization, Article 2 of the Genocide Convention of 1948 was intended to define this type of legislation as genocidal. An original typed copy of the Nuremberg Laws signed by Hitler himself was discovered by the U.S. Army's Counter-Intelligence Corps (CIC) in Bavaria on April 27, 1945; it is now on display at the Skirball Cultural Center in Los Angeles.

Nuremberg Law for the Protection of German Blood and German Honor (September 15, 1935)

Moved by the understanding that purity of the German Blood is the essential condition for the continued existence of the German people, and inspired by the inflexible determination to ensure the existence of the German Nation for all time, the Reichstag has unanimously adopted the following Law, which is promulgated herewith:

157

Article 1.

1) Marriages between Jews and subjects of the state of German or related blood are forbidden. Marriages nevertheless concluded are invalid, even if concluded abroad to circumvent this law.

2) Annulment proceedings can be initialed only by the State Prosecutor.

Article 2.

Extramarital intercourse between Jews and subjects of the state of German or related blood is forbidden.

Article 3.

Jews may not employ in their households female subjects of the state of German or related blood who are under 45 years old.

Source: Nuremberg Law for the Protection of German Blood. Available online. URL: http://www.ess.uwe.ac.uk/documents/gerblood.htm. Accessed April 1, 2007.

Reich Citizenship Law (September 15, 1935)

The Reichstag has unanimously enacted the following law, which is promulgated herewith:

§ 1

1. A subject of the State is a person who enjoys the protection of the German Reich and who in consequence has specific obligations towards it.

2. The status of subject of the State is acquired in accordance with the provisions of the Reich and State Citizenship Law.

§ 2

1. A Reich citizen is a subject of the State who is of German or related blood, who proves by his conduct that he is willing and fit faithfully to serve the German people and Reich.

2. Reich citizenship is acquired through the granting of a Reich Citizenship Certificate.

3. The Reich citizen is the sole bearer of full political rights in accordance with the Law.

§ 3

The Reich Minister of the Interior, in coordination with the Deputy of the Führer will issue the Legal and Administrative orders required to implement and complete this Law.

Nuremberg, September 15, 1935, at the Reich Party Congress of Freedom
The Führer and Reich Chancellor Adolf Hitler
The Reich Minister of the Interior Frick

Source: Reich Citizenship Law. Available online. URL: http://www.ess.uwe.ac.uk/documents/citizen.htm. Accessed April 1, 2007.

Suicide Note of Szmul Zygielbojm (May 11, 1943)

Szmul Zygielbojm (1895–1943) was a Polish Jew who had been active in the labor movement in his homeland and a member of the National Council of the Polish government in exile in London during World War II. Zygielbojm had been in contact with the Jews in the Warsaw ghetto through Jan Karski, the officer who was serving at that time as a courier between the Polish underground resistance and the Polish government in exile. Zygielbojm worked from 1940 through 1943 to convince the various Allied governments to intervene to stop the Holocaust, but committed suicide in May 1943 as a protest against their inaction.

To His Excellency the President of the Republic of Poland, Wladyslaw Raczkiewicz
Prime Minister, General Wladyslaw Sikorski

Mr. President, Mr. Prime Minister,

I am taking the liberty of addressing to you, Sirs, these my last words, and through you to the Polish Government and the people of Poland, and to the governments and people of the Allies, and to the conscience of the whole world:

The latest news that has reached us from Poland makes it clear beyond any doubt that the Germans are now murdering the last remnants of the Jews in

Poland with unbridled cruelty. Behind the walls of the ghetto the last act of this tragedy is now being played out.

The responsibility for the crime of the murder of the whole Jewish nationality in Poland rests first of all on those who are carrying it out, but indirectly it falls also upon the whole of humanity, on the peoples of the Allied nations and on their governments, who up to this day have not taken any real steps to halt this crime. By looking on passively upon this murder of defenseless millions of tortured children, women and men they have become partners to the responsibility.

I am obliged to state that although the Polish Government contributed largely to the arousing of public opinion in the world, it still did not do enough. It did not do anything that was not routine, that might have been appropriate to the dimensions of the tragedy taking place in Poland.

Of close to 3.5 million Polish Jews and about 700,000 Jews who have been deported to Poland from other countries, there were, according to the official figures of the Bund transmitted by the Representative of the Government, only 300,000 still alive in April of this year. And the murder continues without end.

I cannot continue to live and to be silent while the remnants of Polish Jewry, whose representative I am, are being murdered. My comrades in the Warsaw ghetto fell with arms in their hands in the last heroic battle. I was not permitted to fall like them, together with them, but I belong with them, to their mass grave.

By my death, I wish to give expression to my most profound protest against the inaction in which the world watches and permits the destruction of the Jewish people.

I know that there is no great value to the life of a man, especially today. But since I did not succeed in achieving it in my lifetime, perhaps I shall be able by my death to contribute to the arousing from lethargy of those who could and must act in order that even now, perhaps at the last moment, the handful of Polish Jews who are still alive can be saved from certain destruction.

My life belongs to the Jewish people of Poland, and therefore I hand it over to them now. I yearn that the remnant that has remained of the millions of Polish Jews may live to see liberation together with the Polish masses, and that it shall be permitted to breathe freely in Poland and in a world of freedom and socialistic justice, in compensation for the inhuman suffering and torture inflicted on them. And I believe that such a Poland will arise and such a world will come about. I am certain that the President and the Prime Minister will send out these words of mine to all those to whom they are addressed, and that the Polish Government will embark immediately on diplomatic action and explanation of the situation, in order to save the living remnant of the Polish Jews from destruction.

I take leave of you with greetings, from everybody, and from everything that was dear to me and that I loved.

S. Zygielbojm

Source: Suicide note of Szmul Zygielbojm. Available online. URL: http://yad-vashem.org.il/about_holocaust/ documents/part2/doc154.html. Accessed April 2, 2007.

Raphael Lemkin, Definition of Genocide, from *Axis Rule in Occupied Europe,* Chapter 9 (1944) (excerpts)

Lemkin's first extensive definition of genocide comes from the book he published in 1944, Axis Rule in Occupied Europe, *although he first coined the term in 1943. The book is primarily a legal rather than a political analysis of Nazi rule in the countries under German control in the early 1940s. Lemkin had been trained as a lawyer and conceived of genocide as a crime against international law. His concept thus served as one of the legal justifications for the Nuremberg war crimes trials; from 1945 through 1946 he was an adviser to Robert H. Jackson, the chief prosecutor for the United States. Lemkin's book was published by the Carnegie Endowment for International Peace.*

New conceptions require new terms. By "genocide" we mean the destruction of a nation or of an ethnic group. This new word, coined by the author to denote an old practice in its modern development, is made from the ancient Greek word *genos* (race, tribe) and the Latin *cide* (killing), thus corresponding in its formation to such words as tyrannicide, homocide, infanticide, etc. Generally speaking, genocide does not necessarily mean the immediate destruction of a nation, except when accomplished by mass killings of all members of a nation. It is intended rather to signify a coordinated plan of different actions aiming at the destruction of essential foundations of the life of national groups, with the aim of annihilating the groups themselves. The objectives of such a plan would be disintegration of the political and social institutions, of culture, language, national feelings, religion, and the economic existence of national groups, and the destruction of the personal security, liberty, health, dignity, and even the lives of the individuals belonging to such groups. Genocide is directed against the national group as an entity, and the actions involved are directed against individuals, not in their individual capacity, but as members of the national group. . . .

Genocide has two phases: one, destruction of the national pattern of the oppressed group; the other, the imposition of the national pattern of the oppressor. This imposition, in turn, may be made upon the oppressed population which is allowed to remain or upon the territory alone, after removal of the population and the colonization by the oppressor's own nationals.

Denationalization was the word used in the past to describe the destruction of a national pattern. The author believes, however, that this word is inadequate because: *1.*) it does not connote the destruction of the biological structure; *2.*) in connoting the destruction of one national pattern it does not connote the imposition of the national pattern of the oppressor; and *3.*) denationalization is used by some authors to mean only deprivation of citizenship. . . .

Techniques of Genocide in Various Fields

POLITICAL

In the incorporated areas, such as western Poland, Eupen, Malmedy, Moresnet, Luxemburg, and Alsace-Lorraine, local institutions of self-government were destroyed and a German pattern of administration imposed. Every reminder of former national character was obliterated. Even commercial signs and inscriptions on buildings, roads, and streets, as well as names of communities and of localities, were changed to a German form. . . .

Special Commissioners for the Strengthening of Germanism are attached to the administration, and their task consists in coordinating all actions promoting Germanism in a given area. An especially active role in this respect is played by inhabitants of German origin who were living in the occupied countries before the occupation. After having accomplished their task as members of the so-called fifth column, they formed the nucleus of Germanism. . . .

In order further to disrupt national unity, Nazi party organizations were established, such as the Nasjonal Samling Party in Norway and the Mussert Party in the Netherlands, and their members from the local population given political privileges. Other political parties were dissolved. . . . In line with this policy of imposing the German national pattern, particularly in the incorporated territories, the occupant has organized a system of colonization of these areas. In western Poland, especially, this has been done on a large scale. The Polish population have been removed from their homes in order to make place for German settlers who were brought in from the Baltic States, the central and eastern districts of Poland, Bessarabia, and from the Reich itself. . . .

SOCIAL

The destruction of the national pattern in the social field has been accomplished in part by the abolition of local law and local courts and the imposition of German law and courts, and also by Germanization of the judicial language and of the bar. The social structure of a nation being vital to its national development, the occupant also endeavors to bring about such changes as may weaken the national, spiritual resources. The focal point of this attack has been the intelligentsia, because this group largely provides the national leadership and organizes resistance against Nazification. This is especially true in Poland and Slovenia (Slovene part of Yugoslavia), where the intelligentsia and the clergy were in great part removed from the rest of the population and deported for forced labor in Germany. The tendency of the occupant is to retain in Poland only the laboring and peasant class, while in the western occupied countries the industrialist class is also allowed to remain, since it can aid in integrating the local industries with the German economy.

CULTURAL

In the incorporated areas the local population is forbidden to use its own language in schools and in printing. According to the decree of August 6, 1940, the language of instruction in all Luxemburg schools was made exclusively German. The French language was not permitted to be taught in primary schools; only in secondary schools could courses in that language continue to be given. German teachers were introduced into the schools and they were compelled to teach according to the principles of National Socialism. . . .

In order to prevent the expression of the national spirit through artistic media, a rigid control of all cultural activities has been introduced. All persons engaged in painting, drawing, sculpture, music, literature, and the theater are required to obtain a license for the continuation of their activities. Control in these fields is exercised through German authorities. In Luxemburg this control is exercised through the Public Relations Section of the Reich Propaganda Office and embraces music, painting, theater, architecture, literature, press, radio, and cinema. . . .

ECONOMIC

The destruction of the foundations of the economic existence of a national group necessarily brings about a crippling of its development, even a retrogression. The lowering of the standards of living creates difficulties in fulfilling cultural-spiritual requirements. Furthermore, a daily fight literally for bread and for physical survival may handicap thinking in both general and national terms.

It was the purpose of the occupant to create such conditions as these among the peoples of the occupied countries, especially those peoples embraced in the first plans of genocide elaborated by him—the Poles, the Slovenes and the Jews.

The Jews were immediately deprived of the elemental means of existence. As to the Poles in incorporated Poland, the purpose of the occupant was to shift the economic resources from the Polish national group to the German national group. . . .

BIOLOGICAL

In the occupied countries of "people of non-related blood," a policy of depopulation is pursued. Foremost among the methods employed for this purpose is the adoption of measures calculated to decrease the birthrate the national groups of non-related blood, while at the same time steps are taken to encourage the birthrate of the *Volksdeutsche* living in these countries. Thus in incorporated Poland marriages between Poles are forbidden without special permission of the Governor (Reichsstatthalter) of the district; the latter, as a matter of principle, does not permit marriages between Poles.

The birthrate of the undesired group is being further decreased as a result of the separation of males from females by deporting them for forced labor elsewhere. Moreover, the undernourishment of the parents, because of discrimination in rationing, brings about not only a lowering of the birthrate, but a lowering of the survival capacity of children born of underfed parents. . . .

PHYSICAL

The physical debilitation and even annihilation of national groups in occupied countries is carried out mainly in the following ways:

1. Racial Discrimination in Feeding. Rationing of food is organized according to racial principles throughout the occupied countries. "The German people come before all other peoples for food," declared Reich Minister Göring on October 4, 1942. In accordance with this program, the German population is getting 93 per cent of its pre-war diet, while those in the occupied territories receive much less: in Warsaw, for example, the Poles receive 66 per cent of the pre-war rations and the Jews only 20 per cent. The following shows the difference in the percentage of meat rations received by the

Germans and the population of the occupied countries: Germans, 100 per cent; Czechs, 86 per cent; Dutch, 71 per cent; Poles (Incorporated Poland), 71 per cent; Lithuanians, 57 per cent; French, 51 per cent; Belgians, 66 per cent; Serbs, 36 per cent; Poles (General Government), 36 per cent; Slovenes, 29 per cent; Jews, 0 per cent . . .

The result of racial feeding is a decline in health of the nations involved and an increase in the deathrate. In Warsaw, anemia rose 113 per cent among Poles and 435 among Jews. The death rate per thousand in 1941 amounted in the Netherlands to 10 per cent; in Belgium to 14.5 per cent; in Bohemia and Moravia to 13.4. The Polish mortality in Warsaw in 1941 amounted in July to 1,316 in August to 1,729; and in September to 2,160.

2. Endangering of Health. The undesired national groups, particularly in Poland, are deprived of elemental necessities for preserving health and life. This latter method consists, for example, of requisitioning warm clothing and blankets in the winter and withholding firewood and medicine. During the winter of 1940–41, only a single room in a house could be warmed in the Warsaw ghetto, and children had to take turns in warming there. No fuel at all has been received since then by the Jews in the ghetto.

Moreover, the Jews in the ghetto are crowded together under conditions of housing inimical to health, and in being denied the use of public parks they are even deprived of the right to fresh air. Such measures, especially pernicious to the health of children, have caused the development of various diseases. The transfer, in unheated cattle trucks and freight cars, of hundreds of thousands of Poles from Incorporated Poland to the Government General, which took place in the midst of a severe winter, resulted in a decimation of the expelled Poles.

3. Mass Killing. The technique of mass killings is employed mainly against Poles, Russians, and Jews, as well as against leading personalities from among the non-collaborationist groups in all the occupied countries. In Poland, Bohemia-Moravia, and Slovenia, the intellectuals are being "liquidated" because they have always been considered as the main bearers of national ideals and at the time of occupation they were especially suspected of being the organizers of resistance. The Jews for the most part are liquidated within the ghettos, or in special trains in which they are transported to a so-called "unknown" destination. The number of Jews who have been killed by organized murder in all the occupied countries, according to the Institute of Jewish Affairs of the American Jewish Congress in New York, amounts to 1,702,500.

RELIGIOUS

In Luxemburg, where the population is predominantly Catholic and religion plays an important role in national life, especially in the field of education, the occupant has tried to disrupt these national and religious influences. Children over fourteen years of age were permitted by legislation to renounce their religious affiliations, for the occupant was eager to enroll such children exclusively in pro-Nazi youth organizations. Moreover, in order to protect such children from public criticism, another law was issued at the same time imposing penalties ranging up to 15,000 Reichsmarks for any publication of names or any general announcement as to resignations from religious congregations. Likewise in Poland, through the systematic pillage and destruction of church property and persecution of the clergy, the German occupying authorities have sought to destroy the religious leadership of the Polish nation.

MORAL

In order to weaken the spiritual resistance of the national group, the occupant attempts to create an atmosphere of moral debasement within this group. According to this plan, the mental energy of the group should be concentrated upon base instincts and should be diverted from moral and national thinking. It is important for the realization of such a plan that the desire for cheap individual pleasure be substituted for the desire for collective feelings and ideals based upon a higher morality. Therefore, the occupant made an effort in Poland to impose upon the Poles pornographic publications and movies. The consumption of alcohol was encouraged, for while food prices have soared, the Germans have kept down the price of alcohol, and the peasants are compelled by the authorities to take spirits in pay agricultural produce. The curfew law, enforced very strictly against Poles is relaxed if they can show the authorities a ticket to one of the gambling houses which the Germans have allowed to come into existence.

Source: Raphael Lemkin. Definition of Genocide. Available online. URL: http://www.preventgenocide.org/lemkin/ AxisRule1944-1.htm. Accessed March 9, 2007.

Convention on the Prevention and Punishment of the Crime of Genocide (December 9, 1948)

The following is the full English text of the Convention as given by the Office of the High Commissioner for Human Rights of the United Nations. The Convention defines genocide in legal terms and defines the crimes that can be pun-

ished. The Convention, which is still considered a basic standard for defining a given atrocity as genocide, was the result of years of campaigning by Raphael Lemkin. As of 2008, 137 countries have ratified the Convention.

Approved and proposed for signature and ratification or accession by General Assembly resolution 260 A (III)
Entry into force **January 12, 1951, in accordance with article XIII**

The Contracting Parties,

Having considered the declaration made by the General Assembly of the United Nations in its resolution 96 (I) dated 11 December 1946 that genocide is a crime under international law, contrary to the spirit and aims of the United Nations and condemned by the civilized world,

Recognizing that at all periods of history genocide has inflicted great losses on humanity, and

Being convinced that, in order to liberate mankind from such an odious scourge, international co-operation is required,

Hereby agree as hereinafter provided:

Article 1
The Contracting Parties confirm that genocide, whether committed in time of peace or in time of war, is a crime under international law which they undertake to prevent and to punish.

Article 2
In the present Convention, genocide means any of the following acts committed with intent to destroy, in whole or in part, a national, ethnical, racial or religious group, as such:
(a) Killing members of the group;
(b) Causing serious bodily or mental harm to members of the group;
(c) Deliberately inflicting on the group conditions of life calculated to bring about its physical destruction in whole or in part;
(d) Imposing measures intended to prevent births within the group;
(e) Forcibly transferring children of the group to another group.

Article 3
The following acts shall be punishable:
(a) Genocide;
(b) Conspiracy to commit genocide;

(c) Direct and public incitement to commit genocide;

(d) Attempt to commit genocide;

(e) Complicity in genocide.

Article 4

Persons committing genocide or any of the other acts enumerated in article III shall be punished, whether they are constitutionally responsible rulers, public officials or private individuals.

Article 5

The Contracting Parties undertake to enact, in accordance with their respective Constitutions, the necessary legislation to give effect to the provisions of the present Convention, and, in particular, to provide effective penalties for persons guilty of genocide or any of the other acts enumerated in article III.

Article 6

Persons charged with genocide or any of the other acts enumerated in article III shall be tried by a competent tribunal of the State in the territory of which the act was committed, or by such international penal tribunal as may have jurisdiction with respect to those Contracting Parties which shall have accepted its jurisdiction.

Article 7

Genocide and the other acts enumerated in article III shall not be considered as political crimes for the purpose of extradition.

The Contracting Parties pledge themselves in such cases to grant extradition in accordance with their laws and treaties in force.

Source: Convention on the Prevention and Punishment of the Crime of Genocide. Available online. URL: http://www.unhchr.ch/html/menu3/b/p_genoci.htm. Accessed March 3, 2007.

Statute of the International Criminal Tribunal for Rwanda (1996) (excerpt)

The following excerpt from the founding document of the International Criminal Tribunal for Rwanda (ICTR) shows the way in which the 1948 Genocide Convention has been used as a model for legal bodies set up to deal with specific instances of genocide prior to the formation of the International Criminal Court (ICC).

As amended by the Security Council acting under Chapter VII of the Charter of the United Nations, the International Criminal Tribunal for the Prosecution of Persons Responsible for Genocide and Other Serious Violations of International Humanitarian Law Committed in the Territory of Rwanda and Rwandan Citizens responsible for genocide and other such violations committed in the territory of neighbouring States, between 1 January 1994 and 31 December 1994 (hereinafter referred to as "The International Tribunal for Rwanda") shall function in accordance with the provisions of the present Statute.

Article 1: Competence of the International Tribunal for Rwanda

The International Tribunal for Rwanda shall have the power to prosecute persons responsible for serious violations of international humanitarian law committed in the territory of Rwanda and Rwandan citizens responsible for such violations committed in the territory of neighbouring States between 1 January 1994 and 31 December 1994, in accordance with the provisions of the present Statute.

Article 2: Genocide

1. The International Tribunal for Rwanda shall have the power to prosecute persons committing genocide as defined in paragraph 2 of this Article or of committing any of the other acts enumerated in paragraph 3 of this Article.

2. Genocide means any of the following acts committed with intent to destroy, in whole or in part, a national, ethnical, racial or religious group, as such:
   (a) Killing members of the group;
   (b) Causing serious bodily or mental harm to members of the group;
   (c) Deliberately inflicting on the group conditions of life calculated to bring about its physical destruction in whole or in part;
   (d) Imposing measures intended to prevent births within the group;
   (e) Forcibly transferring children of the group to another group.

3. The following acts shall be punishable:
   (a) Genocide;
   (b) Conspiracy to commit genocide;
   (c) Direct and public incitement to commit genocide;
   (d) Attempt to commit genocide;
   (e) Complicity in genocide.

Article 3: Crimes against Humanity

The International Tribunal for Rwanda shall have the power to prosecute persons responsible for the following crimes when committed as part of a widespread or systematic attack against any civilian population on national, political, ethnic, racial or religious grounds:

169

(a) Murder;

(b) Extermination;

(c) Enslavement;

(d) Deportation;

(e) Imprisonment;

(f) Torture;

(g) Rape;

(h) Persecutions on political, racial and religious grounds;

(i) Other inhumane acts.

Article 4: Violations of Article 3 Common to the Geneva Conventions and of Additional Protocol II

The International Tribunal for Rwanda shall have the power to prosecute persons committing or ordering to be committed serious violations of Article 3 common to the Geneva Conventions of 12 August 1949 for the Protection of War Victims, and of Additional Protocol II thereto of 8 June 1977. These violations shall include, but shall not be limited to:

(a) Violence to life, health and physical or mental well-being of persons, in particular murder as well as cruel treatment such as torture, mutilation or any form of corporal punishment;

(b) Collective punishments;

(c) Taking of hostages;

(d) Acts of terrorism;

(e) Outrages upon personal dignity, in particular humiliating and degrading treatment, rape, enforced prostitution and any form of indecent assault;

(f) Pillage;

(g) The passing of sentences and the carrying out of executions without previous judgement pronounced by a regularly constituted court, affording all the judicial guarantees which are recognized as indispensable by civilised peoples;

(h) Threats to commit any of the foregoing acts.

Article 5: Personal Jurisdiction

The International Tribunal for Rwanda shall have jurisdiction over natural persons pursuant to the provisions of the present Statute.

Article 6: Individual Criminal Responsibility

1. A person who planned, instigated, ordered, committed or otherwise aided and abetted in the planning, preparation or execution of a crime referred to in Articles 2 to 4 of the present Statute, shall be individually responsible for the crime.

2. The official position of any accused person, whether as Head of state or government or as a responsible government official, shall not relieve such person of criminal responsibility nor mitigate punishment.

3. The fact that any of the acts referred to in Articles 2 to 4 of the present Statute was committed by a subordinate does not relieve his or her superior of criminal responsibility if he or she knew or had reason to know that the subordinate was about to commit such acts or had done so and the superior failed to take the necessary and reasonable measures to prevent such acts or to punish the perpetrators thereof.

4. The fact that an accused person acted pursuant to an order of a government or of a superior shall not relieve him or her of criminal responsibility, but may be considered in mitigation of punishment if the International Tribunal for Rwanda determines that justice so requires.

Source: Statute of International Criminal Tribunal for Rwanda. Available online. URL: http://69.94.11.53/ENGLISH/basicdocs/statute.html. Accessed March 13, 2007.

DOCUMENTS RELATED TO INTERNATIONAL COURTS

Convention for the Pacific Settlement of International Disputes (First Hague Conference; July 29, 1899) (excerpts)

The Convention for the Pacific Settlement of International Disputes is considered by many scholars to represent the first attempt to establish a secular public international law to maintain peace and to govern the conduct of warfare when attempts at mediation fail. The Convention's most significant accomplishment was the formation of a Permanent Court of Arbitration (PCA), an independent body that still provides resources for resolving disputes among nations although it is not part of the UN system.

TITLE II. ON GOOD OFFICES AND MEDIATION

Article 2

In case of serious disagreement or conflict, before an appeal to arms, the Signatory Powers agree to have recourse, as far as circumstances allow, to the good offices or mediation of one or more friendly Powers.

Article 3

Independently of this recourse, the Signatory Powers recommend that one or more Powers, strangers to the dispute, should, on their own initiative, and as far as circumstances may allow, offer their good offices or mediation to the States at variance.

Powers, strangers to the dispute, have the right to offer good offices or mediation, even during the course of hostilities.

The exercise of this right can never be regarded by one or the other of the parties in conflict as an unfriendly act.

Article 4

The part of the mediator consists in reconciling the opposing claims and appeasing the feelings of resentment which may have arisen between the States at variance. . . .

Article 7

The acceptance of mediation can not, unless there be an agreement to the contrary, have the effect of interrupting, delaying, or hindering mobilization or other measures of preparation for war.

If mediation, occurs after the commencement of hostilities it causes no interruption to the military operations in progress, unless there be an agreement to the contrary.

Article 8

The Signatory Powers are agreed in recommending the application, when circumstances allow, of special mediation in the following form:

In case of a serious difference endangering the peace, the States at variance choose respectively a Power, to whom they intrust the mission of entering into direct communication with the Power chosen on the other side, with the object of preventing the rupture of pacific relations.

For the period of this mandate, the term of which, unless otherwise stipulated, cannot exceed thirty days, the States in conflict cease from all direct communication on the subject of the dispute, which is regarded as referred exclusively to the mediating Powers, who must use their best efforts to settle it.

In case of a definite rupture of pacific relations, these Powers are charged with the joint task of taking advantage of any opportunity to restore peace. . . .

CHAPTER II. On the Permanent Court of Arbitration

Article 20

With the object of facilitating an immediate recourse to arbitration for international differences, which it has not been possible to settle by diplomacy, the Signatory Powers undertake to organize a permanent Court of Arbitration, accessible at all times and operating, unless otherwise stipulated by the parties, in accordance with the Rules of Procedure inserted in the present Convention.

Article 21

The Permanent Court shall be competent for all arbitration cases, unless the parties agree to institute a special Tribunal. . . .

Done at The Hague, the 29th July, 1899, in a single copy, which shall remain in the archives of the Netherlands Government, and copies of it, duly certified, be sent through the diplomatic channel to the Contracting Powers.

[List of Signatories]

Reservations

United States

Under reservation of the declaration made at the plenary sitting of the Conference on the 25th of July, 1899.

Extract from the procès-verbal:

Nothing contained in this convention shall be so construed as to require the United States of America to depart from its traditional policy of not intruding upon, interfering with, or entangling itself in the political questions of policy or internal administration of any foreign state; nor shall anything contained in the said convention be construed to imply a relinquishment by the United States of America of its traditional attitude toward purely American questions.

Source: Convention for the Pacific Settlement of International Disputes. Available online. URL: http://www.yale.edu/lawweb/avalon/lawofwar/hague01.htm. Accessed January 1, 2007.

Statute of International Court of Justice (June 26, 1945) (excerpts)

The International Court of Justice—not to be confused with the International Criminal Court—is the successor body to the Permanent Court of International Justice established by the League of Nations. The ICJ was established by the UN Charter in 1945 and began its work in 1946. It is primarily concerned with settling legal disputes submitted to it by member states of the UN rather than with direct prosecution of war crimes, crimes against humanity, or genocide.

ARTICLE 1.

The International Court of Justice established by the Charter of the United Nations as the principal judicial organ of the United Nations shall be constituted and shall function in accordance with the provisions of the present Statute.

CHAPTER I. ORGANIZATION OF THE COURT

ARTICLE 2

The Court shall be composed of a body of independent judges, elected regardless of their nationality from among persons of high moral character, who possess the qualifications required In their respective countries for appointment to the highest judicial offices, or are jurisconsults of recognized competence in international law.

ARTICLE 3

1. The Court shall consist of fifteen members, no two of whom may be nationals of the same state.

2. A person who for the purposes of membership in the Court could be regarded as a national of more than one state shall be deemed to be a national of the one in which he ordinarily exercises civil and political rights.

ARTICLE 4

1. The members of the Court shall be elected by the General Assembly and by the Security Council from a list of persons nominated by the national groups in the Permanent Court of Arbitration, in accordance with the following provisions.

2. In the case of Members of the United Nations not represented in the Permanent Court of Arbitration, candidates shall be nominated by national groups appointed for this purpose by their governments under the same conditions as those prescribed for members of the Permanent Court of Arbitration by Article 44 of the Convention of The Hague of 1907 for the pacific settlement of international disputes. . . .

ARTICLE 5

1. At least three months before the date of the election, the Secretary-General of the United Nations shall address a written request to the members of the Permanent Court of Arbitration belonging to the states which are parties to the present Statute, and to the members of the national groups appointed under Article 4, paragraph 2, inviting them to undertake, within a given time, by national groups, the nomination of persons in a position to accept the duties of a member of the Court.

2. No group may nominate more than four persons, not more than two of whom shall be of their own nationality. In no case may the number of candidates nominated by a group be more than double the number of seats to be filled.

ARTICLE 6

Before making these nominations, each national group is recommended to consult its highest court of justice, its legal faculties and schools of law, and its national academies and national sections of international academies devoted to the study of law. . . .

ARTICLE 8

The General Assembly and the Security Council shall proceed independently of one another to elect the members of the Court.

ARTICLE 9

At every election, the electors shall bear in mind not only that the persons to be elected should individually possess the qualifications required, but also that in the body as a whole the representation of the main forms of civilization and of the principal legal systems of the world should be assured.

ARTICLE 10

1. Those candidates who obtain an absolute majority of votes in the General and in the Security Council shall be considered as elected.

2. Any vote of the Security Council, whether for the election of judges or for the appointment of members of the conference envisaged in Article 12, shall be taken without any distinction between permanent and non-permanent members of the Security Council. . . .

ARTICLE 12

1. If, after the third meeting, one or more seats still remain unfilled, a joint conference consisting of six members, three appointed by the General Assembly and three by the Security Council, may be formed at any time at the request of either the General Assembly or the Security Council, for the purpose of choosing by the vote of an absolute majority one name for each seat still vacant, to submit to the General Assembly and the Security Council for their respective acceptance.

2. If the joint conference is unanimously agreed upon any person who fulfils the required conditions, he may be included in its list, even though he was not included in the list of nominations referred to in Article 7. . . .

ARTICLE 13

1. The members of the Court shall be elected for nine years and may be reselected; however, that of the judges elected at the first election, the terms of five judges shall expire at the end of three years and the terms of five more judges shall expire at the end of six years.

2. The judges whose terms are to expire at the end of the abovementioned initial periods of three and six years shall be chosen by lot to be drawn by the Secretary-General immediately after the first election has been completed.

3. The members of the Court shall continue to discharge their duties until their places have been filled. Though replaced, they shall finish any cases which they may have begun. . . .

ARTICLE 16

1. No member of the Court may exercise any political or administrative function, or engage in any other occupation of a professional nature.

2. Any doubt on this point shall be settled by the decision of the Court.

ARTICLE 17

1. No member of the Court may act as agent, counsel, or advocate in any case.

2. No member may participate in the decision of any case in which he has previously taken part as agent, counsel, or advocate for one of the parties, or as a member of a national or international court, or of a commission of enquiry, or in any other capacity. . . .

ARTICLE 18

1. No member of the Court can be dismissed unless, in the unanimous opinion of the other members, he has ceased to fulfil the required conditions. . . .

ARTICLE 19

The members of the Court, when engaged on the business of the Court, shall enjoy diplomatic privileges and immunities. . . .

ARTICLE 22

1. The seat of the Court shall be established at The Hague. This however, shall not prevent the Court from sitting and exercising its functions elsewhere whenever the Court considers it desirable.

2. The President and the Registrar shall reside at the seat of the Court.

CHAPTER II. COMPETENCE OF THE COURT

ARTICLE 34

1. Only states may be parties in cases before the Court.

2. The Court, subject to and in conformity with its Rules, may request of public international organizations information relevant to cases before it, and shall receive such information presented by such organizations on their own initiative. . . .

ARTICLE 37

Whenever a treaty or convention in force provides for reference of a matter to a tribunal to have been instituted by the League of Nations, or to the Permanent Court of International Justice, the matter shall, as between the parties to the present Statute, be referred to the International Court of Justice.

ARTICLE 38

1. The Court, whose function is to decide in accordance with international law such disputes as are submitted to it, shall apply:

a. international conventions, whether general or particular, establishing rules expressly recognized by the contesting states;

b. international custom, as evidence of a general practice accepted as law;

c. the general principles of law recognized by civilized nations;

d. subject to the provisions of Article 5, judicial decisions and the teachings of the most highly qualified publicists of the various nations, as subsidiary means for the determination of rules of law. . . .

Source: Statute of International Court of Justice. Available online. URL: http://www.yale.edu/lawweb/avalon/decade/decad026.htm. Accessed April 1, 2007.

London Charter of the International Military Tribunal (August 8, 1945) (excerpt)

The London Charter is the document that set forth the legal justifications for the Nuremberg war crimes trials of 1946 and the standards that were to be applied in conducting the trials. It defines three categories of crimes: War crimes, crimes against humanity, and crimes against peace. The Charter was drafted by three judges, Robert H. Jackson of the United States, Robert Falco of France, and Iona Nikitchenko of the Soviet Union.

I. CONSTITUTION OF THE INTERNATIONAL MILITARY TRIBUNAL

Article 1.

In pursuance of the Agreement signed on the 8th day of August 1945 by the Government of the United States of America, the Provisional Government of the French Republic, the Government of the United Kingdom of Great Britain and Northern Ireland and the Government of the Union of Soviet Socialist Republics, there shall be established an International Military Tribunal (hereinafter called "the Tribunal") for the just and prompt trial and punishment of the major war criminals of the European Axis.

Article 2.

The Tribunal shall consist of four members, each with an alternate. One member and one alternate shall be appointed by each of the Signatories. The alternates shall, so far as they are able, be present at all sessions of the Tribunal. In case of illness of any member of the Tribunal or his incapacity for some other reason to fulfill his functions, his alternate shall take his place.

Article 3.

Neither the Tribunal, its members nor their alternates can be challenged by the prosecution, or by the Defendants or their Counsel. Each Signatory may replace its members of the Tribunal or his alternate for reasons of health or for other good reasons, except that no replacement may take place during a Trial, other than by an alternate.

Article 4

(a) The presence of all four members of the Tribunal or the alternate for any absent member shall be necessary to constitute the quorum.

(b) The members of the Tribunal shall, before any trial begins, agree among themselves upon the selection from their number of a President, and the President shall hold office during the trial, or as may otherwise be agreed by a vote of not less than three members. The principle of rotation of presidency for successive trials is agreed. If, however, a session of the Tribunal takes place on the territory of one of the four Signatories, the representative of that Signatory on the Tribunal shall preside.

(c) Save as aforesaid the Tribunal shall take decisions by a majority vote and in case the votes are evenly divided, the vote of the President shall be decisive: provided always that convictions and sentences shall only be imposed by affirmative votes of at least three members of the Tribunal.

Article 5.

In case of need and depending on the number of the matters to be tried, other Tribunals may be set up; and the establishment, functions, and procedure of each Tribunal shall be identical, and shall be governed by this Charter.

II. JURISDICTION AND GENERAL PRINCIPLES

Article 6.

The Tribunal established by the Agreement referred to Article 1 hereof for the trial and punishment of the major war criminals of the European Axis countries shall have the power to try and punish persons who, acting in the interests of the European Axis countries, whether as individuals or as members of organizations, committed any of the following crimes.

The following acts, or any of them, are crimes coming within the jurisdiction of the Tribunal for which there shall be individual responsibility:

(a) CRIMES AGAINST PEACE: namely, planning, preparation, initiation or waging of a war of aggression, or a war in violation of international treaties, agreements or assurances, or participation in a common plan or conspiracy for the accomplishment of any of the foregoing;

(b) WAR CRIMES: namely, violations of the laws or customs of war. Such violations shall include, but not be limited to, murder, ill-treatment or deportation to slave labor or for any other purpose of civilian population of or in occupied territory, murder or ill-treatment of prisoners of war or persons on the seas, killing of hostages, plunder of public or private property, wanton destruction of cities, towns or villages, or devastation not justified by military necessity;

(c) CRIMES AGAINST HUMANITY: namely, murder, extermination, enslavement, deportation, and other inhumane acts committed against any civilian population, before or during the war; or persecutions on political, racial or religious grounds in execution of or in connection with any crime within the jurisdiction of the Tribunal, whether or not in violation of the domestic law of the country where perpetrated.

Leaders, organizers, instigators and accomplices participating in the formulation or execution of a common plan or conspiracy to commit any of the foregoing crimes are responsible for all acts performed by any persons in execution of such plan.

Article 7.

The official position of defendants, whether as Heads of State or responsible officials in Government Departments, shall not be considered as freeing them from responsibility or mitigating punishment.

Article 8.

The fact that the Defendant acted pursuant to order of his Government or of a superior shall not free him from responsibility, but may be considered in mitigation of punishment if the Tribunal determines that justice so requires.

Article 9.

At the trial of any individual member of any group or organization the Tribunal may declare (in connection with any act of which the individual may be convicted) that the group or organization of which the individual was a member was a criminal organization.

After the receipt of the Indictment the Tribunal shall give such notice as it thinks fit that the prosecution intends to ask the Tribunal to make such declaration and any member of the organization will be entitled to apply to the Tribunal for leave to be heard by the Tribunal upon the question of the criminal character of the organization. The Tribunal shall have power to allow or reject the application. If the application is allowed, the Tribunal may direct in what manner the applicants shall be represented and heard.

Article 10.

In cases where a group or organization is declared criminal by the Tribunal, the competent national authority of any Signatory shall have the right to bring individual to trial for membership therein before national, military or occupation courts. In any such case the criminal nature of the group or organization is considered proved and shall not be questioned.

Source: London Charter. Available online. URL: http://www.yale.edu/lawweb/avalon/imt/proc/imtconst.htm. Accessed April 22, 2007.

Rome Statute Establishing the International Criminal Court (July 17, 1998) (excerpts)

The Rome Statute is the name of the treaty that established the International Criminal Court (ICC) and provided for its entry into force 60 days after its ratification by 60 states. The Rome Statute was opened for signature on July 17, 1998, and received its 60th signature on April 11, 2002. It thus entered into force on July 1, 2002. Unlike the international tribunals for the former Yugoslavia and Rwanda, which will be dissolved when their work is done, the ICC is intended to be a permanent body with the power to prosecute war crimes, crimes against humanity, and genocide committed after July 1, 2002. As of October 1, 2007, 108 nations are parties to the ICC. Former president Clinton signed the treaty at the end of 2000 but did not submit it to the Senate for ratification because of certain reservations about it. The text of Clinton's remarks is included among the documents in chapter 4.

International Documents

PART 1. ESTABLISHMENT OF THE COURT

Article 1: The Court

An International Criminal Court ("the Court") is hereby established. It shall be a permanent institution and shall have the power to exercise its jurisdiction over persons for the most serious crimes of international concern, as referred to in this Statute, and shall be complementary to national criminal jurisdictions. The jurisdiction and functioning of the Court shall be governed by the provisions of this Statute.

Article 2: Relationship of the Court with the United Nations

The Court shall be brought into relationship with the United Nations through an agreement to be approved by the Assembly of States Parties to this Statute and thereafter concluded by the President of the Court on its behalf.

Article 3: Seat of the Court

1. The seat of the Court shall be established at The Hague in the Netherlands ("the host State").

2. The Court shall enter into a headquarters agreement with the host State, to be approved by the Assembly of States Parties and thereafter concluded by the President of the Court on its behalf.

3. The Court may sit elsewhere, whenever it considers it desirable, as provided in this Statute.

Article 4: Legal status and powers of the Court

1. The Court shall have international legal personality. It shall also have such legal capacity as may be necessary for the exercise of its functions and the fulfilment of its purposes.

2. The Court may exercise its functions and powers, as provided in this Statute, on the territory of any State Party and, by special agreement, on the territory of any other State.

PART 2. JURISDICTION, ADMISSIBILITY AND APPLICABLE LAW

Article 5: Crimes within the jurisdiction of the Court

1. The jurisdiction of the Court shall be limited to the most serious crimes of concern to the international community as a whole. The Court has jurisdiction in accordance with this Statute with respect to the following crimes:

(a) The crime of genocide;

(b) Crimes against humanity;

(c) War crimes;

(d) The crime of aggression.

2. The Court shall exercise jurisdiction over the crime of aggression once a provision is adopted in accordance with articles 121 and 123 defining the crime and setting out the conditions under which the Court shall exercise jurisdiction with respect to this crime. Such a provision shall be consistent with the relevant provisions of the Charter of the United Nations.

Article 6: Genocide

For the purpose of this Statute, "genocide" means any of the following acts committed with intent to destroy, in whole or in part, a national, ethnical, racial or religious group, as such:

(a) Killing members of the group;

(b) Causing serious bodily or mental harm to members of the group;

(c) Deliberately inflicting on the group conditions of life calculated to bring about its physical destruction in whole or in part;

(d) Imposing measures intended to prevent births within the group;

(e) Forcibly transferring children of the group to another group.

Article 7: Crimes against humanity

1. For the purpose of this Statute, "crime against humanity" means any of the following acts when committed as part of a widespread or systematic attack directed against any civilian population, with knowledge of the attack:

(a) Murder;

(b) Extermination;

(c) Enslavement;

(d) Deportation or forcible transfer of population;

(e) Imprisonment or other severe deprivation of physical liberty in violation of fundamental rules of international law;

(f) Torture;

(g) Rape, sexual slavery, enforced prostitution, forced pregnancy, enforced sterilization, or any other form of sexual violence of comparable gravity;

(h) Persecution against any identifiable group or collectivity on political, racial, national, ethnic, cultural, religious, gender as defined in paragraph 3, or other grounds that are universally recognized as impermissible under international law, in connection with any act referred to in this paragraph or any crime within the jurisdiction of the Court;

(i) Enforced disappearance of persons;

(j) The crime of apartheid;

(k) Other inhumane acts of a similar character intentionally causing great suffering, or serious injury to body or to mental or physical health. . . .

Article 8: War crimes

1. The Court shall have jurisdiction in respect of war crimes in particular when committed as a part of a plan or policy or as part of a large-scale commission of such crimes.

2. For the purpose of this Statute, "war crimes" means:

(a) Grave breaches of the Geneva Conventions of 12 August 1949, namely, any of the following acts against persons or property protected under the provisions of the relevant Geneva Convention:

(i) Wilful killing;

(ii) Torture or inhuman treatment, including biological experiments;

(iii) Wilfully causing great suffering, or serious injury to body or health;

(iv) Extensive destruction and appropriation of property, not justified by military necessity and carried out unlawfully and wantonly;

(v) Compelling a prisoner of war or other protected person to serve in the forces of a hostile Power;

(vi) Wilfully depriving a prisoner of war or other protected person of the rights of fair and regular trial;

(vii) Unlawful deportation or transfer or unlawful confinement;

(viii) Taking of hostages.

(b) Other serious violations of the laws and customs applicable in international armed conflict, within the established framework of international law, namely, any of the following acts:

(i) Intentionally directing attacks against the civilian population as such or against individual civilians not taking direct part in hostilities;

(ii) Intentionally directing attacks against civilian objects, that is, objects which are not military objectives;

(iii) Intentionally directing attacks against personnel, installations, material, units or vehicles involved in a humanitarian assistance or peacekeeping mission in accordance with the Charter of the United Nations, as long as they are entitled to the protection given to civilians or civilian objects under the international law of armed conflict;

(iv) Intentionally launching an attack in the knowledge that such attack will cause incidental loss of life or injury to civilians or damage to civilian objects or widespread, longterm and severe damage to the natural environment which would be clearly excessive in relation to the concrete and direct overall military advantage anticipated;

(v) Attacking or bombarding, by whatever means, towns, villages, dwellings or buildings which are undefended and which are not military objectives;

(vi) Killing or wounding a combatant who, having laid down his arms or having no longer means of defence, has surrendered at discretion;

(vii) Making improper use of a flag of truce, of the flag or of the military insignia and uniform of the enemy or of the United Nations, as well as of the distinctive emblems of the Geneva Conventions, resulting in death or serious personal injury;

(viii) The transfer, directly or indirectly, by the Occupying Power of parts of its own civilian population into the territory it occupies, or the deportation or transfer of all or parts of the population of the occupied territory within or outside this territory;

(ix) Intentionally directing attacks against buildings dedicated to religion, education, art, science or charitable purposes, historic monuments, hospitals and places where the sick and wounded are collected, provided they are not military objectives;

(x) Subjecting persons who are in the power of an adverse party to physical mutilation or to medical or scientific experiments of any kind which are neither justified by the medical, dental or hospital treatment of the person concerned nor carried out in his or her interest, and which cause death to or seriously endanger the health of such person or persons;

(xi) Killing or wounding treacherously individuals belonging to the hostile nation or army;

(xii) Declaring that no quarter will be given;

(xiii) Destroying or seizing the enemy's property unless such destruction or seizure be imperatively demanded by the necessities of war;

(xiv) Declaring abolished, suspended or inadmissible in a court of law the rights and actions of the nationals of the hostile party;

(xv) Compelling the nationals of the hostile party to take part in the operations of war directed against their own country, even if they were in the belligerent's service before the commencement of the war;

(xvi) Pillaging a town or place, even when taken by assault;

(xvii) Employing poison or poisoned weapons;

(xviii) Employing asphyxiating, poisonous or other gases, and all analogous liquids, materials or devices;

(xix) Employing bullets which expand or flatten easily in the human body, such as bullets with a hard envelope which does not entirely cover the core or is pierced with incisions;

(xx) Employing weapons, projectiles and material and methods of warfare which are of a nature to cause superfluous injury or unnecessary suffering or which are inherently indiscriminate in violation of the international law of armed conflict, provided that such weapons, projectiles and material and methods of warfare are the subject of a comprehensive prohibition and are included in an annex to this Statute, by an amendment in accordance with the relevant provisions set forth in articles 121 and 123;

(xxi) Committing outrages upon personal dignity, in particular humiliating and degrading treatment;

(xxii) Committing rape, sexual slavery, enforced prostitution, forced pregnancy, as defined in article 7, paragraph 2 (f), enforced sterilization, or any other form of sexual violence also constituting a grave breach of the Geneva Conventions;

(xxiii) Utilizing the presence of a civilian or other protected person to render certain points, areas or military forces immune from military operations;

(xxiv) Intentionally directing attacks against buildings, material, medical units and transport, and personnel using the distinctive emblems of the Geneva Conventions in conformity with international law;

(xxv) Intentionally using starvation of civilians as a method of warfare by depriving them of objects indispensable to their survival, including wilfully impeding relief supplies as provided for under the Geneva Conventions;

(xxvi) Conscripting or enlisting children under the age of fifteen years into the national armed forces or using them to participate actively in hostilities. . . .

Source: Rome Statute. Available online. URL: http://www.sovereignty.net/p/gov/iccdoc.htm. Accessed March 3, 2007.

DOCUMENTS RELATED TO SPECIFIC GENOCIDES
Mongol Invasions

Friar William of Rubruck (Willem van Ruysbroeck), *Journey to the Court of the Great Khan Möngke* (1253–1255) (excerpts)

William of Rubruck was a Franciscan friar from what is now northern Belgium who accompanied King Louis IX of France (1215–70) to the Holy Land during the Seventh Crusade (1248). William was the second ambassador that Louis sent to Mongol rulers, seeking alliances against the Abbasid Caliphate in Baghdad. In 1253, William left Acre, a city on the coast of present-day Israel, traveled by ship to Constantinople, and then moved eastward overland to the court of Sartak Khan, a great-grandson of Genghis Khan, who sent him to his father, Batu Khan, whose capital was located along the Volga River. Batu in turn sent William and his interpreter on to Möngke, the great khan, at the central Mongolian capital of Karakorum in Mongolia. William reached Karakorum in the spring of 1254 and returned in 1255 with a letter from the great khan to King Louis, from which the following excerpts are taken. The khan demanded the king's submission with the customary Mongol threats of violence.

Finally, the letter he sends you [King Louis IX] being finished, they called me and interpreted it to me. I wrote down its tenor, as well as I could understand through an interpreter, and it is as follows: "The commandment of the eternal God is, in Heaven there is only one eternal God, and on Earth there is only one lord, Chingis Chan [Genghis Khan]. This is word of the Son of God, Demugin [Temüjin], (or) Chingis 'sound of iron.'" (For they call him Chingis, 'sound of iron,' because he was a blacksmith; and puffed up in their pride they even say that he is the son of God). "This is what is told you. Wherever there be a Mo'al [Mongol], or a Naiman,

186

or a Merkit or a Musteleman [Muslim], wherever ears can hear, wherever horses can travel, there let it be heard and known; those who shall have heard my commandments and understood them, and who shall not believe and shall make war against us, shall hear and see that they have eyes and see not; and when they shall want to hold anything they shall be without hands, and when they shall want to walk they shall be without feet: this is the eternal command of God.

"This, through the virtue of the eternal God, through the great world of the Mo'al, is the word of Mangu Chan [Möngke Khan] to the lord of the French, King Louis, and to all the other lords and priests and to all the great realm of the French, that they may understand our words. For the word of the eternal God to Chingis Chan has not reached unto you, either through Chingis Chan or others who have come after him. . . .

"These two monks, who have come from you to Sartach [Sartak Khan, Batu Khan's son], Sartach sent to Baatu [Batu Khan, one of Jochi's sons and a grandson of Genghis Khan]; but Baatu sent them to us, for Mangu Chan is the greatest lord of the Mo'al realm. Now then, to the end that the whole world and the priests and monks may be in peace and rejoice, and that the word of God be heard among you, we wanted to appoint Mo'al envoys (to go back) with these your priests. But they replied that between us and you there is a hostile country, and many wicked people, and bad roads; so they were afraid that they could not take our envoys in safety to you; but that if we would give them our letter containing our commandments, they would carry them to King Louis himself. So we do not send our envoys with them; but we send you in writing the commandments of the eternal God by these your priests: the commandments of the eternal God are what we impart to you. And when you shall have heard and believed, if you will obey us, send your ambassadors to us; and so we shall have proof whether you want peace or war with us. When, by the virtue of the eternal God, from the rising of the Sun to the setting, all the world shall be in universal joy and peace, then shall be manifested what we are to be. But if you hear the commandment of the eternal God, and understand it, and shall not give heed to it, nor believe it, saying to yourselves: 'Our country is far off, our mountains are strong, our sea is wide,' and in this belief you make war against us, you shall find out what we can do. He who makes easy what is difficult, and brings close what is far off, the eternal God He knows."

Source: W. W. Rockhill. *The journey of William of Rubruck to the eastern parts of the world, 1253–55, as narrated by himself.* Translated from the Latin and edited, with an introduction by William Woodville Rockhill. London: Hakluyt Society, 1900. Available online. URL: http://depts.washington.edu/silkroad/texts/rubruck.html#introduction. Accessed August 12, 2007.

Yusuf ibn Taghri Birdi, *Tamerlane's Invasion of Syria* (1400–1401) (excerpts)

Yusuf ibn Taghri Birdi (1409–70) was the son of an important official of the Mamluk Sultanate of Egypt who became a historian and composed a history of Egypt from the time of the Muslim conquest in 641 until 1469, the year before his death. Taghri Birdi's father had been involved in government affairs at the time of Tamerlane's invasion of Syria; thus Taghri Birdi had access to eyewitness reports of the invasion and the massacres that took place at Aleppo and Damascus. Although Tamerlane (1336–1405) was not a direct descendant of Genghis Khan but married into the khan's family, he was a Mongol by birth and wanted to restore the Mongol Empire to its former size. Tamerlane was a Muslim and considered himself a warrior for the faith; however, most of his wars were conducted against other Muslims. He is estimated to have killed as many as 17 million people in the course of his conquests. Although Taghri Birdi's description of the piles of human heads left by Tamerlane's soldiers was thought at one time to be an exaggeration, later archaeologists have corroborated his report.

[Capture of Aleppo, October 28–November 2, 1400] Only a short time passed before the Syrian forces turned in flight toward the city of Aleppo, with Tamerlane's men in hot pursuit; and a countless number of the inhabitants of Aleppo and others who were on foot perished under the horses' hoofs, for the citizens of Aleppo had gone out from the city to fight Tamerlane, even the women and boys; moreover, as they tried to enter through the city gates people crowded so closely together that they trampled upon one another; and corpses lay there man-high while crowds walked over them. The Syrian viceroys made for the Aleppo citadel and ascended to it, hordes of the inhabitants entering with them; they had previously transported to the Citadel all the property of the men of Aleppo.

Tamerlane's army had in the meanwhile immediately assaulted the city, lighted fires in it, and began to take prisoners, to plunder, and to kill. The women and children fled to the great mosque of Aleppo and to the smaller mosques, but Tamerlane's men turned to follow them, bound the women with ropes as prisoners, and put the children to the sword, killing every one of them. They committed the shameful deeds to which they were accustomed; virgins were violated without concealment; gentlewomen were outraged without any restraints of modesty; a Tatar would seize a woman and ravage her in the great mosque or one of the smaller mosques in sight of the vast multitude of his companions and the people of the city; her father and brother and husband would see her plight and be unable to defend her because of their lack of means to do so and because they were distracted by the torture and torments which they themselves were suffering; the Tatar would then leave the women and another go to her, her body still uncovered. They then put the populace of Aleppo and its troops to the sword, until the mosques and streets were filled with dead, and Aleppo stank with corpses. This continued from the early forenoon of Saturday until the middle of Tuesday, I Rabi' 14 [November 2]. In the meantime the citadel was being subjected to the closest siege and attack, for Tamerlane's armies had mined its walls in a number of places and filled up its moat, so that it was all but captured. . . . The robbery, enslavement, and murder continued in Aleppo daily; trees were cut down, houses were ruined, and mosques were burned. The stench of corpses filled Aleppo and the environs; bodies lay on the ground, overspreading it like a carpet—one could step nowhere without finding dead bodies under his feet. Tamerlane constructed out of the heads of Muslims a number of pulpits about ten cubits in height and twenty in circumference; the human heads which they contained were counted and found to be more than 20,000; the structures were built with the heads protruding and seen by every passer-by.

Tamerlane remained in Aleppo for a month, then departed; he left the city "fallen on its roofs," empty of its inhabitants and every human being, reduced to ruins; the muezzin's call and the prayer services were no longer heard; there was nought there but a desert waste darkened by fire, a lonely solitude where only the owl and the vulture took refuge. . . . The report of the capture of Aleppo by Tamerlane and his siege of the citadel arrived at Cairo, but it was not believed, and the bearer of the news was arrested and imprisoned awaiting future punishment on the charge of falsification. . . .

[After the surrender of Damascus in March 1401, Tamerlane] seized Ibn Muflih and his companions and forced them to write down the names of all the quarters, squares, and streets of Damascus; when they had done so and given the lists to him, he distributed them among his emirs, dividing the city among them. The emirs entered the city with their mamluks and attendants, and each emir settled in his alloted section and then summoned its inhabitants and demanded money of them. At that time there came upon the people of Damascus afflictions beyond description: they were subjected to all sorts of tortures; they were bastinadoed, crushed in presses, scorched in flames, and suspended head down; their nostrils were stopped with rags full of fine dust which they inhaled each time they took a breath so that they almost died. When near to death, a man would be given a respite to recover, then the tortures of all kinds would be repeated, so that the sufferer would envy a companion who had perished under his tortures and would say: "Would that I might die and be at rest from my pain."

And in the meanwhile all his women and daughters and sons were divided among the companions of that emir, and while under torture he would see his wife and daughter ravished and his son defiled; as he cried out in the pain of his torture the boy and girl would cry out in the suffering of their violation. All this took place without any concealment, in broad daylight and in the presence of crowds of people. Indeed, the people of Damascus witnessed tortures of kinds that had never been heard of before. For example, they would take a man and tie a rope around his head, and twist it until it would sink into his flesh; they would put a rope around a man's shoulders, and twist it with a stick until they were torn from their sockets; they would bind another victim's thumbs behind him, then throw him on his back, pour powdered ashes in his nostrils to make him little by little confess what he possessed; when he had given up all, he would still not be believed, but the torture would be repeated until he died; and then his body would be further mutilated in the thought that he might be only feigning death, And some would tie their victim by his thumbs to the roof of the house, kindle a fire under him and keep him thus a long time; if by chance he fell in the flames, he would be dragged out and thrown on the ground till he revived, then he would be thus suspended a second time.

These trials and tortures of the people of Damascus continued for nineteen days, the last being Tuesday, Rajab 28, 803 [March 14, 1401] There perished, during this period of torture and hunger, human beings whose number God (Who is exalted) alone knows. When Tamerlane's emirs knew that nothing was left in the city they went to him, and he asked them: "Have you any more concern with Damascus?" And when they said "No," he granted the city to the followers of the emirs, who entered it on foot on Monday, Rajab 30, with swords drawn from their sheaths. They stole whatever they could lay their hands on, household furniture, etc., took captive all the women of the city, and drove before them, bound with ropes, the men and boys, leaving only the children less than five years old. They then set fire to the dwellings, palaces, and mosques, and as it was a day of high winds the fire spread throughout the city, and the flames almost mounted to the clouds. The fire continued burning for three days and three nights, the last of which was Friday.

Tamerlane (may God curse him) departed from Damascus on Saturday Sha'ban 3 [March 19, 1401], having been there 80 days. The whole city had burned, the roofs of the Umayyad Mosque had fallen in because of the fire, its gates were gone, and the marble cracked—nothing was left standing but the walls. Of the other mosques of the city, its palaces, caravanseries, and baths, nothing remained but wasted ruins and empty traces; only a vast number of young children were left there, who died, or were destined to die, of hunger.

Source: Ibn Taghri Birdi. *The Invasion of Syria by Tamerlane.* Available online. URL: http://www.deremilitari. org/resources/sources/taghri1.htm. Accessed April 12, 2007.

Armenia
The Ten Commandments of the Committee of Union and Progress (1914 or 1915)

The following document was written by an official in the British Foreign Service shortly after the end of World War I. Although the author's identity is uncertain, his report is consistent with accounts from other European diplomats stationed in Istanbul. Taner Akçam describes the German and Austrian ambassadors as fully aware of secret orders given by Talat Pasha contradicting assurances given to the Western diplomats that the Armenians were only being deported and not harmed. Akçam corroborates in his Preface that the Ottoman records were "pruned" after the war.

VERBATIM TRANSLATION. DOCUMENTS RELATING TO COMITÉ UNION AND PROGRES ORGANIZATION IN THE ARMENIAN MASSACRES.

1. The 10 commandments of the COMITÉ UNION AND PROGRES.

(1). Profiting by Arts: 3 and 4 of Comité Union and Progres, close all Armenian Societies, and arrest all who worked against Government at any time among them and send them into the provinces such as Bagdad or Mosul, and wipe them out either on the road or there.

(2). Collect arms.

(3). Excite Moslem opinion by suitable and special means, in places as Van, Erzeroum, Adana, where as a point of fact the Armenians have already won the hatred of the Moslems, provoke organised massacres as the Russians did at Baku.

(4). Leave all executive to the people in the provinces such as Erzeroum, Van, Mumuret ul Aziz, and Bitlis, and use Military disciplinary forces (i.e. Gendarmerie) ostensibly to stop massacres, while on the contrary in places as Adana, Sivas, Broussa, Ismidt and Smyrna actively help the Moslems with military force.

(5). Apply measures to exterminate all males under 50, priests and teachers, leave girls and children to be Islamized.

(6). Carry away the families of all who succeed in escaping and apply measures to cut them off from all connection with their native place.

(7). On the ground that Armenian officials may be spies, expel and drive them out absolutely from every Government department or post.

(8). Kill off in an appropriate manner all Armenians in the Army—this to be left to the military to do.

(9). All action to begin everywhere simultaneously, and thus leave no time for preparation of defensive measures.

(10). Pay attention to the strictly confidential nature of these instructions, which may not go beyond two or three persons.

n.b. Above is verbatim translation—date December 1914 or January 1915.

Source: United Kingdom, Public Record Office, Foreign Office Records, Class 371, Diplomatic Records. Available online. URL: http://www.armenian-genocide.org/br-cup-memo-text.html. Accessed August 15, 2007.

Ambassador Henry Morgenthau's Report on the Deportation of Armenians from Zeitun (July 21, 1915)

The following document is the complete text of one of Ambassador Morgenthau's dispatches to the State Department regarding the Armenian genocide. It is based on eyewitness reports from the American consul in Beirut.

American Embassy,
Constantinople
July 21, 1915
The Honorable
The Secretary of State,
Washington.

Sir:-

I have the honor to transmit herewith two copies of a report received from the American Consul General at Beirut relative to what has been going on in the Zeitoon region of Asiatic Turkey.

I have the honor to be, Sir,
Your obedient servant,
(signed) [U.S. Ambassador to the Ottoman Empire, Henry] Morgenthau
Enclosure: Two copies dated June 20.

A BRIEF STATEMENT OF THE PRESENT SITUATION OF THE ARMENIAN EXILES IN THIS REGION, JUNE 20, 1915.

The deportation began some six weeks ago, with 180 families from Zeitoon; since which time, all the inhabitants of that place and its neighboring villages have been deported: also most of the Christians in Albustan, many from Hadgin, Sis, Kars Pasar, Hassan Beyli and Deort Yol.

The numbers involved are approximately, to date, 26,500. Of these about 5,000 have been sent to the Konieh region, 5,500 are in Aleppo and surrounding towns and villages; and the remainder are in Der Zor, Racca, and various places in Mesopotamia, even as far as the neighborhood of Bagdad.

The process is still going on, and there is no telling how far it may be carried, the orders already issued will bring the number in this region up to 32,000, and there have been as yet none exiled from Aintab, and very few from Marash and Oorfah. The following is the text of the Government order covering the case. Art. 2nd. "The Commanders of the Army, of independent army corps and of divisions may, in case of military necessity and in case they suspect espionage or treason, send away, either or in mass, the inhabitants of villages and towns, and install them in other places."

The orders of Commanders may have been reasonably humane, but the execution of them has been for the most part unnecessarily harsh, and in many cases accompanied by horrible brutality to women and children, to the sick and the aged. Whole villages were deported at an hours notice, with no opportunity to prepare for the journey, not even in some cases to gather together the scattered members of the family, so that little children were left behind. At the mountain village of Geben the women were at the wash tub, and were compelled to leave their wet clothes in the water, and take the road barefooted and half clad just as they were. In some cases they were able to carry part of their scanty household furniture, or implements of agriculture, but for the most part they were neither to carry anything nor to sell it, even where there was time to do so.

In Hadgin well to do people, who had prepared food and bedding for the road, were obliged to leave it in the street, and afterward suffered greatly from hunger.

In many cases the men were (those of military age were nearly all in the army) bound tightly together with ropes or chains. Women with little children in their arms, or in the last days of pregnancy were driven along under the whip like cattle. Three different cases came under my knowledge where the woman was delivered on the road, and because her brutal driver hurried her along she died of hemorrhage. I also know of one case where the gendarme in charge was a humane man, and allowed the poor woman several hours rest and then procured a wagon for her to ride in. Some women became so completely worn out and hopeless that they left their infants beside the road. Many women and girls have been outraged [raped]. At one place the commander of the gendarmerie openly told the men to whom he consigned a large company, that they were at liberty to do what they choose with the women and girls.

As to subsistence, there has been a great difference in different places. In some places the Government has fed them, in some places it has permitted the inhabitants to feed them. In some places it has neither fed them nor permitted others to do so. There has been much hunger, thirst and sickness and some real starvation, and death.

These people are being scattered in small units, three or four families in a place, among a population of different race and religion, and speaking a different language. I speak of them as being composed of families, but four fifths of them are women and children, and what men there are for the most part old or incompetent [disabled].

If a means is not found to aid them through the next few months, until they get established in their new surroundings, two thirds or three fourths of them will die of starvation and disease.

Source: Morgenthau's report on the deportation of Armenians. Available online. URL: http://www.armenian-genocide.org/us-7-21-15-text.html. Accessed August 22, 2007.

Cambodia

"Cambodian Women in the Revolutionary War for the People's National Liberation" (1973) (excerpts)

The following document is a propaganda leaflet directed at women, produced in 1973 by the Khmer Rouge during their campaign against General Lon Nol's government. The identity of the writer is unknown. It was translated by members of the Genocide Study Project at Yale.

Just like the men, Cambodian women, yesterday and today, have contributed greatly to the struggle against foreign aggression in defense of the fatherland. After the anti-national and anti-popular coup d'état on March 18, 1970, the group of traitors Lon Nol, Sirik Matak, and Son Ngoc Thanh sold Cambodia cheap to the U.S. imperialists and allowed them to transform it into a neo-colony and a military base. . . .

In the areas provisionally controlled by the enemy, apart from fascist repression, women are still obliged to cope with the high cost of living, a lack of necessary elementary provisions, notably rice, and find it very difficult to make ends meet. To this are added other worries: their husbands and their sons could be conscripted at any moment at all, their daughters kidnapped and raped by the troops of Phnom Penh and Saigon. The American way of life, a depraved society, and prostitution have poisoned the minds of so many girls and women. More than ever, Cambodian women know that the only possible way to free themselves from this thrall-ring is to join in the struggle with the men, without hesitation or compromise, against the American aggressors and their valets for the national liberation. . . .

Moreover, women in Cambodia possess a legitimate pride in having helped to improve the conditions of women in general. For, arming themselves with their high revolutionary morality and demonstrating supreme revolutionary heroism, they have achieved exploits which our people hold in high esteem. They are thus contributing to tearing apart those backward perceptions of women which still have currency in the world. . . .

Young Women Guerrilla Fighters Overrun an Enemy Post

Village T is situated on the edges of the area provisionally controlled by the enemy in Kompong Speu province. A company of puppet troops set up a position there under the orders of their torturer-captain. Since then, the villagers had to cope with all sorts of trials and exactions. For even the shortest journey, they have to seek permission from the commander of the post. Otherwise they would wind up accused of being agents of the "Khmer Rouges" or the "Vietcong–North Vietnamese" and would be subjected to the worst sorts of torture. Many have come out of such treatment sick, behind, others have gone mad or even died. The families of the prisoners, in order to get their loved ones free, often had to sell what little they had (house, plot of land, buffalo) and even their own children to the torturer-captain the ransom demanded. The villagers must still pay "loans" in the form of money, rice, pork, poultry, which no one dares try to avoid. Worse still, the traitorous captain and his men embark on orgies of rape against the girls and the women of the village.

The inhabitants of this area, victims of exploitation and sorts of robbery by the torturer-captain and his men, have a miserable life full of humiliation. However, despite severe enemy repression day and night, the local branch of FUNK (National United Front of Kampuchea) is still intact, to guide the people in their struggle.

In order to free the villagers from the cruel claws of the eager puppets the American imperialist aggressor, the local branch of the FUNK decided to wipe out the enemy position without endangering the population, in conformity with its wishes.

Representatives of the FUNK branches from surrounding villages met secretly to set in motion a plan to attack the position. One question raised, however, stopped everyone short: "How can we attack the enemy if none of us, even the guerrillas, are armed, because of the continual troops searches of the houses and sweeps into the forest?" When a lively discussion of how to find a solution began, a young girl guerrilla interrupted: "We must take the enemy's arms in order to wipe him out."

"An excellent idea," everyone nodded. "But how are we going to do it?" they asked. "None of us can even approach the enemy position. How, then, could we possibly get inside?" The young girl, with a childish smile on her lips, started explaining in detail how her group intended to outwit the enemy. Everyone approved of her well thought out plan.

A week passed. The carnival atmosphere in village T was quite out of the ordinary. Here, they were putting up a lean-to; there, a kitchen. Over there, they piled up the rice; over there they cut down trees and plants for the decorations. On that day the people from the neighboring villages came to village T in large numbers, some bringing poultry with them, some bringing vegetables. Festival music could be heard from the end of the village to the other. It seemed that a wedding was about to take place.

In the barracks, the soldiers also arranged the tables for a feast. Nothing unusual about that; the parents of the bride and bridegroom had come to the quarters to ask the captain's permission for their children to get married. Permission was granted on condition that the parents organize a feast that same day for he and his men. "But," he added, "I want to be served by the bride herself and all the bridesmaids will wait on my men. None of the others will be allowed into the barracks today." The parents reluctantly decided to give in to the wishes of the traitor.

Three o'clock in the afternoon; twenty people, young and old, men and women, headed towards the barracks, carrying on their heads or on their shoulders the provisions for the feast. When they arrived in front of the post, the sentry stopped them, and told them to put down their loads. He called to other troops inside and they came out to carry in the provisions. Then the sentry ordered our people to go back to the village immediately.

Four-thirty: Ten girls elegantly dressed and accompanied by hefty boys carrying five cases of alcohol, presented themselves at the post. This time, the sentry let the girls in, but stood in the way of the men and ordered them to go back home.

At the sight of the lovely ladies, four plain-clothes officers drinking at a table rejoiced. One of them asked the girls:

"You, girls, can you dance the ramvong?"

"Yes, of course we can," they replied.

This set the four shouting and clapping their hands excitedly.

Then, the captain gave the order to three of the soldiers to stand guard, one at the entrance and the two others at the lookout, while he told the rest to relax at the tables with their rifles by their side, taking turns to do guard duty.

Hearing this order, the girls begged the commander:

"We are afraid of guns. Monsieur le Capitaine, please don't let your men sit down or dance with us with all those rifles! Otherwise how can we generously give you our attention and our dancing?"

At this, laughter filled the room. The officers wanted to appear gallant.

"My darlings, you have nothing to fear from these rifles. We would never use them on girls so lovely and fresh as you all are right now! If we don't carry our guns, how can we defend you when the Khmers Krahom come?" (Khmers Krahom is the popular Cambodian term for Khmer Rouges, or Khmer Reds.)

"Yes," replied the prettiest one, "we agree with you, but we only want you to put your rifles in some place where they won't get in the way when we're dancing."

The captain granted the girls' request and told his men to put their rifles in bundles near the tables.

Then the party started. First the meal was served. The three prettiest girls waited on the officers, the others on the soldiers. They concentrated on being attentive and thought only of one thing; to make them drink as much as possible.

The bell went for the changing of the guard but not one of the merrymaking soldiers took the least notice. They kept on drinking glass after glass and quickly got drunker and drunker. The three angry soldiers on guard came in and sat down at the tables cleared for them by our girls. The drunken soldiers and officers all shouted and sang loudly. They forgot about dancing. All of a sudden, one of the girls clapped her hands three times.

Quick as a flash, without giving the enemy time to work out what was happening, the girls firmly grabbed the gun and pointed them at the soldiers. Simultaneously, one girl fired a shot and ordered the soldiers "Hands up!" They were caught off guard and in no time ten hefty youths, the same ones who had carried the casks of alcohol, charged into the room and tied up the soldiers.

The villagers from round about heard the shots and ran towards the post to find out what had happened. An unexpected but welcome sight met their eyes. They gathered for a meeting in the fields to denounce the crimes committed by the torturer-captain and his whole board, straw dogs for the traitors of Phnom Penh and eager servants of U.S. imperialism. . . .

Village T, as well as the surrounding villages were thus liberated and its inhabitants became masters of their lands, their villages and their communes, and they benefited from their newly-won democratic freedoms.

Source: Yale Cambodian Genocide Project translation of Khmer Rouge propaganda document. Available online. URL: http://www.yale.edu/cgp/kwomen.html. Accessed August 22, 2007.

A Khmer Rouge Personal Life History Questionnaire (1975)

This questionnaire was drawn up by the Santebal, the secret police of the Khmer Rouge, to be filled out by applicants for membership in the Cambodian Communist Party. More than 11,000 completed questionnaires have been located in the Santebal archives. The reader will note that the questionnaire would provide the Khmer Rouge with a great deal of information about the applicant's extended family that could be used to identify enemies of the state. The questionnaire was translated by Ben Kiernan, the present director of the Genocide Studies Program at Yale.

I. About Yourself

1. Original name: Revolutionary name:

2. Place, day, month and year of birth:

3. Sex female or male? Ethnicity:

4. Married or single?

5. Occupation and original class before joining the revolution:

6. Occupation and class after joining the revolution:

7. Had you joined any political organizations prior to joining the revolution? Reason for joining these organizations.

8. When did you join the revolution? Where? Who brought you to join? Reason for joining the revolution.

9. When did you join the Kampuchean Communist Youth League (SYK), the Kampuchean Peasants Association (SKK), the Union (SHC), Democratic Workers and Laborers Association (SKPP)? Where? Who brought you to join? Reason for joining these organizations.

10. When did you join the Party? Where? Who authorized you to join? Reason for joining the Party.

11. What position have you obtained since joining the revolution?

12. What was your educational level during the old regime? In the new regime? What diplomas do you have?

13. What kinds of people did you live and work among? Workers, farmers, intellectuals, capitalists, women, monks? What is your understanding of these groups?

14. Have you studied about the revolution at a seminar or school? What did you study?

15. How many times did Angkar examine and discuss your personal biography and revolutionary lifestyle? How long did it take to both prepare and present it?

16. How clearly do you know your character? To what level? How well do you know your strengths and weaknesses? How have you changed your non-revolutionary character and weaknesses? What is the result?

II. About Your Husband or Wife, if you have one

1. Original name: Revolutionary Name:

2. Ethnicity:

3. Place, day, month and year of birth:

4. Occupation and original class before marriage:

5. Occupation and class after marriage:

6. Did [he/she] use to join a political organization? What is [his/her] political attitude toward the revolution?

7. Has [she/he] joined the revolution yet? When did [she/he] join? Which organization? Currently has what position in the revolution?

8. Does [your spouse] have any political, economic or emotional influence or power over comrade [you]? To what level [extent]?

9. Do you, comrade, have any political, economic, emotional influence or power over your spouse?

10. What is your worldview about love, hatred and marriage? What kind of attachments do these have over you, comrade?

III. About Your Biological Children

1. How many children do you have? How many girls? How many boys? How old are they?

2. How many of them are working or married? What work do they do? What class are they? Have they joined any political organizations? Have they joined the revolution, yet? What is their attitude toward the revolution?

3. How many are dependent [on you] and not yet married? What do they do? Have they joined any political organizations? Have they joined the revolution yet? What is their attitude toward the revolution?

4. What is your standpoint concerning revolutionary worldview in relation to love, hatred, and raising of children?

5. What kind of influence, power and attachment do the children have over you, comrade?

IV. About Your Biological Parents

1. Original name: father/mother Revolutionary name: father/mother

2. Ethnicity: father mother

3. Place, day, month, year of birth, age, living or deceased

    father:

    mother:

4. Occupation and class:

    father:

    mother:

5. Political involvement: Have they joined any political organizations? What is their attitude toward the revolution?

6. What kind of political, economic, material, emotional influence, power and attachment do they have over you, comrade?

7. What influence or power do you, comrade, have on your parents?

V. About Your Parents-in-Law

1. Original name: father-in-law/mother-in-law
Revolutionary name: father-in-law/mother-in-law

2. Place, day, month, year of birth, age, living or deceased

> father-in-law:

> mother-in-law:

3. Occupation and class:

> father-in-law:

> mother-in-law:

4. Political involvement: Have they joined any political organizations? What is their attitude toward the revolution?

5. What kind of political, economic, material, emotional influence, power and attachment do they have over you, comrade?

6. What influence or power do you, comrade, have on your parents-in-law?

VI. About Your Biological Siblings

1. How many siblings do you have? How many sisters? How many brothers? How old are they?

2. Occupation and class of each:

3. Political involvement: Which political organizations have they joined? Have they joined the revolution, yet? What is their attitude toward the revolution?

4. What influence or attachment do they have over you, comrade?

5. What influence do you, comrade, have over each of your biological siblings?

VII. Close Friends and Social Environment You Enjoy Outside of Revolutionary Organizations

1. What very close friends do you have? How many?

2. Occupation and social class of each:

3. Political involvement: What is the political attitude of each toward the revolution?

4. What influence do they have over you, comrade?

5. Which social setting do you most enjoy being part of: workers, farmers, intellectuals, petty bourgeoisie, capitalists, aristocrats, feudalists, foreigners? What political, economic, emotional influence do these groups have over you, comrade?

Source: Santebal (Khmer Rouge secret police) archives, copies held by Cambodian Genocide Program, Yale University, Folder 1, document 1, pp. 5–11. Translated by Ben Kiernan. Available online. URL: http://www.yale.edu/cgp/questionnaire.html. Accessed August 29, 2007.

Rwanda
The Ten Commandments of the Hutu (1990)

The Ten Commandments of the Hutu were first published in Kangura *(Wake Them Up), a radical Hutu Power periodical, in the spring of 1990. They are thought to have been written by Hassan Ngeze, the editor of the publication.* Kangura *itself was launched by Agathe Habyarimana, at that time the wife of the president of Rwanda, and the clique of Hutu Power leaders that surrounded her. The magazine was subsidized financially by the Habyarimana government and printed by state-owned presses.*

1. Every Hutu must know that the Tutsi woman, wherever she may be, is working for the Tutsi ethnic cause. In consequence, any Hutu is a traitor who:
   - Acquires a Tutsi wife;
   - Acquires a Tutsi concubine;
   - Acquires a Tutsi secretary or protégée.
2. Every Hutu must know that our Hutu daughters are more worthy and more conscientious as women, as wives and as mothers. Aren't they lovely, excellent secretaries, and more honest!

3. Hutu women, be vigilant and make sure that your husbands, brothers and sons see reason.

202

4. All Hutus must know that all Tutsis are dishonest in business. Their only goal is ethnic superiority. We have learned this by experience from experience. In consequence, any Hutu is a traitor who:

- Forms a business alliance with a Tutsi
- Invests his own funds or public funds in a Tutsi enterprise
- Borrows money from or loans money to a Tutsi
- Grants favors to Tutsis (import licenses, bank loans, land for construction, public markets . . .)

5. Strategic positions such as politics, administration, economics, the military and security must be restricted to the Hutu.

6. A Hutu majority must prevail throughout the educational system (pupils, scholars, teachers).

7. The Rwandan Army must be exclusively Hutu. The war of October 1990 has taught us that. No soldier may marry a Tutsi woman.

8. Hutu must stop taking pity on the Tutsi.

9. Hutu wherever they be must stand united, in solidarity, and concerned with the fate of their Hutu brothers. Hutu within and without Rwanda must constantly search for friends and allies to the Hutu Cause, beginning with their Bantu brothers.
Hutu must constantly counter Tutsi propaganda.
Hutu must stand firm and vigilant against their common enemy: the Tutsi.

10. The Social Revolution of 1959, the Referendum of 1961 and the Hutu Ideology must be taught to Hutu of every age. Every Hutu must spread the word wherever he goes. Any Hutu who persecutes his brother Hutu for spreading and teaching this ideology is a traitor.

Source: Published in *Kangura,* no. 6. (1990). Available online. URL: http://www.trumanwebdesign.com/~catalina/commandments.htm. Accessed August 22, 2007.

Roméo Dallaire's "Genocide Fax" (1994)

The following is the complete text of the fax that Roméo Dallaire, then Force Commander of the United Nations Assistance Mission for Rwanda (UNAMIR), sent to UN headquarters in New York in January 1994, warning of the potential for genocide in Rwanda. The Interahamwe mentioned in the fax was a radical Hutu paramilitary organization whose name means "those who stand together" in Kinyarwanda, the language of Rwanda. The text of the fax was first published in the New Yorker *in the issue of May 11, 1998.*

OUTGOING CODE CABLE

DATE: 11 JANUARY 1994	
TO: Baril/DPKO/UNATIONS New York	FROM: Dallaire UNAMIR/Kigali
FAX NO: Most Immediate—Code Cable—212-963-9652 Inmarsat:	FAX NO: 011-250-94273
SUBJECT: Request for protection for informant	
ATTN: M[ajor] Gen[eral] Baril	ROOM NO. 2052
Total Number of Transmitted Pages Including This One: 2	

1. Force commander put in contact with informant by very very important government politician. Informant is a top level trainer in the cadre of Intera-hamwe-armed militia of MRND [Mouvement Révolutionnaire National pour le Développement, a political party formed by Juvénal Habyarimana in 1975. The Interahamwe were the militant youth wing of the MRND; the name means "those who attack together" in Kinyarwanda.]

2. He informed us he was in charge of last Saturday's demonstrations which aims were to target deputies of opposition parties coming to ceremonies and Belgian soldiers. They hoped to provoke the RPF [Rwandan Patriotic Front] BN [battalion] to engage (being fired upon) the demonstrators and provoke a civil war. Deputies were to be assassinated upon entry or exit from Parliament. Belgian troops were to be provoked and if Belgians [sic] soldiers resorted to force a number of them were to be killed and thus guar-antee Belgian withdrawal from Rwanda.

3. Informant confirmed 48 RGF [Rwandan government forces] Para GDO and a few members of the Gendarmerie [Rwandan police force] participated in demonstrations in plain clothes. Also at least one minister of the MRND and the sous-prefect [assistant head of a prefecture] of Kigali were in the dem-onstration. RGF and Interahamwe provided communications.

4. Informant is a former security member of the president[ial guard]. He also stated he is paid RF 150,000 per month by the MRND Party to train Interahamwe [members]. Direct link is to chief of staff [of the] RGF and President of the MRND for financial and material support.

5. Interahamwe has trained 1700 men in RGF military camps outside the capital. The 1700 are scattered in groups of 40 throughout Kigali. Since

UNAMIR deployed he has trained 300 personnel in three week training sessions at RGF camps. Training focus was discipline, weapons, explosives, close combat and tactics.

6. Principal aim of Interahamwe in the past was to protect Kigali from RPF. Since UNAMIR mandate he has been ordered to register all Tutsi in Kigali. He suspects it is for their extermination. Example he gave was that in 30 minutes his personnel could kill up to 1000 Tutsis.

7. Informant states he disagrees with anti-Tutsi extermination. He supports opposition to RPF but cannot support killing of innocent persons. He also stated that he believes the president does not have full control over all elements of his old party/faction.

8. Informant is prepared to provide location of major weapons cache with at least 135 weapons. He already has distributed 110 weapons including 35 with ammunition and can give us details of their location. Type of weapons are G3 [battle rifles] and AK47 [assault rifles] provided by RGF. He was ready to go to the arms cache tonight—if we gave him the following guarantee. He requests that he and his family (his wife and four children) be placed under *our* protection.

9. It is our intention to take action within the next 36 hours with a possible H hr of Wednesday at dawn (local). Informant states that hostilities may commence again if political deadlock ends. Violence could take place [on the] day of the ceremonies or the day after. Therefore Wednesday will give greatest chance of success and also be most timely to provide significant input to on-going political negotiations.

10. It is recommended the informant be granted protection and evacuated out of Rwanda. This HQ does not have previous UN experience in such matters and urgently requests guidance. No contact has as yet been made to any embassy in order to inquire if they are prepared to protect him for a period of time by granting diplomatic immunity in their embassy in Kigali before moving him and his family out of the country.

11. Force commander will be meeting with the very very important political person tomorrow morning in order to ensure that this individual is conscious of all parameters of his involvement. Force commander does have certain reservations on the suddenness of the change of heart of the informant to come clean with this information. Recce [reconnaissance] of armed cache and detailed planning of raid to go on late tomorrow. Possibility of a trap not fully excluded, as this may be a set-up against the very very important political person. Force commander to inform SRSG [Special

Representative of the Secretary General of the UN] first thing in [the] morning to ensure his support.

12. Peux ce que veux. Allons-y. [Where there's a will there's a way. Let's go!]

Source: U.S. House of Representatives, Committee on International Relations, Subcommittee on International
Operations and Human Rights, "Hearing: Rwanda: Genocide and the Continuing Cycle of Violence," May 5,
1998. Available online in PDF format [photocopy of original fax]. URL: http://www.gwu.edu/~nsarchiv/NSAEBB/
NSAEBB53/index.html. Accessed August 12, 2007.

The Gacaca Courts of Rwanda (2005)

*The following English-language description of the grassroots system of partici-
pative justice put in place in Rwanda to speed up the trials of persons accused
of participation in the 1994 genocide is taken directly from the Web site of the
National Service of Gacaca Jurisdictions. The spelling and punctuation have
not been changed.*

Context or historical background of Gacaca Courts

For more than 3 decades, the political regimes have, one after the other,
erected sectarianism and ethnical segregation into a system of governance.
That is the reason why persecutions and massacres of innocent populations
have been organised so many times by political leaders who always succeeded in implying large numbers of ordinary citizens.

These heinous crimes have remained unpunished and the culture of
impunity has become part and parcel of the Rwandan socio-political heritage to such an extent that it became easy for those who conceived of the
1994 machiavellian plan of mobilising almost all the population and perpetrating a genocide during which more than a million persons perished in
less than 3 months only.

The Government of National Unity put in place on July 19th, 1994 has
assigned itself the duty of eradicating the culture of impunity: the authors
of the genocide and other crimes against humanity must be brought before
courts and be tried, and the victims must be paid compensation. But, it had
to face a major challenge:

- The judiciary system was completely uprooted by the genocide;
- The portion of the population suspected of participation in the genocide is very large;
- The survivors of the genocide have been left grief-stricken and everyone, the victims as well as the presumed authors of genocide expected

that justice be made as soon as possible. It is in that context that Organic Law n°08/96 of August 30th, 1996 on the organisation of legal proceedings in cases of infrigements that constitute a crime against humanity was elaborated and adopted. The trials begun in December 1996 just after the adoption of the text.

Judicial staff before and after Genocide

REFERENCE PERIOD	JUDGES	PROSECUTORS	OTHER SUPPORTING STAFF (REGISTRARS AND SECRETARIES)
Before 1994	758	70	631
November 1994	244	12	137
After training sessions of 1996	841	210	910

This Organic law established:
- the specialised chambers for genocide crimes in the civil and military courts
- confession procedure and guilt plea for genocide suspects.
- Categorization of genocide defendants:

1st category:
- Planners, organisers, instigators, supervisors of the genocide
- Leaders at the national, provincial or district level, within political parties, army, religious denominations or militia;
- The well-known murderer who distinguished himself because of the zeal which charactarised him in the killings or the excessive wickedness with which killings were carried out.
- People who committed rape or acts of sexual torture.

2nd category:
- Authors, co-authors, accomplices of deliberate homicides, or of serious attacks that caused someone's death.
- The person who—with intention of killing—caused injuries or committed other serious violence, but without actually causing death.

3rd category:
- The person who committed criminal acts or became accomplice of serious attacks, without the intention of causing death.

4th category:
- The person having committed offences against property.

Measures were adopted in order to speed up the trials. These were for example the setting up of a commission responsible for categorization, the mobile teams, the organisation of trials of groups of suspects and itinerant courts. Nevertheless given the large number of files related to genocide, the expected results will never be reached. The courts rapidly became overwhelmed with the large number of genocide related cases in addition to the usual common law cases.

Lessons from this approach:
- The classic justice didn't meet expectations because after approximately a five year period only 6,000 files out of 120,000 detainees were tried.
- At this working speed, it would take more than a century (+ 100 years) to try these detainees.
- It is important to note that justice was also concerning the suspects who were still in the community and in exile; but who could not be arrested due to lack of enough space in the existing prisons and prosecution facilities.
- The conclusion was to look for another alternative solution

The slowness of procedures and the important delay in the trial of these cases represented a serious risk of hindering the efforts made for the reconciliation of the Rwandans. It became clear that it was necessary to modify the strategy and to look for another solution to the problem. His Excellency the President of the Republic, called a reflexion and consulation meeting that has resulted under the inspiration of the traditional context of conflicts resolution in the establishment of the Gacaca Courts.

It is a system of participative justice whereby the population is given the chance to speak out against the committed atrocities, to judge and to punish the authors with the exception of those classified by the law in the first category who will be judged and punished by the ordinary courts according to common law rules.

That kind of justice will be carried out in the context of the Gacaca courts that will sit in Cells, Sectors, Districts and Provinces and will be composed of men and women of integrity elected by their neighbours.

The objectives of the GACACA Courts

The Gacaca Courts have been instituted in order to reach precise objectives:

1. To reveal the truth about what has happened

The unity and reconciliation of the Rwandans that are targetted are based on justice for all. But, this justice can become true only if the truth about the events is established. The way in which the Gacaca Institution has been conceived will allow to discover that truth because:

- The citizens who have been the eyewitnesses of the facts that occurred mainly in their cells will give evidence;
- The list of the names of the victims and those of the authors of the crimes committed will be established;
- Even if the task proves to be difficult, given the fact that now some places are mere ruins, some situations will at least be clarified.

2. To speed up the genocide trials

This problem will be solved because:

- The trials will be made by those who already act as witnesses in the said trials before the specialised courts;
- About 11,000 Gacaca Courts will deal with these genocide trials whereas in classical justice this task was performed by only 12 specialised;
- In front of the eyewitnesses of their deeds, the guilty persons will no more try to deny what has been evidenced.

3. To eradicate the culture of impunity

In their cells, the citizens will play an important role in the reconstruction of the facts and in the accusation of those who perpetrated them. None of those who took part in them will escape punishment. Thus, people will understand that the infringement implies the punishment for the criminal without exception.

4. To reconcile the Rwandans and reinforce their unity

The Gacaca Courts system will allow the population of the same Cell, the same Sector to work together in order to judge those who have participated in the genocide, identify the victims and rehabilitate the innocents. The Gacaca Courts system will thus become the basis of collaboration and unity, mainly because when the truth will be known, there will be no more suspicion, the author will be punished, justice will be done to the victim and to the innocent prisoner who will be reintegrated in the Rwandan society.

5. To prove that the Rwandan society has the capacity to settle its own problems through a system of justice based on the Rwandan custom.
The Rwandan genocide has been perpetrated by Rwandans against their brothers. It is then the responsibility of all the Rwandans with no exception and in the first place to rebuild their society, to settle the disputes related to that genocide especially through the trial of the presumed authors and the reparation of the damage caused to the victims.

Once Gacaca fulfills its mission, it will restore conviviality among Rwandans and they will work for their own and the country's development.

Source: National Service of Gacaca Jurisdictions. Available online. URL: http://www.inkiko-gacaca.gov.rw/En/EnObjectives.htm. Accessed August 2, 2007.

Darfur

Testimony of Secretary of State Colin L. Powell before the Senate Foreign Relations Committee (2004) (excerpt)

On September 9, 2004, then secretary of state Colin Powell reported on the findings of a team of observers from the United States who had interviewed more than 1,000 Darfur refugees living in Chad. He addressed his remarks to the chairman of the committee at that time, Senator Richard Lugar of Indiana. Powell's remarks were controversial because he used the term genocide *to describe the catastrophe in Darfur. Significantly, he noted that an international consensus on the nature of the crisis did not exist: ". . . at this point, genocide is our judgment and not the judgment of the international community." As of 2009, no other permanent member of the United Nations Security Council has agreed with Powell's assessment of the tragedy.*

We have begun consultation in New York on a new resolution that calls for Khartoum to fully cooperate with an expanded AU force and for cessation of Sudanese military flights over the Darfur region. It also provides for international overflights to monitor the situation in Darfur and requires the Security Council to review the record of Khartoum's compliance to determine if sanctions, including on the Sudanese petroleum sector, should be imposed. The resolution also urges the Government of Sudan and the SPLM to conclude negotiations, the Lake Naivasha negotiations, on a comprehensive peace accord.

And, Mr. Chairman, there is, finally, the continuing question of whether what is happening in Darfur should be called genocide.

Since the United States became aware of atrocities occurring in Sudan, we have been reviewing the Genocide Convention and the obligations it places on the Government of Sudan and on the international community and on the state parties to the genocide convention.

In July, we launched a limited investigation by sending a team to visit the refugee camps in Chad to talk to refugees and displaced personnel. The team worked closely with the American Bar Association and the Coalition for International Justice, and were able to interview 1136 of the 2.2 million people the UN estimates have been affected by this horrible situation, this horrible violence.

Those interviews indicated: first, a consistent and widespread pattern of atrocities: Killings, rapes, burning of villages committed by Jingaweit [*sic*] and government forces against non-Arab villagers; three-fourths of those interviewed reported that the Sudanese military forces were involved in the attacks; third, villagers often experienced multiple attacks over a prolonged period before they were destroyed by burning, shelling or bombing, making it impossible for the villagers to return to their villages. This was a coordinated effort, not just random violence.

When we reviewed the evidence compiled by our team, and then put it beside other information available to the State Department and widely known throughout the international community, widely reported upon by the media and by others, we concluded, I concluded, that genocide has been committed in Darfur and that the Government of Sudan and the Jingaweit bear responsibility—and that genocide may still be occurring. . . . We believe in order to confirm the true nature, scope and totality of the crimes our evidence reveals, a full-blown and unfettered investigation needs to occur. Sudan is a contracting party to the Genocide Convention and is obliged under the Convention to prevent and to punish acts of genocide. To us, at this time, it appears that Sudan has failed to do so.

Article VIII of the Genocide Convention provides that Contracting Parties may, I will quote now, "may call upon the competent organs of the United Nations to take action, such action under the Charter of the United Nations as they," the competent organs of the United Nations, "as they consider appropriate, actions as they consider appropriate for the prevention and suppression of acts of genocide or any of the other acts enumerated in Article III" of the Genocide Convention.

Because of that obligation under Article VIII of the Convention, and since the United States is one of the contracting parties; today we are calling on the United Nations to initiate a full investigation. To this end, the United

States will propose that the next UN Security Council Resolution on Sudan request a United Nations investigation into all violations of international humanitarian law and human rights law that have occurred in Darfur, with a view to ensuring accountability.

Mr. Chairman, as I have said, the evidence leads us to the conclusion, the United States to the conclusion; that genocide has occurred and may still be occurring in Darfur. We believe the evidence corroborates the specific intent of the perpetrators to destroy "a group in whole or in part," the words of the Convention. This intent may be inferred from their deliberate conduct. We believe other elements of the convention have been met as well.

Under the 1948 Convention on the Prevention and Punishment of the Crime of Genocide, to which both the United States and Sudan are parties, genocide occurs when the following three criteria are met:

First, specific acts are committed, and those acts include: Killing; causing serious bodily or mental harm; deliberately inflicting conditions of life calculated to bring about physical destruction of a group in whole or in part; imposing measures to prevent births; or forcibly transferring children to another group. Those are specified acts that, if committed, raise the likelihood that genocide is being committed.

The second criteria [sic]: These acts are committed against members of a national, ethnic, racial or religious group; and the third criterion is, they are committed "with intent to destroy, in whole or in part, the group, as such."

The totality of the evidence from the interviews we conducted in July and August, and from the other sources available to us, shows that the Jingaweit and Sudanese military forces have committed large-scale acts of violence, including murders, rape and physical assaults on non-Arab individuals. Second, the Jingaweit and Sudanese military forces destroyed villages, foodstuffs, and other means of survival. Third, the Sudan Government and its military forces obstructed food, water, medicine, and other humanitarian aid from reaching affected populations, thereby leading to further deaths and suffering. And finally, despite having been put on notice multiple times, Khartoum has failed to stop the violence.

Mr. Chairman, some seem to have been waiting for this determination of genocide to take action. In fact, however, no new action is dictated by this determination. We have been doing everything we can to get the Sudanese Government to act responsibly. So let us not be too preoccupied with this designation. These people are in desperate need and we must help them. Call it civil war; call it ethnic cleansing; call it genocide; call it "none of the above." The reality is the same. There are people in Darfur who desperately need the help of the international community.

I expect—I more than expect, I know, that the government of Khartoum in Khartoum will reject our conclusion of genocide anyway. Moreover, at this point, genocide is our judgment and not the judgment of the international community. Before the Government of Sudan is taken to the bar of international justice, let me point out that there is a simple way for Khartoum to avoid such wholesale condemnation by the international community, and that way is to take action—to stop holding back, to stop dissembling.

Source: Testimony of Colin Powell before the Senate Foreign Relations Committee. Available online. URL: http://www.state.gov/secretary/former/powell/remarks/36042.htm. Accessed October 10, 2008.

Luis Moreno-Ocampo, Prosecutor's Application for Warrant of Arrest under Article 58 Against Omar Hassan Ahmad Al Bashir (2008) (excerpts)

On July 14, 2008, Moreno-Ocampo applied for a warrant of arrest in his capacity as prosecutor of the International Criminal Court (ICC) as specified in Article 58 of the Rome Statute, against Omar al-Bashir, the president of Sudan. The arrest warrant states "that there are reasonable grounds to believe" that Bashir "bears criminal responsibility for" genocide, war crimes, and crimes against humanity. The arrest warrant does not allege that Bashir "physically or directly" carried out the crimes; rather it states that "[h]e is the mastermind behind the alleged crimes. He has absolute control." As of late 2008, however, it appears unlikely that the warrant will have any substantial effect on the crisis in Darfur because Sudan does not accept the jurisdiction of the ICC. The following excerpts are from the warrant's summary of the evidence justifying Bashir's arrest for the crimes committed in Darfur.

III. Summary of the Evidence and Information provided in the Prosecution's Application

Consistent with the requirements of Article 58 (2)(d) of the Statute, the Prosecution furnished in the Application "a summary of the evidence" sufficient to establish "reasonable grounds to believe" that Omar Hassan Ahmad AL BASHIR committed crimes within the jurisdiction of the Court.

a. The Context in which Crimes were Committed

Since he assumed power in June 1989, AL BASHIR has engaged in political and military struggles with groups both in Khartoum and in the peripheries of the Sudan seen as threats to his power. In Darfur, he assessed that the

Fur, Masalit and Zaghawa ethnic groups, as socially and politically dominant groups in the province, constituted such threats: they challenged the
economic and political marginalization of their region, and members of
the three groups engaged in armed rebellions. AL BASHIR set out to quell
those movements through armed force and, over the years, also employed a
policy of exploiting real or perceived grievances between the different tribes
struggling to prosper in the difficult Darfur environment. He promoted the
idea of a polarization between tribes aligned with the Government, whom
he labeled "Arabs," and the three groups he perceived as the main threats,
whom he labeled "Zurgas" or "Africans.". . . .

In March 2003, after negotiations and armed action both failed to end
in Darfur a rebellion whose members belonged mostly to the three target
groups, AL BASHIR decided and set out to destroy in part the Fur, Masalit
and Zaghawa groups, on account of their ethnicity. His motives were largely
political. His pretext was a "counterinsurgency." His intent was genocide. The
Fur, Masalit and Zaghawa speak Arabic and share with the majority of the
Darfur population the same religion (Islam). Co-existence and intermarriage
have blurred differences. However historically they occupied specific territories (Dar Fur, Dar Masalit and Dar Zaghawa), and also spoke their own languages, different from one another and from Arabic. Members of the groups
see themselves and are seen by their attackers as different ethnic groups.

b. The crimes
Genocide by killing members of the target groups

From March 2003 up to the date of filing, AL BASHIR's orders giving *carte
blanche* to his subordinates to quell the rebellion and take no prisoners
triggered a series of brutal attacks against the Fur, Masalit and Zaghawa
groups. The Armed Forces, often acting together with Militia/Jangaweed,
singled out for attack those villages and small towns inhabited mainly by
members of the target groups. The attackers went out of their way to spare
from attack villages inhabited predominantly by other tribes considered
aligned with the Government, even where they were located very near villages inhabited predominantly by members of the targeted groups.

The Prosecution has charted all the known attacks that have taken
place from 2003–2008 on an interactive map of Darfur, showing towns,
villages and the tribal composition of the inhabitants (available on the ICC
OTP website). The results show that the overwhelming majority of villages
attacked were inhabited mainly by the target groups. They were clearly
selected for attack.

The Armed Forces and Militia/Jangaweed carried out such attacks jointly
and in a similar pattern throughout the entire period, up to the date of filing.

Typically, the Armed Forces would arrive in trucks and land cruisers mounted with Dshkas, and the Militia/Jangaweed would arrive on camels and horseback. These joint forces would then surround the village and on occasion, the Air Force would be called upon to drop bombs on the village as a precursor to the attacks. The ground forces would then enter the village or town and attack civilian inhabitants. They kill men, children, elderly, women; they subject women and girls to massive rapes. They burn and loot the villages.

The targets are not rebel forces, but the Fur, Masalit and Zaghawa communities. Attacks are typically launched against civilian targets, and do not cease until the town or village, in its entirety, has been victimized and its population forcibly displaced, regardless of the lack of rebel presence or the lack of any valid military objective. . . .

The fate of the displaced persons

Almost the entire population of the target groups has been forcibly displaced following the attacks. Data from refugee camps in Chad and camps for internally displaced persons ("IDP camps") within Darfur confirm that most of those displaced belong to the target groups. As of December 2007, the total number of Sudanese people from Darfur in refugee camps in Chad was approximately 235,000. Of those, there were approximately 110,000 Zaghawa and approximately 103,000 Masalit. Only approximately 7,750 members of the Fur had reached Chad, due to their geographical location in the south of Darfur. According to information, the Fur represent 50% up to the totality of some IDP camps in Darfur. In South Darfur, Kalma camp, near Nyala, which hosts around 92,000 IDPs, there are an estimated 46 to 50,000 Fur, 9,000 Zaghawa and 5,000 Masalit. In West Darfur, Nertiti (Jebel Marra) hosts mostly Fur (about 32,000); Hassa Hissa near Zalingei hosts about 85% Fur (42,500), 10% Zaghawa (5,000), 5% Masalit (2,500) and smaller tribes. The Fur represent 99% (about 30,000) of the population of Hamadiya camp near Zalingei and 90% (about 16,000) in Deleig camp near Wali Sadih. . . . Notwithstanding the evidence that genocide was committed by killing and the infliction of serious bodily and mental harm, the current evidence also shows that the target groups, far from being assisted, are also attacked in the camps. Such attacks, as described below, against such an overwhelming majority of members of the target groups, are a clear indication of AL BASHIR's genocidal intent.

Genocide by causing serious mental harm
to members of the target group

As a result of the attacks to the villages, at least 2,700,000 people, most of them members of the target groups, have been forcibly expelled from their

215

homes. As survivors fled the attacks, they were pursued into deserts, killed or left to die. Those who managed to reach the outskirts of bigger cities and what would become IDP camps are submitted to physical and mental harm, and generally conditions calculated to slowly bring about their destruction.

(i) Thousands of women and girls belonging to the target groups were and continue to be raped in all three States of Darfur by members of the Militia/Jangaweed and Armed Forces since 2003. Girls as young as 5 years old have been raped. A third of the rapes are rapes of children. Underreporting of rape is widespread. Nonetheless, periodic reports and testimonies conclude that rape has been committed systematically and continuously for 5 years. . . . Rape is an integral part of the pattern of destruction that the Government of the Sudan is inflicting upon the target groups in Darfur. As described by the ICTR in the *Akayesu* case, they use rape to kill the will, the spirit, and life itself. Particularly in view of the social stigma associated with rape and other forms of sexual violence among the Fur, Masalit and Zaghawa, these acts cause significant and irreversible harm, to individual women, but also to their communities.

(ii) Massive forced displacement was, and continues to be, conducted in such a manner as to traumatize the victims and prevent the reconstitution of the group. AL BASHIR's criminal plan has violently uprooted at least 2.7 million civilians—principally members of the target groups—from lands on which they and their ancestors had been living for centuries. Victims suffer the trauma of being forced to witness their own homes and possessions destroyed and/or looted and family members raped and/or killed. The victims thereafter endure the anguish of learning that, in many cases, prior homelands have been occupied and resettled by members of other communities—and thus, there is no prospect of ever returning. Organized insecurity in and around the camps by AL BASHIR's forces and agents, including through spying and harassment by members of the Humanitarian Aid Commission ("HAC"), exacerbates the fear of IDPs. The cumulative effect of the crimes described above is that many of the surviving members of the target groups, in particular those in IDP camps, suffer serious mental and/or psychological harm.

Genocide by deliberate infliction on members of the target groups conditions of life calculated to bring about the physical destruction of the group in whole or in part

(i) The attacks on villages across Darfur from March 2003 to the present were designed not only to kill members of the target groups and force them from their lands, but also to destroy the very means of survival of the groups as such. They destroy food, wells and water pumping machines, shelter, crops and livestock, as well as any physical structures capable of sustaining life or commerce. They destroy farms and loot grain stores or set them on fire. The goal is to ensure that those inhabitants not killed outright would not be able to survive without assistance.

(ii) The survivors are not only forced out of their homes, they are also pursued into inhospitable terrain. A victim in the desert overheard one attacker say to another: *"Don't waste the bullet, they've got nothing to eat and they will die from hunger."*

(iii) In addition to persecuting the victims, the attackers spoliate [ruin] their land, now occupied by new settlers: *"This land is liberated and you have no land and no right to cultivate on liberated areas."* Usurpation of the land is often the final blow to the capacity of the target groups to survive in Darfur. Land has always been identified as a key issue, by AL BASHIR himself. . . . Having removed the target groups from their land, and destroyed their means of survival, AL BASHIR encourages and facilitates resettlement of the land by other tribes more supportive of the government, often affiliated with Militia/Jangaweed. The scale of displacements was done in the knowledge of the devastating impact it would have on the fabric of the groups, whose identity is linked with the land. When they were removed from the land, the tribal structure was weakened.

(iv) They also attack the target groups in the camps. AL BASHIR and his subordinates systematically refuse to provide any meaningful aid, and hinder other efforts to bring humanitarian aid to the 2,450,000 civilians displaced. Thus after forcibly expelling members of the target groups from their homes, they subject them to, at best, a subsistence diet and the reduction of essential medical services below minimum requirements. . . .

The overall effect of physical attack, forced displacement, destruction of means of livelihood, and denial of humanitarian assistance was that mortality rates among civilians, including principally members of the target groups, remained at critical levels. Between April and June 2004, as deaths directly caused by violence decreased, mortality rates among displaced populations in Darfur remained elevated because of deficient humanitarian assistance. Overall, at least 100,000 civilians—mostly members of the targeted groups—have already endured "slow death" since March 2003.

Crimes against humanity

Charges of crimes against humanity are also required to represent the full extent of criminal activity in Darfur since 2003, namely the acts of murder, rape, forcible displacement and extermination committed against members of the target groups and other, smaller ethnic groups, such as the Tunjur, Erenga, Birgid, Misseriya Jebel, Meidob, Dajo and Birgo. While the attacks against these groups were carried out on discriminatory grounds, there is insufficient evidence at this time to substantiate a charge of genocide in respect of these groups.

War crimes

At all times relevant to the charges, the Government of the Sudan has been engaged in a military campaign conducted in Darfur against rebel armed forces including the SLM/A and the JEM. Both rebel groups mainly recruit from the Fur, Masalit and Zaghawa tribes. As is well known, the GoS has relied on Militia/Jangaweed.

AL BASHIR also committed, through other persons, the war crime of pillaging towns and villages in Darfur, including but not limited to Kodoom, Bindisi, Mukjar, Arawala, Shataya, Kailek, Buram, Muhajeriya, Siraf Jidad, Silea, Sirba, Abu Suruj and villages in the area of Jebel Mun.

c. The Personal Responsibility of Omar Hassan Ahmad AL BASHIR

AL BASHIR controls and directs the perpetrators. The commission of those crimes on such a scale, and for such a long period of time, the targeting of civilians and in particular the Fur, Masalit and Zaghawa, the impunity enjoyed by the perpetrators, and the systematic cover-up of the crimes through public official statements, are evidence of a plan based on the mobilization of the state apparatus, including the armed forces, the intelligence services, the diplomatic and public information bureaucracies, and the justice system.

Source: Prosecutor's application for arrest warrant for Omar Bashir. Available online. URL: http://www.icc-cpi. int/library/organs/otp/ICC-OTP-Summary-20081704-ENG.pdf. Accessed October 10, 2008.

PART III

Research Tools

6

How to Research Genocide

GETTING STARTED

When researching a large topic like genocide, it is best to narrow the area of study as much as possible. Although there were relatively few books written about either genocide as a general topic or about specific genocides before the 1980s, genocide studies has now become an academic specialty of its own. As of 2008, there are entire journals devoted to genocide studies as well as literally hundreds of books published each year. The amount of material on genocide available on the Internet as well as in printed books and newspaper archives is steadily increasing. In order to keep the area of research manageable, it is a good idea to be specific about

- The specific instance of genocide to be studied. One way to focus the topic is to choose an example of genocide and read an article about it in a general encyclopedia or a specialized encyclopedia such as the two-volume *Encyclopedia of Genocide* edited by Israel Charny (ABC-Clio, Inc., 1999). Another good resource is Dinah Shelton's three-volume *Encyclopedia of Genocide and Crimes against Humanity* (Macmillan Reference, 2005). These resources are intended to provide a general overview of the subject and the main concepts or persons related to it. They will also suggest sources for further reading. If the researcher is interested in a specific person involved in the genocide, a biographical dictionary or encyclopedia will often provide a short article.

- The period of history and the territory where the genocide took place, keeping in mind that it may be necessary to do some further reading to get a general sense of the time, location, and people or groups involved. In regard to ancient and medieval genocides, the reader should remember that present-day Western notions of individuality, human equality, and the value of human life are very recent developments. This fact should not be taken to imply that genocides in the remote past were any less tragic or caused less suffering than more recent genocides, only that those who carried them out did not regard all human beings as equals and their lives as equally precious. In regard to 20th- and 21st-century genocides, the reader will need to look more closely at such features as the use of scientific and military technology in the genocide; reliance on modern methods of transportation for deportations or troop movement; the role of the mass media in spreading propaganda as well as informing outsiders about the genocide; the structure of the government(s) involved; the influence of previous genocides in shaping the perpetrators' decision to use genocide as a political "solution"; and similar matters.

- Distinctive or unusual features of the genocide. Was the genocide largely carried out by an army or paramilitary groups, or was there mass participation? Did the genocide occur before, during, or after wartime? Was only one group targeted for elimination, or were there several? Why were they chosen for elimination? Were scientists and medical professionals used to help carry out the killings, or were they one of the first groups eliminated? Were women among the perpetrators, or were they almost entirely victims? What happened afterward in terms of national and international justice systems? Did the genocide lead to the formation of any new justice organizations or other safeguards against recurrence? Has anyone followed up on the survivors, and, if so, what have the researchers or reporters discovered?

There are many other questions that the reader may want to ask, but these may be useful in beginning the process of gathering material and narrowing the topic.

GATHERING MATERIAL

When gathering material, the researcher must consider how much and what types of documents are needed. A five-minute classroom talk will not need as much research as a 10- or 20-page paper. In addition, the historical period or date of the event, movement, or person of interest will indicate what types of documents will be most helpful. In general, the more recent the genocide, the more current the sources will need to be. An information time line may be useful:

Immediate information about developing situations (minutes to hours old): the Internet

One day to one week: the Internet and general newspapers; some carefully chosen weekly newsmagazines

One month: popular magazines

Several months or more: scholarly journals

A year or more: encyclopedias and similar reference sources; printed books

In general, a genocide like Darfur, which is an ongoing crisis that comes under the heading of current events, requires recent materials that reflect current perspectives on the subject. A topic related to a genocide decades or centuries in the past will require a variety of resources from different time periods. For example, someone researching the genocide in Darfur will begin with Internet news sources, newspapers, and newsmagazines, whereas someone researching the Armenian genocide will consult encyclopedia articles about it, perhaps a biographical dictionary for a brief article about Enver Pasha or Soghomon Tehlirian, general histories of World War I and the 1920s, histories of American diplomacy in the 20th century, and articles about the Armenian genocide in scholarly journals.

In addition, the researcher can choose books and journal articles from different time periods as a way to look for the evolution of different perspectives on the same genocide. To use the Armenian genocide again as an example, it received considerable attention in the American popular press from 1915 through the end of World War I, then was largely forgotten—so much so that Hitler could say in 1937, "Who remembers the extermination of the Armenians?" when he was carrying out his own campaign to eliminate Jews, Roma, the mentally retarded, and other "undesirables." In the 1980s and 1990s, however, the Armenian genocide received fresh attention as the result of comparisons with the Holocaust and the genocides in Cambodia and Rwanda, so much so that some scholars now regard it as the template or pattern that was followed by the planners and perpetrators of later 20th-century genocides.

The reader should note that books, encyclopedias, and scholarly journals are often available on the Internet as well as more current resources. Many school and public libraries subscribe to such database services as *American National Biography,* published by Oxford University Press, or InfoTrac, published by Thomson Gale. InfoTrac is a collection of databases that includes such specific databases as the World Biographical Information System, History Resource Center, Declassified Documents Reference System, National Newspaper Index, Biography Resource Center, and others that are useful in researching topics related to genocide. In addition, several of the genocide studies programs and other institutions listed in Chapter 9 have made articles and visual resources freely available on the Internet as a public service. Some individual scholars, such as R. J. Rummel, have made entire books on genocide available on their Web sites for free download and distribution.

EVALUATING DOCUMENTS

Evaluating materials once they have been gathered is a critical step in researching topics related to genocide.

Document Source

The first consideration is the document's source. Does it come from inside or outside the genocide being studied? If it is an internal document, is it a record of some kind left behind by the perpetrators, such as a military order to deport or kill a certain group of people or notes from a secret meeting, or is it a diary or letters written by a witness? What type of technology was used to produce the document? Was it handwritten, typewritten, telegraphed, or faxed? What language is it written in? If it has been translated into English, is the translation accurate?

If the document comes from outside observers, is it intended for general readers (such as reports in a newspaper, weekly newsmagazine, or posted on an Internet site) or is it written for an academic audience? If it is written for educated readers, is it intended for those with a general interest in the subject or is it written for experts with specialized training or background information? One present difficulty in researching genocide as of the early 2000s, in fact, is that much of the available secondary material is written by scholars for other scholars and is often highly specialized.

Date of Publication

The date of publication is an important item of information in evaluating the completeness or currency of the information it contains. If the topic being researched concerns recent events, newspaper and Internet reports should be arranged in order of the date of publication or posting. The reason for this precaution is that first reports—particularly of tragic or horrifying events—are often inaccurate in some of their details. The first analyses or interpretations of the event are also often wide of the mark. An example of the pitfalls of early analysis was the belief on the part of many Western reporters in 1994 that the Rwanda genocide had to do with tribal enmities going back for centuries. Precisely because genocide is an emotion-laden subject by its very nature, it is important to make sure that the basic facts of any current event are described as accurately as possible in a research study. For this reason it is a good idea to gather news reports from more than one source.

Tone

Tone refers to the style or manner in which a document is written. It is often useful to ask questions in evaluating the tone of a document related to genocide. If the document comes from the perpetrators, is it a dry and matter-of-fact report intended to be circulated among politicians or bureaucrats planning or carrying out the genocide or is it propaganda intended to stir up strong feeling in the general population? Does it indicate that the perpetrators had accepted a conspiracy theory? If the document comes from a witness or survivor, was it written or recorded at the time of the genocide, or is it testimony given months or years after the event? If it is a later testimony, is the witness or survivor writing for or speaking to a law court, a therapist, or a historian? All of these factors can influence the speaker's general tone and the presence or relative absence of open emotion.

Tone is also an important consideration in evaluating documents that originate outside a group, particularly with a subject like genocide. Newspaper editorials or opinions written by columnists about genocide, for example, are usually quite different in tone from news reports because they are intended to persuade the reader to agree with the editor or columnist's viewpoint. This desire to persuade is often particularly evident in editorials that discuss whether a particular event is a "true" or "real" genocide. The Armenian genocide and Darfur are the most common examples of debates over the definition of genocide in the contemporary press. Another important aspect of tone is formality. Scholarly books or journals are typically written in a more formal tone than news reports or popular magazines, which have more freedom to use current slang or colloquial speech.

Reliability

Reliability refers to the integrity or dependability of the text source or visual image in question. A person researching genocide must ask whether there are any doubts about a specific document's overall genuineness. Could the material be faked by a contemporary forger? There have been enough recent instances of document forgery—most notably the fake Hitler diaries sold in 1983 to *Stern,* a German weekly newsmagazine—to justify asking questions about the source of any internal document related to genocide. An electronic version of forgery that sometimes occurs on the Internet is the planting of a fake document on a Web site. In addition to text forgeries, there have also been documented instances of visual forgeries. The invention of Adobe Photoshop and similar image editing programs makes it possible for news photographers to create misleading pictures of current events by adding, exaggerating, or eliminating details in photographs. While photographs reproduced in printed journals or books have usually been checked for accuracy, the same level of checking is difficult to apply to the Internet.

On the other hand, newly discovered documents or documents recently released from previously sealed government archives are sometimes labeled as forgeries by people who are uncomfortable with their contents. For example, Holocaust deniers commonly maintain that records and photographs of the gas chambers in Nazi concentration camps have been faked. Likewise, Russian documents from the 1930s about the famine in the Ukraine, newly available to Western historians since the collapse of the Soviet Union in the 1990s, have been attacked as forgeries by some writers who still defend Stalin's policies.

The age of a document by itself neither guarantees nor disproves the document's reliability. With regard to ancient and medieval genocides, it was common for historians up through the early 1990s to dismiss accounts of massacres written by contemporaries of the Mongol khans or by 16th-century Spanish conquistadors as either propaganda or exaggeration. Recent archaeological digs in Central Asia and Mexico, however, have corroborated the basic reliability of the observers' reports.

The most common problem that a beginning researcher confronts in studying genocide, however, is bias. Bias is a prejudice or tendency of mind that prevents a person from making an objective or impartial judgment. In some cases bias is the result of government censorship. Some Turkish historians of the Armenian genocide, for example, have served time in prison for questioning the Turkish government's official denial of the Armenian genocide. With regard to the Cambodian genocide of 1975–79, the Khmer Rouge's expulsion of all journalists as well as other Westerners from the country and their rigid control of information meant that it was difficult for outsiders to obtain reliable information about the actual course of events.

In other cases, however, bias results from the writer's own prejudices or blind spots. A notorious example of such bias that goes back to the 1930s is that of Walter Duranty (1884–1957), an English-born journalist who served as the *New York Times'* correspondent in Moscow in the 1930s. Duranty acknowledged the brutality of Stalin's government but argued that the dictator's methods were justified because Russians were "Asiatic" and required a heavy-handed ruler. When some British journalists began reporting on the famine in Ukraine in 1933, Duranty published an article in the *Times* referring to their reports as "a big scare story." A professor of history at Columbia University asked to evaluate Duranty's reporting in 2003 described it as uncritical acceptance of Soviet propaganda.[1] Another instance of professional blind spots is related to the genocide in Cambodia. In this instance the bias on the part of the journalists in the country in early 1975 was not primarily political but wishful thinking; many simply did not expect the Khmer Rouge to be as cruel as they turned out to be and later admitted that they had been naïve.[2]

Another problem related to reliability concerns reporting about current events. Most reporters are conscientious professionals who do their best to convey accurate information about breaking news in a straightforward and

226

timely fashion. News reports, however, are sometimes misleading because reporters are not experts on every subject they must cover in the course of their work. In addition, they are usually under pressure to file stories within a very short period of time. In most cases involving genocides in Asia, Africa, or the former Yugoslavia, Western reporters are not fluent in the local language and may have to depend on interpreters or local journalists to explain to them what is happening. One instance of this problem was the Rwanda genocide; the media under the control of the Habyarimana government succeeded in convincing many reporters from Western newspapers that the conflict had to do with "ancient tribal hatreds." While misunderstandings caused by unfamiliarity with a region or its history should not be confused with intentional bias or deliberate slanting of a news report, their occurrence does mean that readers should not assume that current news reports, whether online or in print, are always completely reliable.

SPECIAL CONCERNS
Foreign Languages

There are a few special problems related to researching genocide outside such English-speaking countries as the United Kingdom, Canada, Australia, and the United States. The first concerns the need to use translated materials in almost all cases. Readers who are interested in studying genocides in ancient or medieval history or genocides that took place in Central or South America, Asia, or Africa must depend on good translations if they cannot read the original languages. Even scholars in the field frequently remark that it is almost impossible for one person to master all the different languages required to read original sources related to the Mongol genocides, for example, or the Holocaust. Students who would like to read such primary sources as the *Secret History of the Mongols,* Thucydides' *History of the Peloponnesian War,* Las Casas's *History of the Destruction of the Indies,* or similar works, should consider reading them in more than one translation if possible. For secondary sources that were originally written in another language, it may be helpful to look at the translator's background, experience, or other qualifications.

Statistics

Another major problem in studying genocide is interpreting the death statistics given by various sources. The death tolls for most past genocides vary widely depending on the source consulted. Statistics for ancient and medieval genocides are particularly difficult to evaluate because the size of the original population before the genocide is usually hard to determine. Some governments did not collect what would now be called census information, and most of the records made by those that did have been destroyed over the course of centuries. In addition, there was no standard method of counting population; in some regions only adult males or adult property owners were counted. Historians must often depend on indirect methods of estimating population, such as the studies of parish church records made by Henry Dobyns in trying to calculate the number of Native Americans in the New World before 1500. Other sources used to estimate population size for the ancient, medieval, and early modern periods are land survey records, wills and property deeds, tax collection records, and archaeological evidence.

Genocides from the 20th century present a different type of problem for the statistician; in some cases, records of various types related to genocide exist but are not yet accessible to scholars because they are still housed in sealed government archives. In other cases, the materials include evidence of many different types, ranging from written orders for mass killings and records of medical experiments to photographs of victims prior to execution and human remains discovered in mass graves. Such academic periodicals as the *Journal of Genocide Research* often print articles about such statistical questions as the percentage of the population in Rwanda that participated in the genocide of 1994, and how the author decided which types of evidence provide valid statistical information and which do not. In some cases statistical arguments may be used to define whether or not a humanitarian crisis, such as starvation in Darfur, "counts" as genocide or simply as mass death.[3] The beginning researcher may be helped by consulting the tables of genocides on R. J. Rummel's Web site, taken from his 1997 book *Statistics of Democide* (http://www.hawaii.edu/powerkills/SOD.CHAP1.HTM). Rummel notes that he lists "each source [of statistics for a given genocide], its estimate, and comments qualifying the estimate. From these others can check and evaluate my totals, refine and correct them, and build on this comprehensive set of data." The tables and figures are given on http://www.hawaii.edu/powerkills/NOTE5.HTM#TAB. This online resource allows a beginning researcher to track down the sources of information used to estimate the death toll for a specific genocide and evaluate their reliability for him- or herself.

BIBLIOGRAPHIC RESOURCES
Library of Congress

For researchers interested in historical topics related to genocide, the Library of Congress online catalog at http://catalog.loc.gov/ is a good place to begin. The online catalog has a page of frequently asked questions and another page of tips for basic or guided searching that are useful for beginner researchers. The basic search page allows searching under title, author, keyword, and subject heading. Subject heading refers to the library's system for indexing books and other materials in their holdings by topic. The Library of Congress subject heading system is abbreviated as LCSH and is used by most other large libraries in the United States. LCSH headings are broken down into subheadings by geographical area, historical period, literary category, and others. For example, using genocide in the "subject browse" function yields such LCSH headings as Genocide Africa, Genocide Africa, Central, Genocide Africa Fiction, and so on. Searching under the subhead "Genocide Brazil," for example, yields two specific book titles. Reference librarians in most school and public libraries are usually available to help researchers with questions about finding books through the LCSH system.

U.S. National Archives and Records Administration (NARA)

Researchers interested in documents related to people who came to the United States to escape genocide, or in census records, ship passenger lists, naturalization records, and materials related to Indian removal and the Indian Wars of the 1860s through the 1880s may find NARA a useful resource. The National Archives is an independent agency responsible for the storage and preservation of U.S. government records. Most of NARA's materials are in the public domain and are accessible to the general public. In addition, the agency began in January 2007 to digitize historical documents to make them available online.

Institutional Libraries

Institutional libraries are good places to look for materials on genocide that may not be available in general public libraries. Some large university libraries have online catalogs that can be consulted by off-campus researchers. The libraries of research institutions such as those listed under "Organizations and Agencies" often have large collections of books, pamphlets, videos, survivor testimonies, and other materials related to genocide. In some cases researchers can obtain specific titles through Inter-Library Loan or request the institution to send photocopies of documents, although there is usually a per-page charge for photocopied materials as well as a time delay.

Special Collections

Institutions founded to commemorate a specific genocide frequently have special collections of materials related to it. Yad Vashem in Israel, for example, has over 68 million pages of documents related to the Holocaust, while the United States Holocaust Memorial Museum in Washington, D.C., maintains a registry of Holocaust survivors as well as a library and archives. The

Tuol Sleng Museum of Genocide in Phnom Penh has a collection of several thousand photographs of prisoners taken by the Khmer Rouge before the prisoners were executed. Some special collections are of videotapes rather than print materials; the Fortunoff Video Archive for Holocaust Testimonies is a collection of over 4,300 videotaped interviews with Holocaust survivors, housed in the main library of Yale University. Similarly, there is a small collection of videotaped interviews of survivors of the Armenian genocide at the Armenian Research Center at the University of Michigan in Dearborn.

Periodicals

Most journal articles about genocide are written for specialized academic or professional periodicals in such fields as economics, medicine, psychiatry, psychology, archaeology, and geography as well as in history, political science, and sociology. A beginning researcher can sometimes find an article about genocide in such general-interest publications as *Smithsonian,* the *Atlantic Monthly,* or *National Geographic* written for general readers, but these are the exception rather than the rule. Some students find it helpful to read a chapter-length discussion of a specific genocide in textbooks or collections of essays used in college-level courses on genocide, some of which are listed in the bibliography. The average essay of this type is about 20 or 25 pages long and will provide the reader with a basic outline of the course of events, the names and dates of major figures involved in the genocide, and background information about the historical period and geographical location of the genocide. In many cases a new researcher can narrow the topic of research after reading a chapter-length study and will be able to choose specialized journals for further research on that basis. Some general books on genocide also include recommendations for further reading that cover journal articles as well as books.

INTERNET RESOURCES
Search Engines

The Internet can be used to gather material directly as well as to carry out online searches of library collections or databases. Typing keywords or subject headings into the search function is one way to start. If the researcher is looking for a specific genocide or a specific time period in history, they can add dates to the string. Typing "genocide in colonial North America" will yield more useful results than just "genocide."

There are several popular search engines (also known as information retrieval systems), including Google, Yahoo!, Ask.com (formerly Ask Jeeves), Live Search (formerly MSN Search), and Gigablast. Each search engine uses its own algorithm (a sequence of steps used to program the search), so that different search engines may locate different sets of Web documents from the same keyword search. Some researchers like to use so-called metacrawlers or metasearch engines, which are programs that relay keywords to several search engines at once and then display the combined results on one screen. For example, Dogpile sends keyword searches to Google, Live Search, Ask, and Yahoo! Search. Other recommended metasearch engines are Web-Crawler, Mamma, and MetaCrawler.

A site that may be useful to researchers who are new to the Internet is Search Engine Watch, which has a portion of its site devoted to Web searching tips at http://searchenginewatch.com/facts/. The page includes links to pages on Boolean searching, search engine tutorials, using search engines in foreign languages, a glossary of terms related to search engines, and other useful features.

One of the pitfalls of using search engines to locate information is finding a way to determine whether the information is accurate and unbiased. This problem can be tackled by

a) starting your research at gateway sites on genocide; they link only to reliable sites

b) reading a large variety of Web sites about the specific genocide; after a while, the biased ones can be seen for what they are

c) paying attention to tone; biased sites almost always have an overwrought or hostile tone

Gateway Sites

Gateway sites are Web pages that contain links to more specific pages about an institution or topic. Some gateway sites that are particularly useful to researchers studying genocide are:

- Web Genocide Documentation Centre (http://www.ess.uwe.ac.uk/genocide.htm), maintained by a professor of sociology and psychology at the University of the West of England. The site contains a menu of subject categories on the left-hand side that includes definitions, primary source documents, book reviews, statutes and legal documents, and other resources listed in alphabetical order. Dr. Stein notes that the site focuses on 20th-century genocides and mass killings rather than genocides in the remote past. The site is updated and added to on a regular basis.

- Holocaust and Genocide Links (http://www.webster.edu/~woolflm/genocidelinks.html) is a page maintained by a professor from the Center for the Study of the Holocaust, Genocide, and Human Rights at Webster

University in St. Louis, Missouri. The links are grouped under alphabet-ized headings, beginning with Armenia, the Balkans, Bangladesh, etc. Links under "Additional Resources" at the bottom of the page include those to hate groups on the Internet.

- Prevent Genocide International maintains a page of links to genocide research institutions and advocacy organizations around the world at http://preventgenocide.org/edu/links/ and a second page of links to resources on 20th-century genocides at http://preventgenocide.org/edu/pastgenocides/. This second list is divided into two parts, genocides that occurred prior to 1951, when the Genocide Convention came into force, and those that occurred after 1951.

Blogs

Weblogs, or blogs for short, are an evolving form of online communication that can sometimes be helpful in researching genocide. Blogs began as online diaries posted by individuals but have taken new forms since the early 2000s. There are now group blogs, blogs for people in specific professions, and edi-torial or opinion blogs associated with such online periodicals as *U.S. News & World Report.*

Blogs can be useful sources of opinion about current events related to genocide, particularly for researchers looking for a range or variety of reac-tions to such ongoing crises as those in Darfur or East Timor or for updates on the activities of the United Nations or the International Criminal Court. In addition blogs can be a resource for one type of document closely related to genocide, the survivor narrative or testimony. Some blog writers are the children or grandchildren of genocide survivors and are willing to post their thoughts and experiences about the impact of genocide on later generations. The limitations of blogs are a) the possibility of bias; b) the difficulty in some cases of determining the contributors' background and qualifications; c) the short life span of many blogs.

Institutional Sites

INTERNATIONAL LAW–RELATED

The full English texts of the 1948 Genocide Convention as well as other human rights documents and declarations may be obtained from the Web site of the Office of the United Nations High Commissioner for Human Rights; the index of documents related to international law is located at http://www.ohchr.org/english/law/index.htm. Resolutions of the UN Security Council are available by year at http://www.un.org/documents/scres.htm.

The American Society for International Law (ASIL) maintains an online guide for conducting research in international law as well as databases of international treaties and conventions and ASIL publications. The research guide and the databases can be accessed at http://www.asil.org/resources/index.html.

NATIONAL LAW–RELATED

For historical documents related to the United States, the Avalon Project of the Yale Law School (http://www.yale.edu/lawweb/avalon/avalon.htm) is an excellent resource. The full texts of colonial charters and related documents, diplomatic treaties, presidential addresses and annual messages, U.S. treaties with various Native American tribes, the Hague Conventions and other international documents signed by the United States, and many other collections related to history, law, and diplomacy are available on this site. It also offers a chronology of American history.

Legal cases in the United States can be searched online at FindLaw, http://lp.findlaw.com/. Supreme Court cases, including 19th-century decisions related to Native American land rights, are available at the Legal Information Institute Web site, http://supct.law.cornell.edu/supct/index.html. Specific cases can be searched according to the names of the parties involved or according to the volume number, court, report number, and year assigned to the case.

Although the Federal Bureau of Investigation (FBI) focuses on terrorism, organized crime, and similar offenses rather than genocide itself, its Web site (http://www.fbi.gov/homepage.htm) is a helpful resource for researching individuals who have come to the United States to escape justice for committing genocide and have been tracked down and arrested by the FBI.

RELIGIOUS

Several popes since the beginning of the 20th century have spoken out against genocide in general as well as specific incidents of genocide, including the Armenian genocide of 1915 and the Rwanda genocide of 1994. The official Vatican Web site (http://www.vatican.va/) has the complete texts of all the papal pronouncements on genocide. They are available in French, German, Spanish, and other languages as well as English. The English text of *Mit brennender Sorge* (With Burning Sorrow), the 1937 encyclical in which Pius XI spoke of Nazi religious persecution, is available at http://www.vatican.va/holy_father/pius_xi/encyclicals/documents/hf_p-xi_enc_14031937_mit-brennender-sorge_en.html. Pope John Paul's 1998 presentation, "We Remember: A Reflection on the Shoah," can be read in English at http://www.vatican.va/roman_curia/pontifical_councils/chrstuni/documents/rc_pc_chrstuni_doc _16031998_shoah_en.html.

Online Booksellers

Online booksellers, such as Amazon, Barnes and Noble, and Borders, have search functions that can be used to identify and locate books related to genocide that may not appear in library catalog searches. Amazon and Barnes and Noble also offer used books for sale at lower prices through independent vendors who are registered with them. Some other online booksellers, such as Alibris, specialize in hard-to-find or out-of-print books that may be useful to researchers studying genocides in the remote past.

---

[1] Mark von Hagen, quoted by the Associated Press. "*N.Y. Times* Urged to Rescind 1932 Pulitzer." *USA Today* (10/23/03). Available online. URL: http://www.usatoday.com/news/nation/2003-10-22-ny-times-pulitzer_x.htm. Accessed August 26, 2007.

[2] Samantha Power. *A Problem from Hell: America and the Age of Genocide.* (New York: Basic Books, 2002, pp. 104–106.

[3] See, for example, J. Leaning. "Diagnosing Genocide—The Case of Darfur." *New England Journal of Medicine* 351 (August 19, 2004), pp. 735–738.

7

Facts and Figures

INTRODUCTION

1.1 Ancient, Medieval, and Early Modern Genocides

DATES	LOCATION	PERPETRATORS	VICTIMS	ESTIMATED DEATH TOLL
Babylon, 689 B.C.E.	Mesopotamia (present-day Iraq)	Sennacherib, King of Assyria	Population of the city	100,000
Tyre, 332 B.C.E.	Present-day Lebanon	Alexander the Great	Population of the city	6000 killed; 2000 executed; 30,000 enslaved
Carthage, 146 B.C.E.	Northern Africa	Roman army under Scipio Aemilianus	Population of the city	50,000
Third Servile War, 71 B.C.E.	Italy	Roman army under Marcus Licinius Crassus	Army of former slaves led by Spartacus	60,000 killed; 6000 executed;
Béziers, 1209 C.E.	Southern France	Army of French king	Population of the city	10,000
Merv, 1221	Present-day Turkmenistan	Tule, son of Genghis Khan	Population of the city	1.3 million
Herat, 1222	Northwestern Afghanistan	Genghis Khan	Population of the city	1.6 million
Montségur, 1244	Southern France	Army of French king	Population of the fortress	220

(continues)

(continued)

DATES	LOCATION	PERPETRATORS	VICTIMS	ESTIMATED DEATH TOLL
Baghdad, 1258	Present-day Iraq	Hulagu Khan, grandson of Genghis Khan	Population of the city	90,000–500,000
Delhi, 1394	India	Timur (Tamerlane), a descendant of Genghis Khan	Prisoners of war and population of the city	100,000 prisoners slaughtered before the siege; 1 million civilians after the city falls
Tenochtitlán, 1521	Mexico	Spanish troops under Hernán Cortés	Population of the city	100,000
Mystic, 1637	Connecticut	English settlers and Native Americans under Captain John Mason	Pequot Indians living in the village	400–700

Locations and statistics of pre-18th century genocides

Source: Population estimates from R. J. Rummel. *Death by Government.* (New Brunswick, N.J.: Transaction Publishers, 1994).

1.2 Modern (18th–21st Centuries) Genocides

DATES	LOCATION	PERPETRATORS	VICTIMS	ESTIMATED DEATH TOLL
Vendée, 1796	Western France	Committee of Public Safety	French civilians	250,000
Sand Creek, 1864	Colorado Territory	Colorado militiamen	Cheyenne and Arapaho Indians	180
Hamidian massacres, 1894–96	Turkey	Turkish authorities under Sultan Abdul Hamid II	Armenian, Assyrian, and Greek Christians	100,000– 300,000
Kishinev, 1903	Tsarist Russia (present-day Moldova)	Russian mob, probably state-sponsored	Jews living in the city	47 dead; 500+ wounded
Adana, 1909	Turkey	Turkish govern-ment functionaries, mob violence	Armenians living in the city	20,000–30,000
Armenian genocide, 1915–16	Turkey	Turkish authorities under the Committee of Union and Progress (CUP)	Armenian, Assyrian, and Greek Christians	800,000– 1.5 million
Nanking, 1937–38	China	Soldiers of the Imperial Japanese Army	Chinese civilians in and around the city	150,000– 300,000
Great Purge, 1937–38	Soviet Union	Josef Stalin	Members of the Com-munist Party and army officers sus-pected of being enemies of the state	681,000 executed

(continues)

(continued)

DATES	LOCATION	PERPETRATORS	VICTIMS	ESTIMATED DEATH TOLL
Holocaust, 1941–45	Germany and Eastern Europe	Leaders of the Nazi Party, physicians, and some units of the German armed forces	Jews, Roma, political prisoners, Russian POWs, mentally retarded persons, homosexuals, Jehovah's Witnesses, other minorities	6 to 8 million
Bangladesh, 1971	Southern Asia	Pakistani army	Civilian population of East Pakistan	1 to 3 million
Burundi, 1972	East-central Africa	Tutsis in control of the government	Hutus	250,000
Cambodia, 1975–78	Cambodia	Khmer Rouge	Inhabitants of Phnom Penh and other cities; educated persons; Cham, Vietnamese, and Chinese; members of Khmer Rouge suspected of disloyalty	1 to 2 million
Ethiopia, 1975–87	Northeastern Africa	Derg (a Marxist military junta) under the leadership of Mengistu Haile Mariam	Political opponents of the Derg, Christian clergy, and Ethiopian civilians	50,000–100,000

DATES	LOCATION	PERPETRATORS	VICTIMS	ESTIMATED DEATH TOLL
East Timor, 1975–99	Indonesian archipelago	Indonesian army	Timorese civilians	170,000–200,000
Al-Anfal attacks, 1988	Iraqi Kurdistan	Saddam Hussein and members of Baath Party	Kurdish and Assyrian civilians	100,000–200,000
Rwanda, 1994	East-central Africa	Hutu militiamen and ordinary Hutu citizens	Tutsis and moderate Hutus	800,000–1.1 million
Srebrenica, 1995	Bosnia	Serbian troops and paramilitary units	Bosnian civilians, mostly males	8300
Qahtaniya, 2007	Iraq	Al-Qaeda suicide bombers	Yazidis (members of pre-Islamic religious minority)	572 dead, 1500 wounded

Locations and statistics of genocides between 1796 and 2007.

According to the International Association of Genocide Scholars, "In the 20th century, genocides and state mass murder have killed more people than have all wars." According to R. J. Rummel's statistical tabulations, the democides (his preferred term for government-sponsored genocides) that occurred between 1900 and 1999 took a total of 262 *million* lives. "Just to give perspective on this incredible murder by government, if all these bodies were laid head to toe, with the average height being 5', then they would circle the earth ten times. Also, this democide murdered 6 times more people than died in combat in all the foreign and internal wars of the century. Finally, given popular estimates of the dead in a major nuclear war, this total democide is as though such a war did occur, but with its dead spread over a century."

Source: IAGS Web site. Available online. URL: http://www.genocidescholars.org/home.html. R. J. Rummel. *Death by Government.* (New Brunswick, N.J.: Transaction Publishers, 1994).

1.3 Nazi Extermination Camps and Concentration Camps, 1939–1945

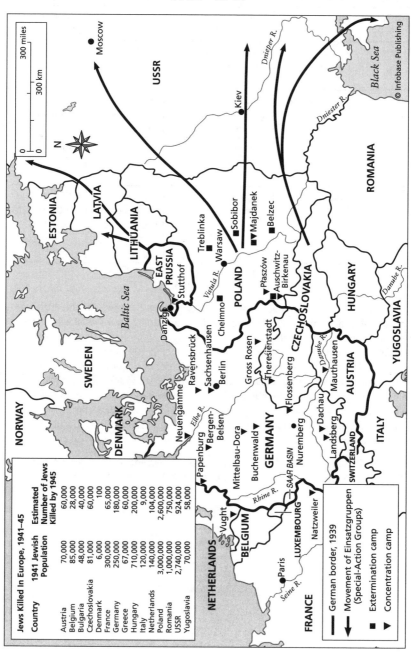

Jews Killed In Europe, 1941–45		
Country	1941 Jewish Population	Estimated Number of Jews Killed by 1945
Austria	70,000	60,000
Belgium	85,000	28,000
Bulgaria	48,000	40,000
Czechoslovakia	81,000	60,000
Denmark	6,000	100
France	300,000	65,000
Germany	250,000	180,000
Greece	67,000	60,000
Hungary	710,000	200,000
Italy	120,000	9,000
Netherlands	140,000	104,000
Poland	3,000,000	2,600,000
Romania	1,000,000	750,000
USSR	2,740,000	924,000
Yugoslavia	70,000	58,000

UNITED STATES

2.1 Sites of Human Cannibalism in the American Southwest

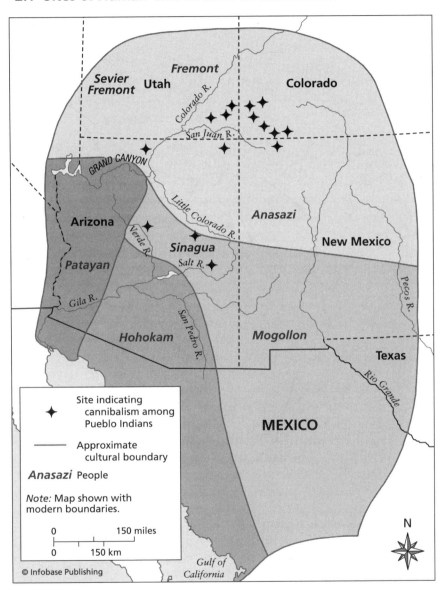

Site indicating cannibalism among Pueblo Indians

Approximate cultural boundary

Anasazi People

Note: Map shown with modern boundaries.

0   150 miles

0   150 km

© Infobase Publishing

2.2 Route of Francisco Coronado's Expedition (1540–1542)

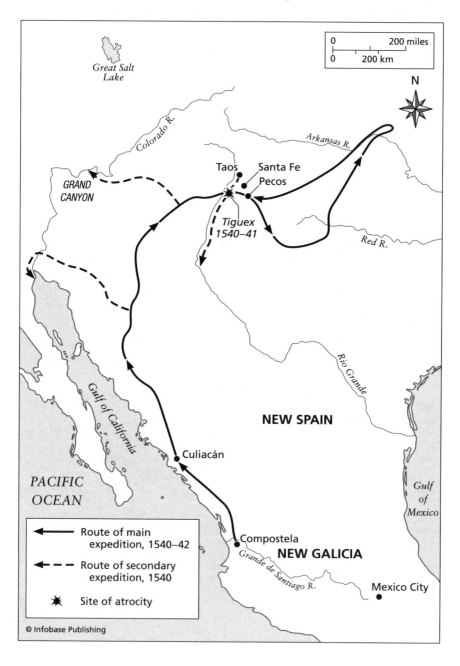

2.3 Route of Paxton Boys' Attack on Conestoga Indians (1763)

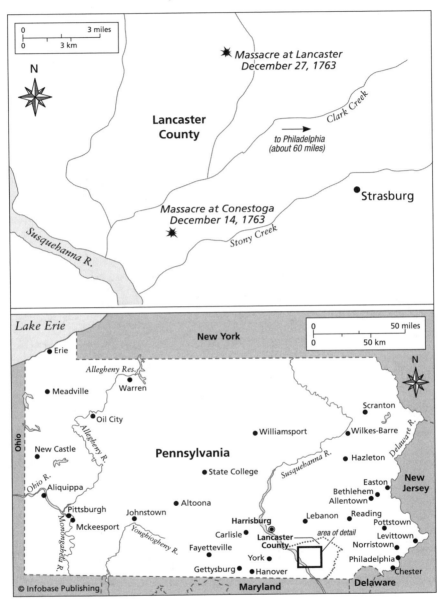

2.4 Route of the Trail of Tears (1838)

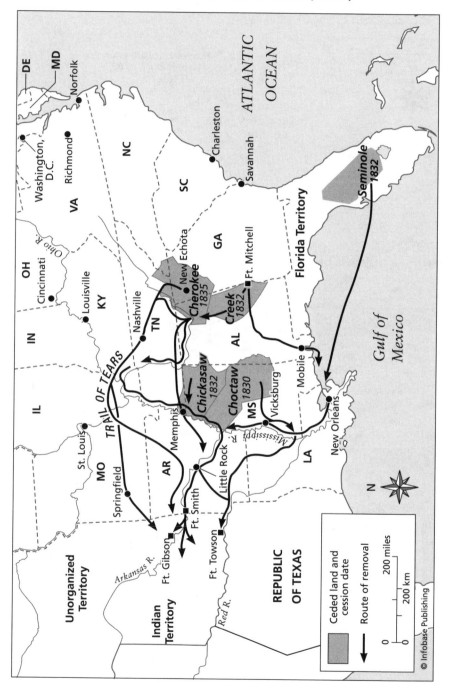

2.5 Location of Sand Creek Massacre (1864)

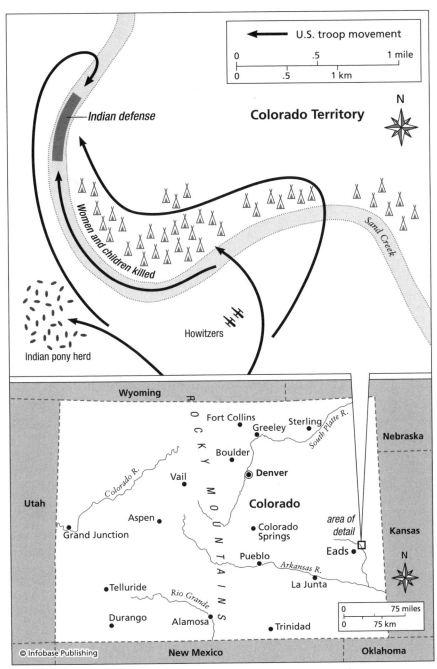

INTERNATIONAL

3.1 Mongol Empire at Its Height (late 13th century)

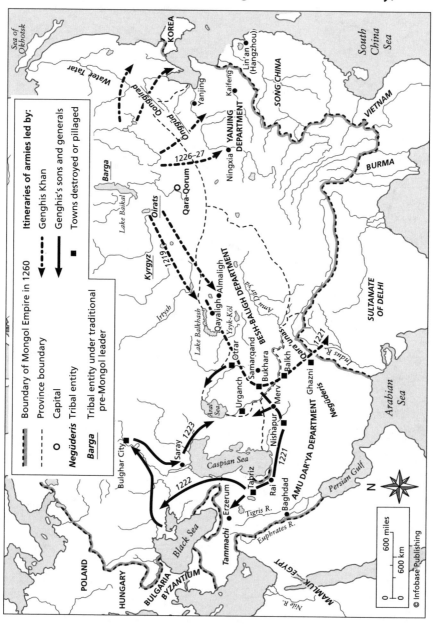

3.2. The Armenian Genocide (1915)

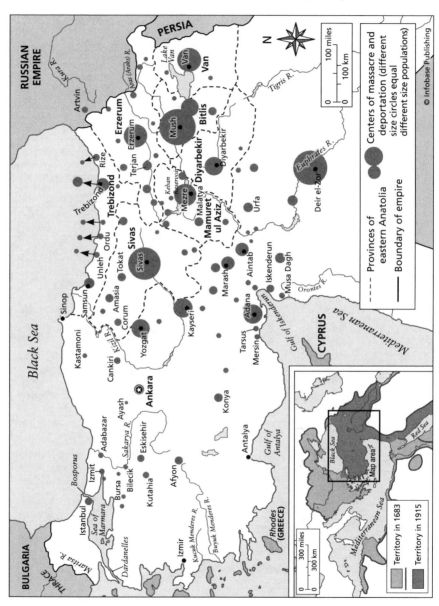

3.3 Mass Graves in Cambodia (1975–1979)

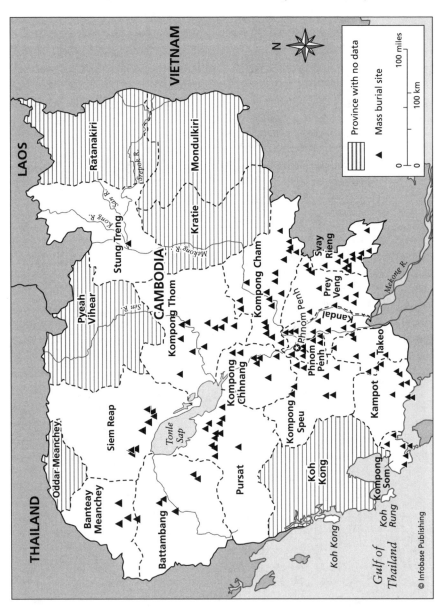

3.4 Mass Graves in Rwanda (1995)

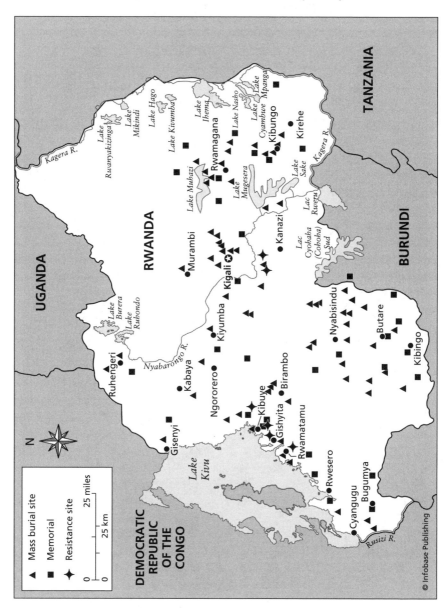

3.5 Confirmed Damaged and Destroyed Villages in Darfur, Sudan (August 2004)

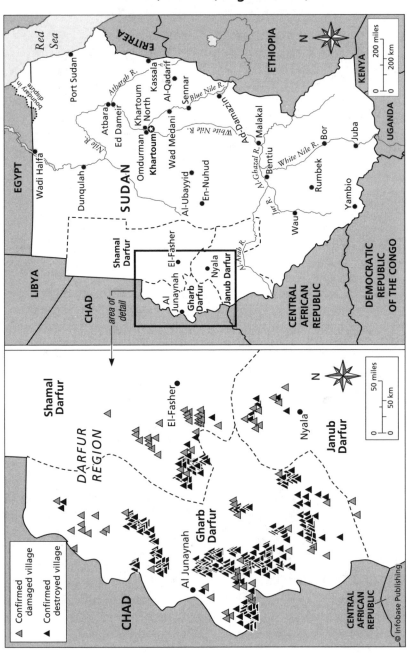

8

Key Players A to Z

JEFFREY AMHERST (1717–1797) Commander of the British forces in North America during the French and Indian War (1754–63). He is best known for his proposal to use smallpox-infected blankets to weaken the Indians during Pontiac's Rebellion in 1763. Amherst was born in Sevenoaks, England, and became a soldier at the age of 14. Amherst assisted in the capture of Quebec City in 1759 and took Montreal in 1760, which effectively ended French rule over North America. He served as the British governor of Canada from 1760 to 1763 and as the nominal Crown governor of Virginia from 1759 to 1768. Amherst was raised to the peerage in 1776 as Baron Amherst of Holmesdale. He refused to accept a field command during the Revolutionary War (1776–83) on the grounds that he had formed friendships with many of the American officers during his years in North America.

KOFI ANNAN (1938–) Seventh secretary-general of the United Nations (1997–2006). He was criticized for his involvement in several scandals related to the UN as well as his handling of the Rwanda genocide and the Darfur crisis. Annan was born in Kumasi, Ghana, together with a twin sister who died in 1991. He is descended from a long line of tribal chiefs and was educated at an elite mission school before coming to the United States to complete his undergraduate education in 1961. He holds a master's degree from MIT's Sloan School of Management. Annan worked as a budget officer for the World Health Organization (WHO) before becoming head of the UN's peacekeeping operations in March 1993. It was in this capacity that he held back the troops and supplies that ROMÉO DALLAIRE requested for dealing with the situation that was unfolding in Rwanda in late 1993 and early 1994. Although Annan was awarded the Nobel Peace Prize in 2001 for his work "for a better organized and more peaceful world," his term as secretary-general was clouded by charges of sexual harassment and misconduct against the UN's high commissioner for refugees and by reports that his son had accepted payments from a Swiss company involved in the Oil-for-Food Program.

251

OMAR AL-BASHIR (1944–)   Military leader and present ruler of Sudan. Born in the Sudanese village of Hosh Bannaga, Bashir completed his secondary studies in Khartoum and attended a military academy in Cairo, Egypt. He became a paratrooper and served in the Egyptian army during its conflict with Israel in 1973. After returning to Sudan, Bashir rose through the ranks of the army to become a general by the early 1980s. He overthrew the democratically elected prime minister in 1989 and assumed the titles of chief of state, prime minister, minister of defense, and chief of the Sudanese armed forces. In 1991 he began to make Sudan an Islamic state by imposing sharia law over the northern part of the country. Bashir is controversial for having allowed Osama bin Laden to live in Sudan from 1991 to 1996 as well as for his support of the Janjaweed in Darfur. Although Bashir made promises to UN representatives in 2004 to disarm the Janjaweed, he has taken few steps to do so as of 2008.

BLACK KETTLE (1801–1868)   Cheyenne tribal leader at the time of the Sand Creek Massacre. Little is known of his early life. He participated in horse-stealing raids against enemy tribes and was made a chief of the Council of Forty-four, the central government of the Cheyenne, in 1854. His role in the series of events that led to the massacre is controversial. Black Kettle was killed in 1868 by troops under the command of George Custer pursuing kidnappers who had taken refuge in his village on the Washita River in present-day Oklahoma.

AHMED CEMAL (CEMAL PASHA) (1872–1922)   Turkish military leader and one of the Three Pashas who ruled Turkey during World War I. Cemal was the son of a pharmacist in the Ottoman army and graduated from the military academy in Istanbul in 1893. He became a staff commander by 1898 but also participated in political administration, becoming the inspector of a railway company as well as receiving further military promotions. He joined the Committee of Union and Progress in 1905. After the CUP took control of the Turkish government in 1913, Cemal became the military commander of Istanbul and minister of the navy. His campaigns during World War I were poorly planned and led to a series of disastrous defeats for Turkey, particularly in Syria. Cemal fled Turkey for Germany in 1918 along with seven other members of the CUP. Condemned to death in absentia after the war for his role in the Armenian genocide, he was shot in Tbilisi (in present-day Georgia) in July 1922 by an agent of Operation Nemesis.

JOHN MILTON CHIVINGTON (1821–1892)   Methodist minister and officer in the U.S. Army in the Colorado Territory during the Civil War, commanding officer of the troops involved in the Sand Creek Massacre of 1864. Chivington was born in Ohio and ordained to the Methodist ministry in 1844. He was forced to leave a congregation he was serving in Kansas in 1856 because his outspoken opposition to slavery led to threatening letters from some of the church members. In 1860 Chivington moved his family to Denver, Colorado, when he became the presiding elder of the Rocky Mountain District of the Methodist Church. When the Civil War broke out in 1861, Chivington was offered a position as a chaplain but refused it because he wanted to fight. He then received a commission as a major in the First Colorado Volunteers and was promoted to the rank of colonel in 1862. After Chivington was disgraced for his role in the Sand Creek Massacre, he returned to Ohio to farm and also worked as the editor of a local newspaper. After an unsuccessful campaign for election to the state legislature, Chivington returned to Denver, where he was employed as a deputy sheriff until he died of cancer in 1892.

FRANCISCO VÁSQUEZ DE CORONADO (ca. 1510–1554)   Spanish conquistador, governor of northern Mexico, and leader of an expedition involved in the first war between Europeans and Native Americans in western North America. Born in Salamanca, Spain, Coronado was the first European to visit the American Southwest. Appointed governor of the province of Nueva Galicia (present-day western Mexico), Coronado set off in 1540 on a search for treasure on the basis of a report from a friar that he had seen a city of gold named Cibola. Coronado's expedition traveled north along the western coast of Mexico, crossed into present-day New Mexico, Arizona, and Colorado, and pressed as far north as the site of present-day Lindsborg, Kansas. Coronado did not find any gold or other treasures but killed several hundred Native Americans in the course of his expedition. He was ordered back to Nueva Galicia in 1542 to put down a rebellion. Coronado resigned his position as governor in 1544 and retired to Mexico City, where he died in 1554.

HERNÁN(DO) CORTÉS (1485–1547)   Spanish conquistador and leader of an expedition from Cuba to the mainland of Mexico. Born into a Spanish family of the lower nobility, Cortés spent two years studying law at the University of Salamanca but quit his studies out of boredom. He moved to Cuba as a young man, where he acquired an encomienda and became the mayor of a small town by 1510. In 1519 he became the captain of an expedition to the mainland of Mexico, where he eventually defeated the Aztec empire by forming a strategic alliance with other native groups. After his victory, Cortés was given a title by the king of Spain but not the position of viceroy that he had hoped to obtain. He returned to Spain in 1541 and died there in 1547, in debt and embittered. His character, as well as the factors that enabled him to overthrow the Aztec empire of central Mexico, is still a subject of controversy because there is relatively little information about his early life.

ÉMERIC CRUCÉ (1590–1648)   French monk and author of *The New Cyneas* (1623), a proposal for the prevention of war through the abolition of standing armies, the creation of a world court, and periodic meetings of representatives from all nations of the known world. He was also an instructor in mathematics in a Parisian secondary school. Crucé proposed the creation of a Council of Ambassadors headquartered in Venice, with the authority to enforce peace by arbitration or to use force to discipline any member of the council that refused arbitration. Crucé was also an early supporter of free trade, believing that international commerce would help to maintain peace.

ROMÉO ALAIN DALLAIRE (1946–   )   Canadian senator, author, humanitarian, and retired lieutenant general. Dallaire was the commander of the ill-fated United Nations peacekeeping force (UNAMIR) in Rwanda at the time of the 1994 genocide. He grew up in Montreal and joined the Canadian army in 1964. He graduated from the Royal Military College of Canada in 1969 with a bachelor's degree. His experience as a member of the French-speaking minority within Canadian military academies sensitized him to ethnic and linguistic conflicts elsewhere in the world. Dallaire took advanced courses and training at military staff colleges in the United States and the United Kingdom. After serving as the commander of several Canadian military units, Dallaire was given command of UNAMIR in 1993. He later recounted his experiences during the Rwandan genocide in his book *Shake Hands with the Devil.* Dallaire suffered from post-traumatic stress disorder after returning from Rwanda in 1994; he was eventually given a medical release from the Canadian military in 2000. He then entered a period of severe depression that lifted when he began to write and speak about his experiences. He testified before the International Criminal Tribunal for Rwanda in 2004 and was appointed to the Canadian senate representing Quebec in 2005. In September 2006, Dallaire became a senior fellow of the Montreal Institute for Genocide and Human Rights Studies (MIGS) at Concordia University.

CHARLOTTE DELBO (1913–1985)   Member of the French Resistance during World War II, witness to the Holocaust, writer, and poet. Born in a suburb of Paris, Delbo was attracted to politics and the theater as a young woman. She joined the French Young Women's Communist League in 1932 and married George Dudach in 1934. She was in Argentina working with a film producer when the Germans invaded France in 1940. She could have remained there until the end of the war but chose to return to Paris and join her husband in his work for the anti-Nazi Resistance. Both were arrested by the Gestapo in March 1942; Dudach was executed in May and Delbo was put on a train to Auschwitz in January 1943 along with 220 other members of the Resistance. Only 49 survived the war; they were released into the care of the Swedish chapter of the Red Cross in the spring of 1945. After recuperating, Delbo returned to Paris, where she wrote memoirs, poetry, and plays about her experiences in the concentration camp. She died of cancer in 1985.

J. HENRY DUNANT (1828–1910)   Swiss businessman and social activist who founded the International Committee of the Red Cross and was instrumental in the First Geneva Convention of 1864. Dunant was born in Geneva into a family of devout Calvinists who were active in social work and caring for orphans. He joined a movement of religious awakening that emphasized generosity to the poor as well as regular Bible study and prayer meetings. Dunant formed a business in 1856 that operated in France's North African colonies. In the course of a journey to meet with Napoléon III, then emperor of France, Dunant came upon the aftermath of a battle between the French and Austrians outside a town in northern Italy. Shocked by the lack of care for the 38,000 casualties, Dunant returned to Geneva with the resolve to establish a neutral organization to care for wounded soldiers. In 1863 Dunant founded the International Committee of the Red Cross (ICRC), together with two physicians, a lawyer, and a general in the Swiss army. Dunant left Geneva in 1867 after his businesses failed and he was forced to declare bankruptcy. His relationships with the other leaders of the Red Cross were strained and difficult in his later years. Dunant was awarded the first-ever Nobel Peace Prize in 1901 for his role in founding the Red Cross. He died in a nursing home in the small Swiss village of Heiden nine years later.

JOHN ELIOT (1604–1690)   Puritan minister and missionary to the praying Indians of Massachusetts. Eliot was born in Hertfordshire, England, and educated at Cambridge University. He arrived in Boston in 1631 and became the minister of the First Church in Roxbury. In 1645 he founded the Latin School in Roxbury, which led him to become involved in the education of Native Americans living nearby as well as in ministry to them. Eliot devised an alphabet for the Indians, wrote a catechism for them, and translated the Bible into their language in 1663. As a cross-cultural missionary, Eliot helped the Indians organize towns in which they could live according to their own tribal customs. Prior to King Philip's War (1675), there were 14 of these praying Indian towns in Massachusetts. Eliot also wrote the first book published in North America on civil government, titled *The Christian Commonwealth* (1659). The General Court of Massachusetts ordered the book to be destroyed in 1661 because its statement that "Christ is the only right Heir of the Crown of England" was offensive to King Charles II (r. 1660–85).

ISMAIL ENVER (ENVER PASHA OR ENVER BEY) (1881–1922)   Military diplomat and leader of the Young Turks during the period of the Armenian genocide. One of the Three Pashas who governed Turkey during World War I, he was born into a wealthy family in Istanbul and graduated from the military academy in 1903. He was sent to Salonika in 1906 after promotion to major; there he met other members of the Committee of Union and Progress and joined the party. In 1910 Enver was sent to Berlin as a military attaché and came to regard the German army as the ideal model for its Turkish counterpart. He became war minister when the Young Turks took control of the Turkish government in a coup in 1913 and married into the royal family of Turkey in 1914. Enver was instrumental in leading Turkey into an alliance with the Central Powers when World War I broke out in the summer of 1914. He was an inept military commander, however, and led the Turkish army into its worst defeat in history in the winter of 1914–15. Enver was dismissed from his position in 1918 when it became obvious that the Central Powers had lost the war. He went into exile in Europe in October 1918 but eventually became involved with a group of Muslim rebels in Russian Turkestan (present-day Tajikistan) who were fighting the new Bolshevik government of Turkestan. Enver was killed in August 1922 when the Russians launched a surprise attack on the rebels' headquarters.

JOHN EVANS (1814–1897)   Physician, educator, and territorial governor of Colorado at the time of the Sand Creek Massacre. Evans was born in Ohio and trained as a physician in Indiana, where he practiced medicine for several years and founded the Indiana Central State Hospital in Indianapolis. He then moved to Chicago, where he taught at Rush Medical College and founded Northwestern University in 1855. He had become a close friend of Abraham Lincoln after moving to Illinois and was appointed by Lincoln as the second governor of Colorado Territory in 1862. In 1864 Evans appointed John Chivington as the officer in charge of the Colorado Volunteers. After the Sand Creek Massacre in November 1864, Evans praised Chivington and his 800 troops for their "valor in subduing the savages." Evans resigned the governorship in 1865 at the request of President Andrew Johnson for his role in attempting to cover up the massacre, but remained popular in Colorado for his perceived toughness in dealing with the Cheyenne and Arapaho. Although Evans was disgraced politically, he played an important role in securing public lands around Denver for railway construction, which helped the city to become a major commercial center by the 1890s.

JEREMIAH EVARTS (1781–1831)   Missionary, opponent of Indian removal, and activist for the rights of the Cherokee Indians prior to their forced removal. Evarts was born in Vermont and graduated from Yale in 1802. He then studied law and was admitted to the bar in 1806. He married the daughter of Roger Sherman, one of the signers of the Declaration of Independence. Evarts was influenced by the Second Great Awakening, an early 19th-century revival movement, and served on the American Board of Commissioners for Foreign Missions from 1812 until his death. He was the editor of a monthly religious magazine in which he published over 200 essays, including 24 on the rights of Native Americans signed under the pen name William Penn. Evarts became an opponent of ANDREW JACKSON's Indian Removal Act of 1830 and tried to organize a group of Congressmen to prevent passage of the bill. Evarts went to South Carolina in 1831 to continue fighting for the rights of the Cherokee, where he died of tuberculosis in May of that year.

GENGHIS KHAN (TEMÜJIN) (ca. 1162–1227) Ruler and military leader of the Mongols, who united the various Mongol tribes and founded the Mongol Empire in Central Asia, which lasted from 1206 to 1368. Born in a mountain range near the current capital of Mongolia, Temüjin was the eldest son of a minor tribal chieftain. His father died when he was still a boy, but the clan refused to acknowledge him as its new chief because he was still a youth. For the next several years he lived in poverty but began a slow ascent to power by offering his services as a vassal to various warlords. By 1200 he had formed a loose confederation of several Mongol tribes, which gave him the title of khan in 1206. He took the name of Genghis Khan at that time. For the next 20 years he extended his empire eastward into China, southward into Afghanistan and India, and westward into central Asia, eastern Russia, and Bulgaria. He died in 1227, possibly as a result of a fall from his horse. He was buried in a secret location with humans as well as horses being sacrificed as part of the ceremonies. According to legend, his funeral escort killed everyone they encountered on the way to the burial site in order to keep its location a secret.

MEHMET ZIYA GÖKALP (1876–1924) Turkish journalist, sociologist, and advocate of Turkish ultranationalism before and during the Armenian genocide of 1915. Gökalp's last name is a pen name, a Turkish word meaning "sky warrior" or "blue warrior." He graduated from a Turkish military academy in 1894. After joining the secret society that eventually became the Committee of Union and Progress, Gökalp was arrested in 1898 and briefly imprisoned. After his release, he founded and published a newspaper in Salonika. He was an official member of the Committee of Union and Progress from 1909 until 1918 and worked closely with TALAT PASHA. Gökalp produced his basic writings between 1911 and 1918, arguing for a Turkey that would adopt the material culture and technology of the West while remaining Muslim in religion and Turkish in culture. His attempt to synthesize Turkish nationalism with Islam and with Western science was a major reason for his becoming the leading intellectual of the CUP. He distrusted the individualism and emphasis on reason associated with the Enlightenment, maintaining that the nation is more important than its individual members. Gökalp was arrested along with 222 other members of the CUP in January 1919. He was deported to the island of Malta for two years, returning to Istanbul in 1921, where he died three years later.

HUGO GROTIUS (1583–1645)   Dutch philosopher, poet, jurist, and the founder of international law. Grotius's book on the laws of war and peace, published in 1625, enunciated a theory of just war that included both a concept of justice in going to war and justice in the conduct of war. A precocious child, Grotius entered the University of Leiden at the age of 11, where he studied under some of the period's outstanding legal scholars. He entered diplomatic service at the age of 15, accompanying a Dutch statesman on a mission to the court of France. Grotius first became involved in international law in 1604, when Dutch merchants seized a Portuguese ship in the Strait of Singapore. He later published a treatise on the freedom of the seas in 1609, a legal principle disputed by the English—which led to a series of naval wars between the Dutch and English. Although Grotius is best known for his three-volume *De jure belli ac pacis* (On the laws of war and peace), published in 1625, he also wrote an important work in 1627 titled *De veritate religionis Christianae* (On the truth of the christian religion). *De veritate* represents the first major Protestant attempt to present rational arguments for the truth of Christianity. Grotius died in exile from his native Holland as the result of a religious controversy; both of his major works were written in Paris after he escaped from imprisonment in a Dutch castle in 1621.

AGATHE HABYARIMANA (1942–   )   Widow of the former president of Rwanda and presently accused of helping to plan the Rwandan genocide of 1994. Born Agathe Kanziga into a Hutu family, she became the power behind the throne during her husband's presidency. The *akazu,* or "little house," of Hutu leaders who surrounded the president was often called *le clan de Madame,* "the First Lady's clique." After her husband was assassinated on April 9, 1994, Agathe Habyarimana was airlifted out of Rwanda by French soldiers and taken to Paris, where the French government gave her a sizable sum of money out of funds allocated for "urgent assistance for Rwandan refugees." Although she was denied political asylum in France in January 2007, she continues to live in a wealthy suburb northwest of Paris.

JUVÉNAL HABYARIMANA (1937–1994)   Rwandan politician and third president of Rwanda. A Hutu, Habyarimana was born into a prominent family in Ruhengeri in northern Rwanda. He became minister of defense during the presidency of Grégoire Kayibanda but overthrew Kayibanda in 1973. Although the coup was publicized as bloodless, Habyarimana is considered responsible for the murder of about 50 members of Kayibanda's group, including Kayibanda and his wife. In 1975 Habyarimana founded the Mouvement révolutionnaire national pour le développement (MRND), the Hutu extremist political party that ruled Rwanda until 1994. Essentially a dictator, Habyarimana favored the Hutus and was surrounded by a clique known as the *akazu,* or "little house," dominated by his wife AGATHE. Habyarimana's regime became shaky in the early 1990s, when a group of exiled Rwandan Tutsis under the leadership of PAUL KAGAME formed the Rwandan Patriotic Front (RPF) and crossed over the border from Uganda, where they had gathered. In April 1994 Habyarimana's private jet was shot down near the Kigali airport. Although the circumstances of the crash are still disputed as of 2007, Habyarimana's assassination touched off the genocide of Rwanda's Tutsis by Hutu extremists.

AHMED HAROUN (1966?–) Sudan's minister of state for humanitarian affairs, wanted by the International Criminal Court (ICC) for war crimes and crimes against humanity in Darfur. A member of the Bargo tribe in western Sudan, Haroun was trained as a lawyer. He was the country's youngest cabinet member at the time he became Sudan's minister of state for the interior in 2003. According to the ICC, Haroun coordinated the Sudanese army and the Janjaweed's attacks on civilians in Darfur between 2003 and 2005, including mass rapes and looting. He is also alleged to have recruited and funded the Jangaweed. The ICC issued an arrest warrant for Haroun in April 2007; however, the government of Sudan refuses to turn him over to the court on the grounds that the ICC has no jurisdiction. In September 2007, he was appointed by the Sudanese government to head an investigation of human rights abuses in Darfur, a move that outraged human rights activists around the world. As of October 2008, Haroun continues to serve as minister of state for humanitarian affairs.

REINHARD HEYDRICH (1904–1942) Head of Adolf Hitler's Reich Security Main Office, Reich governor of Bohemia and Moravia, and architect of the Final Solution. Heydrich was the son of an opera composer and had a lifelong interest in violin music. After high school, Heydrich joined the postwar German navy in 1922 but was dismissed for reasons that have never been explained. In 1931 he was hired by Heinrich Himmler for the Sicherheitsdienst, the Nazi intelligence service; he became its head in 1932. Heydrich was disliked by many for his overbearing ways and hypersensitivity to criticism; Himmler, in fact, nicknamed him GENGHIS KHAN. Heydrich often assisted Hitler in gathering information on political opponents. Following Kristallnacht in November 1938, Heydrich was also given a part in the Third Reich's plans to exterminate the Jews. Heydrich chaired the Wannsee Conference of 1942, in which the construction of the death camps was discussed and planned. He became infamous for his brutality during his brief period as the acting governor of Bohemia and Moravia. On May 27, he was ambushed by two Czech soldiers who threw a bomb at his car. He died of blood poisoning from the bomb fragments eight days later. In retaliation for Heydrich's assassination, the Nazis killed all the males over the age of 16 in two Czech villages on June 10, 1942, and leveled the towns afterward.

ADOLF HITLER (1889–1945)   Chancellor and führer (leader) of Germany from 1933 to 1945 and creator of the Final Solution. Born in Austria, Hitler moved to Vienna to study art after dropping out of high school at age 16. He struggled to make a living selling paintings and postcards and later claimed that he became an anti-Semite during his stay in the city, which had a large Jewish population at that time. Hitler did not become a German citizen until 1932, even though he moved to Munich in 1913 and served in the German Army in World War I (1914–18). In October 1918 he was temporarily blinded by mustard gas and sent to recuperate in a field hospital. He became convinced during his recovery that the purpose of his life was to "save Germany." Some historians think that Hitler's desire to exterminate the Jews was fully formed at the time of this war injury; however, others maintain that his intention did not take final shape until the late 1930s or early 1940s. Hitler became chancellor of Germany in January 1933, took the title of führer in 1934, and assumed supreme command of the armed forces in 1938. In January 1939, Hitler made a speech sometimes referred to as the Prophecy Speech, in which he predicted "the annihilation of the Jewish race in Europe." Some historians regard this speech as marking the beginning of the Holocaust, while others think that Hitler did not make the final decision for genocide until December 1941. As of 2008, no document written by Hitler authorizing the Final Solution has surfaced; however, he is known to have discussed the death camps and gas chambers with his private secretary and his military aide. Hitler committed suicide in Berlin on April 30, 1945, as Russian troops were surrounding his final hiding place.

HULAGU KHAN (1217–1265)   Grandson of Genghis Khan and conqueror of large portions of southwestern Asia. Hulagu was reared to be a warrior like all male members of his family. He was sent by his brother Möngke, Great Khan from 1251 to 1258, to defeat the Muslim states of southwestern Asia that had not yet been subdued by the Mongols. After destroying the sect of the Hashishin (or assassins) in 1256, Hulagu set out in the fall of 1257 with the largest Mongol army ever assembled to take the city of Baghdad, which fell to his troops in February 1258. Hulagu's cruelty to the caliph and his family as well as his utter destruction of the city made him the most feared and despised of all the Mongol rulers in the eyes of Muslims for centuries. Hulagu was not able to defeat the Mamluks of Egypt, however, and after returning to his own lands in 1262, he was drawn into a civil war in 1263 with his cousin Berke, a convert to Islam. Hulagu died in 1265, most likely during a severe attack of epilepsy.

IENG SARY (1922 or 1925–)   Former leader of the Khmer Rouge and deputy prime minister of Democratic Kampuchea from 1975 to 1979. Born Kim Trang in southwestern Vietnam during the early 1920s, he changed his

Vietnamese name to Ieng Sary when he joined the Khmer Rouge. Sary met POL POT during his studies in Paris in the 1950s and eventually became his brother-in-law. After returning to Cambodia, Sary became a schoolteacher before going underground during the Sihanouk regime's crackdown on communists in 1963. He escaped to the jungle near the Thai border after the collapse of Pol Pot's government in 1979 and eventually defected to the present government of Cambodia in 1996. Although Sary had been condemned to death in absentia in 1979, he was officially pardoned by NORODOM SIHANOUK in 1996. In 2006 he was hospitalized in Thailand following a heart attack. He is reported to live in seclusion in Phnom Penh in a villa surrounded by barbed wire and security guards.

ANDREW JACKSON (1767–1845) Seventh president of the United States, known for his involvement with Indian policy. A polarizing military leader who dominated American politics for two decades, Jackson was born shortly after his father's death on the South Carolina frontier. Largely self-educated, Jackson practiced law on the frontier before moving to Tennessee, where he was appointed to the state's supreme court in 1798. It was Jackson's role as a military commander, however, particularly his victory over the British at New Orleans in 1815, that made him a national figure. During his two terms as president (1829–37), Jackson was involved in a number of political controversies over states' rights and the nation's banking system, but it was his policy toward Native Americans that has continued to be controversial. Jackson never publicly advocated removing American Indians by force, but he devoted considerable energy to the negotiation of removal treaties. Almost 70 Indian treaties were ratified during his presidency, more than in any other administration. Perhaps the most distinctive accomplishment of Jackson's administrations is that the United States paid off the national debt in full for the first and only time in its history.

ROBERT HOUGHWOUT JACKSON (1892–1954) United States attorney general, associate justice of the Supreme Court, and chief United States prosecutor for the International Military Tribunal in Nuremberg. Jackson never graduated from a college or law school; he attended law school in Albany for one year of a two-year program and then passed the New York State bar examination in 1913. He became a very successful lawyer in upstate New York and was first appointed to federal office in 1934 by President Roosevelt. In 1936 he became an assistant attorney general in the tax division of the Department of Justice and, in 1938, United States solicitor general, representing the government's cases before the Supreme Court. He was then appointed to the Supreme Court in 1941, where he became noted for his vivid writing style. President Truman appointed Jackson in 1945 as the chief counsel for the United States in the prosecution of the Nazi war criminals at Nuremberg. Jackson is generally considered to have been more effective as a Supreme Court justice than as a prosecutor, as his weakness in cross-examination was evident during the first Nuremberg trial. Jackson resigned as prosecutor in 1946 and returned to the United States. He died in 1954 after a long illness.

PAUL KAGAME (1957–) Founder of the Rwandan Patriotic Front (RPF) and current president of Rwanda. A Tutsi, Kagame fled with his family to Uganda in 1961 following a Hutu uprising and increasing violence against the Tutsi. He received his secondary education in Uganda and joined the National Resistance Army (NRA), a Ugandan guerilla group, in 1979. In 1986 Kagame helped to form the Rwandan Patriotic Front from a group of exiled Tutsi soldiers who had also fought in the NRA. Head of military intelligence after 1986, Kagame became the military leader of the RPF as well in 1990, when his friend Fred Rwigyema was killed. Kagame's troops helped to end the Rwandan genocide in July 1994 by invading the country and taking the capital from Hutu troops. Since his election as president of Rwanda in 2000, Kagame has been accused of involvement in the assassination of President Habyarimana in April 1994, on the grounds that RPF troops were near the Kigali airport at the time. He has also been criticized for Rwanda's participation with Uganda in invading the Democratic Republic of Congo in 1998. Kagame has been highly critical of the UN for its failure to prevent the 1994 genocide; he also caused a diplomatic crisis in 2004 when he openly blamed France for its involvement in the genocide.

IMMANUEL KANT (1724–1804) German philosopher and university professor. Born in what is now East Prussia, Kant entered university at the age of 16 but became a private tutor when his father's death forced him to give up his studies. He began to publish his philosophical writings in 1749 and eventually obtained a university lectureship in 1755, becoming a full professor in 1770. Kant's publication of a treatise on perpetual peace (*Zum ewigen Frieden*) toward the end of his career in 1795 is generally considered the most significant single contribution of the European Enlightenment to modern peace theory. Kant's proposal contained two steps: preliminary articles (stipulations that he regarded as necessary to end hostilities) and definitive articles (foundations for building peace). Unlike most modern peace theorists, Kant did not believe in pure democracy but in representative forms of government. He never discussed universal voting rights (for adults).

JAN KARSKI (1914–2000) Polish resistance leader during World War II and professor of comparative government at Georgetown University. Karski grew up as a Roman Catholic in a neighborhood in Lodz, Poland, that was primarily Jewish. He graduated from the University of Lwow in 1935 with a degree in law and diplomacy. After four years in the Polish diplomatic service, Karski took a position in the ministry of foreign affairs in 1939. When war broke out in September 1939, Karski found his way to Warsaw and joined the resistance movement. In 1940 he organized a courier service, carrying messages from the Polish resistance to the Polish government in exile. In 1942 he conducted secret missions within Nazi-occupied Poland, reporting on the construction of the death camps to President Roosevelt and other high-ranking officials. Many of the persons to whom he spoke found his reports unbelievable, and no action followed. After the war, Karski moved to the United States and began graduate studies at Georgetown University, where he completed his Ph.D. in 1952. He taught courses in comparative government and Eastern European affairs at Georgetown until his retirement in 1992.

GRÉGOIRE KAYIBANDA (1924–1976) Rwandan Hutu politician and president of Rwanda from 1962 to 1973. Kayibanda was born in Tare, in the southern part of Rwanda. Elected president of Rwanda after the country obtained its independence from Belgium, Kayibanda was overthrown in 1973 by Juvénal Habyarimana. About 50 of Kayibanda's supporters were thrown in prison and executed, while Kayibanda and his wife were starved to death in a secret location in 1976.

KHIEU SAMPHAN (1931–) Former head of state of Democratic Kampuchea and one of the most powerful leaders of the Khmer Rouge movement. One of the left-wing Cambodian students in Paris in the early 1950s, Samphan earned a doctoral degree in economics and political science in 1959. He took a faculty position at the University of Phnom Penh but was arrested for publishing a leftist French-language periodical called *L'Observateur.* He fled Cambodia to join Pol Pot in the jungle; he was thought to have been killed by Sihanouk's secret police because he did not make public appearances until 1973. Samphan became the nominal head of state when the Khmer Rouge seized power in 1975, although Pol Pot was the real authority. Samphan survived the successive purges of the Khmer Rouge at the close of the 1970s because of his closeness to Pol Pot. In 1985 he succeeded Pol Pot as the official leader of the remnant of the Khmer Rouge, a position he held until he surrendered to the present government of Cambodia in 1998.

ALI KUSHAYB (?–) This former senior leader of the Sudanese Janjaweed is a member of the Popular Defense Force or PDF. Kushayb, whose title was colonel of colonels, is wanted by the International Criminal Court (ICC) for war crimes and crimes against humanity committed in the Wadi Salih portion of West Darfur in 2003 and 2004. Kushayb is alleged to have led attacks against four villages that included mass rapes and killing as well as looting and property destruction. On May 27, 2007, the ICC issued a warrant for Ali Kushayb's arrest on 51 counts of crimes against humanity and war crimes, including persecution, murder, attacks against the civilian population, and forcible transfer. Kushayb was detained by the Sudanese government shortly after the arrest warrant was issued but was released in April 2008 for lack of evidence.

BARTOLOMÉ DE LAS CASAS (1484–1566) Dominican priest who accompanied the Spanish conquistadores to the New World, witnessed the atrocities they perpetrated against the indigenous populations, and became an advocate for the Indians to King Philip II of Spain. Las Casas was born in Seville, Spain, but traveled with his father to the island of Hispaniola (present-day Haiti and the Dominican Republic) in 1502. There he witnessed the colonists' cruelty to the natives at first hand. He was ordained to the priesthood in 1510 and became a missionary to the Arawak tribe of Cuba in 1512. He joined the Dominican order in 1522 and was sent to Venezuela, where he became well known for his advocacy of the rights of Native Americans. In 1552 he published his *Brief Account of the Destruction of the Indies,* a narrative of the atrocities committed by the Spanish in the New World. Las Casas dedicated the book to King Philip II in hopes that the king would strengthen the ineffective New Laws of 1542, which had been put in place to protect the Indians but were largely ignored by colonial authorities. He made several trips to Spain to plead the cause of the Indians; he died in Madrid on the last of these trips in 1566.

RAPHAEL LEMKIN (1900–1959) Legal scholar, linguist, and advocate for the naming and punishment of genocide. Born into a Jewish family in what is now Lithuania, Lemkin became interested in languages at an early age, mastering nine different tongues by the time he was 14. He studied linguistics as a university undergraduate in Poland and then went to the University of Heidelberg in Germany to study philosophy. He returned to Poland in 1926 to attend law school and became a public prosecutor in Warsaw upon graduation in 1929. In 1933 he presented a paper on what he then called the "crime of barbarity" at an international legal conference in Madrid. This paper contained the nucleus of his later thinking on genocide. Lemkin left Poland in 1940 after the German invasion, fleeing first to Sweden and then to the United States. Although he saved his own life, he lost 49 family members in the Holocaust. During the 1940s and early 1950s, Lemkin lectured at law schools in the United States and worked tirelessly for the passage of the Convention on the Prevention and Punishment of the Crime of Genocide after the formation of the United Nations in 1945. The Convention was finally adopted by the General Assembly in 1948. Lemkin was nominated seven times for the Nobel Peace Prize between 1950 and his death in 1959 but was never awarded it.

LON NOL (1913–1985)   Cambodian military leader and politician who opposed the Khmer Rouge prior to their takeover of Cambodia in 1975. Educated in French schools within Cambodia, Lon Nol was originally trained for the civil service but entered the military instead, becoming a provincial governor by 1946 and later minister of defense. From 1966 to 1967 and from 1969 to 1972 he was prime minister of Cambodia. He proclaimed himself president of the newly formed Khmer Republic after a coup against Prince NORODOM SIHANOUK in March 1970. A fanatically intense Buddhist, Nol was anticommunist but also corrupt and repressive. He suspended parliament in 1971 and proclaimed himself prime minister and defense minister as well as president in 1972. Increasingly unpopular with the Cambodian people, Nol neglected the training and equipment of his army as well. His forces gradually lost ground to the Khmer Rouge, who were backed by China as well as better trained. Reduced to holding little more than the area around Phnom Penh, Nol resigned his offices at the beginning of April 1975. He went into exile in Hawaii but moved in 1979 to Fullerton, California, where he died in 1985.

JOHN MASON (ca. 1600–1672)   Leader of the Connecticut and Massachussetts troops in the Pequot War (1637), and later deputy governor of Connecticut. Born in England, Mason came to New England in 1630. He moved in 1635 from the Massachusetts Bay Colony to a settlement along the Connecticut River. Tensions between the colonists and the Pequots, the local Native American tribe, led to bloodshed and the Pequot War of 1637, in which Mason led an expedition against the Pequot village at Mystic. The tribe was virtually destroyed in the war, as many of those who survived the attack on the village were sold into slavery. Mason became deputy governor of the Connecticut colony after the war and later wrote an account of the assault on Mystic.

HENRY MORGENTHAU SR. (1856–1946)   American ambassador to the Ottoman Empire from 1913 to 1916. Born in Mannheim, Germany, Morgenthau came to the United States with his family as a child of 10. He graduated from Columbia Law School and made a large amount of money in real estate. He became treasurer of the national Democratic Party in 1912 and was reappointed in 1916. Disappointed in his attempts to secure help from the U.S. government to help the Armenians in 1915, Morgenthau turned to American churches and the Rockefeller Foundation. He attended the Paris Peace Conference as an adviser on Eastern Europe and the Middle East. Although Morgenthau's official dispatches to Washington during the Armenian genocide are still important primary sources for historians, his autobiography,

Ambassador Morgenthau's Story (1919), has been criticized for its inclusion of wartime propaganda stories about Kaiser Wilhelm I that were shown after the war to be fabrications.

MUHAMMAD ALA AD-DIN (MUHAMMAD II) (d. 1221)   Last ruler of the Khwarezmian Empire before its conquest by GENGHIS KHAN. Muhammad was the son of a slave who had first gained his freedom and then became viceroy of a small province called Khwarezm, in present-day Uzbekistan. Muhammad inherited his father's lands in 1200 and began expanding his territory across central Asia, conquering Persia in 1205 and the Khitan Empire to the east by 1212. He attempted to depose the caliph of Baghdad in 1216 but failed when his army was caught in a snowstorm attempting to cross a mountain range on its way southward. In 1218 Muhammad executed emissaries sent to him by Genghis Khan, who was seeking a trade agreement with him. In revenge the khan led an army against Muhammad in 1220 and destroyed the Khwarezmian Empire by the end of 1221. Muhammad fled to an island in the Caspian Sea, where he died of a lung infection in January 1221.

NEOLIN (birth and death dates unknown)   Spiritual leader of the Lenni Lenape (Delaware) Indians in eastern Ohio. Neolin was known as the Delaware Prophet or the Enlightened One by his own people; the British called him the Imposter. Around 1761 Neolin had a vision of an angry God who told him to create a religion that would bring Native Americans back to their traditional ways; they should renounce alcohol, polygamy, and the use of European-made goods (including cloth, tools, and weapons). Neolin's best-known follower was Pontiac, the leader of a 1763 rebellion against the British. Neolin's fate after Pontiac's Rebellion collapsed in 1766 is unknown.

ÖGEDEI KHAN (1186–1241)   Third son of GENGHIS KHAN by his principal wife Börte and second great khan of the Mongol Empire. Ögedei ruled the empire at the time of its greatest territorial expansion westward into Europe. He is said to have been his father's favorite son for his intelligence and steadiness of character as well as his outgoing and charismatic personality. Ögedei's success as a ruler was also related to his humility; he knew his limitations and trusted the generals that he had found to be most capable rather than forcing his own ideas on them. His armies were so successful in defeating eastern European rulers that historians maintain that only his death in 1241 prevented all of Europe from coming under Mongol rule. In addition, Ögedei's restoration of political stability in central Asia led to the reopening of the Silk Road and the resumption of profitable trade between China and the West.

POL POT (SALOTH SAR) (1925–1998)   General secretary of the Khmer Rouge and prime minister of Democratic Kampuchea (Cambodia) from 1976 to 1979. Born into a moderately wealthy family of mixed Chinese and Khmer ancestry, Pot was educated in a Roman Catholic school in Phnom Penh. Although he gained admission to a competitive academy, he did not do well in liberal arts courses. Switching to engineering, he won a scholarship to the prestigious École Française de Radioélectricité (EFR), a private technological and engineering school in Paris, where he studied from 1949 through 1953. During his student years in Paris, Pot joined a secret communist cell called the Cercle Marxiste, which had taken over the local Cambodian student association. Pot was a poor student and failed his examinations three times, which forced him to return to Cambodia in 1953. When he became involved with the Cambodian communist groups, he found that they were largely run by the Vietnamese Communist Party. He became the leader of an underground Cambodian nationalist splinter group but went into hiding in 1963 when his name was published on a list of Cambodian leftists. His group renamed itself the Communist Party of Kampuchea (CPK) at a secret meeting in 1966. Pot took advantage of the political turmoil within Cambodia and armed conflict between Cambodia and Vietnam in the early 1970s to strengthen what had become the Khmer Rouge movement, leading to the eventual defeat of the Lon Nol government and the capture of Phnom Penh in 1975. Pot was forced to flee the country he had renamed Democratic Kampuchea in 1979 after he had provoked a war with Vietnam. He took refuge in a jungle area near the Thai border, where he continued to lead a small group of Khmer Rouge until he was placed under house arrest by TA MOK. He is said to have died of a heart attack in April 1998 after hearing a Voice of America broadcast declaring that the Khmer Rouge were planning to hand him over to an international tribunal, although rumors persist that he was murdered by Ta Mok.

FRANÇOIS PONCHAUD (1939–   )   French missionary priest in Cambodia and author of the first major eyewitness account of the Cambodian genocide. Born in Sallanches, France, he was one of 12 children in a devoutly Roman Catholic family. He began his seminary studies in 1958 but left the next year to carry out his required military service as a paratrooper in Algeria. Returning to France in 1961, Ponchaud completed his studies for the priesthood and entered the Jesuit order. He felt a call to missionary work in Asia and applied through the Missions Étrangères de Paris (Foreign missions of Paris), which sent him to Cambodia in the early 1970s. He lived among the people in a poor area of Phnom Penh known as Tuol Kork; he was there in April 1975 when the Khmer Rouge entered the capital and forced its inhabitants to evacuate. Ponchaud was confined on the grounds of the French embassy for three weeks before the Khmer Rouge expelled him from Cambodia. Once across the border in Thailand, Ponchaud began to record the stories that refugees told him of Khmer Rouge mass executions and other atrocities. In 1977 he published *Cambodia Year Zero,* a book that confronted the West with the evidence of genocide in Cambodia. Ponchaud returned to Cambodia in 1979 after the collapse of Pol Pot's regime.

POPÉ (PO'PAY) (ca. 1630–ca. 1691)   Tewa religious figure and leader of the Pueblo revolt against the Spanish in 1680. Popé was born in Ohkay Owingeh (formerly known as San Juan Pueblo) around 1632. He was one of 47 Tewa who were accused of sorcery in 1675 by Spanish colonial officials. Two of the accused were hanged, one committed suicide, and the others were sentenced to public whipping and imprisonment. They were, however, released by the Spanish governor shortly afterward. Popé returned home in anger and moved to Taos Pueblo, where the revolt of 1680 was planned. The Pueblo revolt was successful, driving the Spanish out of Santa Fe and most of New Mexico. Popé installed himself in the Palace of the Governors in Santa Fe and attempted to stamp out all vestiges of Spanish rule, from Christian churches and symbols to livestock and cultivation of wheat and barley. He also collected annual tribute from each pueblo and forced Indians who had been married in Christian ceremonies to divorce their wives and marry other women according to Native traditions. The date of Popé's death is uncertain; it is given variously as 1688 and 1691.

WILLIAM PROXMIRE (1915–2005)   United States senator from Wisconsin from 1957 to 1989 and strong proponent of the Genocide Convention. A graduate of Yale University and the Harvard Business School, Proxmire worked for the Military Intelligence Service during World War II. He moved to Wisconsin after the war and became a reporter for the Madison *Capital Times.* Proxmire served in the Wisconsin state assembly for a year (1951–52) and later ran unsuccessfully several times for the governorship. He was elected to the United States Senate in a special election in 1957 to complete the term of Senator Joseph McCarthy and won reelection five times. Proxmire still holds the Senate record for the number of consecutive roll call votes cast: 10,252 (between April 1966 and October 1988). In addition to his early opposition to the Vietnam War, his support of campaign finance reform, and his Golden Fleece Awards for wasteful government spending, Proxmire was also known for giving daily speeches on the importance of the Genocide Convention from 1967 until 1986, when the Senate finally ratified it. The act of ratification was named the Proxmire Act in his honor. He died of Alzheimer's disease in 2005.

JOHN RIDGE (SKAH-TLE-LOH-SKEE, YELLOW BIRD) (1792–1839) Leader of the Ridge party or treaty party that signed the Treaty of New Echota against the wishes of Chief JOHN ROSS and other Cherokee leaders. Born in what is now Rome, Georgia, Ridge was sent north to school. He married Sarah Bird Northup, a woman whom he met while attending school in Cornwall, Connecticut. Intermarriages between the Cherokee and people of French, English, or Scots-Irish ancestry were common in the late 18th and early 19th centuries. Ridge became the leader of the so-called Ridge party, a minority faction within the Cherokee nation that saw migration to the West as the only way to preserve the nation, rather than attempting to retain the land that had been illegally annexed by the state of Georgia. Cherokee of mixed ancestry generally supported the Ridge party, while full-blooded Cherokee were more likely to support John Ross. Ridge moved to present-day Oklahoma before the forced removal of the Cherokee in 1838. He was assassinated in June 1839 by angry Cherokee for his part in the tribe's forced removal.

JOHN ROSS (KOOWESKOOWE, THE EGRET) (1790–1866) Principal chief of the Cherokee Nation, who led the Cherokees from 1828 to 1860 and drafted their first constitution after their forced removal to Oklahoma. In terms of genetics, Ross was seven-eighths Scots-American and spoke the Cherokee language poorly; it is often remarked that he resembled ANDREW JACKSON in background and economic position more than he did most members of the Cherokee nation. Ross was born in Turkeytown, Alabama, the son of a trader who allowed him to mingle with other Cherokee but also wanted him to have a rigorous education. After completing his schooling in Tennessee, Ross served in a Cherokee regiment during the War of 1812. Although he had several business ventures, most of his wealth came from a plantation farmed by slaves. Ross's rise to leadership of the Cherokee nation indicated the tribe's recognition that education and the ability to speak English was vital in protecting its interests at the national level. Ross made several trips to Washington before and during his tenure as principal chief of the Cherokee nation, a position he held from 1827 until his death. Although Ross was not able to prevent the split within the tribe that developed in the 1830s over negotiations with the federal government or the RIDGE party's signing of the Treaty of New Echota, he was able to convince General Winfield Scott to allow him to supervise the removal of the Cherokee. After the Cherokee nation was resettled in Oklahoma, Ross led the establishment of farms, businesses, schools, and tribal colleges.

WINFIELD SCOTT (1786–1866) General of the U.S. Army and leader of the troops sent to Georgia in May 1838 to begin the forced removal of the Cherokee to Indian Territory (present-day Oklahoma). Scott turned over the supervision of the removal to Chief John Ross in August 1838. Scott, who served as an active-duty general for 47 years (longer than any other soldier in American history), later became famous for his role in the Mexican War (1846–48) and for his tactical plan to defeat the Confederacy in the Civil War.

SIHANOUK, KING (NORODOM SIHANOUK) (1922–) Former ruler of Cambodia, presently given the title of King-Father since his abdication in 2004. He has held the greatest variety of elected and hereditary positions of any living politician in the world. He was educated in French-run schools in Cambodia and succeeded his grandfather as king of Cambodia in 1941. His effective period of rule lasted from 1953, when Cambodia gained its independence from France, to 1970, when his government was overthrown by LON NOL. Sihanouk's policies varied from siding with China and Vietnam in the early 1960s to cracking down on left-wing political groups in 1966 and 1967. When his balancing act began to fail in the late 1960s, Sihanouk was deposed while he was traveling outside Cambodia. He fled to China and began to support the Khmer Rouge in their opposition to Lon Nol. After the fall of Phnom Penh in 1975, the Khmer Rouge imprisoned Sihanouk, releasing him only when the Vietnamese invaded Cambodia in December 1978. In 1982 Sihanouk became president of an unstable coalition of resistance groups during the Vietnamese occupation of Cambodia. Following UN-sponsored elections in 1993, Cambodia's National Assembly voted to restore the monarchy, and Sihanouk again became king. He abdicated in favor of one of his sons in 2004, on the grounds of failing health.

SON SEN (1930–1997) Member of the Central Committee of the Communist Party of Kampuchea and hand-picked successor to POL POT as ruler of Democratic Kampuchea. Sen was born in southern Vietnam to a family of Chinese as well as Vietnamese ancestry. He was educated in Phnom Penh and won a scholarship to study in Paris, where he joined the circle of left-wing Cambodian students led by Pol Pot. After returning to Cambodia, Sen became the head of the National Teaching Institute as well as a member of the underground Communist Party. He left Cambodia in 1963 to avoid arrest by NORODOM SIHANOUK's secret police. By 1972 he had become chief of staff of the Khmer Rouge and was rewarded with the posts of deputy prime minister and minister of defense after the Khmer Rouge seized power in 1975. After the fall of Pol Pot's regime in 1979, Sen reassumed control of the Khmer Rouge and directed operations against the Vietnamese occupation army. In 1992 he was removed from power by TA MOK. Sen was murdered together with his family in 1997 on Pol Pot's orders during Pot's attempt to regain control of the Khmer Rouge from Ta Mok.

MEHMET TALAT (or TALAAT) PASHA (1874–1921) Leader of the Young Turks, minister of the interior in the last years of the Ottoman Empire, and chief architect of the Armenian genocide of 1915. Talat was the son of a high-ranking officer in the Ottoman army and received a privileged education. He joined the staff of the telegraph company in Edirne, his birthplace, but was arrested in 1893 for subversive political activity. He was actively involved in the resistance movement against Sultan Abdul Hamid II after that point. After serving on the staff of the Ottoman postal service, Talat entered the Turkish parliament after the Young Turk revolution of 1908. In July 1909 he became the minister of internal affairs and secretary-general of the Committee of Union and Progress (CUP) in 1912. Together with ENVER PASHA and DJEMAL PASHA, Talat was a member of the triumvirate known as the Three Pashas that ruled Turkey between 1913 and the end of World War I. More than the other two leaders, Talat is considered to bear primary responsibility for the Armenian genocide of 1915. He resigned his office in October 1918 when the Central Powers were known to be close to signing an armistice with the Allies and fled to Berlin. He was condemned to death in absentia by an Ottoman military tribunal in 1919 and killed by Soghoman Tehlirian in Berlin in 1921 as part of Operation Nemesis.

TA MOK (CHHIT CHOEUN) (1926–2006)   One of the higher-level military leaders of the Khmer Rouge during and after the Cambodian genocide of 1975–78. Born into a prosperous family of mixed Chinese and Khmer descent, he originally intended to become a Buddhist priest but joined the Khmer Rouge instead in 1964. He became the group's chief of staff by the late 1960s and a member of its central committee. He earned the nickname "The Butcher" for the massacres he organized in the zones of Cambodia that he controlled and for the internal purges of the Khmer Rouge that he carried out. After POL POT's regime collapsed in 1979, Ta Mok continued to control a sizable group of the remaining Khmer Rouge troops. In 1997 Ta Mok took control of one faction within the Khmer Rouge, named himself supreme commander, and placed Pol Pot under house arrest. Pol Pot died in his custody in 1998, leading to suspicions that Ta Mok had killed him. Ta Mok was captured near the Thai border by Cambodian troops in 1999. He was charged with crimes against humanity in 2002 but died in military prison in 2006 before he was brought to trial.

RAOUL GUSTAV WALLENBERG (1912–1947?)   Swedish diplomat credited with rescuing tens of thousands of Hungarian Jews from the Holocaust. The son of a Swedish naval officer, Wallenberg received his secondary education in Sweden but went to the University of Michigan in 1931 to study architecture. Unable to find a position as an architect in Sweden, he worked for a construction firm in South Africa for several years and at a branch office of the Holland Bank in Haifa, Israel. In 1936 he returned to Sweden and took a position with a Central European trading company owned by a Hungarian Jewish businessman. When the outbreak of World War II prevented the

271

owner of the company from traveling in Axis-occupied Europe, Wallenberg went as his representative. When Nazi Germany began deporting Jews from Hungary in 1944, Wallenberg was able to rescue several thousand of them (possibly as many as 15,000) by issuing them protetive passports from the Swedish embassy that identified them as Swedish nationals waiting to return to Sweden. Wallenberg was arrested by the Soviets in 1945 on suspicion of being an American spy. He is said by some Russian officials to have been executed in 1947. Other witnesses, however, claimed to have seen him in a prison in Leningrad as late as 1987.

THOMAS WOODROW WILSON (1856–1924)   Twenty-eighth president of the United States, architect of the League of Nations, and proponent of an idealistic foreign policy. Trained as a lawyer, Wilson served as president of Princeton University and governor of New Jersey before his election to the presidency in 1912. He was narrowly reelected in 1916. In spite of earlier promises to keep the United States out of World War I, he led the country into war on the basis of Germany's use of unrestricted submarine warfare. He also instituted the first effective draft in 1917 in order to supply troops for the battlefronts in France. In the later phases of the war, Wilson became actively involved in peace negotiations, going to Paris in 1919 to help define the Treaty of Versailles and establish the League of Nations. By refusing to cooperate with the Republicans in Congress after 1918, however, Wilson destroyed any possibility that the United States would either ratify the treaty or join the league. He collapsed of a stroke in 1919 and remained paralyzed on his left side; the full extent of his disability was kept secret from the public until his death in 1924, three years after he left the White House.

SZMUL ZYGIELBOJM (1895–1943)   Leader of the Polish government-in-exile during World War II. Born in what was then the Russian Empire, Zygielbojm left home at the age of 12 and moved to Chelm, where he became a metalworker and got involved in the Jewish labor movement. He was invited to Warsaw in 1920 to serve as the secretary of the Jewish metalworkers' union. He edited the union journal and took on other positions of importance in the labor movement. When World War II began in September 1939, Zygielbojm fled first to Belgium and then to the United States, where he worked for a year and a half trying to convince various leaders of the importance of helping the Jews in Nazi-occupied Poland. In 1942 Zygielbojm returned to London, where he joined the cabinet of the Polish government in exile. He committed suicide in May 1943 as an act of protest against the indifference of the Allied governments to the Holocaust.

9

Organizations and Agencies

This chapter provides contact information for various types of groups related to the study of genocide. They include research centers; museums and memorial institutions; humanitarian and relief agencies; political action organizations; and bodies related to international law.

RESEARCH AND STUDY ORGANIZATIONS

Armenian National Institute (ANI)
URL: http://www.armenian-genocide.org
1140 19th Street NW
Suite 600
Washington, DC 20036
Phone: (202) 383-9009

The establishment of the ANI was first proposed by the Armenian Assembly of America in 1996 and opened in 1997 as the Armenian National Institute. It kept that name when it merged with the Armenian Genocide Museum and Memorial in 2003. The ANI is a nonprofit organization incorporated in the District of Columbia that collects documentation (including photographs, books, and manuscripts) about the Armenian genocide of 1915 from government and personal archives. It maintains educational programs, legal research, outreach to scholarly organizations, and publications as well as documentation of the genocide.

Center for Holocaust and Genocide Studies
(Centrum voor Holocaust en Genocidestudies)
URL: http://www.chgs.nl/index_eng.html
Herengracht 380
1016 CJ Amsterdam
The Netherlands
Phone: +31(0) 20 523-3808

The Center was founded in 2002 jointly by the University of Amsterdam and the Netherlands Institute for War Documentation, part of the Royal Netherlands Academy of Arts and Sciences. It defines its primary purpose as university teaching and scholarly research on genocide in general and the Holocaust in particular. The Center offers an interdisciplinary master's degree program through the University. It also presents lectures and other educational activities for the general public.

Center for Holocaust and Genocide Studies (CHGS)
University of Minnesota
URL: http://www.chgs.umn.edu
100 Nolte Hall West
315 Pillsbury Drive
Minneapolis, MN 55455
Phone: (612) 624-0256

The CHGS was established on the campus of the University of Minnesota in 1997, funded partly by private donors and partly by the university's College of Liberal Arts. It conducts educational programs on the Holocaust for elementary and high school teachers, hosts visiting scholars in the field of genocide studies, and assists local communities of displaced Cambodians, Bosnians, Native Americans, Sudanese, and Rwandans. The CHGS also maintains a large library of materials on the Holocaust, including videotapes as well as books and private papers, which are made available to visiting researchers.

Genocide Studies Program (GSP)
Yale University
URL: http://www.yale.edu/gsp
c/o Barbara A. Papacoda
P.O. Box 208206
New Haven, CT 06520-8206
Phone: (203) 432-3410

The GSP is presently housed near the center of the Yale campus in the MacMillan Center for International and Area Studies. Established in 1994, the program offers seminars and conferences related to policy issues as well as the history and sociology of genocide. It has supported the publication of seven books and 34 working papers since 1994. It has also provided support for researchers from East Timor, Cambodia, and Rwanda as well as other countries affected by recent genocides. The GPS Web site contains papers and other materials in Thai, Khmer, Serbo-Croatian, Armenian, and Indonesian as well as French, Italian, and English.

Inforce Foundation
URL: http://mail.inforce.org.uk:8080/
Melbury House
Bournemouth University
1–3 Oxford House
Bournemouth BH8 8ES
United Kingdom
Phone: +44 (0) 1793 78-5266

Inforce, which stands for International Forensic Centre of Excellence, was founded in 2001 to provide forensic expertise for locating and identifying the victims of such crimes as genocide, crimes against humanity, and war crimes. Inforce provides training for medical specialists from post-conflict regions so that they can undertake their own investigations, as well as sending its own experts when requested. In addition to helping to recover and identify victims of genocide, Inforce also assists in identifying the victims of such large-scale fatalities as natural disasters, transportation accidents, and terrorist attacks.

Institute for the Study of Genocide (ISG)
International Association of Genocide Scholars (IAGS)
URL: http://www.isg-iags.org
John Jay College of Criminal Justice
899 Tenth Avenue, room 325
New York, NY 10019

The ISG is an independent nonprofit organization chartered by the University of the State of New York in 1982. Its purpose is to research and provide policy analyses on the causes, the results, and the prevention of genocide. It publishes a newsletter and working papers, as well as holding periodic conferences and serving as a consultant to other organizations. The Institute helped to organize the International Association of Genocide Scholars (IAGS) in 1995. Although the IAGS is considered an independent affiliate of the ISG, the two organizations share a Web site. The IAGS meets twice each year to hold interdisciplinary conferences on comparative studies of genocide, the prevention and punishment of genocide, other human rights violations, and similar topics. Membership in the IAGS is open to research scholars, graduate students, and other interested people around the world.

International Society for Traumatic Stress Studies (ISTSS)
URL: http://www.istss.org
60 Revere Drive, suite 500

Northbrook, IL 60062
Phone: (847) 480-9028

Founded in 1985, the ISTSS is the largest interdisciplinary professional society in the world dedicated to understanding the causes of severe emotional trauma as well as its treatment and prevention. Members include physicians and psychiatrists, psychologists, clergy, nurses, social workers, and researchers concerned with trauma. The society publishes a research journal, *Journal of Traumatic Stress,* and a quarterly newsletter. It works with the United Nations in countries torn by war and genocide to provide education for policymakers and train mental health professionals in those countries to care for the victims of violence.

Minorities at Risk (MAR) Project
URL: http://www.cidcm.umd.edu/mar/
Center for International Development and Conflict Management
0145 Tydings Hall
University of Maryland
College Park, MD 20742
Phone: (301) 405-6983

The Minorities at Risk (MAR) Project, based on campus at the University of Maryland, monitors and analyzes politically active communal groups in all countries with a current population of at least 500,000. The project is designed to store information for researchers in a standardized format that helps them to compare various groups and thus to gain a clearer understanding of conflicts between specific groups. The MAR Project tracks 284 politically active ethnic groups as of 2007 along several dimensions, including politics, economic concerns, and cultural characteristics. The project also maintains historical analyses, risk assessments, and chronological outlines of each group in its dataset.

Montreal Institute for Genocide and Human Rights Studies (MIGS)
Concordia University
URL: http://migs.concordia.ca
1455 De Maisonneuve Blvd. West
Montreal, Quebec
H3G 1M8 Canada
Phone: (514) 848-2424 ext. 2404

MIGS was established in 1986 within the departments of history and sociology/anthropology at Concordia. More recently it has formed relationships with the university's departments of communications, political science, geography, and English. MIGS takes a historical and comparative approach to the study of genocide, publishing occasional papers as well as hosting workshops and conferences. Many of its publications are available online on its Web site. It is presently supported by a combination of private donations and outside grants. Roméo Dallaire became a senior fellow of MIGS in 2006.

Ontario Consultants on Religious Tolerance (OCRT)
URL: http://www.religioustolerance.org
Box 27026
Kingston, ON K7M 8W5
Canada
Mailing address for readers in the United States:
OCRT
P.O. Box 128
Watertown, NY 13601-0128
Fax: (613) 547-9015

The OCRT is a group of volunteers from different religious traditions who maintain a Web site intended to provide accurate information about religious groups and expose frauds or false information. They state that their postings are reviewed by people familiar with the subject who represent different points of view. They also state that the role of religion in genocide is one reason for maintaining the site: "[People] also need to learn the shadow side of religion: how religious beliefs have contributed to hatred, intolerance, discrimination, as well as: mass murders and genocides in such places as Nazi Germany, Bosnia, East Timor, Kosovo, Northern Ireland, the Middle East, Sudan and countless other countries." The group no longer posts a telephone number in its contact information because of death threats.

U.S. National Archives and Records Administration (NARA)
URL: http://www.archives.gov/
8601 Adelphi Road
College Park, MD 20740-6001
Phone: (866) 272-6272

NARA is an independent agency of the federal government charged with preserving and documenting United States government and historical records. These include presidential proclamations and executive orders as well as census records, ship passenger lists, naturalization records, and military records from the Revolutionary War through the beginning of the 20th century—including materials related to Indian removal and the Indian Wars of the 1860s through the 1880s. Most of NARA's materials are in the public domain and are accessible to the general public. The agency began in January 2007 to digitize historical documents to make them available online. On July 30, 2007, NARA announced that it would make several thousand historical films available for purchase through a subsidiary of Amazon.com.

Zoryan Institute for Contemporary Armenian Documentation and Research
URL: http://www.zoryaninstitute.org
2286 Massachusetts Avenue
Cambridge, MA 02140
Phone: (617) 497-6713

Zoryan Institute of Canada, Inc.
URL: http://www.zoryaninstitute.org
255 Duncan Mill Road, Suite 310
Toronto, ON
M3B 3H9 Canada
Phone: (416) 250-9807

The Zoryan Institute has two centers, one founded in 1982 in the United States and a second incorporated in Canada in 1984. Both branches of the institute support documentation and study in three major areas: the Armenian genocide of 1915; the Armenian Diaspora; and Armenia from 1920 to the present. It sponsors research of contemporary as well as past events and makes its collections available to journalists and filmmakers as well as scholarly researchers. The Zoryan Institute has produced a videotape on the Armenian genocide as well as publishing over 20 scholarly books, three of them devoted to survivors' accounts.

MUSEUMS AND MEMORIAL INSTITUTIONS

American Indian Genocide Museum
URL: http://www.aigenom.com/index.html
11013 Fuqua
PMB #178
Houston, TX 77089-2519
Phone: (281) 841-3028

The AIGM is a relatively young organization that is still seeking a permanent home for its collection of documents and artifacts related to the extermination of Native Americans. It has a small space for its present collection but can accommodate visitors who wish to see the collection and call in advance. As of 2007, the AIGM focuses on educational events: an annual film festival at Rice University, art and sculpture exhibits, and traveling displays. The organization sets up information booths at fairs and other cultural events in the Houston area.

Armenian Genocide Museum–Institute (AGMI)
URL: http://www.genocide-museum.am/index.html
Tsitsernakaberd Memorial Complex
Yerevan 0028
RA, Armenia
Phone: (+374 10) 39 09 81

AGMI is part of the Tsitsernakaberd Memorial Complex, a site that contains a large memorial obelisk erected to honor the victims of the 1915 genocide, a memorial wall, and a hall containing an eternal flame. The AGMI building was constructed in 1995 to commemorate the 80th anniversary of the genocide. Overlooking Mount Ararat, it was deliberately built directly into a hillside in order not to detract from the nearby genocide monument. AGMI presently functions as a part of Armenia's National Academy of Sciences. In addition to publishing scholarly works on the genocide and housing a research library, AGMI offers guided tours to visitors in Armenian, Russian, English, French, and German.

Cambodian American Heritage Museum and Killing Fields Memorial
Cambodian Association of Illinois (CAI)
URL: http://www.cambodian-association.org/
2831 West Lawrence Avenue
Chicago, IL 60625
Phone: (773) 878-7090

CAI was established as a nonprofit organization in 1976 by a group of volunteers to meet the needs of refugees from the Khmer Rouge who had settled in the Chicago area. As of 2007 it serves 5,000 Cambodian refugees living in Illinois, 3,000 of them in Chicago. It offers bilingual programs to assist the refugees in completing citizenship requirements, continuing their education, and finding employment. CAI also sponsors day camps and youth programs for Cambodian students at the junior high and high school level, offers home health care and homemaking assistance for seniors, and maintains a museum and Killing Fields memorial that opened in 2004. In addition, CAI offers a genocide curriculum for classroom use that was developed by Chicago's Northside College Preparatory High School.

Kigali Memorial Centre
URL: http://www.kigalimemorialcentre.org/

c/o The Aegis Trust
P.O. Box 7251
Kigali
Rwanda

The Kigali Memorial Centre was opened in April 2004 on the 10th anniversary of the Rwandan genocide. Built by a joint partnership between the Kigali city council and the Aegis Trust, the center holds a permanent exhibition about the Rwandan genocide as well as materials related to other genocides. It is maintained almost entirely by goodwill donations from friends and visitors. In addition to housing documentation of the Rwandan genocide, the center maintains an area where survivors may bury their murdered friends and relatives. As of 2007, over 250,000 victims have been buried at the site. The center's other major focus is educational programs for the children of Rwanda, in order to help them cope with the aftereffects of the genocide whether or not they are old enough to remember it directly.

Museum of the Cherokee Indian
URL: http://www.cherokeemuseum.org/
P.O. Box 1599
Cherokee, NC 28719
Phone: (828) 497-3481

The Museum of the Cherokee Indian maintains a historical museum of the Cherokee Nation that includes a new exhibit with special media effects as well as a large collection of artifacts and an education department for teachers, including graduate-level courses in Cherokee history and culture and courses in the Cherokee language. The museum is also an official interpretive site for the Trail of Tears National Historic Trail, authorized by Congress in 1987 and maintained by the National Park Service. The trail, which is open to the general public, covers more than 2,200 miles of land and water routes across nine southeastern states.

Northern Cheyenne Sand Creek Massacre Site Project
URL: http://www.sandcreek.org/index.htm
P.O. Box 1350
600 Cheyenne Avenue South
Lame Deer, MT 59043
Phone: (406) 477-8026

The focus of this project, sponsored by the Northern Cheyenne tribe, is to provide the general public with historical information about the Sand Creek Massacre. The project office is currently developing and implementing programs for the education of members of the tribe as well as the public. The project committee is also assisting the National Park Service and the State of Colorado in the ongoing development of the Sand Creek Massacre National Historic Site near Eads, Colorado.

Tuol Sleng Museum of Genocide
[no official Web site]
Corner of Street 113 and Street 350
Phnom Penh, Cambodia

The Tuol Sleng Museum of Genocide is one of the most frequently visited sites in the Cambodian capital. At one time a high school named for an ancestor of Norodom Sihanouk, the five buildings that formed the school complex were turned into the notorious Security Prison 21, or S-21, by the Khmer Rouge in 1975. *Tuol Sleng* means "Hill of the Poisonous Trees" in Khmer. The prisoners included Australians, Englishmen, Frenchmen, and Americans, Vietnamese, as well as Cambodians. Of the 17,000 to 20,000 people who were sent to Tuol Sleng between 1975 and 1979, there are only eight known survivors. After being tortured to confess to nonexistent crimes, the prisoners were put to death with crowbars, pickaxes, machetes, and other handheld tools. They were not shot because bullets were considered too valuable to be used for executions. Tuol Sleng was turned into a museum in 1980, a year after the Khmer Rouge were driven out of Phnom Penh; the buildings have been kept as they were when the executioners left. Although Tuol Sleng does not have its own official Web site, there are several sites with slideshows and prisoner photographs from the museum available on the Internet.

United States Holocaust Memorial Museum
URL: http://www.ushmm.org
100 Raoul Wallenberg Place SW
Washington, DC 20024-2126
Phone: (202) 488-0400

Dedicated in 1993, the Holocaust Museum is located along the National Mall close to the Washington Monument. In addition to a permanent exhibition about the Holocaust, the museum maintains a registry of Holocaust survivors, a learning center, library, and archives, a Wall of Remembrance, and two theaters in which plays, lectures, musical performances, and interviews with public figures are presented. The museum also sponsors campus outreach programs and leadership training programs for medical, legal, and religious professionals concerned about genocide. The museum has actively campaigned to raise public awareness of the present crisis in Darfur as well as provide information about the Holocaust and other genocides in history.

Yad Vashem
The Martyrs' and Heroes' Remembrance Authority
URL: http://www.yadvashem.org
P.O.B. 3477
Jerusalem 91034
Israel
Phone: 972 (2) 6443400

Yad Vashem was founded in 1953 by an act of the Israeli Knesset to document the history of the Holocaust, preserve the memory of the 6 million victims, and educate people about the importance of preventing future genocides. Yad Vashem's archives are the largest repository of Holocaust-related material in the world, with 68 million pages of documents, hundreds of videotaped interviews with Holocaust survivors, and 300,000 photographs. Its library contains 112,000 volumes and is open to visitors; residents of Israel have limited borrowing privileges. Yad Vashem also maintains an international school for Holocaust studies, an institute for Holocaust research, an art museum, and a publishing house that has produced over 200 volumes as of 2009. A popular spot for visitors is the Avenue and Garden of the Righteous among the Nations, which honors non-Jews who risked their lives to help Jews during the Holocaust.

HUMANITARIAN AND RELIEF AGENCIES

Fondation Chirezi (FOCHI)
URL: http://ourcongo.net/intro.01.htm
Kiliba Village
Democratic Republic of Congo
Phone (Burundi): +257 970-193
Phone (DR Congo): +243 813 201-607

FOCHI was founded in 2003 by Floribert Kazingufu Kasirusiru (Flory Zozo), a Christian minister, to build a non-killing society and protect women and children in the Great Lakes region of Africa. This region includes the eastern part of the Democratic Republic of Congo as well as Rwanda and Burundi. Four million people have been killed since 2004 in the Great Lakes region because of war. *Chirezi* is the Swahili word for caregiver and summarizes the organization's emphasis on building a sense of community in this part of Africa and healing the wounds of war. FOCHI is presently constructing a refuge for children orphaned by AIDS or war called the Farm of Hope. It also supplies war widows and other women's groups with tools and seeds for agriculture and conducts seminars for clergy and schoolteachers in peacemaking. The Web site is available in French as well as English.

International Committee of the Red Cross (ICRC)
URL: http://www.icrc.org/
19, avenue de la Paix
CH 1202 Geneva
Phone: +41 (22) 734-6001

The ICRC is a private humanitarian movement that is the oldest organization within the international Red Cross/Red Crescent movement. It is also one of a few organizations in the world that is a nongovernmental sovereign entity; it is not an NGO in the ordinary sense of that term. Founded in Geneva, Switzerland, in 1863, by Henry Dunant and a committee of four other concerned men, the ICRC seeks to meet the needs of refugees, civilians, prisoners of war, and other noncombatants in civil wars as well as international conflicts. It has been awarded the Nobel Peace Prize three times since 1917. The ICRC is committed to maintain neutrality and impartiality in assisting victims of war in accord with the Geneva Conventions. It identifies its core tasks as monitoring the compliance of warring nations with the Geneva Conventions; organizing nursing care for those wounded in battle; supervising the treatment of prisoners of war; helping to search for persons missing in war; protecting and caring for civilians in wartime; and acting as a neutral intermediary between warring powers.

Médecins Sans Frontières
URL: http://www.msf.org/
Rue de Lausanne 78
CP-116-1211
Geneva 21, Switzerland
Phone: +41 (22) 849-8400

Médecins Sans Frontières (MSF) is an international humanitarian aid organization that provides emergency medical assistance to populations in danger in more than 70 countries. Known as Doctors Without Borders in the United States, it is internationally recognized for its assistance in preventing epidemics in developing countries as well as caring for the victims of war, genocide, and natural disasters. MSF was founded in 1971 by Bernard Kouchner and a small group of French physicians, in part in response to what they considered the Red Cross's overemphasis on neutrality at the expense of victims' welfare. As of 2007, MSF uses the services of about 3,000 physicians each year. Most of its funding comes from private donors, with government agencies and foundations providing about 20 percent. The organization received the Nobel Peace Prize in 1999 for its work during the 1994 Rwanda genocide as well as other crisis situations.

World Food Programme (WFP)
URL: http://www.wfp.org/english/
Via C.G. Viola 68
Parco dei Medici
00148 Rome
Italy
Phone: +39-06-65131

WFP is the United Nations' frontline agency for dealing with global hunger. As of 2007, it is the world's largest humanitarian agency, delivering food to 90 million people in 80 countries each year. In 2006 it distributed 4 million metric tons of food to hungry people around the world. The origins of the WFP go back to a conference of the UN's Food and Agricultural Organization (FAO) held in 1961, when then-Senator George McGovern (1922–   ) proposed the establishment of an international food aid program under UN sponsorship. The WFP was set up on a trial basis in 1963 and given permanent status in 1965. In addition to providing food directly to people in war- or famine-torn regions, the WFP also works to improve nutrition through agricultural education and self-help projects. Most of its assistance is directed toward women and children, however, with the eventual goal of eliminating child hunger around the world.

World Health Organization (WHO)
URL: http://www.who.int/en/
Avenue Appia 20
CH - 1211 Geneva 27
Switzerland
Phone: +41 (22) 791 2111

WHO is the well-known health authority of the United Nations. It was founded in 1948 as the successor organization to the Health Organization established by the League of Nations between the two world wars. WHO's major task is the treatment of disease, especially infectious disease, around the world. In addition to providing vaccines and medications in war-torn regions as well as developing countries, WHO also offers technical support in monitoring and assessing health trends. In 1979 WHO declared that smallpox, a once fearsome disease, had been wiped out; polio is on the way to complete eradication as of 2007. WHO carries out health campaigns, such as a current program to discourage smoking, and compiles the *International Classification of Diseases*

(ICD), a diagnostic handbook used by physicians around the world. A searchable file of the ICD is available on the WHO Web site.

POLITICAL ACTION ORGANIZATIONS

The Aegis Trust
URL: http://www.aegistrust.org/index.php
The Holocaust Centre
Laxton, Newark
Nottinghamshire NG22 0PA
United Kingdom
Phone: +44 (0) 1623 836627

Aegis is a private trust that was launched in the United Kingdom in 2000 by James and Stephen Smith. The trust, whose name derives from the Greek word for shield, describes itself as "an independent, international organization, dedicated to eliminating genocide." It emerged from the family's experience of the UK Holocaust Centre, established in 1995. The Smiths were aware from their work with the centre that genocide is a gradual process that unfolds over a period of time. As the Holocaust Centre was prepared to open in 1994, the genocide in Rwanda and ethnic cleansing in Bosnia provided an ironic commentary on the failure of the international community to prevent repetitions of the Holocaust. Aegis presently supports the Kigali Memorial Centre in Rwanda as well as an active program to help the people of Darfur.

Cambodian Genocide Group (CGG)
URL: http://www.cambodiangenocide.org
567 West 125th Street, suite 3B
New York, NY 10021
Phone: (203) 809-7197

The CGG is an international nonprofit student group focused on study and analysis of the Cambodian genocide of 1975–79. It has two primary purposes: fostering debate and discussion of the genocide among students and scholars and working to support the present Cambodian genocide tribunal to bring a measure of justice for the victims. The CGG maintains a Reconciliation Project, collecting and documenting testimonies from survivors of the genocide as a historical resource for researchers and human rights advocates, and as evidence to be presented to the genocide tribunal in Cambodia. The CGG is supported by four universities in Canada and by Columbia University's School of International and Public Affairs in New York City. The Web site is available in both French and English.

International Campaign to End Genocide
Genocide Watch
URL: http://www.genocidewatch.org
P.O. Box 809
Washington, DC 20044
Phone: (703) 488-0222

Genocide Watch describes itself as the coordinating organization of the International Campaign to End Genocide (ICEG), which is an international coalition of antigenocide groups and organizations. The purpose of Genocide Watch is "to raise awareness and influence public policy concerning potential and actual genocide . . . [and] to build an international movement to prevent and stop genocide." The online documents and other publications of Genocide Watch are intended to educate the general public as well as government leaders. The organization specializes in assessment and analysis of high-risk situations in order to provide policy makers with recommendations for specific action before genocide occurs. It also supports the formation of a standing UN Rapid Response Force for speedy and effective interventions once a massacre begins. ICEG's member groups include the Aegis Trust, the Montreal Institute for Genocide and Human Rights Studies, the Yale Genocide Studies Program, Inforce, Minority Rights Group International, and the Cambodian Genocide Group.

Minority Rights Group International (MRG)
URL: http://www.minorityrights.org/
54 Commercial Street
London E1 6LT
United Kingdom
Phone: +44 (0)20 7422 4200

MRG, founded in England in 1965, is an organization devoted to protecting human rights and increasing awareness of the needs of nondominant ethnic, religious and linguistic groups—which may not necessarily be numerical minorities. MRG's work includes programs to help indigenous and tribal peoples, migrant communities, and refugees; it provides advocacy, legal advice, research, and training for minority organizations in other countries. Since 2004 MRG has published 15 studies on the rights of specific minorities in countries ranging from China, Iraq, and Turkey to Hungary, Kosovo, India, and Bosnia. MRG is an accredited nongovernmental organization (NGO) with the UN and with the African Commission on Human and People's Rights.

Protect Darfur Campaign
URL: http://www.protectdarfur.org/
[no other contact information]

The Protect Darfur campaign was started in March 2005 to keep the ongoing crisis in Darfur at the forefront of the world's attention. It is coordinated by the Aegis Trust and supported by the Pears Foundation, a charitable trust established in the United Kingdom by the Pears family in 1991. The Protect Darfur Web site includes a campaign statement that readers can sign, downloadable posters and Web site banners, multimedia presentations about Darfur, interviews with survivors, and regular news updates about the region.

Simon Wiesenthal Center
URL: http://www.wiesenthal.com/site/
1399 South Roxbury Drive
Los Angeles, CA 90035
Phone: (310) 553-9036 or (800) 900-5036

The Simon Wiesenthal Center is a Jewish international human rights organization accredited as an NGO by the United Nations and the Council of Europe. It is headquartered in California but maintains offices in Argentina, Israel, France, and Canada as well as the United States. Named for Simon Wiesenthal (1908–2005), a survivor of the Nazi death camps who devoted his life to hunting down such perpetrators of genocide as Adolf Eichmann, the center was established in 1977 and opened its Museum of Tolerance in 1993. The museum offers an all-day educational experience for schoolteachers and children about the importance of tolerance in preventing future genocides. The center also sponsors the New York Tolerance Center, a professional development facility for training educators and local government officials, and a national institute against hate crimes that trains law enforcement professionals with assistance from the U.S. Department of Justice.

ORGANIZATIONS RELATED TO NATIONAL AND INTERNATIONAL LAW AND JUSTICE

American Society of International Law (ASIL)
URL: http://www.asil.org
2223 Massachusetts Avenue NW
Washington, DC 20008
Phone: (202) 939-6000

ASIL was founded in 1906 as a nonprofit, nonpartisan, educational membership organization. It was chartered by Congress in 1950 and is a founding member of the American Council of Learned Societies. It is presently an official consultant to the Economic and Social Council of the United Nations. ASIL has about 4,000 members drawn from 100 nations as of 2007, including students of international law as well as lawyers, judges, and international civil servants. The organization conducts outreach programs as well as offering educational seminars for international legal professionals and publishing a scholarly journal, the *American Journal of International Law*. ASIL also maintains a useful research tools page on its Web site, which gives readers access to an electronic database of international treaties, a guide to conducting online research, and a database of ASIL publications.

Hague Academy of International Law
URL: http://www.hagueacademy.nl/
Peace Palace
Carnegieplein 2
2517 KJ, The Hague
The Netherlands
Phone: 0031 (70) 302-4152

The academy was founded in 1923 with funds from the Carnegie Foundation in Washington, D.C. It is not a university or degree-granting institution. It presently maintains a research center (open for one month around mid-August to high-level researchers) and offers summer courses in public and private international law. Its location in the Peace Palace allows students and researchers to meet judges and legal experts associated with the International Court of Justice, the International Criminal Court, and other bodies of international law currently situated in The Hague. In 2004 the academy introduced seminars in advanced studies in international law for practicing lawyers who need continuing education in a rapidly changing field.

International Court of Justice (ICJ)
URL: http://www.icj-cij.org/
Peace Palace
2517 KJ, The Hague
The Netherlands
Phone: +31 (0) 70 302-2323

The ICJ is the primary permanent judicial body of the United Nations, established by the UN's charter in 1945. It is the successor of the Permanent Court of International Justice (sometimes called the World Court), which was set up by the League of Nations in 1922 and operated until 1940. The present ICJ is housed in the Peace Palace in The Hague together with the Hague Academy of International Law. It has two official languages, French and English. The ICJ should not be confused with the International Criminal Court (ICC); the ICJ does not prosecute criminal cases but focuses on legal disputes submitted by member states of the UN. It also offers advisory opinions on legal matters submitted to it by the UN's General Assembly and by other international agencies. The ICJ consists of 15 judges who serve nine-year terms, elected by the UN General Assembly and the UN Security Council.

International Criminal Court (ICC)
URL: http://www.icc-cpi.int
P.O. Box 19519
2500 CM, The Hague
The Netherlands
Phone: +31 (0) 70 515-8515

The ICC was established in July 2002 when its founding document, the Rome Statute of the International Criminal Court, came into force. It is intended to be a permanent tribunal for the prosecution of genocide, war crimes, and crimes against humanity rather than an ad hoc body like the ICTR and ICTY, which will be dissolved when their tasks are completed. The ICC can exercise jurisdiction only over cases in which the accused person is a national of a state that has signed the Rome Statute; the alleged crime took place on the territory of such a state; or the crime has been referred to the ICC by the UN's Security Council. In addition, the ICC cannot prosecute crimes committed before July 1, 2002. As of October 2007, 105 nations are members of the ICC; China, India, and the United States have not joined. The ICC has opened investigations into four situations involving charges of genocide: Northern Uganda, the Democratic Republic of the Congo, the Central African Republic, and Darfur.

International Criminal Tribunal for Rwanda (ICTR)
URL: http://69.94.11.53/
Arusha International Conference Centre
P.O. Box 6016
Arusha, Tanzania
Phone: +255 (27) 250-5000 or 256-5062

The ICTR, like the ICTY, is an ad hoc international court formed for the specific purpose of prosecuting genocide, war crimes, and crimes against humanity committed in Rwanda between January 1 and December 31, 1994. The tribunal was established over a period of four years by Resolutions 955, 978, and 1165 of the UN Security Council. The ICTR's Completion Strategy designates 2008 as the closing date for all first-stage trials and 2010 as the date for completion of all the court's work. As of late 2008, however, the ICTR has noted that these goals may need to be changed.

International Criminal Tribunal for the Former Yugoslavia (ICTY)
URL: http://www.un.org/icty/
Churchillplein 1
2517 JW, The Hague
The Netherlands
Phone: +31 (70) 512-5000

The ICTY is an ad hoc court, which means that it was formed for a specific purpose and is not a permanent legal body. It was formed in 1993 by Resolution 827 of the UN Security Council, to try four categories of crimes committed on the territory of the former Yugoslavia since 1991: breaches of the Geneva Conventions, crimes against humanity, genocide, and violations of the laws or customs of war. The maximum sentence it can impose is life imprisonment. Although the tribunal has not handed down any indictments since March 2004, it intends to complete all trials by the end of 2009 and all appeals by the end of 2010.

National Service of Gacaca Jurisdictions
URL: http://www.inkiko-gacaca.gov.rw/En/EnIntroduction.htm
P.O. Box 1874
Kigali
Rwanda
Phone: (250) 586648; 586647

The National Service is the body responsible for coordinating the activities of the grassroots gacaca courts of Rwanda, put in place by the government to assist the national prosecutors in speeding up the trials of those who participated in the genocide of 1994 and to provide a form of participative justice alongside retributive justice at the national level. The gacaca courts are organized according to cells or sectors in terms of area of jurisdiction. They have three tasks: collection of information about genocidal activities in their cell or sector; categorizing the type and severity of the offenses involved; and trying cases that fall within their competence, high-level offenders being referred to the national courts.

Office of the High Commissioner for Human Rights (OHCHR)
United Nations Office at Geneva
URL: http://www.unhchr.ch
8–14, avenue de la Paix
Phone: +41 (22) 917-9000
Fax: +41 (22) 917-9022

The OHCHR is a department within the United Nations Secretariat. Its mission is to promote and protect the full enjoyment, by all people in all member nations, of all human rights recognized in the Charter of the United Nations as well as in international human rights treaties and agreements. It also has a mandate to prevent human rights violations, including trafficking in human persons, involuntary disappearances, arbitrary executions, religious persecution, forced migrations, slavery, and other abuses that frequently accompany genocide. The priorities of the OHCHR are set by the UN's General Assembly.

10

Annotated Bibliography

The annotated bibliography on genocide is divided into the following broad subject areas:

General Historical Studies

General Works on Genocide

International Law and Justice

Medical, Psychiatric, and Psychological Studies

Specific Genocides (in historical order)

   Genocides in the Ancient World

   Mongol Invasions

   Genocides in the Americas before 1600

   Genocides in the Americas after 1600

   Armenia

   The Holocaust

   Cambodia

   Rwanda

   Darfur

   Other Specific Genocides

Each of these areas is subdivided into three subsections: Books and Book Chapters; Articles; and Web Documents. Some areas also contain a fourth subsection, Films.

GENERAL HISTORICAL STUDIES
Books and Book Chapters

Ahlstrom, Sydney E. *A Religious History of the American People.* New Haven, Conn.: Yale University Press, 1972. Ahlstrom's history, which won the National Book

Award for 1973, has been used as a basic introduction to American church history at the seminary level. Although it ends with the 1970s, it is still a useful guide to earlier periods in the religious history of the United States. The first part of the book is especially useful for students interested in relations between Europeans and Native Americans, as it contains a lengthy section on the European roots of American Christianity, thus giving the reader an opportunity to compare differences among French, British, and Spanish attitudes toward missionary activity.

Anderson, Fred. *Crucible of War: The Seven Years' War and the Fate of Empire in British North America, 1754–1766.* New York: Knopf, 2000. Anderson's book has become a classic account of a European war that "broke the mold" of previous European dynastic conflicts because it began on American soil and permanently changed the balance of power in the New World in favor of Great Britain. The book is also noteworthy for highlighting the role of the Iroquois and other Native American tribes during the war. It is long (912 pages), but well-organized, plentifully illustrated, and written for general readers rather than specialists in diplomatic or military history.

Botkin, Daniel B. *Beyond the Stony Mountains: Nature in the American West from Lewis and Clark to Today.* New York: Oxford University Press, 2004. Primarily a comparison of the present landscape of the American West with the natural features documented by the Lewis and Clark expedition (1804–06), Botkin's account includes some telling observations about the prevalence of animal-borne diseases in the 19th-century West and their impact on Native Americans.

Diamond, Jared. *Guns, Germs, and Steel: The Fates of Human Societies.* New York: W. W. Norton, 2005. Diamond's book, first published in 1997, sparked controversy among historians because of its assertion that European and Asian civilizations have tended to dominate the globe because of their geographical and environmental advantages over the other continents. The Eurasian landmass, according to Diamond, possessed both plant and animal species suitable for cultivation and domestication, which allowed it to support a larger population, encouraged the development of cities and trade routes, and speeded up technological progress. Diamond has been criticized for what some consider his environmental determinism, although he argues that a geographical explanation of the dominance of some societies over others is not a justification of that dominance.

Fenn, Elizabeth A. *Pox Americana: The Great Smallpox Epidemic of 1775–81.* New York: Hill and Wang, 2001. Fenn's book is a noteworthy study of the role of contagious disease in changing the course of history. She argues that the colonists might well have lost the Revolutionary War if George Washington had not insisted that his troops be vaccinated against smallpox. Tracing the course of the epidemic that broke out along the eastern seaboard in 1775, Fenn notes that the colonists had weaker immune systems than the British troops sent to fight them. The disease was particularly devastating to black slaves in the South as well as to white civilians and Native Americans; moreover, because of increased contact among Native Americans with British soldiers as well as with colonists, the disease spread as far as the Pacific Northwest and Mexico before it finally burned itself out in 1781.

Hanson, Victor David. *Carnage and Culture: Landmark Battles in the Rise of Western Power.* New York: Anchor Books, 2002. Hanson's book is a well-written introduction to key battles in Western history, designed for the general reader rather than the specialist. Choosing a range of different naval as well as land battles from Salamis in 480 B.C.E. to the Tet offensive of 1968, Hanson describes the political background of each battle as well as the tactics and weapons involved. Some of the details are fascinating, such as Hanson's vivid description of the hellish conditions aboard 16th-century ships. The chapter on Cortés's defeat of the Aztecs at Tenochtitlán in 1521 is particularly useful to readers interested in the role of military technology in the disintegration of Native American groups after the coming of Europeans.

Kagan, Donald. *The Peloponnesian War.* New York: Viking Penguin, 2003. Kagan's book is a useful account of a civil war in ancient Greece that set some unhappy precedents for later genocides. A one-volume condensation of Kagan's four-volume scholarly treatment of the war, *The Peloponnesian War* introduces the general reader to a turning point in the history of Western warfare. The Athenians' treatment of the survivors of their campaign to conquer the island of Melos is sometimes considered the first well-documented instance of genocide. Kagan narrates the Greeks' gradual turn away from democratic development toward a collapse of the basic institutions and standards of civilization.

Morton, Frederic. *A Nervous Splendor: Vienna 1888/1889.* New York: Penguin Books, 1980. Morton's book is a rich and fascinating account of the long-term antecedents of the Holocaust, and as such is worth reading by anyone interested in tracing the rise of Nazi Germany back beyond World War I. Morton traces the complex cultural and political currents that made late 19th-century Vienna a nursery of anti-Semitic prejudice as well as the city that produced such major figures as Sigmund Freud, Gustav Mahler, Theodor Herzl, and many other composers, artists, and intellectuals. The author weaves information about the ethnic hatreds that festered (and still fester) within southeastern Europe into the story of a troubled imperial family. While the center of the book is Crown Prince Rudolf's suicide at Mayerling in January 1889, the last chapter closes with an eerie reference to a folk belief that Rudolf would be "reborn as a child entering the world at Eastertide. . . . On Saturday, April 20 . . . [there was] the thin cry of a baby born that afternoon. The parents were Alois and Klara Hitler. They named their little one Adolf."

Singh, Simon. *The Code Book: The Science of Secrecy from Ancient Egypt to Quantum Cryptography.* New York: Anchor Books, 1999. Singh's book is an interesting historical introduction to the science of codebreaking; the chapters on the decipherment of the Zimmermann telegram of 1915 and the breaking of the German military code used during World War II show the relevance of codebreaking in recent history. Readers interested in Native American history, however, will be particularly drawn to Singh's discussion of the Navajo code talkers of World War II, willing to use their indigenous language as a code language for radio transmissions in the Pacific theater in spite of the tribe's history of harsh treatment at the hands of settlers and the Union Army in the 19th century. The Navajo code is one of the few in the history of decipherment that was never broken by outsiders.

Taylor, Charles. *Sources of the Self: The Making of the Modern Identity.* Cambridge, Mass.: Harvard University Press, 1989. Taylor's book is not easy reading but none-theless offers a thorough and convincing account of the historical development of the modern Western understanding of human beings. This understanding is fun-damental to most contemporary human rights and antigenocide organizations, so much so that it is easy to take it for granted as the way people "should" feel about the value of all human life and the worth of each individual. Taylor shows clearly that the Western notion was gradually extended from members of a specific tribe to male members of various elite groups to women, children, minorities, and finally all humanity; and that this universality is an accomplishment to be main-tained, not a given to be treated carelessly. Readers who are particularly interested in philosophical questions about human nature related to genocide will want to read Taylor's discussion of the possible conflicts between justice and goodwill in the final chapter.

Terraine, John. *The Great War.* Ware, England: Wordsworth Editions Ltd., 1999. The book offers a brief but satisfactory chronological outline of the major military cam-paigns of World War I (1914–18) for general readers. Terraine's descriptions of the Gallipoli campaign of 1915, which he calls "The Great 'If,'" and Enver Pasha's disas-trous defeat by the Russians at Sarikamish in January 1915 are useful background for understanding the mindset of Turkish ultranationalists prior to the Armenian genocide. In addition, the book's discussion of the war's sheer destructiveness in terms of human life lends support to the theory that it made genocide in general a plausible course of action to such perpetrators as Hitler and Stalin.

Wood, Michael. *In the Footsteps of Alexander the Great: A Journey from Greece to Asia.* Berkeley and Los Angeles: University of California Press, 1997. This book is a text version of a PBS documentary series on Alexander also broadcast in 1997. The descriptions of Alexander's sack of Tyre and his massacres of civilian populations in India are chilling evidence that the ancient world had its own versions of genocide.

GENERAL WORKS ON GENOCIDE
General Encyclopedias

Charny, Israel W., editor in chief. *Encyclopedia of Genocide,* 2 vols. Santa Barbara, Calif.: ABC-CLIO, 1999. This 720-page encyclopedia, which consists of entries from over 100 contributors, is divided into two parts. The first is devoted to definitions of genocide and the study of genocide. The essays in this part deal primarily with the use of such concepts as democide and the significance of the Holocaust. The second part of the encyclopedia consists of an alphabetical list of genocidal events from the Adana massacre of 1909 to mass killings in the former Yugoslavia. The editor is the executive director of the Institute on the Holocaust and Genocide in Jerusalem and one of the cofounders of the International As-sociation of Genocide Scholars.

Horvitz, Leslie Alan, and Christopher Catherwood. *Encyclopedia of War Crimes and Genocide.* New York: Facts On File, 2006. This is a concise one-volume encyclopedia for general readers with over 400 entries arranged alphabetically, an introduction, and appendices. The first author is a freelance writer who specializes in scientific and medical topics. The second author is an instructor at the University of Richmond's School for Continuing Education who has written several books on 20th-century history and church history.

Shelton, Dinah L., editor in chief. *Encyclopedia of Genocide and Crimes against Humanity*, 3 vols. Detroit, Mich.: Macmillan Reference, 2005. This three-volume encyclopedia covers events and judicial decisions up through 2004, thus including more recent material than Charny's 1999 work. It also covers a wider range of groups and topics, including entries on such subjects as videotaped testimonies, banned and stolen art, and hate speech. The entries are all arranged alphabetically rather than divided into sections. The writing is academic in tone rather than popular and is aimed at educated adult readers. The editor is currently a professor of international law at the George Washington University Law School.

Books and Book Chapters

Bartov, Omer. "Seeking the Roots of Modern Genocide: On the Macro- and Micro-history of Mass Murder." In *The Specter of Genocide: Mass Murder in Historical Perspective*, edited by Robert Gellately and Ben Kiernan. New York: Cambridge University Press, 2003, pp. 75–96. Bartov's chapter discusses both the positive aspects and the drawbacks of comparing different genocides. He notes that the comparative approach often leads to misguided political conclusions about the material being studied and that it also does not shed much light on the involvement of smaller communities in genocides. He suggests adding what he terms community studies to the investigation of large-scale genocides in order to understand better how genocidal policies designed at the top levels of a government are actually put in place at the local level.

Gellately, Robert, and Ben Kiernan. "Investigating Genocide." In *The Specter of Genocide: Mass Murder in Historical Perspective*, edited by Robert Gellately and Ben Kiernan. New York: Cambridge University Press, 2003, pp. 373–380. This chapter outlines the various definitions and legal principles involved in the study of genocide as well as the different approaches a researcher can take to study the subject. It is useful to the general reader just beginning to study genocide.

Jones, Adam. *Genocide: A Comprehensive Introduction.* New York: Routledge, 2006. Designed as a college-level textbook for the study of genocide, this introduction provides the reader with a general introduction and overview of the causes of genocide, background information and a chronology of events of major genocides, and some chapters at the end on gendercide, the sociology and anthropology of genocide, psychological studies of genocide, and international justice. The maps are particularly useful for readers unfamiliar with the geography of the countries involved.

Power, Samantha. *A Problem from Hell: America and the Age of Genocide.* New York: Basic Books, 2002. Power's book has become standard reading for students of 20th-century genocides; it was awarded a Pulitzer Prize in nonfiction as well as the Raphael Lemkin Award from the Institute for the Study of Genocide. Power, currently director of the Carr Center for Human Rights Policy at Harvard, began her career as a war correspondent in the Balkans and later became an academic analyst, not only of genocide itself, but also of the psychological as well as political reasons underlying governmental reluctance to intervene. *A Problem from Hell* has been called a "damning" book, but Power is just as unsparing in her criticism of the media's role in downplaying atrocities as of the government's repeated refusals to take direct action in Armenia, the Holocaust, Cambodia, Bosnia, and Rwanda. Her chapter on Raphael Lemkin is required reading for anyone interested in his role in defining genocide and placing it on the agenda of international justice.

Rosenbaum, Alan S. *Is the Holocaust Unique? Perspectives on Comparative Genocide*, 2nd ed. Boulder, Colo.: Westview Press, 2001. Rosenbaum's collection of essays has been controversial since the first edition was published in 1995 because he allowed his contributors "to speak in a wholly uncensored or even uncorrected way." This generosity allows the reader to encounter a wide variety of viewpoints on "this ongoing and sometimes impassioned debate." Some essays may irritate or provoke readers, but even the more challenging or abrasive contributions compel one to think through one's own position at a deeper level.

Rummel, R. J. *Death by Government.* New Brunswick, N.J.: Transaction Publishers, 1994. Rummel is a professor emeritus of political science at the University of Hawaii who coined the term *democide*, explained in this book, to describe mass murder by government. Rummel's studies of death by government have led to what some call Rummel's Law, namely the statistic that six times as many people died at the hands of their own governments during the 20th century as were killed in combat. Rummel has noted that "if all these bodies [of 20th-century victims of democide] were laid head to toe, with the average height being 5', then they would circle the earth ten times. Also, this democide murdered 6 times more people than died in combat in all the foreign and internal wars of the century. Finally, given popular estimates of the dead in a major nuclear war, this total democide is as though such a war did occur, but with its dead spread over a century."

Stannard, David E. "Uniqueness as Denial: The Politics of Genocide Scholarship." In *Is the Holocaust Unique? Perspectives on Comparative Genocide*, 2nd ed., edited by Allan S. Rosenbaum, pp. 245–290. Boulder, Colo.: Westview Press, 2001. Stannard's chapter is an attack on scholars who consider the Holocaust as morally as well as historically unique.

Print Articles

Darity, W. A., and C. B. Turner. "Family Planning, Race Consciousness, and the Fear of Race Genocide." *American Journal of Public Health* 62 (1972): pp. 1,454–1,459. This article has been cited in medical journals as an example of the misuse of the term *genocide*.

Web Documents

Fussell, Jim. "Group Classification on National ID Cards as a Factor in Genocide and Ethnic Cleansing." Seminar presentation, Yale University Genocide Studies Program,

November 15, 2001. Available online. URL: http://www.preventgenocide.org/prevent/removing-facilitating-factors/IDcards/. Accessed August 15, 2007. Fussell's presentation is an instructive analysis of the ways in which national ID cards can be abused to facilitate genocide when they include information about the bearer's religious or ethnic identity. The outstanding examples that he cites are Germany during the Holocaust and Rwanda in 1994. Fussell documents contemporary instances in a number of countries in which members of specific groups may be identified by religion or ethnicity on the ID card itself, be required to carry an additional ID card conveying this information, or be given an ID card of a distinctive color. His point is not that ID cards as such are a precondition of genocide but that they can heighten awareness of group differences and thereby increase the likelihood of polarization between groups within troubled societies.

Jonassohn, Kurt. "How I Came to the Study of Genocide." Montreal Institute for Genocide and Human Rights Studies (MIGS) Occasional Papers, September 1998. Available online. URL: http://migs.concordia.ca/occpapers/study.html. Accessed 1/8/2007. This is Jonassohn's personal account of his background as a Jew in Cologne, Germany, in the 1930s, his studies in London during World War II, and his move to Canada and eventual foundation of the Montreal Institute for Genocide and Human Rights Studies (MIGS).

Lemkin, Raphael. "Genocide." *American Scholar* 15 (April 1946): pp. 227–230. Available online. URL: http://www.preventgenocide.org/lemkin/americanscholar1946.htm. Accessed March 9, 2007. This is Lemkin's detailed discussion of genocide for the educated public, first published after World War II.

———. "Genocide—A Modern Crime." *Free World* 4 (April 1945): pp. 39–43. Available online. URL: http://www.preventgenocide.org/lemkin/freeworld1945.htm. Accessed March 9, 2007. This is an online version of an article Lemkin wrote for the general public a year before his longer article in *American Scholar.*

Stanton, Gregory H. "The Eight Stages of Genocide." Available online. URL: http://www.genocidewatch.org/eightstages.htm. Accessed March 1, 2007. Stanton's typology of the eight stages of genocide has been frequently reproduced in various books and research papers and is worth noting even though the reader will find that relatively few genocides in history fit neatly into the eight stages.

Sylva, Douglas A. "The Lost Girls." *Weekly Standard* (3/21/07). Available online. URL: http://www.theweeklystandard.com/Content/Public/Articles/000/000/013/415gcfae.asp. Accessed March 28, 2007. Sylva is reporting on an instance of gendercide—here, the selective abortion and infanticide of female children in China and India—and the reluctance of the UN to condemn it because abortion rights are seen as more important than saving the lives of girls.

INTERNATIONAL LAW AND JUSTICE
Books and Book Chapters

Kuper, Leo. "The United States Ratifies the Genocide Convention." In *The History and Sociology of Genocide: Analyses and Case Studies,* edited by Frank Chalk and Kurt

Jonassohn, pp. 422–425. New Haven, Conn.: Yale University Press, 1990. Kuper's essay, reprinted from *Internet and the Holocaust and Genocide* (1989), makes the point that ratification of the Genocide Convention by itself is meaningless without meaningful provision for punishment of offenders. Since the Convention, in Kuper's opinion, lacks realistic provisions for punishment, the United States should use its resources as a superpower to prevent genocides from occurring. Kuper's specific suggestions include restraining trade with offending governments or withholding foreign aid.

Web Documents

Bolton, John H. "American Justice and the International Criminal Court." (11/3/03). Available online. URL: http://www.state.gov/t/us/rm/25818.htm. Accessed April 12, 2007. Written before Bolton's appointment as the United States' representative to the UN, this transcript of his remarks to the American Enterprise Institute outline the position that giving jurisdiction over Americans abroad to the ICC "runs contrary to fundamental American precepts and basic Constitutional principles of popular sovereignty, checks and balances, and national independence."

Kissinger, Henry. "The Pitfalls of Universal Jurisdiction: Risking Judicial Tyranny." *Foreign Affairs* (July/August 2001). Available online. URL: http://www.globalpolicy.org/intljustice/general/2001/07kiss.htm. Accessed April 12, 2007. Kissinger's article makes a distinction between the application of universal standards of justice to such crimes as genocide and the concept of universal jurisdiction for the International Criminal Court, which he considers open to abuse. As he sees it, the present structure of the ICC allows for "legal principles to be used as weapons to settle political scores." He also calls attention to President Clinton's reservations about the ICC.

Rehnquist, William H. "Remarks of the Chief Justice, American Law Institute Annual Meeting." (5/17/04). Available online. URL: http://www.supremecourtus.gov/publicinfo/speeches/sp_05-17-04a.html. Accessed April 12, 2007. Rehnquist's address is a helpful summary of Robert Jackson's role as a prosecutor in the Nuremberg war crimes trials of 1946 as well as a thoughtful analysis of the importance of Jackson's work.

Roosevelt, Grace. "A Brief History of the Quest for Peace: Pacifism and Just War Theory in Europe from the 16th to the 20th Centuries." Available online. URL: http://www.globalpolicy.org/reform/intro/1999jinx.htm. Accessed April 4, 2007. A readable and useful introduction and summary for general readers unfamiliar with the medieval and early modern background of just war theory and pacifist thought.

Stanton, Gregory H. "The Cambodian Genocide and International Law." Monograph #41, Yale University Southeast Asia Studies. New Haven, Conn.: Yale University, 1993. Available online. URL: http://www.genocidewatch.org/THE%20CAMBODIAN%20GENOCIDE%20AND%20INTERNATIONAL%20LAW.htm. Accessed January 20, 2007. Although the international justice system has moved forward in regard to Cambodia since this article was written, it is still a good example of the way in which each new instance of genocide forces people to reexamine the present state of international law and suggest improvements.

——. "Perfection Is the Enemy of Justice: A Response to Amnesty International's Critique of the Draft Agreement between the U.N. and Cambodia." *Bangkok Post* (2003). Available online. URL: http://www.yale.edu/cgp/resources.html. Accessed January 20, 2007. In this article Stanton maintains that genocide trials in Cambodia should proceed as rapidly as possible so that justice can be done before the death of the perpetrators, rather than waiting for a "perfect" international court or tribunal to be structured.

MEDICAL, PSYCHIATRIC, AND PSYCHOLOGICAL STUDIES
Books and Book Chapters

Baumeister, Roy F. *Evil: Inside Human Violence and Cruelty.* New York: W. H. Freeman and Co., 1999. The author is currently president of the American Psychological Association (APA). Baumeister's book represents a social scientist's attempt to understand evil, including genocide, from actual incidents rather than literature or films. His main purpose is "to understand the causal processes that produce evil actions." In order to do this, Baumeister calls attention to what he calls "the magnitude gap," that is, the vast difference between victims' and perpetrators' view of genocide and other evil deeds. He maintains that understanding the causality of evil, one must begin with the perpetrator's perspective, which minimizes or trivializes the consequences of the act. Further, he argues that an important mechanism leading to genocide is the inaction and silence of bystanders: "The lack of response by bystanders is often a crucial factor in the promotion of evil, and victims [of genocide] at least can recognize this fact."

Beck, Aaron T. *Prisoners of Hate: The Cognitive Basis of Anger, Hostility, and Violence.* New York: HarperCollins, 1999. Dr. Beck is well known for his development of cognitive-behavioral therapy as a treatment for depression. In this book he seeks to extend his clinical findings to the treatment of violence. Beck deals with group as well as individual disturbances, describing what he calls "collective illusions" in chapter 9. He maintains that groups are more likely than individuals to stereotype others to the point of creating massive misperceptions of them. On the basis of his clinical experience with paranoid patients, Beck regards the outer display of hate and hostility in members of extremist and genocidal groups as a cover for inner vulnerability. He recommends the training of a new generation of psychologists and psychiatrists to deal specifically with genocide, ethnic cleansing, and other forms of violence between ethnic, racial, or political groups.

Blass, Thomas. *The Man Who Shocked the World: The Life and Legacy of Stanley Milgram.* New York: Basic Books, 2004. Blass's book is the first full-length biography of Stanley Milgram, the professor of psychology whose experiments on obedience in the early 1960s led to disturbing conclusions about the effectiveness of moral principles in the face of social pressure. Milgram, who was a Jew, was drawn to investigate the question of obedience to authority by reading about the Holocaust.

Gaylin, Willard. *The Rage Within: Anger in Modern Life.* New York: Simon & Schuster, Inc., 1984. Gaylin, a psychiatrist, describes the structures in the central nervous system and the biochemistry involved in human anger as well as the social forces in the modern world that trigger anger in humans. Gaylin's central notion is that anger is a major problem in modern societies because of the number of factors that stimulate it (envy, perceptions of injustice and inequality, the rise in street crime, reduced sources of pride and feelings of competence, and many others) and the comparatively small number of socially acceptable outlets for it.

Herman, Judith, M.D. *Trauma and Recovery,* 2nd ed. New York: Basic Books, 1999. The author is a clinical professor of psychiatry at Harvard Medical School specializing in the treatment of victims of genocide as well as other forms of violence. The book outlines the steps in the treatment and recovery of severely traumatized persons.

Laub, Dori, M.D. "Bearing Witness or the Vicissitudes of Listening." In Shoshana Felman and Dori Laub, M.D., *Testimony: Crises of Witnessing in Literature, Psychoanalysis, and History,* New York: Routledge, 1992, pp. 57–74. Dr. Laub was a child survivor of the Holocaust who is presently a clinical professor of psychiatry specializing in the treatment of Holocaust survivors and other victims of massive psychological trauma. He discusses the accounts of survivors as a form of testimony or witness; that is, as "testifying . . . to the very secret of survival and of resistance to extermination" even when the accounts may contain historical inaccuracies in some of their details. The remainder of the chapter analyzes the therapist's task as listener, the survivor's fear that the traumatic events will recur, and the hazards for the therapist in confronting his or her own reactions to the survivor's testimony.

Lifton, Robert J. *Destroying the World to Save It: Aum Shinrikyō, Apocalyptic Violence, and the New Global Terrorism.* New York: Henry Holt and Co., 2000. Dr. Lifton is a well-known professor of psychiatry who has written several books on the psychological problems of people in the modern era, including studies of Nazi doctors, survivors of Hiroshima, and Vietnam veterans. This book on the Aum Shinrikyō cult in Japan deals not only with the role of the guru in such a group but also with the group's fascination with death and apocalyptic violence, expressed as a collective "urge to kill the world." Lifton introduced the term *omnicide,* a word he coined to describe the wish to kill everyone in the world, in this book.

———. *The Nazi Doctors: Medical Killing and the Psychology of Genocide.* New York: Basic Books, 2002. Lifton's study of the physicians involved in medical experiments under Hitler's regime was first published in 1986. Taking his material from interviews with the accused doctors as well as archival records, Lifton traced the identification of mass murder as a form of "healing" the body of the German nation from the Nazis' sterilization and euthanasia of their own citizens in the 1930s to mass extermination of European Jews and other 'racial undesirables.' His account of the psychological process of "doubling," which allowed doctors who were not basically mentally ill to rationalize experimentation on and eventual killing of human beings, is widely used to explain the participation of highly educated professionals in genocide.

Nafte, Myriam. *Flesh and Bone: An Introduction to Forensic Anthropology.* Durham, N.C.: Carolina Academic Press, 2002. Nafte's book is an introduction to the basic techniques used to identify the victims of a genocide or other disaster as well as determine the cause of death.

Wexler, Bruce E., M.D. *Brain and Culture: Neurobiology, Ideology, and Social Change.* Cambridge, Mass.: MIT Press, 2006. Wexler's book is an attempt to pull together recent discoveries about the human nervous system to explain the way people interact with their environments and their need to keep their external environments aligned with their internal psychological structures. He maintains that much of the genocidal conflict in the world since the beginning of the 20th century is the outcome of "battles for control of the cultural environment"—people "fight for the opportunity to create external structures that fit with their internal structures, and to prevent others from filling their environments with structures and stimulation that conflict with their internal structures." The book is not easy reading because it is filled with technical terms, but offers considerable food for thought.

Print Articles

Courtois, Christine, Ph.D. "Vicarious Traumatization of the Therapist." *National Center for PTSD Newsletter* (Spring 1993), pp. 8–9. This article is one of the earliest reports of post-traumatic stress among therapists treating victims of genocide and other mass disasters.

Palm, K. M., M. A. Polusny, and V. M. Follette. "Vicarious Traumatization: Potential Hazards and Interventions for Disaster and Trauma Workers." *Prehospital Disaster Medicine* 19 (January–March 2004), pp. 73–78. This article is a report on the high levels of post-traumatic stress disorder among rescue workers after genocides as well as other large-scale disasters. It also discusses suggestions for lowering the risk of PTSD among rescuers.

Pham, P. N., H. M. Weinstein, and T. Longman. "Trauma and PTSD Symptoms in Rwanda: Implications for Attitudes toward Justice and Reconciliation." *Journal of the American Medical Association* 292 (8/4/04), pp. 602–612. The authors are part of a research group based at Tulane University. Their findings were based on interviews with more than 2,000 survivors of the Rwandan genocide of 1994. They reported that those with the least exposure to traumatic suffering were more likely to believe in the possibility of reconciliation and accept the work of the gacaca courts, while those exposed to a greater number of traumatic events favored the International Criminal Tribunal for Rwanda rather than the national or gacaca courts and were much less hopeful about the possibilities for reconciliation and healing within Rwanda.

Vinck, P., P. N. Pham, E. Stover, and H. M. Weinstein. "Exposure to War Crimes and Implications for Peace Building in Northern Uganda." *Journal of the American Medical Association* 298 (8/1/07), pp. 543–554. Written by the same group as the preceding article on survivors of the Rwandan genocide, this article discusses findings from the ongoing conflict in northern Uganda. The researchers report that survivors diagnosed with post-traumatic stress disorder (PTSD) or depression are much more likely to approve of violent methods for ending the war than nonviolent ones.

Annotated Bibliography

Zerjal, T., Y. Xue, G. Bertorelle, et al. "The Genetic Legacy of the Mongols." *American Journal of Human Genetics* 72 (March 2003), pp. 717–721. This article is a technical article written by geneticists for other medical researchers but is important because it has been cited by journalists in recent popular articles about Genghis Khan and his impact on later history.

Zimbardo, Philip. "When Good People Do Evil: The Milgram Experiments Revisited." *Yale Alumni Magazine* 70 (January/February 2007): pp. 40–47. This article, written by an eminent psychologist who is best known for his 1971 experiment in using undergraduate subjects as "prisoners" and "guards" in order to study the effects of unequal power on human behavior, is an account of Stanley Milgram's famous experiments on obedience 45 years later. Milgram's experiments were profoundly upsetting to many psychologists because they demonstrated that almost all people can be manipulated into violent or genocidal behavior by making changes in their social situation (peer groups as well as authority figures).

Web Documents

Enzensberger, Hans Magnus. "The Radical Loser." Originally published in German in *Der Spiegel,* 11/7/05. English translation available online. URL: http://www.signandsight.com/features/493.html. Accessed March 3, 2007. Enzensberger's lengthy article is an analysis of the type of individual in contemporary society most likely to be attracted to terrorist or genocidal movements. The author's basic hypothesis is that the very success of modern technology and science in removing many of the ills that people in the past had to accept as a matter of course has made the remaining problems seem less bearable, and that unhappy individuals find it relatively easy to form or join groups that share their sense of righteous anger.

Gross, Paul R. "Exorcising Sociobiology." *The New Criterion* 19 (February 2001). Available online. URL: http://www.newcriterion.com/archive/19/feb01/pgross.htm. Accessed January 15, 2007. The author is discussing the tendency among some professors in the social sciences to ignore the biological dimension of human nature and to make false accusations of genocide against anthropologists in the field. The article discusses a specific instance of the misuse of the word *genocide* for political purposes.

Ruedenberg-Wright, Luci. "The Second and Third Generation: Where Do We Go from Here?" Paper delivered at the 29th annual conference of the Association for Jewish Studies, Boston, Mass., December 21–23, 1997. Available online. URL: http://www.lrw.net/~lucia/pubs/ajs/. Accessed March 25, 2007. This paper is a discussion of the intergenerational impact of the Holocaust.

Films

Milgram, Stanley. *Obedience.* Producer unknown. 45 minutes. 1965. VHS format. This film is the only authentic footage of Milgram's famous experiment on obedience conducted at Yale. Available from Penn State Media Sales at http://www.mediasales.psu.edu/.

SPECIFIC GENOCIDES
Genocides in the Ancient World
BOOKS AND BOOK CHAPTERS

Chalk, Frank, and Kurt Jonassohn. "On Cases from Antiquity." In *The History and Sociology of Genocide: Analyses and Case Studies.* New Haven, Conn.: Yale University Press, 1990, pp. 58–64. This chapter from a well-regarded book on historic instances of genocide discusses the problems of understanding cases of genocide in the ancient world, from the relative scarcity of source material to the difficulties in interpreting the documents that do survive.

PRINT ARTICLES

Kiernan, Ben. "The First Genocide: Carthage, 146 B.C." *Diogenes* 203 (2004): pp. 27–39. This article is a historical account of the Roman destruction of Carthage at the end of the Third Punic War. The author notes that most of what is known about the genocide comes from sources that were lost for centuries and not rediscovered until the 15th century. He maintains that the attitudes of such Roman leaders as Cato toward Carthage are comparable to those of perpetrators of more recent genocides.

WEB DOCUMENTS

Caesar, Julius. *The Gallic Wars.* Translated by W. A. McDevitte and W. S. Bohn. Available online. URL: http://classics.mit.edu/Caesar/gallic.html. Accessed January 15, 2007. A basic primary source for understanding the Roman attitude toward warfare and territorial expansion.

Thucydides. *History of the Peloponnesian War.* Translated by Richard Crawley. Available online. URL: http://classics.mit.edu/Thucydides/pelopwar.html. Accessed January 15, 2007. Thucydides is still an important source for understanding long-term war as one possible prelude to genocide.

Mongol Invasions
BOOKS AND BOOK CHAPTERS

Atwood, Christopher P. *Encyclopedia of Mongolia and the Mongol Empire.* New York: Facts On File, 2004. Atwood's work is intended as a reference encyclopedia for students at the college level on the history of Mongolia from the second century B.C.E. to 2003, as well as a guide to the history of the Mongol Empire during the 13th and 14th centuries. The author, a professor of Mongolian history at Indiana University, has included a guide to pronunciation as well as maps and illustrations.

Cleaves, Francis Woodman. *The Secret History of the Mongols.* Cambridge, Mass.: Harvard University Press for the Harvard-Yenching Institute, 1982. Cleaves's translation is the first complete English translation of the *Secret History,* originally written in Mongolian. Cleaves chose to use archaic and formal language in his translation, however, and most recent readers prefer the livelier English translation by Igor de Rachewiltz.

Annotated Bibliography

Juvayni, Ala'iddin Ata-Malik. *The History of the World-conqueror.* Translated by John Andrew Boyle. Manchester, England: Manchester University Press, 1958. Juvayni (sometimes spelled Juvaini) (1226–83) is a standard primary source for biographies of Genghis Khan or histories of the Mongols. He was a Persian who served as a minor official of the Mongol Empire under Hulagu Khan and accompanied him during the siege of Baghdad in 1258.

Lewis, Bernard. *The Assassins: A Radical Sect in Islam.* New York: Basic Books, 2002. Lewis's study of the Assassins involved peeling away earlier European misconceptions of them as primarily targeting Crusaders. Lewis was able to show that the sect primarily targeted Muslim rulers who were thought to be insufficiently pious or orthodox rather than outsiders. He also debunked the legend that the Grand Master of the Assassins obtained his men's loyalty by drugging them with hashish or other narcotics. Lewis's account, however, is sufficiently detailed about the actual targeted killings to help the reader understand why the Mongols wanted the sect destroyed.

de Rachewiltz, Igor. *The Secret History of the Mongols: A Mongolian Epic Chronicle of the Thirteenth Century.* Boston and Leiden: Brill, 2004, 2006. De Rachewiltz's translation of the *Secret History* has largely replaced Cleaves's earlier work because it is more readable. This edition is accompanied by scholarly notes and commentary.

Saunders, J. J. *The History of the Mongol Conquests.* London: Routledge & Kegan Paul, 1971. Saunders's book is the standard academic history of Genghis Khan and his heirs, thoroughly researched and widely available in college libraries. Saunders tries to balance the destructiveness of the Mongols with an estimation of their positive contributions to civil administration and international trade.

PRINT ARTICLES

Guzman, Gregory. "Christian Europe and Mongol Asia: First Medieval Intercultural Contact between East and West." *Essays in Medieval Studies* 2 (1985), pp. 227–244. This article is essentially a summary of the ways in which the Mongol invasions of Europe in 1240–41 forced significant changes in the West's understanding of and dealings with the East.

Sinor, Denis. "The Inner Asian Warriors." *Journal of the American Oriental Society* 101 (1981), pp. 135–144. Originally delivered as a lecture to a scholarly society, this article is a detailed description of the cultural background, training, equipment, and military tactics of the Mongol armies. The author makes the point that these were mass citizen armies rather than professional or conscripted fighting forces.

WEB DOCUMENTS

Dalintai. "The Art of War under Chinggis Qahan (Genghis Khan)." Included as an appendix to *The History and the Life of Chinggis Khan: The Secret History of the Mongols.* Translated by Urgunge Onon. Leiden: Brill, 1990. Available online. URL: http://www.deremilitari.org/resources/articles/onon.htm. Accessed June 24, 2007. Dalintai is an Uighur scholar whose discussion of Genghis Khan's religious beliefs and his military strategy was included as an appendix to a biography of the khan. The author, who is a specialist in Mongolian history, lists 16 military tactics that he considers distinctive features of Mongol warfare. (Readers should note that Uighurs, most of whom are Muslims living in Central Asia, have only one given name.)

Frazier, Ian. "Annals of History: The Invaders." *The New Yorker* (4/25/05). Available online. URL: http://www.newyorker.com/fact/content/articles/050425fa_fact4. Accessed January 8, 2007. Frazier's lively article is taken from a popular magazine and is written for nonspecialists. It looks at Hulagu Khan's destruction of Baghdad from the angle of the present war in Iraq.

Friar John of Plano Carpini. *History of the Mongols* (excerpts). Available online. URL: http://www.deremilitari.org/resources/sources/carpini.htm. Accessed June 2, 2007. These are excerpts from the *History of the Mongols,* a book written by a Franciscan friar who was sent by Pope Innocent IV in 1245 to visit the court of the great khan. The pope was concerned to learn about the Mongols after their destructive invasions of Hungary and Poland in 1240–41. Friar John describes the techniques of Mongol warfare as well as suggestions to European rulers for successful resistance to future invasions.

Marquand, Robert. "Mongolia's Marauding Son Gets a Makeover." *Christian Science Monitor* (5/10/02). Available online. URL: http://www.csmonitor.com/2002/0510/p01s04-woap.html. Accessed July 1, 2007. This is a popular journalistic account of Genghis Khan's transformation from ruthless tyrant into the founding father of Mongolia. The article is illustrated with a painting depicting a youthful and idealistic Genghis Khan, taken from a Mongolian art exhibition celebrating his 840th birthday.

Oestmoen, Per Inge. "The Yasa of Chingis Khan: A Code of Honor, Dignity and Excellence." Available online. URL: http://www.coldsiberia.org/webdoc9.htm. Accessed July 2, 2007. Oestmoen precedes the translations of extant fragments of the Yasa with an introductory essay explaining why he regards it as an admirable code of law.

Sinor, Denis. "The Mongols in the West." *Journal of Asian History* 33 (1999). Available online. URL: http://www.deremilitari.org/resources/articles/sinor1.htm. Accessed July 22, 2007. The author seeks to provide the general reader with a basic outline of the Western campaigns of the Mongols and their long-term as well as short-term impact on European history. It is a good introduction to the subject for nonspecialists.

Venegoni, L. "Hülägü's Campaign in the West—(1258–1260)." *Transoxiana: Journal Libre de Estudios Orientales,* Webfestschrift Marshak, 2003. Available online. URL: http://www.transoxiana.org/Eran/Articles/venegoni.html. Accessed July 25, 2007. This article is taken from a collection of essays presented to Boris Marshak, an eminent scholar of Central Asian history, on his 70th birthday. Venegoni's article follows Hulagu Khan's campaign in Iran and Mesopotamia from his conquest of the Assassins to the defeat of his troops at the battle of Ain Jalut. The English is awkward in places but the article is nonetheless useful in providing a basic account of the course of events and the major figures involved.

Wingfield-Hayes, Rupert. "Mongolia's Cult of the Great Khan." *BBC News* (8/12/03). Available online. URL: http://news.bbc.co.uk/2/hi/programmes/from_our_own_correspondent/3144099.stm. Accessed July 15, 2007. This is another popular news article on the revival of Genghis Khan as a Mongolian hero. The Web page contains a link to an audio presentation by Wingfield-Hayes.

Genocides in the Americas Before 1600
BOOKS AND BOOK CHAPTERS

Leblanc, Steven A. *Prehistoric Warfare in the American Southwest.* Salt Lake City: University of Utah Press, 1999. This is a scholarly evaluation of the archaeological evidence for recurrent ethnocidal warfare in the American Southwest before the coming of Spanish colonists. The chapters are divided according to time period and illustrated with many maps, photographs, and line drawings of weapons that have been unearthed as well as pottery depicting battle scenes. The last chapter of the book is particularly valuable for its discussion of the impact of warfare and group massacres on the Native American societies of the Southwest.

Malotki, Ekkehart. *Hopi Tales of Destruction.* Lincoln: University of Nebraska Press, 2002. This book is a collection and translation of Hopi folk accounts and oral histories of civil war and war with external enemies that led to the destruction of seven different villages from 1250 C.E. through the 17th century. Like the preceding book, *Hopi Tales of Destruction* shows that Native Americans did not learn about ethnocide from Europeans; they had already practiced it when the first white settlers came into the Four Corners area. The author presently teaches languages at Northern Arizona University.

Mann, Charles C. *1491: New Revelations of the Americas before Columbus.* New York: Knopf, 2005. Mann's book is a readable and informative summary of recent discoveries about Native American cultures before contact with Europeans. These scholarly reevaluations include evidence that there were large cities in the Americas before Columbus, not just small isolated villages; that the epidemics of the 16th century killed more Native Americans than had been previously thought; that the calendars and timekeeping systems of the Inca, Maya, and Aztecs were more sophisticated than their European counterparts; and that the Amazon basin is not an unspoiled wilderness but has been settled and managed by humans for thousands of years before the arrival of Europeans. The book's chapters are arranged by topic rather than chronology and can be read in any order.

Turner, Christy G., II, and Jacqueline A. Turner. *Man Corn: Cannibalism and Violence in the American Southwest.* Salt Lake City: University of Utah Press, 1999. The Turners' book stirred up a major controversy among anthropologists and historians of the American Southwest because of its assertion that the condition of human bones and other artifacts discovered at 14 sites in the Four Corners region points to the practice of genocidal cannibalism among the tribes that once inhabited the region. Many scholars were disturbed by the implication that the Indians of the Southwest were not necessarily peaceful agriculturalists.

PRINT ARTICLES

Darling, J. Andrew. "Mass Inhumation and the Execution of Witches in the American Southwest." *American Anthropologist*, New Series, 100 (September 1998): pp. 732–752. This article attempts to argue that the signs of injury to human remains found in the ancient pueblos of the Southwest were caused by execution for witchcraft rather than genocidal killing followed by cannibalism.

WEB DOCUMENTS

"Cannibals of the Canyon." *PBS Secrets of the Dead.* Available online. URL: http://www.pbs.org/wnet/secrets/html/e4-menu.html. Accessed January 8, 2007. Site includes a transcript of the original telecast under the "Additional Resources" menu. A video of the program for home use is also available from PBS.

Hartigan, Rachel. "Dying for Dinner? A Debate Rages Over Desert Cannibalism." *U.S. News and World Report* (7/24/00). Available online. URL: http://www.usnews.com/usnews/doubleissue/mysteries/anasazi.htm. Accessed January 8, 2007. This article is a brief news account over the debate among archaeologists of the American Southwest about the practice of ethnocide and cannibalism in the region before the coming of Europeans.

Mann, Charles C. "1491." *Atlantic Monthly* (March 2002). Available online. URL: http://cogweb.ucla.edu/Chumash/Population.html. Accessed February 26, 2007. This article is a condensed version of Mann's book on the Americas before Columbus.

Stevenson, Mark. Associated Press, (1/23/05). Available online. URL: http://www.livescience.com/history/human_sacrifice_050123.html. Accessed April 12, 2007. A brief account of recent forensic evidence from Mexico supporting 16th-century Spanish accounts of human sacrifice and cruel methods of executing prisoners among the Maya and Aztecs. The scientific evidence includes the discovery of human blood and genetic material on the floors of Aztec temples as well as human bones showing signs of cannibalism.

Genocides in the Americas after 1600

BOOKS AND BOOK CHAPTERS

Barkan, Elazar. "Genocides of Indigenous Peoples: Rhetoric of Human Rights." In *The Specter of Genocide: Mass Murder in Historical Perspective,* edited by Robert Gellately and Ben Kiernan. New York: Cambridge University Press, 2003, pp. 117–139. Barkan's chapter examines the appropriateness of describing the destruction of tribes and civilizations in the Americas in the 16th and 17th centuries as genocides, both in terms of intentionality and in terms of identifying the perpetrators. He also notes the many differences among European colonies with regard to size, geographic location, and the characteristics of the various European nations that sent out colonists. Barkan concludes that much of the current discussion of colonial genocides is overly general and uses heated language that tends to polarize readers rather than clarifying the important histories under discussion.

Annotated Bibliography

Cashin, Edward J., ed. *A Wilderness Still the Cradle of Nature: Frontier Georgia.* Savannah, Ga.: Beehive Press, 1994. Cashin's book is a collection of primary source documents related to the forced removal of the Cherokee in 1838 and the Trail of Tears.

Ehle, John. *Trail of Tears: The Rise and Fall of the Cherokee Nation.* New York: Anchor Books, 1988. Ehle's is an older book on the forced removal of the Cherokee in 1838 but is still one of the most read, as it tells the story in a lively and interesting fashion and never loses sight of the human dimension of the tragedy. It contains excerpts from letters and diaries kept by Winfield Scott and his soldiers that show that most of them did their best to be as humane as possible to the Cherokees; most of the harsh treatment the tribe received was from opportunistic traders and the Georgia militia. The photographs in the center of the book include pictures of the houses of the various Cherokee leaders as well as the chiefs themselves.

Ellis, Jerry. *Walking the Trail: One Man's Journey along the Cherokee Trail of Tears.* Lincoln: University of Nebraska Press, 1991. Ellis's book is a personal account of a contemporary journey along the Trail of Tears rather than a history of the trail. The author is a direct descendant of a Cherokee family that walked the trail in 1838.

Greene, Jerome A., and Douglas D. Scott. *Finding Sand Creek: History, Archaeology, and the 1864 Massacre Site.* Norman: University of Oklahoma Press, 2004. This is a book-length account of the archaeological and historical research that finally led to the identification of the Sand Creek Massacre site in 1999. The book opens with an excellent summary chapter of the events leading up to the 1864 massacre and the people involved in the tragedy. Readers interested in archaeological techniques and documentation will particularly enjoy this book.

Hagan, William T. *Theodore Roosevelt and Six Friends of the Indian.* Norman: University of Oklahoma Press, 1997. This is a useful and unsparing historical account of six men who advised Theodore Roosevelt on Indian policy during his administration. Although these advocates for Native Americans, who included the novelist Hamlin Garland as well as journalists and civil servants, were able to obtain modest protections for the Indians from land-hungry white settlers and businessmen, neither they nor Roosevelt were able to do as much for the Indians as they had hoped. The author is a retired professor of history at the University of Oklahoma.

Hoig, Stan. *The Sand Creek Massacre.* Norman: University of Oklahoma Press, 1961. Hoig's history of the Sand Creek Massacre has been generally accepted as the standard documentary text since it was published over 40 years ago. More recent historians, however, maintain that Hoig did not give enough attention to the behavior of the Cheyenne Dog Soldiers and their responsibility for provoking a harsh response on the part of the settlers and the government.

Luthin, Herbert W., ed. *Surviving through the Days: Translations of Native California Stories and Songs.* Berkeley: University of California Press, 2002. This book is a collection of poems, songs, and narratives from the oral traditions of Native Americans in California, transcribed from dictation and then translated by a team of editors. The first chapter is an informative introduction to the characteristics of Native American oral literature to help the reader fully appreciate its beauty and complexity.

Michno, Gregory F. *Battle at Sand Creek: The Military Perspective.* El Segundo, Calif.: Upton and Sons, 2004. This book is an expansion of Michno's journal articles on Sand Creek, with particular attention to the military equipment and tactics involved.

Nash, Gary. "Cultures Meet in Seventeenth-Century New England." In *The History and Sociology of Genocide: Analyses and Case Studies,* edited by Frank Chalk and Kurt Jonassohn. New Haven, Conn.: Yale University Press, 1990, pp. 181–193. Nash discusses the role of the Puritan theory of land possession in order to explain why friction developed between the English colonists and the Native Americans in New England. The Puritans accepted a European legal theory called *vacuum domicilium* (literally, "empty of households"), which held that land that was not "settled" belonged to those who set up households in a "civilized" manner, Thus they regarded the lands of nomadic tribes as theirs by right.

Richter, Daniel K. *Facing East from Indian Country: A Native History of Early America.* Cambridge, Mass.: Harvard University Press, 2001. This book, which was nominated for the Pulitzer Prize in history, reverses the usual emphasis in colonial history on the westward movement of European settlers to take a closer look at the process through the eyes of Native Americans. They had to struggle to make sense of the newcomers and cope with the biological and environmental changes that the settlers brought with them. The author, a professor of history at the University of Pennsylvania, regards the Revolutionary War as the critical event that made it impossible for Native Americans and European Americans to live together peacefully.

Roustang, François, S. J. *Jesuit Missionaries to North America: Spiritual Writings and Biographical Sketches.* Translated by Sr. M. Renelle. San Francisco, Calif.: Ignatius Press, 2006. This collection of biographies of Jean de Brébeuf and his companions is helpful in understanding the differences between the French and Spanish approaches to missionary activity among Native Americans as well as tracing the development of Catholic missions in French-speaking Canada.

Rozema, Vicki, ed. *Voices from the Trail of Tears.* Winston-Salem, N.C.: J. F. Blair, 2003. Rozema's book begins with a historical outline of the Cherokee removal of 1838, but most of the book is a collection of primary source documents related to the Trail of Tears—letters and diaries written by Cherokee as well as whites. Each set of documents is preceded by a historical introduction.

Stannard, David E. *American Holocaust: The Conquest of the New World.* New York: Oxford University Press, 1993. Stannard's book has been controversial since its publication, not least for its comparison of the loss of Native American lives since 1500 to the Nazi Holocaust. In so doing, Stannard prompted vigorous ongoing discussion among genocide scholars about the appropriateness of comparing one instance of genocide to others. Stannard continues to take the position that there is nothing unique about the Holocaust and that anyone who maintains its uniqueness is doing so in order to preserve an unearned position of moral superiority. Barkan's chapter listed above includes a discussion of Stannard's work.

Annotated Bibliography

Wood, Nancy, ed. *The Serpent's Tongue: Prose, Poetry, and Art of the New Mexico Pueblos.* New York: Dutton Books, 1997. This book is a beautifully illustrated and instructive collection of visual art as well as poetry and personal narratives from the northern pueblos of New Mexico. Some of the most poignant accounts and artworks deal with the Indians' suffering at the hands of the Spanish settlers.

PRINT ARTICLES

Abler, Thomas S. "Iroquois Cannibalism: Fact Not Fiction," *Ethnohistory* 27 (Autumn 1980): pp. 309–316. This article documents the archaeological and documentary evidence that the Iroquois practiced cannibalism on members of other tribes as well as white settlers.

Dobyns, Henry F. "Estimating Aboriginal American Population: An Appraisal of Techniques with a New Hemispheric Estimate," *Current Anthropology* 7 (1966): pp. 395–416. Dobyns's article has proved to be a controversial landmark in the study of New World populations in the colonial period. Working from parish registers of baptisms and funerals in Mexico and Peru, Dobyns came to the conclusion that previous estimates of Indian populations before contact with Europeans had been far too low, and that the Americas had supported about 100 million people before 1500. Dobyns's revised figures are still a subject of dispute among historians and archaeologists.

WEB DOCUMENTS

D'Souza, Dinesh. "The Crimes of Christopher Columbus." *First Things* 57 (November 1995): pp. 26–33. Available online. URL: http://www.firstthings.com/ftissues/ ft9511/dsouza.html. Accessed January 8, 2007. This article is an examination of the tendency of contemporary scholarship to interpret the 15th- and 16th-century voyages of exploration in purely negative terms. After examining a number of current distortions of the historical record, the author concludes that "the aspiration of an authentic multicultural education [should be] to help us move from opinion to knowledge, to climb out of the darkness into the illuminating light of the sun," rather than to replace previous biased accounts of colonial American history with a new set of biases.

Lowensteyn, Peter. "The Role of the Dutch in the Iroquois Wars." Available online. URL: http://www.lowensteyn.com/iroquois/index.html. Accessed April 4, 2007. This is a detailed historical analysis of the ways in which the Iroquois (and other tribes in eastern North America) were not as powerless as they are sometimes thought to have been in their dealings with Europeans; rather they were skilled in playing off the various European powers against one another. The page contains maps and illustrations as well as text.

Michno, Gregory F. "Cheyenne Chief Black Kettle." *Wild West* (December 2005). Available online. URL: http://www.historynet.com/culture/wild_west/3418666. html. Accessed March 22, 2007. Michno's article is a useful counterbalance to the customary portrayal of the chief as a man of peace and a wise leader. He documents the chief's dishonesty in some negotiations and ineptness in others and concludes, "[Contemporary] Americans' perceptions of the past are the result of

311

continuous bombardment by films and books that perpetuate myths but do not provide the historical accuracy that would enable us to understand our past. It is time to drop the legend and print the fact, even if the reputations of such legendary figures as Black Kettle must suffer."

———. "Sand Creek Massacre: The Real Villains." *Wild West* (December 2003). Available online. URL: http://www.historynet.com/culture/wild_west/3025016.html. Accessed March 22, 2007. Like the preceding article, this one offers a challenge to the usual depiction of the Sand Creek Massacre as "an epic struggle between good and evil," with John Chivington as the central villain. Michno's sifting of the historical evidence is a good example of the need for care in evaluating reports of genocides. He concludes that "Blame, if it must be placed, should be on the politicians who sought to destroy their enemies for personal aggrandizement, on the crooked agents and traders for fomenting discontent [among the Indians], and on [Major Ned] Wynkoop for setting the stage for disaster."

Morley, Judy Mattivi. "Our People: Southern Arapahos Are Part of Boulder's Spirit." Available online. URL: http://www.getboulder.com/visitors/articles/southernarapahoe.html. Accessed April 3, 2007. This is an online article from a regional Colorado newspaper about the Arapaho and Cheyenne tribes and the effect of the Sand Creek Massacre on them. The author teaches history at the University of Colorado.

Whitacre, Christine. "The Search for the Site of the Sand Creek Massacre," *Prologue* 33, no. 2 (Summer 2001). Available online. URL: http://www.archives.gov/publications/prologue/2001/summer/sand-creek-massacre-1.html. Accessed April 2, 2007. *Prologue* is the quarterly magazine of the National Archives. This article is a description of the National Park Service's inclusion of Cheyenne and Arapaho chiefs and elders in the search for the exact location of the Sand Creek Massacre of 1864, and their contributions to the archaeological and historical studies required for the search.

Armenia

BOOKS AND BOOK CHAPTERS

Akçam, Taner. *A Shameful Act: The Armenian Genocide and the Question of Turkish Responsibility.* Translated by Paul Bessemer. New York: Henry Holt and Company, 2006. Taner Akçam is a historian and sociologist who is presently a visiting professor at the University of Minnesota. One of the first Turkish scholars to confront the role of his government in the Armenian genocide, Akçam was a prisoner of conscience in Turkey from 1975 to 1976 and was granted political asylum in Germany, where he completed his Ph.D. As of 2007 he has been harassed or had his lectures disrupted at various stops on his lecture tours in Canada and the United States. *A Shameful Act* is his best-known history of the Armenian genocide for general readers.

Arlen, Michael J. *Passage to Ararat.* St. Paul, Minn.: Ruminator Books, 1975. Michael J. Arlen is the son of Michael Arlen (1895–1956), a writer of the 1920s known for *The Green Hat* and a few other society novels, who was born Dikran Kouyoumjian but changed his name after moving to England. *Passage to Ararat* is the son's account of his trip to Armenia, the homeland of his father's extended family, to find out why his father had tried to deny his Armenian heritage. The book has become a classic account of the impact of genocide across generations and its profound effects even on those who were indirect survivors of the killing.

Balakian, Peter. *Black Dog of Fate: A Memoir.* New York: Broadway Books, 1997. Balakian's book is similar to Arlen's in that it is a memoir of a second-generation Armenian-American who discovers the history of the genocide that affected his family after he finishes college in the 1970s. It contains a number of poems that the author, presently a professor of English literature, wrote in the course of listening to his aunts' accounts of their escape from Armenia in 1915 after their father's murder.

———. *The Burning Tigris: The Armenian Genocide and America's Response.* New York: HarperCollins, 2003. This book is Balakian's historical account of the Armenian genocide of 1915 rather than a personal memoir. The author begins with a detailed discussion of the Hamidian massacres of 1894–96 and the response of Americans to them in order to show that genocide has not always been met with minimization or denial; in fact, he maintains that the Hamidian massacres were responsible for "the emergence of international human rights in America."

Bloxham, Donald. "Determinants of the Armenian Genocide." In *Looking Backward, Moving Forward: Confronting the Armenian Genocide,* edited by Richard G. Hovannisian. New Brunswick, N.J.: Transaction Publishers, 2003, pp. 23–50. This book chapter offers an outline of the major political factors involved in the Armenian genocide, focusing on the Ottoman Empire's relationships with other powers before World War I and the role of the CUP in the genocide.

Dadrian, Vahakn N. "The Comparative Aspects of the Armenian and Jewish Cases of Genocide: A Sociohistorical Perspective." In *Is the Holocaust Unique? Perspectives on Comparative Genocide,* 2nd ed., edited by Alan S. Rosenbaum. Boulder, Colo.: Westview Press, 2001, pp. 133–168. Dadrian is considered by many the leading contemporary historian of the Armenian genocide of 1915. This chapter compares the Armenian genocide with the Holocaust of the 1940s. Dadrian outlines both similarities and differences between the two cases, thus providing a good example of the comparative approach to genocide studies.

Hovannisian, Richard G., ed., *The Armenian Genocide in Perspective.* New Brunswick, N.J.: Transaction Publishers, 1986. One of the earliest group studies of the Armenian genocide, this book is a collection of 12 essays on the genocide from experts in a wide range of different fields, including psychiatry, religion, ethics, and literature as well as history and political science.

———. "Bitter-Sweet Memories: The Last Generation of Ottoman Armenians." In *Looking Backward, Moving Forward: Confronting the Armenian Genocide.* New Brunswick, N.J.: Transaction Publishers, 2003, pp. 113–124. Hovannisian reviews the material collected by the UCLA Armenian Oral History project, begun in the 1970s to interview survivors of the 1915 genocide before their testimonies were lost. The interviews, in his opinion, corroborate the documentary evidence from Turkish government archives that the deportations and massacres were centrally planned and followed a consistent pattern throughout Armenia.

Jacobs, Steven J. "Raphael Lemkin and the Armenian Genocide." In *Looking Backward, Moving Forward: Confronting the Armenian Genocide,* edited by Richard G. Hovannisian. New Brunswick, N.J.: Transaction Publishers, 2003, pp. 125–135. This chapter discusses the role of the Armenian genocide in prompting Lemkin to make it his central life concern and describes two of Lemkin's yet-unpublished manuscripts about the genocide, one of them book length.

Kiernan, Ben. "Twentieth-Century Genocides: Underlying Ideological Themes from Armenia to East Timor." In *The Specter of Genocide: Mass Murder in Historical Perspective,* edited by Robert Gellately and Ben Kiernan. New York: Cambridge University Press, 2003, pp. 29–40. This chapter interprets the Armenian genocide as reflecting a desire for territorial expansion and purification to offset the widespread sense of decline and loss within the Ottoman Empire. Kiernan emphasizes the Turks' feelings of humiliation from the loss of various provinces to Austria, Italy, and Russia between 1908 and 1912 as an important factor in the genocide of 1915.

Kirakossian, Arman J., ed. *The Armenian Massacres 1894–1896: U.S. Media Testimony.* Detroit, Mich.: Wayne State University Press, 2004. Kirakossian's book is a compilation of 35 documents that appeared in the American media at the time of the Hamidian massacres. Written by diplomats, missionaries, and scientists as well as journalists, these reports helped to educate the American public about the Armenians' suffering under Ottoman rule and their struggle for independence. Thus news reports of the genocide of 1915 found Americans ready and eager to intervene and to help the survivors.

Melson, Robert. "The Armenian Genocide as Precursor and Prototype of Twentieth-Century Genocide." In *Is the Holocaust Unique? Perspectives on Comparative Genocide,* 2nd ed., edited by Alan S. Rosenbaum. Boulder, Colo.: Westview Press, 2001, pp. 119–131. Melson argues in this chapter that the Armenian genocide served as the basic model of later genocides because its "territorial and national aspects, which distinguish it from the Holocaust, make it an archetype for ethnic and national genocides in the Third World as well as in the post-Communist states."

———. "Provocation or Nationalism?" In *The History and Sociology of Genocide: Analyses and Case Studies,* edited by Frank Chalk and Kurt Jonassohn. New Haven, Conn: Yale University Press, 1990, pp. 266–289. This essay is an attempt to answer scholars who argue that the Armenians provoked the genocide of 1915—a theory that was first proposed by Bernard Lewis in his 1961 book on *The Emergence of Modern Turkey.* Melson argues that "both the perpetrator and victim and [the history of] their relations must be examined for a complete explanation."

Miller, Donald E., and Lorna Touryan Miller. *Survivors: An Oral History of the Armenian Genocide.* Berkeley: University of California Press, 1999. The Millers began transcribing the interviews with survivors of the 1915 genocide recorded in this book in 1978, in a race against time. In addition to providing the reader with a basic historical outline of the genocide, the authors provide some interpretation of the survivors' testimonies in the final chapters of the book. They came up with six types of response that they found among the survivors: denial and repression; outrage and anger; desires for revenge or restitution; a wish for reconciliation coupled with a moral demand that the Turks should acknowledge the genocide; resignation and feelings of hopelessness; and trying to find reasons for what happened (rationalization).

Payaslian, Simon. "The United States Response to the Armenian Genocide." In *Looking Backward, Moving Forward: Confronting the Armenian Genocide*, edited by Richard G. Hovannisian. New Brunswick, N.J.: Transaction Publishers, 2003, pp. 51–80. This chapter is a brief outline of topics covered in much greater depth in Balakian's book *The Burning Tigris*. Payaslian focuses on Ambassador Henry Morgenthau and three other figures in the Wilson administration: Abram I. Elkus, who succeeded Morgenthau as ambassador to the Ottoman Empire, William Jennings Bryan, Wilson's first secretary of state, and Robert Lansing, who succeeded Bryan at the State Department.

Verhoeven, Joe. "The Armenian Genocide and International Law." In *Looking Backward, Moving Forward: Confronting the Armenian Genocide*, edited by Richard G. Hovannisian. New Brunswick, N.J.: Transaction Publishers, 2003, pp. 137–155. Verhoeven's chapter is a study of the evolution of the UN's application of the Genocide Convention since its adoption in 1948 in order to explore the possibility of international recognition of the atrocity as a genocide, and the possibility of compensation for the remaining survivors.

Winter, Jay. "Under Cover of War: The Armenian Genocide in the Context of Total War." In *The Specter of Genocide: Mass Murder in Historical Perspective*, edited by Robert Gellately and Ben Kiernan. New York: Cambridge University Press, 2003, pp. 189–213. Winter's chapter is an analysis of the meaning of "total war" and a discussion of its applicability to the Armenian genocide.

PRINT ARTICLES

Kalayjian, A. S., S. P. Shahinian, E. L. Gergerian, and L. Saraydarian. "Coping with Ottoman Turkish Genocide: An Exploration of the Experience of Armenian Survivors." *Journal of Traumatic Stress* 9 (January 1996): pp. 87–97. This study, which consisted of interviews with 40 survivors of the 1915 genocide, was concerned with the effects of Turkey's ongoing denial of the genocide as well as the survivors' coping strategies. The researchers reported that resentment, rage, and hatred were the most common responses to Turkey's position.

Lewis, Bernard. "Europe and the Turks: The Civilization of the Ottoman Empire." *History Today* (October 1953), pp. 673–680. This article is an attempt to correct common Western misconceptions of the Ottoman Empire as either completely corrupt or uncivilized. The reader should note that it was written before the controversies of the 1980s and later regarding Turkish recognition of the Armenian genocide.

———. "History Writing and National Revival in Turkey." *Middle Eastern Affairs* 4 (1953), pp. 218–227. Lewis discusses the role of Turkish nationalism in stimulating historical research in Turkey both before and after the Armenian genocide.

———. "A Taxonomy of Group Hatred." *Transit* 16 (Winter 1998–99), pp. 3–13. Lewis's analysis of religion (and other factors) as a source of hatred between different groups is helpful in understanding the historical background of the Armenian genocide even though the article does not focus on Armenia as a specific instance of intergroup hatred.

WEB DOCUMENTS

Ahmaranian, John, compiler. "Editorial Cartoons of the Armenian Genocide." Available online. URL: http://www.chgs.umn.edu/Histories__Narratives__Documen/ Armenian_Genocide/armenian_genocide.html. Accessed March 9, 2007. An interesting visual resource for readers interested in media coverage of the 1915 genocide at the time of its occurrence.

Armenian Library and Museum of America, Watertown, Mass. "The Armenians: Shadows of a Forgotten Genocide." Available online. URL: http://www.chgs.umn. edu/Histories__Narratives__Documen/The_Armenians/the_armenians.html. Accessed March 9, 2007. This is the index of a multipage Web document on the Armenian genocide created by the Armenian Library and Museum of America in Watertown, Massachusetts, and the Holocaust Research Center and Archives of Queensborough Community College in Bayside, New York.

BBC News. "Turkish-Armenian Writer Shot Dead." (1/19/07). Available online. URL: http://news.bbc.co.uk/2/hi/europe/6279241.stm. Accessed July 27, 2007. This is the BBC's news account of Hrant Dink's assassination in January 2007.

Danielyan, Emil. "Nobel Laureates Call for Armenian-Turkish Reconciliation." Radio Free Europe (4/10/07). Available online. URL: http://www.rferl.org/features article/2007/4/F1CACD86-B6BF-413F-B6AD-6C423454F845.html. Accessed July 28, 2007. A news report on the efforts of Elie Wiesel and other Nobel Prize winners to urge Turkey to recognize the Armenian genocide as a step toward better relations between the two nations.

EurActiv. "Parliament Faces Crucial Enlargement Decisions." (9/25/06). Available online. URL: http://www.euractiv.com/en/enlargement/parliament-faces-crucial-enlargement-decisions/article -158105. Accessed July 28, 2007. This is an article on the European Union's decision not to press Turkey to acknowledge the Armenian genocide as a precondition for admission to the EU.

FILMS

Goldberg, Andrew. *The Armenian Genocide.* Directed by Andrew Goldberg. 60 minutes. Two Cat Productions, 2006. Available in printed film or DVD format. This documentary consists of interviews with Peter Balakian, Vahakn Dadrian, Taner Akçam, and survivors of the Armenian genocide as well as archival film footage from 1915.

The Holocaust

BOOKS AND BOOK CHAPTERS

Anissimov, Myriam. *Primo Levi: Tragedy of an Optimist.* Woodstock, N.Y.: The Overlook Press, 1998. This is a full-length biography of a noted Italian Jewish author who survived the concentration camps only to suffer depression in his later years and take his own life. The biography includes numerous excerpts from Levi's writings about the Holocaust.

Annotated Bibliography

Bauer, Yehuda. "The Evolution of Nazi Jewish Policy, 1933–1938." In *The History and Sociology of Genocide: Analyses and Case Studies,* edited by Frank Chalk and Kurt Jonassohn. New Haven, Conn: Yale University Press, 1990, pp. 332–353. This chapter organizes Nazi policies toward the Jews chronologically in order to clarify its broad outlines for nonspecialist readers. It is a good introduction for readers who are not already familiar with the course of events during the five years between Hitler's rise to power in 1933 and the eve of World War II.

Browning, Christopher R. *The Origins of the Final Solution.* London: William Heinemann, 2004. Browning takes the position in this book that the Nazis did not have a premeditated plan for genocide when they took control of the German government in 1933. He views the Final Solution as the outcome of German victories in the first two years of World War II and the use of Poland as a "laboratory for [Nazi] racial policy."

Burleigh, Michael. *Ethics and Extermination: Reflections on Nazi Genocide.* Cambridge: Cambridge University Press, 1997. Burleigh's book is a collection of nine of his essays, grouped under three headings: the German fascination with eastern Europe and Russia; the Nazi program of euthanasia and its relationship to current thinking about euthanasia; and the Nazi final solution of mass extermination of the Jews.

Butz, Arthur R. *The Hoax of the Twentieth Century: The Case against the Presumed Extermination of European Jewry,* 3rd ed. Chicago: Theses & Dissertations Press, 2003. Butz's book is a well-known example of Holocaust revisionism. In the preface to the 2003 edition, Butz, who is not a trained historian, describes his approach to the topic and his reasons for his position. Castle Hill Publishers has made the full 500-page manuscript available for free download in either HTML or PDF format at http://www.vho.org/GB/Books/thottc/. Accessed August 15, 2007.

Delbo, Charlotte. *Auschwitz and After,* translated by Rosette C. Lamont. New Haven, Conn.: Yale University Press, 1995. This book is an English translation of three essays written by Charlotte Delbo after her release from Auschwitz—"The Measure of Our Days," "Useless Knowledge," and "None of Us Will Return." The volume includes a fine introduction by Lawrence Langer.

Faurisson, Robert. *Écrits révisionnistes, 1974–1998,* 4 vols. Pithiviers: Ed. privée, 1999. These volumes are a collection of Faurisson's writings on the Holocaust. Over the years he has attracted considerable attention for his denial of the existence of the gas chambers and his claim that Anne Frank's diary could not have been written by a child. Faurisson was removed from his teaching position in 1991 after the French government passed a law against Holocaust denial.

Gellately, Robert. "The Third Reich, the Holocaust, and Visions of Serial Genocide." In *The Specter of Genocide: Mass Murder in Historical Perspective,* edited by Robert Gellately and Ben Kiernan. New York: Cambridge University Press, 2003, pp. 241–263. Gellately's approach to the Holocaust is similar to Browning's in that he interprets it as a reaction to the demands of fighting World War II rather than the outcome of a master plan prepared in the early 1930s.

Gilbert, Martin. *The Righteous: The Unsung Heroes of the Holocaust.* New York: Henry Holt & Co., 2003. Gilbert's book is a series of thumbnail biographies, arranged by country, of ordinary people (clergy, schoolteachers, farmers, sewer workers, musicians, shopkeepers, and many others). Gilbert has also written general histories of the Holocaust but thought that the existence of altruism in a hellish period of history should not be forgotten. The book notes that many of the Jews who were saved from the concentration camps were helped by a series of rescuers (rather than just one person) who moved them from one hiding place to another, somewhat like the Underground Railroad of the American Civil War.

Hilberg, Raul. "The Anatomy of the Holocaust." In *The Holocaust: Ideology, Bureaucracy, and Genocide. The San José Papers,* edited by Henry Friedlander and Sybil Milton. New York: Kraus International Publications, 1980, pp. 85–102. Hilberg is known for his emphasis on the role of the bureaucracy of the Nazi state in the series of events that led to the Holocaust. His chapter on the anatomy of the Holocaust traces the steps from identifying the Jews as such to imposing economic sanctions, then forcing the Jews into ghettos or other types of housing that separated them from other Germans, and then beginning the process of physical extermination. Like Browning, Hilberg saw the outbreak of World War II, in particular the German invasion of Russia in 1941, as the final trigger of the Holocaust.

Irving, David J. C. *Hitler's War.* New York: Avon Books, 1990. Irving is a controversial author not only because of his denial of the Holocaust but also because of charges by other historians that he has deliberately misinterpreted or distorted historical evidence. He served a 10-month prison sentence in Austria in 2006 for glorifying the Nazis. *Hitler's War* received a number of unfavorable reviews when it was first published but has continued to sell well because it is written in a lively and nonacademic style.

Katz, Steven T. "The Uniqueness of the Holocaust: The Historical Dimension." In *Is the Holocaust Unique? Perspectives on Comparative Genocide,* 2nd ed., edited by Alan S. Rosenbaum. Boulder, Colo.: Westview Press, 2001, pp. 49–68. In this chapter, Katz discusses three events that have been compared to the Holocaust—the depopulation of Native Americans after the coming of Europeans, the 1930–33 famine in Ukraine, and the Armenian genocide of 1915—and explains why he does not consider them comparable to the Holocaust. He maintains, however, that "in arguing for the uniqueness of the Holocaust, [he is] *not* making a *moral* claim, in other words, that the Holocaust was more evil than the other events discussed."

Plant, Richard. *The Pink Triangle: The Nazi War against Homosexuals.* New York: Henry Holt, 1986. Plant's book has become the standard scholarly English-language source for understanding the Nazi determination to exterminate homosexuals as well as Jews, Roma, and other minorities. The author was born in Germany in 1910 and emigrated to the United States in 1938. His book attributes the Nazi policy toward homosexuals to Heinrich Himmler, the head of the SS and the Gestapo, rather than to Hitler himself.

Rosenberg, Harvey. *Raoul Wallenberg.* New York: Holmes & Meier, 1995. Rosenberg's is still the basic book-length biography of Wallenberg available in English. The

1995 edition is an updated version of the first edition (1982), to take into account material related to Wallenberg's fate released from Soviet archives after the collapse of the Soviet Union.

Samuels, Shimon. "Applying the Lessons of the Holocaust." In *Is the Holocaust Unique? Perspectives on Comparative Genocide*, 2nd ed., edited by Alan S. Rosenbaum. Boulder, Colo.: Westview Press, 2001, pp. 209–220. Samuels prefers to focus attention on the relevance of the Holocaust as a preventive "early-warning system for mass murder" against its recurrence. Later sections of the chapter discuss the evolution of international law since the Holocaust and the question of restitution for the survivors of genocide.

Weissmark, Mona Sue. *Justice Matters: Legacies of the Holocaust and World War II.* New York: Oxford University Press, 2004. Weissmark, the daughter of Holocaust survivors, is a clinical psychologist who undertook a research project in 1992 to bring together other adult children of survivors with sons and daughters of Nazis. *Justice Matters* is an exploration of the ways in which ethnic hatreds and resentments are transmitted across generations, and the fact that legal systems do not remove emotional pain even when they try to restore justice.

Wood, E. Thomas, and Stanislaw M. Jankowski. *Karski: How One Man Tried to Stop the Holocaust.* New York: John Wiley and Sons, 1994. This biography of Karski, written by an American and a Polish journalist, was the first book-length account of Karski's work available in English. It is well written for the general reader and includes a guide to people mentioned in the book as an appendix.

PRINT ARTICLES

Krell, R. "Child Survivors of the Holocaust—Strategies of Adaptation." *Canadian Journal of Psychiatry* 38 (August 1993): pp. 384–389. This is a psychiatric study of Holocaust survivors who were children during their imprisonment. The author notes that they have adopted different coping strategies from those used by survivors who were adults during World War II and that most child survivors have gone on to live productive and emotionally stable lives.

WEB DOCUMENTS

Anti-Defamation League (ADL). "Holocaust Imagery and Animal Rights." (8/2/05). Available online. URL: http://www.adl.org/Anti_semitism/holocaust_imagery. asp. Accessed March 21, 2007. This press release explains the ADL's objection to material produced by animal rights organizations that compared laboratory experimentation on animals or the killing of animals for food to the Holocaust.

Associated Press. "Nobel Laureate Accosted at San Francisco Peace Forum." *San Francisco Examiner* (2/9/07). Available online. URL: http://www.examiner.com/ a-556256~Nobel_laureate_accosted_at_peace_conference. html. Accessed February 9, 2007. A brief news report about a Holocaust denier's attack on Elie Wiesel in a San Francisco hotel lobby.

Clark, Laura. "Teachers Drop the Holocaust to Avoid Offending Muslims." *Daily Mail* (4/2/07). Available online. URL: http://www.dailymail.co.uk/pages/live/articles/ news/news.html?in_article_id=445979&in_page_id=1770. Accessed April 4, 2007.

A news article on a British government report about teachers suppressing study of the Holocaust to avoid upsetting Muslim pupils. "The findings have prompted claims that some schools are using history as a vehicle for promoting political correctness."

Farragher, Thomas. "Vengeance at Dachau." *Boston Globe* (7/1/01), p. A1. Available online. URL: http://graphics.boston.com/globe/nation/packages/secret_history/ index5.shtml. Accessed January 28, 2007. Farragher's article is a five-part account of the revenge taken by a unit of the 45th Infantry Division after liberating the Nazi concentration camp at Dachau in April 1945. Farragher used recently declassified government documents to reopen an investigation into the massacre of the German soldiers and guards at the camp. The Web pages contain links to video clips of a documentary made in 1990 with some of the surviving veterans.

Gambetta, Diego. "Primo Levi's Last Moments." *Boston Review* 24 (Summer 1999). Available online. URL: http://www.bostonreview.net/BR24.3/gambetta.html. Accessed March 22, 2007. This article revisits the question of the writer's suicide and concludes that it was an accident caused by side effects of the medications prescribed for Levi to treat his recurrent depression.

"The Holocaust on Trial." PBS Nova Online. Transcript available online. URL: http:// www.pbs.org/wgbh/nova/holocaust/. Accessed January 8, 2007. The program, which was originally aired on October 31, 2000, refers to a recent trial in the United Kingdom as a starting point for exploring the issue of Holocaust denial.

Morris, Benny. "Essay: This Holocaust Will Be Different." *Jerusalem Post* (1/15/07). Available online. URL: http://www.jpost.com/servlet/Satellite?apage=1&cid=116746776 2531&pagename=JPost%2FJPArticle%2FShowFull. Accessed January 21, 2007. The author, a professor of Middle Eastern history at Ben-Gurion University, maintains that Iran's quest for nuclear power has a second Holocaust as its ultimate goal.

FILMS

Lanzmann, Claude. *Shoah.* Produced and directed by Claude Lanzmann. 9.5 hours. Les Films Aleph, 1985. Printed film. Considered the definitive documentary about the Holocaust, Lanzmann's film is a series of interviews with survivors, bystanders, and perpetrators of the Holocaust. One of the high points of the film, in the minds of many viewers, is Lanzmann's interview with Jan Karski, the Polish courier who slipped into the Warsaw ghetto and the death camp at Belzec in order to take information about the genocide to the West.

Cambodia
BOOKS AND BOOK CHAPTERS

Becker, Elizabeth. *When the War Was Over: The Voices of Cambodia's Revolution and Its People.* New York: Simon and Schuster, 1986. Becker was a reporter for the *Washington Post* in Cambodia in the early 1970s who was expelled along with other Westerners in 1975. Allowed to return briefly in 1978, she was traveling together with Richard Dudman, another journalist, and Malcolm Caldwell, a university lecturer sympathetic to the Khmer Rouge, when Caldwell was shot shortly before the group was due to leave. Her book is an account of her years as a correspondent in Cambodia.

Bizot, François. *The Gate.* Translated by Euan Cameron. New York: Alfred A. Knopf, 2003. Bizot was a French scholar of Khmer pottery and Buddhism in Cambodia in the early 1970s when the Khmer Rouge were slowly gaining power. In 1971 he was accused of being an American spy and put into a Khmer Rouge prison; he is the only known Westerner to escape from one. Four years later, he worked together with François Ponchaud to help a group of French and Cambodians escape from Phnom Penh. His memoir is painful but necessary reading for anyone concerned about genocide.

Chandler, David P. *The Tragedy of Cambodian History: Politics, War, and Revolution Since 1945.* New Haven, Conn.: Yale University Press, 1991. This book was written as a sequel to the author's longer history of Cambodia that was published in 1983. It provides useful background information that readers may find helpful before tackling more detailed works on the Khmer Rouge regime.

Kiernan, Ben. "External and Indigenous Sources of Khmer Rouge Ideology." In *The Third IndoChina War: Conflict between China, Vietnam and Cambodia, 1972–1979,* edited by O. Arne Westad and Sophie Quinn. London: Routledge, 2006, pp. 187–206. This chapter is an academic analysis of the mixture of Marxist and home-grown ideas that characterized the political thought of the Khmer Rouge leaders.

———. *The Pol Pot Regime: Race, Power and Genocide in Cambodia under the Khmer Rouge, 1975–1979,* 2nd ed. New Haven, Conn.: Yale University Press, 2002. Detailed and written by an academic for other specialists in the field. General readers should read overviews of the Cambodian genocide before tackling this book.

Kissi, Edward. "Genocide in Cambodia and Ethiopia." In *The Specter of Genocide: Mass Murder in Historical Perspective,* edited by Robert Gellately and Ben Kiernan. New York: Cambridge University Press, 2003, pp. 307–323. This chapter compares the regime of the Derg in Ethiopia with that of the Khmer Rouge in Cambodia to revisit the general question of defining genocide. The author concludes that defining the Derg's killings of opponents as genocide is questionable because they were random rather than systematic and because the Derg's political opponents also committed massacres.

Ponchaud, François. *Cambodia Year Zero.* Translated by Nancy Amphoux. London: Allen Lane, 1978. Ponchaud's book has become a basic primary source for researchers of the Cambodian genocide. The first book-length account to be published in the West about the brutality of the Khmer Rouge regime, it was based on the author's interviews with Cambodian refugees in Thailand as well as his own observations before he was expelled from Cambodia by the Khmer Rouge.

PRINT ARTICLES

Burton, Charles. Book review of *Revolution and Its Aftermath in Kampuchea,* edited by David Chandler and Ben Kiernan. *Pacific Affairs* 57 (Fall 1984), p. 532.

Clayton, Thomas. "Education under Occupation: Political Violence, Schooling, and Response in Cambodia, 1979–1989." *Current Issues in Comparative Education* 2 (11/15/99), pp. 1–12. This is an article written for educators about the destruction of the Cambodian educational system during the period of Vietnamese occupation.

Hinton, D. E., V. Pich, D. Chhean, and M. H. Pollack. "'The Ghost Pushes You Down': Sleep Paralysis-type Panic Attacks in a Khmer Refugee Population." *Transcultural Psychiatry* 42 (March 2005): pp. 46–77. The authors are discussing culture-specific symptoms of post-traumatic stress disorder in Cambodian refugees. This research group, based at Massachusetts General Hospital, has published a series of articles on PTSD and its specific symptoms in survivors of the Khmer Rouge genocide.

WEB DOCUMENTS

Carvin, Andy. *Southeast Asia Diary: A Day in the Killing Fields* (11/8/97). Available online. URL: http://www.edwebproject.org/seasia/killingfields.html. Accessed March 18, 2007. This is an account by a British Jew of his visit to the genocide museum at Tuol Sleng.

Channer, Alan. "Priest of Many Frontiers: Alan Channer Meets François Ponchaud, the Catholic Priest Who Brought the Cambodian Genocide to the Attention of the World." *For a Change* (December–January 1999). Available online. URL: http://findarticles.com/p/articles/mi_m0KZH/is_6_12/ai_30125891. Accessed July 7, 2007. This article is a profile of Ponchaud and his present work as a missionary as well as his role in writing *Cambodia Year Zero*.

Kyne, Phelim. "François Ponchaud: The Priest Who Exposed Pol Pot to the World." *Taipei Times* (4/16/00), p. 5. Available online. URL: http://www.taipeitimes.com/News/asia/archives/2000/04/16/32499. Accessed July 5, 2007. This news article about Ponchaud discusses the Vietnamese leaders' use of his book as a political tool for their own purposes after 1979 as well as his current thinking about genocide trials in Cambodia.

Thayer, Nate. "Dying Breath: The Inside Story of Pol Pot's Last Days and the Disintegration of the Movement He Created." *Far Eastern Economic Review* (4/30/98). Available online. URL: http://www.cybercambodia.com/dachs/killing/polpot.html. Accessed July 30, 2007. Originally printed in the *Far Eastern Economic Review,* Thayer's description of the end of Pol Pot's life is combined with his accounts of conversations with Ta Mok, who "gives the impression of being increasingly out of touch with reality, seeing enemies everywhere and unwilling to compromise." In July 1997 Thayer obtained the only interview that Pol Pot gave a Westerner between 1979 and his death in 1998.

FILMS

Kurtis, Bill. *Investigative Reports: Return to the Killing Fields.* 50 minutes. Arts & Entertainment Home Video, 2000. DVD format. Shot on site in Cambodia, this reexamination of Pol Pot's regime 25 years after its takeover of Cambodia features a number of interviews with people who witnessed the Khmer Rouge's systematic massacres, including survivors of the killing fields and those who actually carried out the torture and killing.

Rwanda
BOOKS AND BOOK CHAPTERS

Dallaire, Roméo, with Brent Beardsley. *Shake Hands with the Devil: The Failure of Humanity in Rwanda.* New York: Carroll & Graf, 2004. Dallaire's book is a basic source for understanding what happened in Rwanda in 1994. Although Dallaire had to be persuaded to write it because he was still recovering from PTSD in the early 2000s as well as trying to put his family life back together, he decided to tell his story as what he calls a cri de coeur rather than a straightforward military account or an academic analysis. Brent Beardsley was Dallaire's operations manager during the UNAMIR mission in 1994 and has contributed to other documentaries about the Rwandan genocide.

Mamdani, Mahmood. *When Victims Become Killers: Colonialism, Nativism, and the Genocide in Rwanda.* Princeton, N.J.: Princeton University Press, 2001. Mamdani is a third-generation East African scholar of Asian descent. Born in Uganda, he was educated in the United States and is presently the director of the Institute for African Studies at Columbia University. *When Victims Become Killers* represents an attempt to understand the 1994 genocide in Rwanda as the outcome of Rwanda's colonial past and to explain the reasons for the unprecedented involvement of large masses of the population as killers.

Melson, Robert. "Modern Genocide in Rwanda: Ideology, Revolution, War, and Mass Murder in an African State." In *The Specter of Genocide: Mass Murder in Historical Perspective,* edited by Robert Gellately and Ben Kiernan. New York: Cambridge University Press, 2003, pp. 325–338. Melson is well known for his studies of the Armenian genocide of 1915. Like Mamdani, Melson sees the roots of the Rwandan genocide in the colonial period, when the European powers turned the apparent physical differences between Hutus and Tutsis into class and political differences.

Melvern, Linda. *Conspiracy to Murder: The Rwandan Genocide.* New York: Verso, 2004. *Conspiracy to Murder* is Melvern's second book about the Rwanda genocide of 1994. She traces the planning of the genocide to the group of Hutu extremists surrounding President Habyarimana and his wife as well as the role of France and Egypt in supplying arms to the Hutus. The book is informative but may be difficult for readers who are not already familiar with the people involved, as it has no glossary of major figures and is not organized chronologically.

———. *A People Betrayed: The Role of the West in Rwanda's Genocide.* London: Zed Books, 2000. This book was Melvern's first book on the Rwanda genocide. An investigative journalist for the London *Sunday Times* at the time of the genocide, Melvern has served as a consultant to the International Criminal Tribunal for Rwanda and is presently the second vice-president of the International Association of Genocide Scholars. *A People Betrayed* is more accessible to the general reader than Melvern's later book because it is more of a narrative account than a report of investigative findings.

Prunier, Gérard. *The Rwanda Crisis: History of a Genocide*. New York: Columbia University Press, 1995. Gérard Prunier is a Belgian scholar who earned his Ph.D. in African studies at the University of Paris in 1981. He is a specialist in the history of Ethiopia and presently director of the French Centre for Ethiopian Studies in Addis Ababa. His account of the Rwandan genocide of 1994 was his first book on the subject of genocide in Africa, followed by a book on Darfur in 2005, and one on the genocide in the Republic of Congo in 2006. Prunier was one of the first Western scholars to perceive that the genocide in Rwanda was not produced by ancient tribal hatreds but by a combination of political chaos and repression, Western bungling during the colonial period, overpopulation, and economic problems.

Scherrer, Christian P. *Genocide and Crisis in Central Africa*. Westport, Conn.: Praeger, 2002. Scherrer is a Dutch scholar who is currently head of the Ethnic Conflict Research Project, an independent research project founded in 1987. He conducted investigations in Rwanda for the UN High Commissioner on Human Rights after the 1994 genocide. Scherrer focuses on the prevention of ethnic violence as central to resolving conflicts elsewhere in Africa as well as in Rwanda.

PRINT ARTICLES

Graybill, Lyn S. "Ten Years After, Rwanda Tries Reconciliation." *Current History* (May 2004), pp. 202–205. This article is a brief introduction to and summary of the first years of the gacaca courts in Rwanda.

Hagengimana, A., D. Hinton, B. Bird, M. Pollack, and R. K. Pitman. "Somatic Panic-Attack Equivalents in a Community Sample of Rwandan Widows Who Survived the 1994 Genocide." *Psychiatry Research* 117 (1/25/03): pp. 1–9. This is a study of the high rate of panic attacks among Rwandan women widowed in the 1994 genocide and the distinctive physical focus of their panic attacks.

WEB DOCUMENTS

BBC News. "Rwanda Starts Prisoner Releases." (7/29/05). Available online. URL: http://news.bbc.co.uk/2/hi/africa/4726969.stm. Accessed August 2, 2007. This article is a brief news report about the release of persons accused of genocide in Rwanda due to overcrowding in the prisons and the case overload in the national courts.

Chrétien, Jean-Pierre. "RTLM Propaganda: The Democratic Alibi." In *The Media and the Rwandan Genocide*, edited by Allan Thompson. London: Pluto Press and Fountain Publishers, 2007. Available online. URL: http://www.idrc.ca/en/ev-108180-201-1-DO_TOPIC.html. Accessed August 22, 2007. This chapter from a larger book on the role of mass media in the 1994 genocide focuses on the hate radio station, *Radio-Télévision Libre des Milles Collines* (RTLM), and the role of its broadcasts in spreading the ideology of Hutu Power.

Frontline Interview: General Roméo Dallaire. (4/1/04). Available online. URL: http://www.pbs.org/wgbh/pages/frontline/shows/ghosts/interviews/dallaire.html. Accessed March 14, 2007. This is the text version of PBS's *Frontline* interview with Roméo Dallaire. It ends with Dallaire's insistence on taking responsibility for the failure of the UNAMIR mission: ". . . in command there is no 'sort of in command'. . . . What could I have done better, well, we can discuss that for hours. But there's one thing for damn sure: I was in the field, I commanded, I did not convince, I lost soldiers and 800,000 people died. And there's no way of taking that away."

Gbadamassi, Falila. "Kigali accuse Agathe Habyarimana de génocide: L'ancienne Première Dame du Rwanda menacée de poursuites judiciaries." *Afrik.com* (4/1/04). Available online [in French]. URL: http://www.afrik.com/article7171.html. Accessed August 10, 2007. This is a news article on recent attempts by the Rwandan government to bring Agathe Habyarimana to justice for her role in the 1994 genocide.

"How the Mighty Are Falling: The Beginning of the End of Impunity for the World's Once All-Powerful Thugs." *Economist* (7/5/07). Available online. URL: http://www.economist.com/world/international/displaystory.cfm?story_id=9441341. Accessed August 12, 2007. This article is an update on the work of the International Criminal Court (ICC) and the two international criminal tribunals for the former Yugoslavia and Rwanda respectively.

Kabanda, Marcel. "*Kangura*: The Triumph of Propaganda Refined." In *The Media and the Rwandan Genocide*, edited by Allan Thompson. London: Pluto Press and Fountain Publishers, 2007. Available online. URL: http://www.idrc.ca/en/ev-108184-201-1-DO_TOPIC.html. Accessed August 22, 2007. Kabanda is a Rwandan historian who has contributed this chapter on *Kangura*, a bimonthly French-language newspaper that was established in 1990 and quickly gained a reputation as the voice of Hutu extremism. He provides a detailed analysis of the ideology underlying *Kangura*'s articles and editorials as well as a historical account of earlier mass killings in Rwandan history that provided precedents for the killers in 1994. Readers should note that the entire book from which this chapter is taken is available online; a list of the individual chapters may be found at http://www.idrc.ca/en/ev-106013-201-1-DO_TOPIC.html.

Melvern, Linda. "The West Did Intervene in Rwanda, On the Wrong Side." *The Guardian* (4/5/04). Available online. URL: http://www.guardian.co.uk/rwanda/story/0,,1185980,00.html. Accessed August 2, 2007. This article, published just before publication of Melvern's book on the planning of the Rwandan genocide, summarizes her findings: ". . . a corrupt, vicious and violent oligarchy in Rwanda planned and perpetrated the crime of genocide, testing the UN each step of the way. . . . [I]t is not the case [, however,] that foreign powers were absent, but rather that their involvement was entirely limited to serving their own ends."

Power, Samantha. "Bystanders to Genocide." *Atlantic Monthly* (September 2001). Available online. URL: http://www.theatlantic.com/doc/200109/power-genocide. Accessed March 14, 2007. This article is an early version of the chapter on the Rwandan genocide in the author's book *A Problem from Hell*.

Sellström, Tor, and Lennart Wohlgemuth. *The International Response to Conflict and Genocide: Lessons from the Rwanda Experience*, Study 1: Historical Perspective: Some Explanatory Factors. Uppsala, Sweden: Nordic Africa Institute, 1996. Available online. URL: http://www.reliefweb.int/library/nordic/book1/pb020d.html. Accessed August 5, 2007. This is a book-length study first posted in 1996 about the Rwanda genocide. It contains detailed historical and cultural information about the background of the genocide as well as a chronological account of events. The study was carried out in the hopes that the international community could learn better ways of dealing with so-called complex emergencies—situations of violent conflict involving political breakdown, population displacement, and widespread suffering. The authors note that "a complex emergency tends to be very dynamic, characterized by rapid changes that are difficult to predict."

World Food Programme (WFP). "Where We Work—Rwanda." Available online. URL: http://www.wfp.org/country_brief/indexcountry.asp?country=646. Accessed August 2, 2007. A brief description of the UN's largest agency and its specific work in relieving hunger in Rwanda. It supplies some useful background information on the country's geography and demographics.

FILMS

Dallaire, Roméo. *Shake Hands with the Devil: The Journey of Roméo Dallaire.* Directed by Peter Raymont. 90 minutes. White Pine Pictures, 2004. Format: DVD. Available in French under the title *J'ai serré la main du diable.* This film is a documentary based on Dallaire's autobiographical account of the Rwandan genocide and his role as the commander of the ill-fated UNAMIR mission. The film won a prize at the annual Sundance film festival in 2005.

Darfur

BOOKS AND BOOK CHAPTERS

Prunier, Gérard. *Darfur: The Ambiguous Genocide.* Ithaca, N.Y.: Cornell University Press, 2005. Prunier's book is one of the few book-length treatments of the Darfur crisis available as of 2008 and the most useful one for general readers. It offers a glossary of Arabic terms and a helpful introductory chapter about the history, geography, and ethnic groups of Darfur along with maps and a list of abbreviations.

PRINT ARTICLES

Kessler, Glenn, and Colum Lynch. "U.S. Calls Killings in Sudan Genocide." *Washington Post* (9/10/04), p. A1. This is a news article about the controversy stirred up by then-secretary of state Colin Powell's reference to the killings in Darfur as genocide and his naming the government of Sudan and the Jangaweed as the perpetrators.

Leaning, J. "Diagnosing Genocide—The Case of Darfur." *New England Journal of Medicine* 351 (8/19/04), pp. 735–738. The author notes that the Genocide Convention of 1948 does not provide statistical criteria for distinguishing between genocide and mass killing and discusses Darfur as a case study in the difficulty of defining genocide.

WEB DOCUMENTS

Allott, Daniel. "A Non-Credible Threat: Why Khartoum Continues to Kill." *Weekly Standard* (3/23/07). Available online. URL: http://weeklystandard.com/Content/

Public/Articles/000/000/013/409tpapb.asp. Accessed March 27, 2007. This is a news article summarizing the ineffectiveness of UN attempts to stop the killing in Darfur and the floating of proposals to have NATO or such individual nations as France intervene.

BBC News. "African Troops Killed in Darfur." (4/2/07). Available online. URL: http://news.bbc.co.uk/2/hi/africa/6517791.stm. Accessed September 10, 2007. This is a brief news report about the spreading violence in Darfur in the spring of 2007.

———. "UN Backs New Darfur Peace Force," (8/1/07). Available online. URL: http://news.bbc.co.uk/2/hi/africa/6925187.stm. Accessed August 18, 2007. A news report on the UN's establishment of UNAMID, a peacekeeping mission in Darfur that absorbed the African Union peacekeeping force at the end of December 2007.

Hertzke, Allen D. "The Shame of Darfur." *First Things* 156 (October 2005): pp. 16–22. Available online. URL: http://www.firstthings.com/ftissues/ft0510/articles/hertzke. html. Accessed January 8, 2007. This article focuses on the role of religious groups as part of a grassroots movement to stop the genocide in Darfur but also offers a good summary history of Darfur and the evolution of the current crisis.

Marquand, Robert. "World Court's Big Move on Darfur." *Christian Science Monitor* (2/28/07). Available online. URL: http://www.csmonitor.com/2007/0228/p01s02woaf.html?s=t5. Accessed March 3, 2007. This is a news article about the prosecutor of the International Criminal Court (ICC) and his handing down an indictment against a Sudanese government official and the Jangaweed on 51 counts of war crimes and crimes against humanity in Darfur.

Moreno-Ocampo, Luis. "Instrument of Justice: The ICC Prosecutor Reflects," *Jurist* (1/24/07). Available online. URL: http://jurist.law.pitt.edu/forumy/2007/01/instrument-of-justice-icc-prosecutor.php. Accessed April 12, 2007. Moreno-Ocampo's article was written as a guest editorial for the journal of the University of Pittsburgh School of Law. Writing for the general reader, he outlines the history and present role of the International Criminal Court and discusses the court's investigations into Uganda, the Democratic Republic of Congo, and Darfur.

Packer, George. "International Inaction." *New Yorker* (10/9/06). Available online. URL: http://www.newyorker.com/archive/2006/10/09/061009ta_talk_packer. Accessed August 9, 2007. Packer's update on the situation in Darfur notes the curious fact that Arabs are now complaining that Darfur is just one more example of Western opposition to Muslims: "Darfur, where an Arab government unleashed Arab militias to commit massacres against Muslim African farmers, has joined the growing list of Arab grievances—against the West."

Power, Samantha. "Dying in Darfur: Can the Ethnic Cleansing in Sudan Be Stopped?" *New Yorker* (8/30/04). Available online. URL: http://www.newyorker.com/archive/2004/08/30/040830fa_fact1. Accessed April 9, 2007. Power's lengthy article is written in the same readable style as her book, *A Problem from Hell*. The article begins with a description of the Jangaweed's massacre of the inhabitants of a small village in early 2004 and proceeds through a history of the Darfur conflict as of the summer of 2004. The author then summarizes her interviews with several tribal leaders and Sudanese officials.

———. "Missions." *New Yorker* (11/28/05). Available online. URL: http://www.new
yorker.com/archive/2005/11/28/051128ta_talk_power. Accessed August 12, 2007.
This article is Power's report on the African Union's attempt to stop the ongoing
fighting in Darfur by sending in its own mission in May 2004, which had to be
expanded but was still inadequate, and proposals to send an international force
from the UN. She quotes Roméo Dallaire to the effect that at least 44,000 troops
would be needed to protect people still living in Darfur and allow the refugees in
Chad to return home safely.

Other Specific Genocides

BOOKS AND BOOK CHAPTERS

Barenblatt, Daniel. *A Plague upon Humanity: The Secret Genocide of Axis Japan's Germ
Warfare Operation.* New York: HarperCollins, 2004. Barenblatt's is a book-length
account of Japan's Unit 731, a secret facility for medical experiments on human
beings that began operation in 1932, during Japan's invasion of China, and was
not closed down until the end of World War II in 1945. The unit intentionally infected thousands of Chinese prisoners with anthrax, bubonic plague, cholera, and
other deadly contagious diseases. It also developed biological bombs that were
dropped on Chinese villages. About 250,000 people, including Allied prisoners of
war, passed through Unit 731; the great majority died.

Bird, Kai, and Martin J. Sherwin. *American Prometheus: The Triumph and Tragedy
of J. Robert Oppenheimer.* New York: Vintage Books, 2006. This biography of
the famous physicist presents him as a complex individual who was never able
to reconcile his interest in scientific experimentation for its own sake with the
results of his work on the atomic bomb in 1945. The book raises some disturbing long-term questions about the moral implications of contemporary scientific
research.

Brackman, Arnold C. *The Other Nuremberg: The Untold Story of the Tokyo War
Crimes Trials.* New York: William Morrow and Co., 1987. Brackman was a
young correspondent for United Press International when he covered the Tokyo
war crimes in 1946 and 1947. The book contains excerpts from the courtroom
transcripts as well as a chronological account of the war and the crimes for
which seven of the defendants were executed. It also has brief biographies of the
defendants in an appendix.

Chang, Iris. *The Rape of Nanking: The Forgotten Holocaust of World War II.* New York:
Penguin Books, 1998. Chang's book is considered the definitive recent account of
Japan's genocidal activities in China in the late 1930s. Readers should be warned
that the photographs in the center of the book are graphic and may be upsetting
to some. The author was a casualty of her research, committing suicide in 2004
in the middle of a project interviewing American veterans who had suffered as
prisoners of war at the hands of the Japanese in the 1940s.

Conquest, Robert. *The Great Terror: Stalin's Purge of the Thirties,* rev. ed. New York:
Macmillan, 1973; and *The Great Terror: A Reassessment.* London: Hutchinson,

1990. Conquest is a former member of the British Communist Party and historian of Soviet Russia best known for these two books on Stalin's atrocities. He has also written on the human-made famine in the Ukraine in the 1930s (*Harvest of Sorrow*, 1986). The earlier book on Stalin's purges was controversial because most historians believed that Stalin had purged only a relatively small group of Party leaders; Conquest's claim that as many as 20 million Russians died as a result of Stalin's policies in the 1930s seemed incredible. However, access to state archives opened after the collapse of the Soviet Union in 1990 allowed Conquest to confirm the findings reported in his earlier book, and his evaluation of Stalin's regime is no longer questioned by mainstream historians.

Hull, Isabel V. "Military Culture and the Production of 'Final Solutions' in the Colonies: The Example of Wilhelminian Germany." In *The Specter of Genocide: Mass Murder in Historical Perspective*, edited by Robert Gellately and Ben Kiernan. New York: Cambridge University Press, 2003, pp. 141–162. Hull's chapter discusses the German colonial genocide of the Herero in eastern Africa in 1904 in terms of the role of the military in the atrocity. The genocide had not been ordered by civilian authorities in Berlin. Hull examines the German army's preference for unlimited use of force in dealing with the Herero and identifies several factors in the military culture of Germany at the beginning of the 20th century that set it apart from the armies of other European nations.

McCormack, Gavan. "Reflections on Modern Japanese History in the Context of the Concept of Genocide." In *The Specter of Genocide: Mass Murder in Historical Perspective*, edited by Robert Gellately and Ben Kiernan. New York: Cambridge University Press, 2003, pp. 265–286. McCormack's chapter is concerned to examine the concept of genocide itself in order to determine whether the war crimes of imperial Japan in the 1930s can be considered genocidal. Within Japan itself, there is a tendency on the part of scholars to accuse the West of holding double standards in regard to genocide and to maintain that the numbers of civilians killed by the Japanese in Korea and China were the tragic result of conventional warfare rather than the deliberate destruction of a national group. The author concludes the chapter with a reflection on the ongoing difficulty of arriving at a definition of genocide that will cover all historical instances of mass killing.

Morris, James. "The Final Solution, Down Under." In *The History and Sociology of Genocide: Analyses and Case Studies*, edited by Frank Chalk and Kurt Jonassohn. New Haven, Conn: Yale University Press, 1990, pp. 205–222. Morris's chapter, originally published in *Horizon* in 1972, concerns an unusual case of what might be called unintentional genocide. Tasmania is an island near the southern coast of Australia whose original inhabitants were at first hunted down by European settlers who were mostly former convicts, because the island had been used by the British as a penal colony. Ironically, in an attempt to save the 44 survivors, the British authorities moved them to a settlement at Oyster Cove in 1847, where the native Tasmanians gradually died out. A similar situation is said to have occurred in Canada, in that attempts to protect an indigenous population actually led to their dwindling and eventual extinction.

Tokudome, Kinue. "The Holocaust and the Japanese Atrocities." In *Is the Holocaust Unique? Perspectives on Comparative Genocide*, 2nd ed., edited by Alan S. Rosenbaum. Boulder, Colo.: Westview Press, 2001, pp. 195–207. Tokudome's chapter maintains that the Japanese medical experiments and other atrocities of World War II do indeed merit comparison to the Holocaust. He describes the hostile reception Iris Chang's book received in Japan and the refusal of many Japanese scholars to consider the mass killings that took place in China as genocide. Tokudome, a writer and journalist, notes, "It was my profound experience of learning about the Holocaust . . . that awoke me to the realization of my own country's dark history."

Weller, George, and Anthony Weller. *First into Nagasaki: The Censored Eyewitness Dispatches on Post-Atomic Japan and Its Prisoners of War.* New York: Crown Publishing Group, 2006. Anthony Weller is the son of George Weller, a Pulitzer Prize–winning reporter who covered World War II in the Pacific and died in 2002. Weller's eyewitness accounts of the destruction of Nagasaki in August 1945 and his interviews with American prisoners of war tortured by the Japanese were censored by the military in the late 1940s but retrieved from a manuscript copy by his son.

PRINT ARTICLES

Madley, Benjamin. "Patterns of Frontier Genocide 1803–1910: The Aboriginal Tasmanians, the Yuki of California, and the Herero of Namibia." *Journal of Genocide Research* 6 (June 2004): pp. 167–192. This article is a comparative study of three different genocides of indigenous groups from three different time periods on three different continents. The author believes that all three examples follow a common pattern of invasion by settlers, insurgency on the part of the native groups, and imprisonment of the natives on reservations resembling concentration camps.

WEB DOCUMENTS

Associated Press. "*N.Y. Times* Urged to Rescind 1932 Pulitzer." *USA Today* (10/22/03). Available online. URL: http://www.usatoday.com/news/nation/2003-10-22-ny-times-pulitzer_x.htm. Accessed August 26, 2007. A news report about Walter Duranty's misleading articles in the *New York Times* in the 1930s about Stalin's policies and the famine in Ukraine and calls by contemporary historians and journalists to revoke the Pulitzer Prize that Duranty had been awarded for his biased reporting in 1932.

Brass, Paul R. "Organised Riots & Structured Violence in India." *The Hindu* (8/23/06). Available online. URL: http://www.hindu.com/2006/08/23/stories/2006082307241000.htm. Accessed January 18, 2007. This is an op-ed piece by a British scholar who has researched communal violence in India since the early 1960s. Brass maintains that what are called Hindu-Muslim "riots" in the Western press are really pogroms and verge on being genocidal.

Case, David. "The Land That Knew Hell." *Yale Alumni Magazine* (November–December 2003). Available online. URL: http://www.yalealumnimagazine.com/

issues/03_11/easttimor.html. Accessed January 20, 2007. This article is a profile of Ben Kiernan, a professor of comparative genocide at Yale and the founder of the Genocide Studies Program (GSP), the first of its kind in the United States. Kiernan's interview with the president of East Timor, who discusses the atrocities perpetrated on his people, is the centerpiece of the article.

Hancock, Ian. "Jewish Responses to the Porrajmos." Available online. URL: http://www.chgs.umn.edu/Histories_Narratives_Documen/Roma__Sinti_Gypsies_/Jewish_Responses_to_the_Porraj/jewish_responses_to_the_porraj.html. Accessed March 9, 2007. Hancock is a leading expert on the Porrajmos and has written a number of articles on it. Some visual materials related to the Porrajmos (photographs of Roma children used in medical experiments, Roma inmates of Auschwitz, etc.) may be viewed at http://chgs.umn.edu/histories/victims/romaSinti/index.html. Accessed August 22, 2007.

Kristof, Nicholas D. "Unmasking Horror—A Special Report: Japan Confronting Gruesome War Atrocity." *New York Times* (3/17/95). Available online. URL: http://query.nytimes.com/gst/fullpage.html?res=990CE2D71630F934A25750C0A963958260&sec=health&spon=&pagewanted=print. Accessed January 20, 2007. Kristof is a well-known columnist for the *New York Times*. In this article he describes the medical experiments and vivisection performed on Chinese prisoners of war during World War II by Japanese surgeons in the infamous Unit 731—including experiments with poison gas or infecting the prisoners with bubonic plague and then cutting them open without anesthetic to trace the course of the infection through the body.

Windschuttle, Keith. "The Fabrication of Aboriginal History." *The New Criterion* 20 (September 2001). Available online. URL: http://www.newcriterion.com/archive/20/sept01/keith.htm. Accessed January 15, 2007. Windschuttle's work is an example of the importance of questioning accepted versions of history when doing genocide research. The author maintains that most of the evidence for genocides in Australia and Tasmania "turns out to be highly suspect. Most of it is very poorly founded, other parts are seriously mistaken, and a good deal of it is outright fabrication." The remainder of the article contains a detailed analysis of atrocity stories first published in the 19th century and later shown to be false.

11

Chronology

This chapter presents a list of significant events and dates related to genocides and international justice. It begins with genocides in ancient and medieval history that are important in understanding contemporary atrocities and the attempts to prevent them. The reader should note for the ancient and medieval periods that there were doubtless other genocides that went unrecorded, either because there were no survivors or because the accounts that were written were later destroyed. The modern period includes significant dates for genocides that are not discussed at length in the text; they are included here to help the reader understand not only the frequency of genocides but also their interconnection. Many of the perpetrators of recent genocides referred to earlier mass killings in order to excuse or justify their own behavior.

689 B.C.E.

- Sennacherib, king of Assyria, takes the city of Babylon after a lengthy siege. The city is thought to have been the largest in the world at that time and probably the first human city to reach a population of 200,000. Sennacherib is said to have slaughtered civilians until the streets were clogged with corpses and to have diverted the waters of the Euphrates into the city in order to wipe it out completely.

587 B.C.E.

- Nebuchadnezzar II (r. 605–562 B.C.E) takes the city of Jerusalem after a lengthy siege. He destroys the temple and deports the leading citizens to Babylon.

416 B.C.E.

- Athenian troops take the island of Melos, the southwesternmost island of the Cyclades, during the Peloponnesian War. To punish the Melians for not contributing to the Athenian war effort against Sparta, the soldiers kill all the men of military age and sell the women and children into slavery.

Chronology

332 B.C.E.

- Alexander the Great takes Tyre, a Phoenician city in what is now Lebanon, in late spring after a seven-month siege. The Greek soldiers kill about 8,000 men, while the 30,000 women, children, and foreigners in the city are sold into slavery. Alexander orders another 2,000 Tyrians to be crucified (a form of execution he had invented) along the causeway leading from the ruined city.

216 B.C.E.

- *August 2:* Hannibal of Carthage defeats a Roman army twice the size of his forces at Cannae in southeastern Italy during the Second Punic War. Between 50,000 and 70,000 Roman soldiers are killed and another 11,000 captured. The memory of Cannae—one of the costliest battles in military history in terms of lives lost—helps to explain the Roman cruelty toward Carthage half a century later.

146 B.C.E.

- The Third Punic War between Rome and Carthage ends with Scipio Aemilianus's capture of the North African city after a three-year siege. Fifty thousand civilians are allowed to leave the city unharmed before the Romans' final assault on the Byrsa (the central citadel); another 50,000 are thought to have either died in the fires that consumed the city or survived to be sold into slavery.

73–71 B.C.E.

- The Third Servile War (slave rebellion), also known as the Gladiator War or the War of Spartacus, is a two-year conflict between a force of 120,000 escaped gladiators and other slaves and the armies of the Roman republic. The slaves and gladiators are initially successful in raiding the Italian countryside and routing Roman forces. In the second year of the war, the slave army defeats two new Roman armies under the consuls Lucius Gellius and Lentulus Clodianus. It is not until Marcus Licinius Crassus takes command of the legions in 71 B.C.E. that Spartacus's army is decisively defeated. It is estimated that about 60,000 slaves were killed in the final combat. The 6,000 survivors are crucified along the Appian Way between Rome and Capua.

52 B.C.E.

- *October 2:* Surrender of the Gallic fortified city of Alesia (probably the modern Chaux-des-Crotenay; others place it at Alise-Sainte-Reine) gives Julius Caesar's troops a decisive victory over a confederation of Gallic tribes led by Vercingetorix. It is thought that as much as a third of the population of pre-Roman Gaul (contemporary France, Switzerland, and southern Belgium) died of starvation or disease as a result of the Roman campaigns between 56 and 52 B.C.E.

70 C.E.

- *September 7*: The Roman general Titus (ruled as emperor from 79 to 81) takes Jerusalem, burns the city, destroys the Second Temple, and kills or disperses the inhabitants. Estimates of the death toll range between 60,000 and 1 million people.

301 C.E.

- Armenia becomes the first sovereign nation in the world to adopt Christianity as its official state religion.

311 C.E.

- *April 30:* Emperor Galerius issues the Edict of Toleration, which ends the Roman government's persecution of Christianity. In return for this benefit, he asks Christians "to pray to their God for our safety, for that of the republic, and for their own, that the republic may continue uninjured on every side, and that they may be able to live securely in their homes."

989

- The Synod of Charroux, a meeting of local clergy at a Benedictine abbey on the border between La Marche and Aquitaine, decrees the first *Pax Dei* or Peace of God, which granted immunity from violence at the hands of warring nobles to noncombatants who could not defend themselves. The first form of the *Pax Dei* applied to peasant farmers and to clergy, with women and children added within a few years. The nobles were forbidden to beat or rob the defenseless, steal farm animals, and burn houses or churches.

1027

- The Council of Toulouges in Roussillon, presided over by Oliba, the bishop of Vic (a town near present-day Barcelona), decrees the Truce of God, or *Treuga Dei*. The truce forbids the conduct of warfare on Sundays and holy days and is gradually extended to cover the entire season of Lent and the Fridays of the other weeks of the year.

1090–1120

- Approximate dates of cannibalized human remains found in Chaco Canyon and other Anasazi sites in the Four Corners region of the American Southwest.

1099

- *July 15:* Leaders of the First Crusade take Jerusalem after a six-week siege. The inhabitants of the city, some Christians as well as Jews and Muslims, are slaughtered indiscriminately. About 40,000 people are thought to have died in the massacre.

Chronology

1206

- Genghis Khan unites a group of nomadic tribes in northeastern and central Asia to form the nucleus of the Mongol Empire. He is acknowledged as khan, or supreme military leader, at a council of Mongol chieftains.

1209

- The Western Xia dynasty of China surrenders to Genghis Khan after a three-year invasion and acknowledges him as its overlord.
- *July 22:* Béziers, a city in southwestern France, is the first town to be sacked and destroyed during the Albigensian Crusade. The French army burns the city, including the cathedral, and massacres all the inhabitants, "sparing neither age nor sex," as a contemporary chronicler recorded. It is estimated that as many as 10,000 people were slaughtered.

1211

- Genghis Khan begins the expansion of his empire into eastern China, India, Afghanistan, Persia, and Russia. Estimates of the Chinese death toll alone are 18.4 million people.

1219

- The Mongols cross the Tien Shan Mountains, entering the Khwarezmid Empire of Shah Ala ad-Din Muhammad. The campaign marks the beginning of Genghis Khan's expansion into Islamic states and also the first time the Mongols used wholesale slaughter of conquered populations as a tactic to terrorize others.

1221

- The city of Merv in what is now Turkmenistan surrenders to the Mongols under Tule, the son of Genghis Khan, without a fight. In spite of the fact that the city offered no resistance, the Mongols butcher the inhabitants, including cats and dogs as well as hundreds of thousands of refugees who had fled to the city. The death toll may have reached as high as 1.3 million human beings.

1222

- Genghis Khan's army slaughters 1.6 million people in the city of Herat in northwestern Afghanistan, using only hand weapons (clubs, swords, and arrows).

1227

- *August 18:* Genghis Khan dies in western China. His body is returned to Mongolia for burial. According to later legend, the funeral escort killed everyone they encountered on their journey so that no one would know for certain where the khan was buried.

1244

- *March:* The Cathar fortress at Montségur in southern France falls to the troops of the French king after a siege of several months. About 220 survivors of the siege are burned alive en masse at the foot of the mountain when they refuse to renounce their faith.

1258

- *January 29:* The Mongol leader Hulagu Khan, who has assembled the largest Mongol army in history, begins the siege of Baghdad.
- *February 10:* Baghdad falls to the Mongols, ending the Abbasid caliphate. One descendant flees to Egypt, where the caliphate continues as a shadow institution. The massacre of the city's population followed; estimates of the death toll range between 90,000 and half a million.

1260

- *September 3:* The Mongol army is defeated by the Mamluk Turks at the battle of Ain Jalut (in present-day Israel). This battle is the first time the Mongols are defeated by another power; it also leads to civil war among Genghis Khan's descendants and the eventual end of the Mongol Empire.

1346

- A Tartar khan throws the bodies of his soldiers who have died of bubonic plague over the walls of Kaffa, a city in the Crimea under siege by his troops. It is thought that Genoese merchants fleeing Kaffa carried the plague to Western Europe, thus causing the pandemic known as the Black Death.

1398

- *December 17:* Timur the Lame, a descendant of the Mongol khans known to the West as Tamerlane, invades India in the fall of 1398. He has 100,000 Indian prisoners of war slaughtered before the siege of Delhi in December. After Delhi falls to the invaders, most of the inhabitants are killed. The final death toll may have reached as high as 1 million people.

1400

- *September:* Timur begins his invasion of Syria.
- *October 30:* Aleppo falls to the invaders. Timur's army plunders the city and massacres the inhabitants; at least 20,000 people are killed.

1401

- *February 25*: Timur's troops enter Damascus and begin a two-week reign of terror. After this massacre, Timur is declared an enemy of Islam by other Muslim rulers.

- *July 23*: Timur takes Baghdad and orders his soldiers to bring him two severed heads apiece. A pyramid of 90,000 human heads is constructed outside the ruined city. The total death toll from Timur's campaigns is estimated at 17 million people.

1432

- Thai troops under King Ayuthaya capture the Cambodian capital of Angkor, sack the city, and carry off 90,000 prisoners. The Khmer kings then move their capital to Phnom Penh.

1453

- *May 29*: Constantinople falls to the Ottoman Turks under Sultan Mehmed II after a siege lasting seven weeks. The loss of the city causes the Western European monarchies to look toward the Atlantic as the sea route to the East. Mehmet adopts the title of caliph to justify his conquest of other Muslim countries.

1492

- *January 2*: The city of Granada falls to the troops of Ferdinand and Isabella, thus ending 800 years of Islamic rule over southern Spain.
- *August 3–October 12*: Christopher Columbus leaves the port of Palos de la Frontera in Spain and makes his first voyage across the Atlantic. The voyage ends when a sailor sights the island of San Salvador at 2 A.M. on October 12.

1520

- *May 10*: A massacre takes place in the Aztec capital city of Tenochtitlán after Hernán Cortés leaves the city in the temporary charge of his deputy governor, Pedro de Alvarado. The Aztec nobility gathered to celebrate a festival known as Toxcatl, in honor of one of their major gods. According to Spanish sources, the massacre occurs when the Spanish soldiers interrupt a hideous act of human sacrifice. According to the Aztec sources, the Spaniards attacked the nobles in order to take the gold ornaments they were wearing.

1521

- *August 13*: Spanish troops under Hernán Cortés overrun the Aztec capital city of Tenochtitlán after a siege beginning on May 26. Much of the city is destroyed, along with 100,000 of its inhabitants. Smallpox and typhus epidemics decimate the survivors of the Aztec Empire, reducing a population estimated at 19 million in 1520 to less than 2 million by 1581.

1529

- *September 29–October 14*: The Ottoman Turks under Sultan Suleiman I (Suleiman the Magnificent) besiege Vienna. They are finally driven away by the defenders led by Nicholas, Graf von Salm. The failure of the siege marks the high point of Ottoman power in Europe.

1539

- *May 30*: The Spanish explorer Hernando de Soto lands on the coast of Florida near what is now Tampa Bay, bringing 300 pigs along with his 600 soldiers and 200 horses. De Soto's pigs introduce a variety of zoonotic (animal-borne) diseases previously unknown in North America, decimating the indigenous populations from the Carolinas to Texas.

1540–1541

- Francisco Vásquez de Coronado leads a force of Spanish troops against the Indians of the 12 Tiguex pueblos lying on both sides of the Rio Grande in what is now New Mexico. The Tiguex War is the first war between Europeans and Native Americans in the American West.

1566

- *July 17*: Bartolomé de Las Casas dies in Madrid.

1592–1598

- Toyotomi Hideyoshi, a warlord who unifies Japan after several centuries of civil war, invades Korea repeatedly over a period of seven years. The ears and noses of 40,000 Koreans, civilians as well as soldiers, are brought back to Kyoto and placed in a monument called the Mimizuka or Ear Mound. Some historians estimate that as many as 1 million Koreans were killed during the Japanese invasions.

1625

- Hugo Grotius, a Dutch lawyer and philosopher in exile in France, publishes *De jure belli ac pacis libri tres* (Three books on the law of war and peace), dedicated to King Louis XIII of France. Grotius sets forth a theory of just war and the proper conduct of war that stands at the beginning of Western thought about international law.

1637

- *May 26*: A force of 90 English settlers under the command of Captain John Mason, together with about 300 braves from the Niantic, Narragansett, and Mohegan tribes, surround the Pequot village at Mystic, Connecticut, in retaliation for the murder of a trader named John Oldham. The village is set on fire to prevent the inhabitants—mostly women and children—from escaping. Between 400 and 700 Pequots died in the Mystic massacre.

1649

- *March 16*: Members of the Iroquois tribe attack and destroy St. Louis, a village of Huron Indians in what is now Ontario, Canada. Jean de Brébeuf, a French Jesuit missionary, is tortured and burned to death along with the captured Hurons. The Iroquois perform an act of cannibalism on the remains of their victims.
- *September 12*: The Ottoman Turks under Kara Mustafa Pasha are defeated at the gates of Vienna by a combined army led by the Duke of Lorraine and Jan Sobieski, the king of Poland. Mustafa Pasha is executed in December for losing the battle.

1663

- John Eliot publishes the Bible in the language of the Massachusett Indians. It is the first Bible printed in North America in any language.

1675

- *June 20*: Beginning of King Philip's War, a yearlong conflict between white settlers in southern New England, leading to the death of 600 colonists and 3,000 Native Americans.

1680

- *August 10*: Beginning of the Pueblo Revolt, an uprising of the Taos, Picuris, and Tewa Indians against the Spanish settlers in and around Santa Fe. The Indians' chief grievance is the Spaniards' suppression of their traditional folk religion. The Spanish settlers flee to El Paso. Popé, the leader of the revolt, installs himself in the Palace of the Governors in Santa Fe. He dies in 1688.

1692

- *September 14*: Diego de Vargas, the new governor of the Spanish colony in Santa Fe, agrees to peace with the Pueblo Indians and promises clemency provided they swear allegiance to the King of Spain and return to Christianity. Both sides keep their promises.

1699

- *January 26*: The Treaty of Carlowitz is signed, ending the Austro-Ottoman War (1683–97). The Ottoman Empire agrees to give up various territories in Europe to Austria, Poland, and Venice. The treaty indicates that the balance of power between an Islamic empire and the West is shifting in favor of the West. The Ottoman Empire enters on a long period of gradual decline, leading to a sense of humiliation and inferiority on the part of its leaders.

1754

- *May 28*: Opening skirmishes of the French and Indian War near present-day Uniontown, Pennsylvania. A French officer is killed by a group of Virginia militiamen under the command of George Washington.

1760

- *September 8*: The governor of New France surrenders Montreal (and effectively all of French Canada) to Lord Jeffrey Amherst, thus ending the fighting in North America in the French and Indian War.

1763

- *February 10*: The Treaty of Paris is signed, formally ending the French and Indian War.

- *December 14*: The Paxton Boys, a group of Scots-Irish frontiersmen, murder six Susquehannock Indians living in the village of Conestoga in southeastern Pennsylvania. On December 27, they march northeastward to Lancaster and murder the surviving Conestoga who had been placed there by Governor John Penn for protection. The death of these Indians marks the extinction of the tribe.

1775–1782

- A major smallpox epidemic ravages the eastern seaboard of North America from British Canada to Florida, killing whites, black slaves, and Native Americans alike.

1795

- The philosopher Immanuel Kant publishes *Zum ewigen Frieden* (On perpetual peace), a philosophical proposal for the establishment of a world federation of free nation-states.

1796

- *March*: The French Revolutionary Committee of Public Safety succeeds in crushing a three-year revolt in the Vendée, a region along the western coast of France. Sometimes considered the first modern genocide because of its ideological motivation, the massacre of the inhabitants of the Vendée is estimated to have killed as many as 250,000 out of a total population of 800,000. One of the Committee's innovations was the "national bath," a form of execution in which people were tied up and loaded onto barges that were then sunk in the Loire River. One such barge contained over 400 children.

1827

- *July 26*: The Cherokees of Georgia draw up their own constitution and declare themselves a sovereign nation.

Chronology

1830

- *May 28*: President Andrew Jackson signs into law the Indian Removal Act, passed by Congress only after bitter debate.

1831

- *May 10*: Jeremiah Evarts dies of tuberculosis in Charleston, South Carolina.

1835

- *December 29*: Leaders of a faction within the Cherokee Nation known as the Ridge Party sign the Treaty of New Echota, according to which the federal government agrees to pay the Cherokees $4.5 million for their lands in Georgia and Alabama, pay for the costs of their relocation, and give them land in Indian Territory (present-day Oklahoma).

1838

- *May 23*: Deadline for voluntary removal of the Cherokee tribe.
- *May 26*: Beginning of the forcible removal of the Cherokees of Georgia by federal troops under the command of Winfield Scott.
- *July 25*: Scott agrees to turn over the relocation of the tribe to Chief John Ross. The transfer of authority becomes effective in August.

1839

- *March*: The last of the Cherokee groups to leave Georgia arrives in Indian Territory.
- *June 22*: Three leaders of the Ridge Party are ambushed and killed for their role in signing the Treaty of New Echota.

1858

- *July*: Gold is discovered near Pike's Peak, Colorado, setting off the Colorado gold rush. The sudden influx of 100,000 prospectors and other new settlers adds to the tensions between whites and Indians on the Colorado frontier.

1863

- *January 29*: A detachment of the Union Army under the command of Colonel Patrick Edward Connor massacres about 250 Shoshone warriors at the confluence of Bear River and Beaver Creek near present-day Preston, Idaho. After the men of the tribe were killed, the soldiers proceed to rape and kill women and children.
- *February 17*: J. Henry Dunant, a Swiss businessman who has been traveling throughout Europe to promote the idea of a neutral humanitarian society to care for injured soldiers in wartime, meets with two Swiss doctors, a lawyer, and an army general to found the International Committee of the Red Cross.

1864

- *July 11*: Four members of the Nathan Hungate family are murdered by a group of Cheyenne and Arapaho Indians on their ranch near Denver. The killing creates panic among the white settlers in Colorado Territory.
- *August 11*: Governor John Evans of Colorado issues a proclamation calling on all citizens of the territory to kill all Indians and seize their property.
- *August 22*: Adoption of the First Geneva Convention by 16 European nations. The Convention, whose official title is "A Convention for the Amelioration of the Condition of the Wounded in Armies in the Field," is intended to save the lives of injured combatants in warfare and protect civilians rendering aid.
- *August 29*: Black Kettle, a chief of the Cheyenne, sends a letter to the authorities at Fort Lyon offering to exchange seven captives taken by Arapahos to his village for assurances of peace.
- *November 29*: Troops of the Colorado militia under the command of Colonel John Chivington attack and massacre the Cheyenne and Arapaho Indians in Black Kettle's village at Sand Creek, killing about 180 persons, mostly women, children, and elderly men.

1865

- *April 23*: Silas Soule is shot and killed outside his home in Denver, Colorado, by Charles Squires, a soldier thought by some to have been hired by some of Chivington's men to murder Soule.
- *November 10*: Henry Wirz, the only former Confederate soldier executed for war crimes after the Civil War, is hanged in front of the U.S. Capitol for conspiracy to impair the lives of Union prisoners of war. Twenty-eight percent of the Union soldiers held at the prison run by Wirz near Andersonville, Georgia, died of disease, malnutrition, and abuse by guards. Wirz's trial in the summer of 1865 was the first trial for war crimes in modern history and set a precedent for the Nuremberg War Crimes Tribunal after World War II.

1868

- *November 27*: Black Kettle is killed by cavalry under the command of George A. Custer in pursuit of Cheyenne who had taken captives into Black Kettle's village.

1870

- *January 23*: Major Eugene Baker, an officer of the U.S. Army with a known history of alcoholism, raids a camp of the Piegan Indians camped along the Marias River in northwestern Idaho. As the men of the tribe are out hunting, Baker's soldiers kill 173 people, mostly women and children, with another 140 women and children captured.

1881

- *March 13*: Czar Alexander II of Russia is assassinated by a bomb thrown by a left-wing revolutionary. Hessia Helfmann, a young Jewish girl, is arrested for her part in the assassination plot. The czar's death is followed by three years of anti-Semitic pogroms in Russia.

1894–1896

- Between the summer of 1894 and August 1896, the government of the Ottoman Empire carries out a series of peacetime massacres of Armenians, killing between 100,000 and 300,000 people. These mass killings are usually called the Hamidian massacres (after the name of the sultan, Abdul Hamid II), to distinguish them from the Armenian genocide of 1915.

1899

- *May 18*: Opening of the First International Peace Conference at The Hague.
- *July 29*: Signing of the first Hague Convention on settlement of international disputes and the laws of war on land. The convention enters into force on September 4, 1900.

1901

- *December 10*: J. Henry Dunant is awarded the first Nobel Peace Prize, which he shares with Frédéric Passy, the founder and president of the first French peace society.

1903

- *April 6–7*: The killing of a Christian boy (by a relative, it was later discovered) around the time of the Russian Orthodox celebration of Easter touches off a pogrom in the city of Kishinev (in present-day Moldova). Forty-seven Jews are killed and 500 others wounded. The Russian government does nothing to stop the rioters until the third day of violence. The Kishinev pogrom is considered the first state-sponsored act of violence against Jews in the 20th century.

1904

- *January 12*: Beginning of Herero revolt in German South-West Africa (present-day Namibia) under the leadership of Samuel Maharero. The tribesmen attack German settlers, killing about 120 people, including women and children, and burning several farms.
- *August 11*: German troops, although outnumbered by a ratio of 3 to 1, defeat the Herero at the Battle of Waterberg. The Germans capture almost all the wells and water holes, forcing the surviving Herero into the Omaheke desert, where many die of starvation and dehydration.

1905

- *July 21*: A group of Armenian patriots attempts to assassinate Sultan Abdul Hamid II with a car bomb outside a mosque; the attempt fails because the bomb timer goes off before the sultan arrives for Friday prayers. Twenty-six bystanders are killed and 58 wounded.

1907

- *June 15*: Opening of the Second Peace Conference at The Hague.
- *October 18*: Signing of the Second Hague Convention, which enters into force on January 26, 1910.

1908

- *July 3*: The Young Turks, a collection of various groups committed to reforming the Ottoman Empire, revolt against the sultan, who capitulates on July 23 and agrees to restore the parliament, which had not met since 1876.

1909

- *March*: Abdul Hamid II stages a countercoup against the Young Turks, pledging to restore the caliphate, the traditional privileges of Muslims within the Ottoman Empire, and Islamic law.
- *April 1*: Beginning of violence in Adana province, leading to the massacre of 20,000–30,000 Armenians by the end of April.
- *April 27*: Abdul Hamid II is finally deposed as the ruler of the Ottoman Empire. His brother succeeds him as Sultan Mehmed V.

1912

- *October 8*: Outbreak of First Balkan War. The Ottoman Empire suffers the loss of Macedonia and Thrace to a coalition of Greece, Serbia, and Bulgaria. In order to cope with resettling Muslim refugees from the lost territories, the government begins ethnic cleansing of Armenians living in Anatolia (the Asian portion of Turkey). The territorial losses of the war also strengthen the government's belief that the army should be exclusively Muslim.

1913

- *January 23*: The Three Pashas (Talat Pasha, Enver Pasha, and Cemal Pasha) carry out a coup that restores the Committee of Union and Progress to power. They form a one-party dictatorship and rule as a triumvirate.

1914

- *June 28*: Archduke Franz Ferdinand, the heir apparent of Austria-Hungary, and his wife are assassinated in Sarajevo, the capital of Bosnia, by a Serb student named Gavrilo Princip. The assassination is followed by a series of diplomatic maneuvers that end in Austria-Hungary's declaration of war on Serbia on July 28, Russian mobilization of its armed forces on July 31, Germany's declaration of war on Russia on August 1, Germany's declaration of war on France on August 3, and Germany's invasion of Belgium on August 4. Great Britain declares war on Germany for violating Belgian neutrality that same day.

- *November 11*: The Ottoman Empire enters World War I on the side of the Central Powers.
- *December 29*: Beginning of the battle of Sarikamish, in which Russia inflicts a devastating defeat on the Turkish army. The battle ends on January 4, 1915. It serves as a partial pretext for the Armenian genocide.

1915

- *February 19*: Beginning of the Gallipoli campaign, in which a joint British and French expedition attempts to capture the Ottoman capital of Istanbul by going overland across the Gallipoli peninsula. The defeat and eventual withdrawal of the Allied forces (in January 1916) leads to a new surge of nationalist feeling among the Turks.
- *April 19*: Beginning of the siege of Van.
- *April 24*: The government of Turkey arrests nearly 300 leading Armenian intellectuals.
- *May 7*: A German submarine torpedoes the RMS *Lusitania*, a British vessel with 128 Americans aboard. The ship sinks in only 18 minutes, causing the death of most of the passengers. Although the United States does not enter World War I for another two years, public opinion turns sharply against Germany.
- *May 24*: Great Britain, France, and Russia issue a joint declaration accusing Turkey of "crimes against humanity"—the massacres of Armenians—and state that they will hold members of the Ottoman government "personally responsible" for their part in the massacres.
- *May 29*: The central committee of the CUP passes the Tehcir Law or Temporary Law of Deportation.

1917

- *January 16*: Arthur Zimmermann, the foreign secretary of the German Empire, sends a coded telegram to Heinrich Eckardt, the German ambassador in Mexico, instructing Eckardt to approach the Mexican government with a proposal to form an alliance against the United States. The telegram is intercepted by the British, decoded by a naval intelligence group, and relayed to the British foreign minister, who in turn delivers the contents to the United States ambassador in London.

- *April 6*: The United States declares war on Germany and enters World War I on the side of the Allied Powers.

1918

- *March 3*: The new Bolshevik government of Russia signs the Treaty of Brest-Litovsk with the Central Powers. The treaty takes Russia out of World War I and cedes Finland, parts of Poland, and the Baltic countries to Germany and Austria-Hungary.
- *October 30*: The armistice of Mudros ends hostilities between the Ottoman Empire and the Allied Powers.
- *November 11*: An armistice between Germany and the Allied Powers is signed in the forest of Compiègne, to take effect at 11 A.M. The armistice marks the effective end of World War I.

1919

- *January 18*: Opening of the Paris Peace Conference.
- *February 14*: Woodrow Wilson completes the initial draft of the Covenant of the League of Nations.
- *June 28*: Signing of the Treaty of Versailles, considered the official end of World War I. Part I of the treaty establishes the League of Nations.
- *November 19*: The United States Senate votes against joining the League of Nations.

1920

- *January 10*: First official meeting of the League of Nations.
- *January 21*: Closing of the Paris Peace Conference.
- *March 19*: The U.S. Senate refuses to ratify the Treaty of Versailles.
- *August 10*: Signing of the Treaty of Sèvres, between the Ottoman Empire and the European Allies of World War I. Turkey is compelled to recognize an independent Armenia and to cede certain disputed territories to Greece. The treaty is nullified by the Turkish nationalist movement and the founding of a republican state in Turkey in 1922.
- *November 15*: The League of Nations holds its first general assembly after it moves to new headquarters in Geneva, Switzerland.

1921

- *March 14*: Soghomon Tehlirian, a survivor of the Armenian genocide, assassinates Talat Pasha, the former Turkish minister of the interior, whom Tehlirian considered responsible for the death of his family. The killing reawakens Raphael Lemkin's interest in drafting an international law against mass murder based on ethnicity or nationality. Tehlirian is acquitted by a Berlin jury on grounds of temporary insanity.

1923

- *July 24*: Signing of the Treaty of Lausanne. The treaty secures international recognition of the new Republic of Turkey, settles boundary disputes between Greece and Turkey, and provides for a population exchange between the two countries that involves about 2 million people. The population exchange, known in Greece as the Asia Minor Catastrophe, is carried out in 1923, creating large-scale suffering for both Greek and Turkish nationals.

1929

- *July 27*: Signing of the Third Geneva Convention, titled "A Convention Relative to the Treatment of Prisoners of War." The Convention entered into force on June 13, 1931.
- *October 22–24*: Collapse of the New York Stock Exchange, ending the economic boom of the late 1920s, setting off a chain reaction in banking systems and stock exchanges around the world, and leading into the Great Depression of the 1930s. Hitler's rise to power in Germany was made possible in part by the impact of the depression on the German economy.

1932–1933

- Famine kills between 5 and 6 million people in the rural areas of Ukraine as the result of the policies of Joseph Stalin, the Soviet dictator. In addition to the forced collectivization of land, Stalin refuses to send humanitarian aid to the stricken region. The Holodomor, as it is known, is sometimes called the Ukrainian genocide.

1933

- *January 30*: Hitler is appointed Chancellor of Germany by President Paul von Hindenburg.
- *March 23*: Passage of the Enabling Act, which essentially places the legislative powers of the Reichstag (German parliament) in the chancellor's hands. The act permits the chancellor and his cabinet to deviate from the constitution of the German republic and to issue laws without submitting them to the Reichstag for approval.
- *July 14*: Hitler's regime promulgates the Law for the Prevention of Hereditarily Diseased Offspring, which mandates the sterilization of persons with schizophrenia, epilepsy, chronic alcoholism, mental retardation, Huntington's disease, and other diseases or mental disorders known (or thought at the time) to be inherited. By 1935 over 300,000 people had been forcibly sterilized.

1934

- **December 1**: Sergei Kirov, a member of the Central Committee of the Russian Communist Party, is assassinated in Leningrad. Stalin uses the murder as an excuse to hunt down "enemies of the state" within the party, beginning with its elites. Over 1,500,000 people are arrested and 681,000 executed during the so-called Great Purge of 1937–38. Stalin's purge sets a precedent for Pol Pot's purge of the Khmer Rouge in 1977.

1935

- **September 15**: The government of Nazi Germany passes the Nuremberg laws in two major parts: the "Laws for the Protection of German Blood and German Honor," which forbid intermarriage between Jews and "citizens of German or kindred blood," and the "Reich Citizenship Law," which stripped Jews in Germany of their citizenship.

1936

- **January 3**: The Nuremberg laws forbidding intermarriage between German non-Jews and Jews are extended to the Gypsies.
- **March 7**: Jews and Gypsies in Germany are deprived of the right to vote in elections.

1937

- **December 13**: Nanking falls to the Imperial Japanese army, which begins a six-week massacre of civilians as well as Chinese soldiers and prisoners of war. The death toll is estimated to be between 150,000 and 300,000 people.

1938

- **March 12**: The Anschluss Österreichs—Austria is formally and forcibly annexed by Nazi Germany. It ceases to exist as a fully independent nation until 1955.
- **November 9–10**: Kristallnacht, or the Night of Broken Glass. Ordinary citizens and Nazi storm troopers throughout Germany and parts of Austria attack Jewish homes, stores, and synagogues with sledgehammers. Thirty thousand Jewish men are taken to concentration camps and over 1600 synagogues are set on fire.

1939

- **September 1**: Germany invades Poland. World War II begins when France and Great Britain declare war on September 3.

1941

- **July 31**: Reinhard Heydrich, the chief of Hitler's Reich Security Main Office and one of the architects of the Holocaust, gives an official order for the killing of "all Jews, Gypsies, and mental patients." This directive is considered by some scholars to mark the beginning of the Holocaust.

- **December 7**: The Japanese attack the U.S. Pacific Fleet at the naval base in Pearl Harbor on the island of Oahu, Hawaii. Congress declares war on Japan the next day, December 8.

1942

- **January 20**: Heydrich chairs the Wannsee Conference, a meeting of senior Nazi officials held at a villa in the Berlin suburb of Wannsee, to plan the so-called Final Solution of the Jewish Question.
- **June 4**: Heydrich dies in Prague of massive blood poisoning following an assassination attempt on May 27.

1942–1945

- Some 21,000 out of 50,000 Allied prisoners of war die during transport to Japanese POW camps in so-called hellships. Thirty-four percent of POWs in Japanese camps die from maltreatment, compared with 4 percent in German prison camps.

1943

- **May 12**: Szmul Zygielbojm, a leader of the Polish government-in-exile who had tried to persuade the Allies to accept more Jewish refugees and to bomb Auschwitz, commits suicide in London after his proposals are rejected.

1944

- **August 1**: Ziguenernacht: A mass killing in which 4,000 Gypsies are gassed and burned in one mass action at Auschwitz-Birkenau.
- **November**: The Carnegie Endowment for International Peace publishes Raphael Lemkin's book, *Axis Rule in Occupied Europe*, which introduces the term *genocide*.

1945

- **April 25**: The United Nations Conference on International Organizations begins in San Francisco.
- **May 7**: General Alfred Jodl signs the instrument of unconditional surrender of all German armed forces to the Allied powers in Rheims, France. Victory in Europe Day (VE Day) is celebrated on May 8.
- **June 26**: The Charter of the United Nations is signed by the 50 nations represented at the San Francisco conference.
- **August 6**: The first atomic bomb is dropped on Hiroshima, Japan.
- **August 8**: The London Charter of the International Military Tribunal (IMT) is issued, stipulating the procedures by which members of the European Axis

powers (Germany and Italy) could be tried. It defined three categories of crimes: war crimes, crimes against peace, and crimes against humanity.

- *August 9*: The second atomic bomb is dropped on Nagasaki. The immediate death toll from both bombs is estimated to have been between 100,000 and 200,000 people. Many survivors of the initial blasts die later from radiation poisoning.

- *August 15*: The Allied nations celebrate Victory in Japan (VJ) Day.

- *September 2*: Japanese representatives sign the formal document of surrender aboard the USS *Missouri* in Tokyo Bay.

- *October 24*: The United Nations comes into existence when the five permanent members of the Security Council (the Republic of China, France, the Soviet Union, the United Kingdom, and the United States) and a majority of the other signatories ratify the Charter of the United Nations.

1946

- *October 16*: Execution by hanging of German war criminals sentenced to death at the Nuremberg trials. Hermann Göring cheats the executioner by swallowing a capsule of potassium cyanide on the evening of October 15.

1947

- *July 16*: Raoul Wallenberg is executed by firing squad in Lubyanka Prison in Moscow, according to the November 2000 report of a Russian investigative commission.

1948–1987

- Kim il-Sung, the Communist dictator of North Korea, carries out a series of purges, mass executions, and forced labor of civilians that are thought to have cost between 710,000 and 3.5 million lives during his rule.

1948

- *June 2*: Seven defendants in the Nuremberg Doctors' Trial are executed by hanging for war crimes and crimes against humanity; specifically, for performing medical experiments on prisoners of war without the subjects' consent and for participation in the mass murder of concentration camp inmates.

- *December 9*: The General Assembly of the United Nations approves the Convention on the Prevention and Punishment of the Crime of Genocide by unanimous vote.

- *December 22*: Hideki Tōjō is executed by hanging for ordering the murders of 8 million civilians in countries under Japanese rule as well as inhumane experiments and murders of tens of thousands of Allied prisoners of war. Five other high-ranking generals and one civilian diplomat die with him.

Chronology

1949

- **August 12**: Signing of the Third and Fourth Geneva Conventions, which amend the 1929 document concerning the treatment of prisoners of war and also provide for the protection of civilians and others in the category of "protected persons."

1951

- **January 12**: The Convention on the Prevention and Punishment of the Crime of Genocide enters into force as international law.

1959

- **August 28**: Raphael Lemkin collapses and dies of a heart attack in New York City.

1961

- **October 26**: Grégoire Kayibanda, a Hutu politician from southern Rwanda, becomes the first elected president of the new nation.

1962

- **June 1**: Adolf Eichmann is hanged at Ramla prison in Israel for crimes against humanity. His body is cremated and his ashes scattered over the Mediterranean in international waters, so that there could be no memorial nor any one nation identified as his burial place.

1967

- **January 11**: Senator William Proxmire delivers his first speech on the Senate floor urging ratification of the 1948 genocide convention. He makes a total of 3,211 speeches over a period of 19 years on the subject.

1970

- **March 18**: Norodom Sihanouk is deposed from power in Cambodia and replaced by Lon Nol, head of the armed forces.
- **April 29**: American forces begin the bombing of North Vietnamese sanctuaries in Cambodia.

1971

- **March 26**: Bangladesh (then East Pakistan) declares its independence from West Pakistan, following a general strike in opposition to the president's suspension of the national assembly.
- **March 27**: The West Pakistani army declares war on East Pakistan, concentrating on eliminating the Bangladeshis within its own ranks, Hindus living in Pakistan, and anyone supporting Bangladeshi independence. Between 1 and 3 million people are killed.

- **December 3**: India invades East Pakistan in support of the independence movement.
- **December 16**: The West Pakistani army surrenders.
- **December 17**: East Pakistan is established as an independent nation.

1972

- **January 11**: East Pakistan formally changes its name to Bangladesh.
- **April 29**: Beginning of genocide of Hutus in Burundi by the Tutsi minority, which nonetheless controlled the army. It is estimated that 250,000 people were killed during April and May 1972.

1973

- **July 5**: Major General Juvénal Habyarimana overthrows the Rwandan government of Grégoire Kayibanda.

1974

- **September 12**: The Derg, a Marxist military junta, overthrows Emperor Haile Selassie of Ethiopia. Civil war between the Derg and various opposition parties breaks out the following year and lasts until 1987. Between 50,000 and 100,000 people are killed in the fighting. The Derg's campaign is sometimes known as the Red Terror.

1975

- **April 1**: Lon Nol resigns as head of state and leaves Phnom Penh, the capital of Cambodia.
- **April 17**: The Khmer Rouge enter Phnom Penh in force. Within hours, they begin to evacuate the city, forcing the entire population into the countryside to work on collective farms. They rename the country Democratic Kampuchea.
- **November 28**: East Timor declares its independence from Portugal.
- **December 7**: Indonesia invades East Timor.

1978

- **December 22**: Malcolm Caldwell, a Scottish Marxist who has visited Cambodia with two other Western journalists, is murdered after his personal interview with Pol Pot.
- **December 25**: Vietnam begins a full-scale invasion of Cambodia.

1979

- **January 7**: Vietnamese forces enter Phnom Penh; Pol Pot and other Khmer Rouge leaders flee across northern Cambodia into Thailand.

Chronology

1980

- *May 4*: Death of Tito (Josip Broz), president of the Socialist Federal Republic of Yugoslavia (SFRY). The loose federation begins a slow process of internal decline and dissolution.

1981

- *October 5*: Raoul Wallenberg is made an honorary citizen of the United States for his role in rescuing Hungarian Jews from the Holocaust.

1983–1984

- Darfur suffers two years of famine when the annual rains fail, leading to a loss of almost 100,000 people out of a total population of 3.1 million.

1986

- *February 11*: Senator Bob Dole is able to bring the 1948 genocide convention to a full Senate vote. At this point in time, 97 nations had ratified the convention ahead of the United States.

1988

- *February 23*: Official beginning of al-Anfal attacks on Iraqi Kurdistan by Iraqi troops commanded by members of the Baath Party of Saddam Hussein. Between 180,000 and 200,000 Kurds are killed by mass executions by firing squads, forced deportations, and chemical warfare.
- *March 15–19*: Iraqi airplanes drop chemical bombs containing mustard gas, tabun, sarin, hydrogen cyanide, and VX on Halabja, a city in Iraq about eight miles from the Iranian border. Between 1,000 and 5,000 people are killed in the attack, which is considered the largest-scale use of chemical weapons on a civilian population in modern times.
- *May*: Outbreaks of fighting in Darfur; first references to the Janjaweed (armed groups of thugs). About 9,000 people are killed in what are considered tribal conflicts.
- *September 6*: End of al-Anfal attacks.
- *October 19*: The Senate passes the Genocide Convention Implementation Act, also known as the Proxmire Act, which is signed into law by President Ronald Reagan on November 4.

1989

- Vietnamese forces finally leave Cambodia.

1990

- *August 2*: Iraqi troops invade Kuwait.

1991

- *January 17*: Beginning of Operation Desert Storm (the Gulf War), a coalition of 12 nations to remove the Iraqis from Kuwait.
- *February 28*: End of the Gulf War.
- *May*: Mengistu Haile Mariam, leader of the Ethiopian Derg, flees to Zimbabwe to escape opposition forces advancing on the capital of Addis Ababa.
- *June 25*: Croatia, one of six states that comprised the former Yugoslavia, declares its independence of the Socialist Federal Republic of Yugoslavia (SFRY).
- *June 27*: Slovenia declares its independence of the SFRY; fighting breaks out.
- *July 6*: End of the Ten-Day War for Slovenia's independence.
- *November 12*: Indonesian troops massacre 250–400 East Timorese civilians in a cemetery following a funeral Mass in Dili, the capital of East Timor. The massacre is caught on videotape by a British journalist and shown on television; it turns world opinion against Indonesia.
- *November 18–21*: About 260 Croats (including POWs and civilians) are taken from a hospital and massacred by members of the Yugoslav People's Army (JNA) near the city of Vukovar in northeastern Croatia.

1992

- *January 15*: Croatia is recognized as an independent state by the European Union.

1993

- *May 25*: The United Nations Security Council establishes the International Criminal Tribunal for the Former Yugoslavia (ICTY) at The Hague. The tribunal is given jurisdiction over four types of crimes committed anywhere on the territory of the former Yugoslavia since 1991: violations of the 1949 Geneva Conventions; war crimes; genocide; and crimes against humanity.
- *August 4*: The Arusha Accords are signed between the government of Rwanda and the Rwandan Patriotic Front to end the three-year civil war.
- *October 5*: The UN Security Council establishes the United Nations Assistance Mission for Rwanda, or UNAMIR, to monitor the cease-fire and other provisions of the Arusha Accords, and to coordinate humanitarian assistance.

1994

- *January 11*: Roméo Dallaire, the commander of the UN peacekeeping forces in Rwanda, sends his famous "genocide fax" to the UN headquarters in New York City. It is never brought to the attention of the Secretary General.
- *April 6*: The airplane carrying the presidents of Rwanda and Burundi, Juvénal Habyarimana and Cyprien Ntaryamira, is shot down.

Chronology

- *April 7*: Hutu gunmen begin to track down and kill moderate Hutu and Tutsi leaders. Dallaire is told not to intervene.
- *April 21*: The UN Security Council votes to slash Dallaire's peacekeeping force from 2,100 soldiers to 270.
- *April 27*: Pope John Paul II is the first world leader to describe the killing in Rwanda as a genocide.
- *June 23*: Operation Turquoise: The French government sends 2,500 soldiers to set up a safe zone in southwestern Rwanda.
- *July 4*: RPF troops under the leadership of Paul Kagame enter Kigali.
- *July 17*: End of the Rwandan genocide; an estimated 800,000 people have been killed. Later estimates raise the death toll to a million.
- *July 19*: The RPF government of national unity is sworn in.
- *November 8*: The UN Security Council establishes the International Criminal Tribunal for Rwanda (ICTR). The ICTR's mandate is the prosecution of crimes that occurred in Rwanda between January 1 and December 31, 1994.

1995

- *July 11–16*: Serbian troops massacre about 8,300 Bosnian male civilians in the region of Srebrenica. The atrocity represents the largest mass killing in Europe since the end of World War II.
- *August 28*: A Serb mortar shell strikes the Markale, the marketplace in Sarajevo, killing 37 civilians and wounding another 90. The attack became the stated reason for the NATO air strikes that began two days later.
- *August 30–September 20*: Operation Deliberate Force, a sustained air campaign carried out by NATO to protect designated "safe areas" in Bosnia from the Serb armed forces.
- *December 14*: The Dayton Agreement, also known as the General Framework Agreement for Peace in Bosnia and Herzegovina, is signed in Paris, thus ending the Bosnian war.

1996

- *March 8*: The United Nations officially ends UNAMIR's mission in Rwanda.
- *April 22*: A group of radicalized Albanians calling itself the Kosovo Liberation Army (KLA) carries out four attacks on Serbian police and civilians.
- *December*: Bishop Carlos Felipe Ximenes Belo and José Ramos-Horta, foreign minister in exile, receive the Nobel Peace Prize for their work toward ending the conflict in East Timor.

1997

- *March 2*: The president of Albania declares a state of emergency as riots break out due to an economic crisis.

- **March 28**: The UN sends a force of 7,000 soldiers to restore order in Albania. The troops leave on August 11. Meanwhile, the country's military stockpiles are looted and sent to the KLA in Kosovo.
- **June 10**: Son Sen, at one time deputy prime minister of Democratic Kampuchea, is murdered along with 13 members of his family on Pol Pot's orders.

1998

- **March 16**: Edward Cardinal Cassidy, president of the Holy See's Commission for Religious Relations with the Jews, presents for publication the document, "We Remember: A Reflection on the Shoah."
- **April 16**: Pol Pot dies under house arrest near the Thai border, ostensibly of heart failure. Some observers maintain that he committed suicide, as the Khmer Rouge had agreed to turn him over to an international tribunal.
- **May 31**: Police from the Serbian ministry of the interior and troops from the former Yugoslavia begin an offensive to drive the KLA from Kosovo.
- **July 17**: The Rome Statute establishing the International Criminal Court is adopted by the General Assembly of the United Nations.
- **October 2**: Jean-Paul Akayesu, a Rwandan politician, is sentenced to life imprisonment by the International Criminal Tribunal for Rwanda (ICTR) for acts of genocide marked by sexual violence against women. His conviction marks the first time that mass rape was officially condemned as a genocidal act intended to destroy a group.

1999

- **January 15**: A clash between KLA guerillas and Yugoslav troops in the village of Račak in Kosovo leads to the death of 45 Albanian civilians. The Yugoslav forces are accused of a deliberate massacre. The Račak incident is later charged as a war crime against Slobodan Milošević, then president of the Federal Republic of Yugoslavia.
- **March 6**: The Cambodian army captures Ta Mok near the Thai border. He is brought back to Phnom Penh and put in a military prison.
- **March 24–June 11**: NATO bombing of Kosovo. The Serbs step up their ethnic cleansing campaign in Kosovo. By April, 850,000 Albanians have fled the province.
- **April 6**: Indonesian militiamen massacre 200 out of several thousand refugees taking shelter in the parish church in Liquiçá in East Timor.
- **May**: The Sand Creek Massacre Project, a federally funded multidisciplinary team consisting of historians and archaeologists from the National Park Service and representatives from the Cheyenne and Arapaho Tribes, successfully completes its identification of the site of the Sand Creek Massacre.

- **August 30**: The citizens of East Timor vote in a popular referendum for complete independence from Indonesia. The vote is followed by attacks by Indonesian militiamen on Timorese civilians; at least 1,500 are killed.
- **September 20**: Australia sends troops to Dili at the head of an international peacekeeping force.
- **September 27**: Indonesia yields control of East Timor to the international force.

2000

- **June 9**: The *New York Times* publishes a statement by over 126 scholars of the Holocaust affirming that the Armenian genocide is "an incontestable historical fact" and urging Western governments to recognize it as such.
- **June 20**: Roméo Dallaire is found intoxicated under a park bench in Hull, Quebec, suffering from combining alcohol with antidepressant medications prescribed for post-traumatic stress disorder following his release from the Canadian military in April 2000. He is rushed to a nearby hospital.

2002

- **May 20**: East Timor obtains official recognition as a sovereign state, the Democratic Republic of Timor-Leste.
- **July 1**: The International Criminal Court comes into legal existence when the Rome Statute of 1998 goes into effect.

2003

- **February 26**: A group that calls itself the Darfur Liberation Front (DLF) takes credit for an attack on the town and rural district of Golo (sometimes spelled Golu) in western Sudan. This attack is usually considered the beginning of the contemporary crisis in Darfur.
- **March 11**: The International Criminal Court holds its inaugural session.
- **March 20**: Beginning of Operation Iraqi Freedom.
- **July**: Intensification of armed conflict in Darfur as the Janjaweed is used as a counterinsurgency force.
- **December 13**: Saddam Hussein is captured by American troops near his hometown of Tikrit.

2004

- **March–April**: A major humanitarian crisis arises as 100,000 refugees flee from Darfur across the border to Chad. Several thousand people, mostly from the non-Arab population, have already been killed and about a million driven from their homes.
- **June 23**: The International Criminal Tribunal for the Former Yugoslavia declares that the Srebrenica massacre of 1995 was an act of genocide.

- *October 8*: Kofi Annan, Secretary General of the United Nations, appoints a five-member panel to investigate charges that genocide has taken place in Darfur. The group is given three months to report on the situation. Annan has refused to use the term *genocide* in connection with Darfur, which would place the UN under legal obligation to act.

- *November 9*: Iris Chang, the author of the first major English-language work on the Nanking massacre, commits suicide following a severe episode of depression. Her notes indicate that her depression was in large part a reaction to the disturbing historical material she had been working with.

2005

- *August 2*: The location of the Sand Creek Massacre is officially recognized as a National Historic Site.

- *September 22*: A statue of Popé, the Tewa leader of the Pueblo revolt of 1680, is presented by the state of New Mexico to the National Statuary Hall Collection in Washington, D.C., and dedicated in the rotunda of the United States Capitol.

- *October 11*: Three former officers of the Yugoslav People's Army are put on trial at The Hague for the Vukovar massacre of 1991.

2006

- *March 10*: Slobodan Milošević dies in prison in The Hague awaiting trial for crimes against humanity.

- *July 26*: Ta Mok, the director of the massive purges in the Eastern Zone of Cambodia in 1978, dies of natural causes in a military hospital.

- *September 4*: Members of the European Parliament vote to ask Turkey to recognize the Armenian deportations and massacres of 1915–16 as a genocide as a precondition for admission to the European Union. This requirement is dropped on September 27.

- *September 8*: Concordia University in Montreal appoints Roméo Dallaire a senior fellow at the Montreal Institute for Genocide and Human Rights (MIGS).

- *December 12*: Mengistu Haile Mariam, the Marxist former head of the Derg, is found guilty of genocide by Ethiopia's Federal High Court.

- *December 30*: Saddam Hussein is executed by hanging in Baghdad after being convicted by an Iraqi court for crimes against humanity.

2007

- *January 4*: The government of France refuses political asylum to Agathe Habyarimana, the widow of Juvénal Habyarimana.

- *January 11*: Mengistu is sentenced to life in prison for the crime of genocide; Zimbabwe refuses to extradite him.

- *January 19*: Hrant Dink, a Turkish Armenian editor and journalist, is assassinated in front of the offices of the newspaper he edited for trying to improve relations between Turks and Armenians, including dialogue about the Armenian genocide.
- *February 1*: Elie Wiesel, a Holocaust survivor and scholar who won the Nobel Peace Prize in 1986, is attacked in a hotel elevator in San Francisco by a Holocaust denier. The suspect is arrested in New Jersey on February 17.
- *February 27*: The prosecutor of the International Criminal Court indicts a high-ranking Sudanese minister of the interior and a leader of the Jangaweed militia on 51 counts of war crimes and crimes against humanity.
- *April 9*: Fifty-three Nobel laureates sign an open letter urging the Turkish government to acknowledge that the 1915–18 mass killings and deportations of Armenians under the Ottoman Empire constituted genocide.
- *April 14*: An exhibit in the visitors lobby of the UN building in New York titled "Lessons from Rwanda" about the 1994 genocide is removed when Turkey objects to the exhibit's mention of the Armenian genocide of 1915.
- *April 27*: The site of the Sand Creek Massacre is officially dedicated as a national historic site.
- *April 27*: The International Criminal Court (ICC) issues a warrant of arrest for Ahmed Haroun for war crimes and crimes against humanity committed in Darfur between 2003 and 2005.
- *May 27*: The ICC issues a warrant for the arrest of Ali Kushayb, leader of the Jangaweed, on 51 counts of war crimes and crimes against humanity committed in West Darfur in 2003 and 2004. Kushayb is taken into custody by the Sudanese government.
- *July 27*: The UN's World Food Programme reports increasingly frequent attacks by armed bandits on food convoys in Darfur.
- *July 31*: The UN Security Council approves the formation of the United Nations African Union Mission in Darfur (UNAMID), which will take over the African Union Mission in Sudan (AMIS) on December 31, 2007. UNAMID will include 19,500 troops and 3,700 police.
- *August 14*: Four coordinated suicide bomb attacks in the Iraqi towns of Qahtaniya and Siba Sheikh Khidir target a Kurdish religious minority, the Yazidi, who are considered infidels by Muslim fundamentalists. The bombs kill 572 people and injure another 1,500. Some Iraqi observers condemn the attacks as genocidal.
- *September 7*: The government of Sudan appoints Ahmed Haroun to head a committee investigating human rights abuses in Darfur.
- *September 19*: Cambodian troops arrest Nuon Chea, one of the few surviving leaders of the Khmer Rouge who was close to Pol Pot, in his house near the

Thai border. Chea is considered to bear heavy responsibility for the organized killing of 1.7 million Cambodians between 1975 and 1979.

- *October 24*: Secretary of State Condoleezza Rice urges Congress to drop a resolution on the Armenian genocide in order not to jeopardize U.S. strategic ties with Turkey.

2008

- *April*: Ali Kushayb is released from custody by the government of Sudan on the grounds of lack of evidence for his war crimes.
- *April 22*: The United Nations undersecretary for humanitarian affairs reports that the UN figures for the death toll in Darfur may be too low by as much as 50 percent.
- *June 12*: The Swedish parliament defeats a resolution for recognition of the Armenian genocide.
- *July 14*: Luis Moreno-Ocampo, the International Criminal Court's prosecutor for Darfur, asks the ICC for an arrest warrant for Omar al-Bashir on grounds of "criminal responsibility" for genocide, war crimes, and crimes against humanity in Darfur.
- *July 31*: The United Nations Security Council extends the mandate of UNAMID to July 31, 2009.
- *August 14*: The Cambodia Tribunal formally indicts Kaing Guek Eav, or Duch, the former head of the Khmer Rouge prison camp at Tuol Sleng, for crimes against humanity.
- *September 15*: The United States announces its intention to help fund the Cambodia Tribunal.
- *October 8*: Rwanda announces plans to turn the former home of Juvénal Habyarimana into a museum to promote reconciliation.
- *December 18*: The UN International Tribunal for Rwanda (ICTR) sentences Colonel Théoneste Bagosora, the alleged mastermindehind the 1994 massacre of thousands in Rwanda, and two codefendants to life imprisonment for genocide, crimes against humanity, and war crimes.

2009

- *February*: Duch goes on trial in Phnom Penh, Cambodia.
- *March*: The ICC issues and arrest warrant for Sudanese president Omar al-Bashir.

12

Glossary

This chapter presents terms that often arise in discussions of historical and contemporary cases of genocide, as well as names of groups or terms found in accounts of specific genocides.

akazu   a word that means "little house" in Kinyarwanda, the language of Rwanda. It refers to the group of Hutu leaders surrounding the president of Rwanda and his wife in the early 1990s who planned the genocide of 1994.

Angkar   a term for the leadership of the KHMER ROUGE during the Cambodian genocide of 1975–78. The term can be roughly translated as "the Organization."

atrocity   a general term used to describe an intentional act of killing, whether of an individual or a group, that is excessively brutal, cruel, or in violation of most traditional moral principles. The more precise terms CRIME AGAINST HUMANITY and WAR CRIME are preferred in international law.

autogenocide   the mass killing of a country's citizens by its own government or people. The term was coined in the 1970s to describe the massacres of Cambodians by the KHMER ROUGE.

base people   a term used by the KHMER ROUGE to refer to the Cambodian peasantry, whom they idealized as the "true" or "pure" Cambodians.

biological warfare   the use of any bacterium, virus, fungus, or other disease-causing organism as a weapon of war or genocide.

blood libel   the allegation that a group practices human sacrifice and/or uses the blood of its victims in various rituals. Jews have historically been the most frequent victims of blood libels, but other groups have been accused as well.

caliphate   the institution of a unified Islamic state. Prior to its abolition in 1924 by the secular government of Turkey, the caliphate represented a succession of rulers who were descended from Mohammed and held spiritual as well as temporal authority. After 1517 the Ottoman rulers took the title of caliph as well as sultan.

chauvinism   a term that refers to blind or fanatical ultranationalism. The name is derived from Nicolas Chauvin, a soldier in a 19th-century French play characterized as excessively devoted to Napoléon. The members of the COMMITTEE OF UNION AND PROGRESS have been described as Turkish chauvinists.

chétés groups of criminals released from Turkish prisons during the genocide of 1915 to attack and kill Armenians along the routes of deportation.

collective guilt the notion that an individual or group should bear guilt or accept responsibility for wrongdoing committed by other members of the group, whether ancestors or contemporaries. Collective guilt is often used to justify genocide.

Committee of Union and Progress (CUP) a Turkish political organization that began as a secret society among medical students in 1889. It became a formal political party in 1906 and ruled Turkey between 1908 and 1918. Originally in favor of liberal reforms, the CUP adopted an ultranationalist ideology and helped to bring Turkey into World War I on the side of the Central Powers.

crime against humanity a term used in international law to refer to large-scale persecution of or atrocities committed against a group of people. The phrase was first used in reference to the Armenian genocide in 1915.

decimation a historical term that refers to a form of punishment carried out in the Roman army against mutineers or cowards, in which every 10th soldier in the cohort to be punished was selected by lot and clubbed or beaten to death by the others. The journalistic use of the term to mean a drastic reduction in population (usually much more than a 10th) is disapproved by many scholars.

democide a term coined by a contemporary political scientist, R. J. Rummel, to refer to the murder of any person or people by a government. According to Rummel, democide may include POLITICIDE, GENOCIDE, or MASS MURDER.

denaturalization stripping or depriving a person or group of their rights and duties as citizens of a country. The NUREMBERG LAWS of 1935 are examples of denaturalization.

deportation the expulsion from a country of an individual or group whose presence is considered unlawful or prejudicial. The term is also used to refer to the forcible resettlement of a group of people within a different part of a country. Deportation on the basis of religion or ethnicity is sometimes called POPULATION TRANSFER.

Derg the committee or council of military leaders that ruled Ethiopia between 1974 and 1987. It imprisoned and executed thousands of people without trial.

dhimmi a non-Muslim living under sharia law who pays the JIZYA in exchange for protection. *Dhimmis* had fewer rights than Muslims and were often required to wear special clothing for identifications. The Armenians under the Ottoman Empire were considered *dhimmis*.

Einsatzgruppen the German word for the paramilitary groups that were formed by Hitler's security organization (the Schutzstaffel or SS) during World War II to execute Jews, Roma, and other civilians in occupied Eastern Europe.

eliticide the systematic elimination of the educated classes of a country as well as wealthy persons. The Cambodian genocide is an example of eliticide.

encomienda the Spanish word for the labor system that was instituted in the Spanish colonies of North and South America. The *encomendero* (person who managed the *encomienda*) was technically a trustee who had authority to tax the Indians under his authority and demand labor from them; he did not have direct ownership over their land. The *encomienda* system was replaced after 1791 by the hacienda system, which was based on direct ownership of land.

epidemic an outbreak of a communicable disease that affects large numbers of people within a community or region. Epidemics are generally regarded as more localized or smaller in scale than PANDEMICS.

ethnic cleansing a term that refers to government practices or policies aimed at the displacement or removal of a specific ethnic group from a specific territory. It is often used to describe forcible population transfers associated with gross violations of human rights. Although ethnic cleansing may lead to instances of genocide, it should not be used as a synonym for genocide.

ethnocide a term used to describe a subtype of genocide based on ethnicity; some scholars also use the term to describe the destruction of the culture or language of a group whether or not mass killings occur.

eugenics a social philosophy that deals with the improvement, usually through selective mating, of inherited human characteristics in order to improve the species. It has been used at various times during the 20th century to justify the forced sterilization of people with genetic defects, the killing of institutionalized people, and genocide.

ex post facto law a law applied retroactively to criminalize actions that were not crimes at the time the act was committed, to redefine acts as more serious crimes, to change or increase punishments for specific crimes, or to alter the rules of evidence to make conviction more likely. Some legal experts regarded the Nuremberg and Tokyo tribunals' definitions of war crimes and crimes against humanity as examples of ex post facto law.

extradition the surrender by one state of a person charged with a crime to another state with jurisdiction to try the criminal charges. Many perpetrators of genocide have avoided extradition to stand trial for their crimes.

femicide the selective killing of women or girls on the basis of their sex. The most common form of femicide is the selective infanticide of female infants in cultures that value male children more highly. HONOR KILLINGS are another form of femicide.

gacaca **courts** a type of genocide court that is unique to Rwanda. Based on traditional village procedures for community justice, the *gacaca* courts were established by the Rwandan government in 2001 to speed up the process of punishing perpetrators of the 1994 genocide. *Gacaca* can be translated as "justice on the grass."

gendercide   the selective killing of either males or females on the basis of their sex.

ghetto   a term that denotes an area of a city where Jews were formerly forced to live. It has since been extended to mean any area of any city in which a minority group is forced to remain for economic reasons. The term *ghettoization* is sometimes used to describe the Nazis' forcible confinement of Jews in the ghettos during World War II prior to sending them to the death camps.

Holocaust   the word most commonly used in English-language histories for the Nazis' planned attempt to exterminate the Jews (and other persecuted groups) during World War II. Some writers, however, prefer the Hebrew term SHOAH on the grounds that *holocaust* is derived from a Greek word for burned sacrificial offerings to pagan gods. The Holocaust did not become the standard term of reference for Hitler's genocide until the 1950s, although it was first used in 1942.

Holocaust denial   the belief that the Holocaust (and mass killings of other victims of the Nazis) either did not occur at all or did not occur on the scale attested by current scholarship. It is sometimes called Holocaust revisionism.

Holodomor   the Ukrainian name for the human-made famine of 1932–33, which killed 5–6 million people in the rural areas of Ukraine. It is sometimes called the Ukrainian genocide.

honor killing   the murder of a female member of a family by male members who regard her as having dishonored the family by refusing to enter an arranged marriage, associating with men outside the clan or religion, attempting to divorce an abusive husband, or being the victim of sexual assault. Honor killings are one form of FEMICIDE.

human sacrifice   the killing of human beings, usually in a highly ritualized manner, in order to please or appease gods or spirits. The Mongols practiced human sacrifice when one of their khans died.

Hutu Power   a political ideology supported by the AKUZU and Hutu extremists that helped to bring about the Rwandan genocide of 1994. Hutu Power was aggressively promoted by the Rwandan media, both print and broadcast.

ideology   a way of thinking or the content of thinking characteristic of a person, a group, a political movement, or a culture.

infanticide   the intentional killing of newborn members of a species by members of the same species, whether humans or other animals. The selective killing of female infants is considered a form of FEMICIDE.

Ittihadism   another name for the nationalist ideology adopted by the COMMITTEE OF UNION AND PROGRESS in the years leading up to World War I. It is derived from the CUP's name in Turkish, *Ittihad ve Terakki Cemiyeti*.

Glossary

Janjaweed an Arabic word used to describe the armed bands of militiamen involved in the conflicts in Darfur, western Sudan, and eastern Chad. The word is variously translated as "devils on horseback," "thieving hordes," or "bandits."

jihad an Islamic term derived from a root that means "to strive" or "to struggle." It has a range of meanings, from inward spiritual struggle to perfect one's faith to political movements or war regarded as divinely ordained. The Turkish government referred in 1915 to the Armenian genocide as a jihad. In the present conflict in Darfur, jihad is usually interpreted as holy war by the government in Khartoum.

jizya a tax paid by non-Muslim people living under Muslim rule in return for protection and as a sign of subjection.

junta a group of persons that controls a government after a revolutionary seizure of power. The Derg in Ethiopia and the Three Pashas in Turkey are examples of juntas.

Kampuchea the name used for Cambodia by the KHMER ROUGE from 1975 to 1979.

khan the title given by medieval Mongol clans to their chieftains or rulers.

Khmer Rouge the name of the Communist party that ruled Cambodia between 1975 and 1979. The name means "Red Khmer" in French.

killing fields a term used for a number of sites in Cambodia that were used for mass executions and burials by the KHMER ROUGE between 1975 and 1979.

Kristallnacht a pogrom that took place throughout Germany and parts of Austria in November 1938. The German word is sometimes translated into English as the "Night of Broken Glass," a reference to the windows of Jewish homes, businesses, and synagogues that were smashed by the rioters.

laws of war a collection of general rules and principles, some customary for millennia and others defined more recently in international documents, governing the justifications for going to war *(jus ad bellum)* and acceptable conduct during war *(jus in bello)*. The laws of war were first discussed in a systematic form by Hugo Grotius in the 17th century and given international force by the Second Hague Convention of 1907.

mass murder a general term that is used to refer to the intentional killing of a number of people at or about the same time. It may or may not be an act of genocide. The U.S. Bureau of Justice defines a mass murder as "the murder of four or more victims at one location, within one event."

millet a term used in the Ottoman Empire prior to World War I to refer to legally protected religious minorities. People were bound to their *millet* by their religious affiliation rather than their ethnicity. The Armenians were the largest *millet* within the empire before the 1915 genocide.

new people the term used by the KHMER ROUGE for Cambodian civilians, usually from urban areas, who were forced into rural communes, turned into agricultural slave laborers, and sometimes executed en masse during the period from 1975 to 1979.

nongovernmental organization (NGO) an organization that is not directly affiliated with any government. Many NGOs are humanitarian groups, often dependent on volunteers, and are sometimes called nonstate actors or NSAs. The term NGO originated with the United Nations Charter in 1945.

Nuremberg laws a set of laws passed by the government of Nazi Germany in 1935 to denaturalize the Jews and other racial minorities living in Germany. In 1936 the Nuremberg laws were extended to Gypsies.

omnicide a term coined by the psychiatrist Robert J. Lifton in the late 1990s to refer to the intentional killing of the entire human race.

pandemic an outbreak of a contagious disease that occurs over a wide geographic area and affects an unusually high proportion of the population.

pogrom a violent riot, either spontaneous or organized, that includes the organized massacre of helpless people—usually Jews, although the term has also been applied to attacks on Gypsies under the Nazi regime and to the murder of ethnic Greeks by a Turkish mob in Istanbul in 1955. The English word is derived from the Russian word for *wreaking havoc* or *devastation.*

politicide a form of mass killing in which people are executed for their political or ideological beliefs. It differs from genocide in that racial, ethnic, or cultural groups are not targeted as such.

population transfer the forcible movement of a large group of people from one region to another by state policy or international authority, most frequently on the basis of ethnicity or religion. Population transfer is sometimes called population exchange when two populations are being transferred in opposite directions across the same border at the same time.

Porajmos (Porrajmos) a term coined by the Roma (Gypsy) people to describe the Nazi attempt to kill the Gypsies of Europe during World War II. The term literally means *devouring.* The genocide of the Gypsies is also known as the SAMUDARIPEN or *mass killing.*

Praying Indians a term that refers to the members of the Massachusett and associated tribes who were converted to Christianity by John Eliot and his coworkers in the 17th century. The Praying Indians formed and settled in towns that they governed according to their own tribal laws and customs as well as biblical guidelines.

repatriation the restoration or return of prisoners of war to their country of origin or citizenship after the end of hostilities, or the return of refugees to their homelands as a matter of government policy. Repatriation may be either voluntary or compulsory.

restorative justice an approach to crime and punishment that focuses on crimes (including genocide) as offenses against individuals and communities rather than the state, in order to promote reconciliation. Punishments typically take the form of restitution or community service rather than imprisonment. The GACACA courts of Rwanda represent a form of restorative justice.

retributive justice   an approach to criminal justice that maintains that punishment tailored to the severity of the crime is a morally appropriate response. The severity of the crime may be measured by the extent of harm done to the victim(s) as well as its moral offensiveness. High-level planners or perpetrators of genocide are usually tried and sentenced according to retributive justice.

righteous Gentiles   a term used to describe non-Jews who risked their lives to rescue Jews from extermination by the Nazis during World War II.

Roma (also Romani)   the preferred term for the ethnic group known in some English-speaking countries as Gypsies (a term derived from the mistaken belief that the Roma originated in Egypt). There is no connection between the ethnic group known as Roma and the nation or language of Romania.

second-degree genocide   a term used by some scholars to refer to mass death caused by starvation or disease associated with war or conquest, even though the loss of life is not directly intended or desired.

shamanism   a type of traditional religion that emphasizes communication with the spirit world through healers or magicians (shamans) who are thought to have special powers to interpret omens, control the weather, and cure disease. The Mongols in the time of Genghis Khan practiced a form of shamanism.

sharia   the Arabic word for Islamic law, which is held to regulate all of life; thus sharia covers business contracts and social matters as well as religious rituals and obligations. The main sources of the law are the Quran, the hadith, applications of previous rulings to new situations, and the consensus of the ulama.

Shoah   the Hebrew term for the HOLOCAUST. It means "catastrophe" or "catastrophic upheaval."

Sufism   a mystical form of Islam that emphasizes direct experience of God and religion of the heart. It began around Basra (in present-day Iraq) around 1000 A.D. Sufism is considered heretical or apostate by fundamentalist Muslims. The Muslim population of Darfur is primarily Sufi, which is one reason for the conflict between the farmers of Darfur and the central government of Sudan.

tribunal   a generic word for a forum or court of justice. International legal bodies that are formed to try cases involving genocide or crimes against humanity are often called tribunals to underscore the fact that they are not courts with ordinary national or local jurisdiction.

triumvirate   a ruling group of three members. The name comes from the Latin words for "three" and "men." The Three Pashas who ruled Turkey between 1913 and 1918 are an example of a triumvirate.

urbicide   the deliberate destruction of a city in order to attack a group's cultural identity. The Mongols' complete destruction of the cities they captured and the deportation of the inhabitants of Phnom Penh in 1975 are considered instances of urbicide.

vicarious traumatization   a form of post-traumatic stress disorder that affects some rescue workers, therapists, and others who treat survivors of genocide.

victor's justice   a term applied to the conduct of a victorious nation following a war in which the victor is seen as applying a more lenient standard in judging the conduct of its own troops than the standard applied to the troops of the defeated enemy. The Nuremberg and Tokyo war crimes trials after World War II have been criticized as examples of victor's justice.

vigilante justice   a term used to describe vengeance or the taking of law into one's own hands by private individuals who regard existing law enforcement as inadequate. The English *vigilante* comes from the Spanish word for a watchman. Operation Nemesis following the Armenian genocide is an instance of vigilante justice.

vivisection   the dissection of or performance of surgery on a living animal or human being, typically without anesthesia. The Japanese practiced vivisection on Chinese and Allied prisoners of war during World War II.

war crime   a violation of the laws of war, punishable under international law whether the crimes were committed by military personnel or civilians. The International Criminal Court was formed in 2002 to prosecute war crimes committed on or after July 1, 2002. Former heads of state indicted for war crimes include Karl Dönitz (Germany) and Hideki Tōjō (Japan) after World War II; Slobodan Milošević (former Yugoslavia) in the early 2000s; and Charles Taylor (Liberia) in 2006.

xenophobia   hatred of foreigners and foreign influence. The Cambodian genocide is considered to have been motivated in part by xenophobia.

yassa (or *yasa*)   the code of law promulgated by Genghis Khan and intended to be enforced by his son Chagatai. The word *yassa* means "command" or "decree" in Mongolian. Although there are no surviving written copies of Genghis's code, it was considered to be in advance of its time in its tolerance of different religions and the high position it accorded to women.

Year Zero   the term used by the KHMER ROUGE for 1975, the first year of their new revolutionary calendar. It is thought that they borrowed the concept of a new calendar from the leaders of the French Revolution, who declared 1792 (when the monarchy was abolished) to be the Year One. The Year Zero signaled the beginning of the KHMER ROUGE's ELITICIDE, or purging of intellectuals and educated persons.

Young Turks   a loose coalition of reform groups that wanted to modernize the administration of the Ottoman Empire in the late 1880s. Most of the Young Turks eventually joined the COMMITTEE OF UNION AND PROGRESS.

zoonosis (plural, **zoonoses**)   any infectious disease that can be transmitted from animals, whether wild or domesticated, to humans. The catastrophic depopulation of the Americas after the entry of Europeans is sometimes attributed to zoonoses carried by the animals brought by the conquistadors and other explorers.

Index

Page numbers in **boldface** indicate major treatment of a subject. Page numbers followed by *f* indicate figures. Page numbers followed by *m* indicate maps. Page numbers followed by *b* indicate biographical entries. Page numbers followed by *c* indicate chronology entries. Page numbers followed by *g* indicate glossary entries.

Index

Index

Index

Index

Index

Index